Application of Chaos and Fractals to Computer Vision

Authored By

Michael E. Farmer

University of Michigan-Flint
Flint, MI
USA

DEDICATION

To my wife Shweta and my son Patrick for their amazing love and support

CONTENTS

Author Biography

Michael Farmer as an Associate Professor in the Departments of Computer Science, Engineering Science and Physics at the University of Michigan in Flint. Prior to joining the University of Michigan, held numerous advanced engineering positions in the industry. He received his B.S. degree from Columbia University in Applied Physics, an M.S. degree from the University of Michigan in Physics, an M.S. degree in the Management of Technology from the University of Minnesota, and a Ph.D. degree from Michigan State University in Computer Science. His research interests include motion and context-based image segmentation and object tracking, and temporal accumulation of evidence. He is a senior member of the IEEE and ACM. He holds twenty-five patents in radar and vision systems for a variety of applications including military surveillance, precision agriculture, and automotive safety. He also has over thirty scholarly publications in computer vision, pattern recognition, and artificial intelligence.

FOREWORD

Computer Science, Computer Engineering, Electrical Engineering, Biomedical Engineering, Mechanical Engineering, and Civil Engineering, together with physics, cognitive psychology, evolutionary biology and mathematics have been involved in computer vision to solve many theoretical and practical problems. For example, understanding of human vision as well as vision of terrestrial animals, underground creatures, underwater animals, and flying animals could be very helpful in developing improved computer vision algorithms for various "smart" autonomous machines such as terrestrial vehicles, mobile robots, underground drones, submersibles, and constellations of small satellites, including nano-, pico-, and femtosatellites. Another fundamental reason for the quest to develop better computer vision is the expanding interest in cognitive dynamical systems. While adaptive control systems constituted the foundation of the previous revolution in systems, cognitive dynamical systems appear to be the next.

This book is right in the center of such developments. It is motivated by the need to solve many fundamental issues in computer vision, including static and moving object segmentation, scene registration and tracking, as well as object classification. Its approach is also matching the requirements of dynamic systems by including not only the three classic stable states (point, cyclic and toroidal stability), but also the fourth stable state, chaos. Under special conditions and driving functions, chaos can develop in a system to affect its behavior either negatively or positively. The positive impact is explored in the book using aperiodic forcing functions to induce temporal chaotic-like behavior (in image sequences) and spatial chaotic-like behavior (in image textures). This approach is of interest to many researchers today. Since the phase-space trajectories (behavior) of chaotic systems is fractal and multi-fractal, their analysis must also be multi-fractal. The book uses this approach to detect chaotic behavior in a system. This approach could also be used to quantify the behavior in order to improve it. Since a multi-fractal analysis is necessarily based on information-theoretic arguments, it often is superior to energy-based approaches in quantification of complexity of systems and their behavior. An example of the use of a unified approach to multi-fractal analysis of phase-space self-affine objects is presented in Chapter 5.

Since this well-crafted and unique book is supported by many examples, illustrations and images, it is easy to read and understand even though it deals with very difficult scientific and technical matters. It should be of interest to many students, researchers and practitioners not only in the area of computer vision, but also to the broader audience of mechatronics, robotics, secure and resilient systems, as well as adaptive, perceptual and cognitive systems.

Witold Kinsner

Cognitive Systems Laboratory
Department of Electrical and Computer Engineering
University of Manitoba
Manitoba
Canada

PREFACE

Computer vision has been an active area of research in the Computer Science community for well over half a century. Various areas of research within this community such as image segmentation and object recognition continue to be actively pursued. These areas continue to prove challenging in terms of developing general approaches to broad classes of problems. Approaches that are promising in the laboratory and on standard data sets often fail to meet expectations in real world applications. Researchers have derived motivation for their algorithmic approaches from a variety of other research fields including, physics, physiology, psychology, evolutionary biology, and mathematics. Approaches inspired by physics include optical flow which is obviously based on fluid flow theory and normalized graph cut which is loosely based on coupled oscillators models. Likewise, numerous mathematically inspired models such as probability distribution mixture models, fractal analysis, support vector machines, and optimization theory have been employed. Approaches inspired by physiology obviously include neural networks, while evolutionary biology has inspired genetic algorithms and swarm-based algorithms.

In parallel over the past thirty years researchers in dynamical systems and physics have explored the field of chaos theory where complex system behaviors have been understood as emerging from relatively simple mathematical constructs. This research has found a place in a broad variety of applications such as weather analysis, mechanical vibration analysis, and electrical signals in biological neural pathways. Much of the biological research has been conducted in perception systems such as nasal and optical systems. Because of these efforts in explaining biological neural systems through chaotic dynamics it was quite natural that researchers began exploring adding chaos theory to artificial neural networks and this has been a common approach for enhancing neural network algorithmic performance.

Chaos theory to date, however, has been focused predominantly on applications to neural networks in the computer vision community. Some researchers have applied chaos theory to peripheral tasks such as image compression, but it has not found a home in the traditional computer vision tasks such as segmentation, image registration, or feature extraction. In this text we will remedy this shortcoming. We explore applying concepts from chaos theory to all aspects of computer vision including static and moving object segmentation, scene registration and tracking, as well as neural and genetic algorithm approaches to object classification.

One powerful concept that has arisen from the research in biological neural systems is the concept of the aperiodic forcing function that when applied to a system can create complex chaos-like behavior. This concept will be exploited throughout this text both for generating temporal chaotic-like behavior in image sequences as well as for generating spatial chaotic-like behavior in image textures. In particular, we will demonstrate that illumination effects in image scenes can be modeled by linear forcing functions while motion, contextual change and image texture can be modeled with these aperiodic forcing functions. We will exploit this distinct difference in forcing functions to develop approaches to computer vision applications. This is a dramatically different approach from algorithms to date which intentionally linearize these various effects with a variety of approximations. In this text we will embrace the inherent non-linearities present in complex image scenes and by analyzing them using the tools from chaos theory we will discover approaches that are inherently immune to illumination change. Results from a variety of real-world applications using datasets collected by numerous researchers throughout the world will demonstrate the efficacy of the proposed approaches.

One interesting result of this book is that we will present algorithms to solve a broad range of vision tasks all based on this common theme of chaos theory. Tasks that in the past have been analyzed using significantly different algorithms such as motion segmentation and texture analysis will be processed using the common approach of chaos theory. This text provides the first attempt to develop a fully unified view of computer vision tasks, with the various tasks being manifestations of temporal or spatial chaos, and a common toolset of algorithms are applicable across all of the tasks.

ACKNOWLEDGEMENTS

The author would like to acknowledge the efforts of his students that worked on the underlying research within this book and served as co-authors on numerous papers. These students are Sushma Kittali, Cheng Yuan, David Shugars, and Jason Rieman. Additionally, the author would like to acknowledge the efforts of the students that helped with the proof-reading and indexing of the text, namely Ben Hart and Logan Shumaker. Other students assisted with research by running MATLAB simulations, namely Matthew Medon and Samuel Atkins. The author would also like to thank the University of Michigan-Flint Office of Research and Creative Activities for their generous funding of portions of this research and travel funding to attend some of the conferences to present the results of the published papers. Lastly, the author would like to thank the reviewers of this text for their thorough and thoughtful review of this text and many invaluable comments.

CONFLICT OF INTEREST

The author confirms that this eBook contents have no conflict of interest.

Michael Edward Farmer

Associate Professor of Computer Science
Department of Computer Science, Engineering and Physics
207 Murchie Science Building
303 E. Kearsley Street
Flint, Michigan
USA
E-mail: farmerme@umflint.edu

CHAPTER 1

Introduction

Abstract: Computer vision has been an active area of research in computer science for over fifty years. Much progress has been made on many fronts by researchers proposing a variety of algorithms motivated by many other fields of science, including mathematics, physics, physiology, and biology. These algorithms are often focused on specific tasks such as image segmentation, classification, or image registration. Some common approaches to many algorithms is that they employ a variety of linearizing approximations to simplify the computations. Chaos theory is a field of research that provides insight into how dynamical systems can exhibit radically different behaviors from seemingly similar initial conditions. It is based on the ideas of non-linear dynamics and provides a set of tools for understanding these complex behaviors. In this text we embrace the non-linear foundations of chaos theory and employ them to solve a broad variety of computer vision applications.

Keywords: Chaos theory, information, phase space, biological vision systems.

Chaos theory has been successfully used to model many naturally occurring processes in the natural sciences [1], and most recently found success in modeling the biological neural activity [2]. Specifically, neural processes related to sensory perception have been shown to produce chaotic and multi-fractal signals, that create distinct basins of attraction [2-5]. Despite the interest in chaos for describing neural perceptual activity, there has been relatively little work in applying chaos theory to computer vision. A few exceptions to this include with the application of chaos to artificial neural networks, lossy image compression, image watermarking, and image encryption [6-8]. The related field of multi-fractal analysis has been more widely used in a variety of image-related applications including texture analysis, image coding and change detection in image sequences [9-17]. Likewise multi-fractal analysis has been extensively used in one-dimensional signal analysis such as coast-line analysis, man-made object detection in rough seas using radar signals, and electro-encephalograph (EEG) analysis [18-20]. In the aforementioned applications the authors applied fractal analysis directly to time series and image with mixed results. In texture analysis for example, multi-fractal analysis of grayscale images was found lacking in terms of its ability to correctly classify various textures. This text introduces a complementary approach of applying multi-fractal analysis to the phase space

Michael E. Farmer

trajectory of imaging systems rather than to the actual grayscale images themselves. By doing this we will be able to detect the possible presence of chaos and chaotic-like behavior *versus* deterministic behavior. We will see that many of these same applications for which direct multi-fractal analysis was applied can be more effectively analyzed in phase space. This is because many of the behaviors being sought after in these imaging systems can be modeled as being produced by underlying non-linear chaos-like dynamics.

Various schemes for computer vision have been proposed over the past forty years, but few of these have provided a common underlying mathematical foundation for performing a variety of computer vision tasks. The application of chaos-based analysis to these systems provides a unique approach to computer vision that will address a broad range of computer vision tasks from attention direction through object tracking and object classification. We will show that analysis in phase space of both image sequences temporally and single images spatially provides us a unique mechanism for understanding the creation and distribution of ***information*** in images. The presence of temporal chaos is well known and discussed in many of the references in the text such as [21, 22], but the existence of spatial chaos will also be demonstrated to be important for texture analysis. It has been demonstrated in physical systems such as defects in solid state physics by Coullet, *et al.*, [23]. Employing the concept of information creation in an image sequence or information content within an individual image is in contrast to traditional approaches such as optical flow and traditional texture analysis methods that simply seek to directly model the behavior of grayscale values. It is the understanding of the information creation and content in images that will make the methods proposed in this text well suited to detecting meaningful behaviors captured in the grayscale values of images.

We will see that one unique aspect of analyzing image sequences in phase space is that it provides a robust mechanism for isolating the effects of motion and contextual change in image sequences from the effects of spatio-temporal illumination changes. Spatio-temporal illumination change is defined in Fig. **1** [24]. Traditional and popular vision algorithms such as optical flow for motion segmentation are founded on the premise of image constancy where the only changes are due to motion and not due to illumination changes [25]. Clearly many real-world computer vision applications such as outdoor surveillance cannot realistically assume image constancy. Even subsequent vision models such as mixture-model approaches that try to mitigate the effects of changing illumination are still based on an underlying assumption of the ability to separate the effects of motion and illumination in the grayscale domain. The mixture-based approaches model the effects of illumination by proposing they manifest themselves with different amplitude characteristics [26-31]. Unfortunately these approaches usually limit the behavior of illumination change to be only slowly changing. The chaos-based approach advocated throughout this text provides a unified mathematical framework for illumination and contextual or motion-based change. We note that each of these effects is derived from a fundamentally different mathematical structure where one is highly linear and the other is highly ***non-linear***. This then allows motion and illumination to be clearly differentiated in phase space even when their effects in the grayscale domain may be very difficult to differentiate. This different mathematical structure comes from modeling the motion of objects through an image scene as creating an aperiodic forcing function which imparts chaos-like behavior on the imaging sensor, while illumination is caused by a simpler linear forcing function.

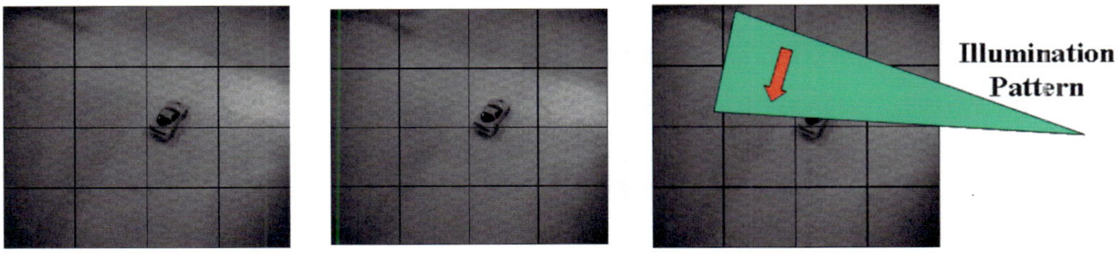

(a) (b) (c)

Figure 1: Spatio-temporal illumination: (a) first image, (b) second image, and (c) graphic showing moving light band.

The proposed chaos theory approach to computer vision in this text also provides interesting insights into another common problem, namely texture analysis. The findings of Coullet [23] for spatial chaos provide a motivation for applying chaos-based approaches to texture analysis. In this case the underlying surface being imaged serves as an aperiodic forcing function that generates the image detected by the imaging sensor. Thus different textures are the result of different aperiodic forcing functions. Interestingly, we will see that the grey-level co-occurrence matrix is structurally equivalent to the spatial phase plot of the image. Consequently, one significant aspect of the approach of employing principles from chaos theory is that it provides a unification of the two distinct approaches to texture analysis, namely statistical analysis using co-occurrence matrices and model-based analysis using image-domain fractal analysis. We will show that while historically treated as very distinct approaches they can be considered intimately related if the co-occurrence matrix is simply replaced by the phase plot. Both approaches define texture as occurring due to underlying complex phenomena, either *via* an aperiodic forcing function described by Velazquez [5] or *via* a fractional dimension Brownian noise advocated by Pentland [10]. Both mechanisms, however, generate behaviors in the images that are intimately related, namely chaos and fractals.

The approaches proposed in this text embrace the non-linear processing and non-linear system modeling inherent in the chaos-based approaches. This makes the approaches here unique in computer vision and much of computer science in general, where linear processing and linearizations in applications to simplify problems are the norm [27-35]. This dedication to linearization, while convenient from an implementation viewpoint, is somewhat puzzling given the proven efficacy of neural networks. These networks derive their computation power from the non-linearities embedded in the sigmoidal activation functions. Nonetheless widespread adoption of non-linear approaches is rare. There have been a few researchers that have begun to embrace non-linear processing, and particularly the adoption of underlying models of non-linear dynamics and chaos-based analysis. Lindgren, *et al.,* proposed using chaos-based approaches to speech recognition which is traditionally based on linear processing based on Fourier spectra and cepstral analysis [36]. Additionally, very recently Fotopoulou *et al.,* proposed performing phase space analysis on object boundaries in image processing for the purpose of object classification [37]. Interestingly, the use of information *via* measuring the mutual information between image pairs for registration has proven to be very effective for a broad range of imaging applications [38]. The application of chaos theory can be considered the next step along this path of recognizing that not only is information content important, but the change in information content is important. There is a tangible connection between information creation and the various important phenomena in image processing such as change detection, texture analysis, registration, et cetera and chaos theory provides a powerful toolset for analyzing these changes in information [1, 39].

The motivation for the proposed chaos-theoretic approach to computer vision adopted in this text was derived from integrating research in biological vision systems both at the micro-system level and the macro-system level. At the micro-system level biological vision systems have been shown to employ neural signals that exhibit chaotic behavior. Research in biological neural signals has demonstrated interesting chaos-like behavior of the time series that are propagated through the neural pathways [3-5, 20]. At the macro-system level psycho-perceptive models of biological vision systems have adopted tiered hierarchies. Past approaches in artificial intelligence, such as the subsumption architecture, advocated layered approaches to problem solving. Unfortunately, the emergence of high performance low cost computing resources has led more recent researchers to much more monolithic solutions to artificial vision systems [5, 33]. It is this integration of both microscopic and macroscopic features of biological vision systems that is an approach uniquely adopted in this book. It is also the unique feature that allows multi-fractal analysis of the phase space trajectories of the image sequences to be applied at a variety of levels of the vision hierarchy to accomplish increasingly complex tasks.

This text will first introduce the macroscopic and microscopic models of biological vision systems in Chapter 2. In Chapter 3 it will then introduce the key principles of chaos-based signal analysis. It will address fractal and multi-fractal analysis of phase spaces both at the global and local levels. Chapter 4 will introduce the critical differences between changes in image streams due to illumination *versus* contextual and motive change which provides the remaining sections of the book the phenomenological foundations critical to their success. Chapter 5 through Chapter 8 will then address the application of this chaos-based analysis to each level of the vision stack. Chapter 9 will address the higher level task of object tracking and how chaos can be used to enhance registration-based tracking. Chapter 10 finally will address the application of chaos theory to object classification. This chapter will discuss the benefits of employing chaos in traditional neural network architectures as well as using chaos to enhance random processes associated with genetic algorithms and other optimization algorithms.

CHAPTER 2

Biological Vision Systems – Architecture and Signal Characteristics

Abstract: Biological vision systems have been successfully modeled as hierarchical systems with lower level subsystems performing simpler tasks such as attention direction towards moving objects, and higher level subsystems performing tasks such as tracking, object recognition and scene understanding. Likewise robotics researchers have found great utility in layered systems such as the subsumption architecture. Within biological sensing systems there has been the detection of chaotic signals within the neural pathways. Chaotic systems have some unique behaviors such as basins of attraction that allow systems to quickly transit between states. Additionally, small changes to chaotic signals can lead to dramatic changes in the outputs which can make sensing organs very sensitive to subtle events. Researchers to date tend to focus on either the use of the macroscopic models or the microscopic models in their avenues of research. We will uniquely adopt both the structural macroscopic model of biological systems as well as the chaotic microscopic nature of biological systems in this text. Dividing the complex vision task into a hierarchy will allow us to address increasing levels of complexity, yet show how chaos-based methodologies can be applied through all of these levels.

Keywords: Neural signals, neural pathways, basins of attraction, visual cortex.

BIOLOGICAL MOTIVATIONS FOR A CHAOTIC APPROACH

Biological vision systems have been widely analyzed by researchers both at a macroscopic level and microscopic levels. The fields of psychology and psycho-perception have been responsible for the macroscopic analysis and modeling of vision systems with models of attention direction, change detection, saliency, et cetera. Likewise neurobiologists have analyzed and modeled vision systems at the microscopic level with the detailed characterization neural signals and neural structures. The computer vision approach advocated in this text derives motivations from both ends of this spectrum. From the macroscopic level we adopt the concept of a vision stack and the ideas of pre-attentive through post-attentive vision tasks which operate on varying levels of consciousness in the human visual system [40, 41]. From the microscopic level we adopt the idea that the underlying signals have chaotic behavior, particularly with regard to the switching of attention in perception and recognition tasks [3, 4, 42].

Michael E. Farmer

VISION SYSTEM PROCESSING ARCHITECTURE

There is considerable evidence from neuro-cognitive research that infers that the biological cortex is organized in layers [40, 41, 44]. Very loosely, the lower levels, such as the primary visual cortex or V1 layer, are responsible for lower-level functionality. More complex behaviors which require increasing intelligence are accomplished by higher layers of cortex. The specific details of the signals transmitted between these layers are not generally well understood. A highly simplified view of the layered cortical model is provided in Fig. **2**. Cauller adds that there is also a parallel organization of the sensor pathways as they extend through the cortex [44]. One manifestation of this parallel structure is the existence of two major processing streams, the ventral and the dorsal streams which transmit signals from the early visual areas to the rest of the human brain. In this model the dorsal stream computes 'vision for-action'. Vision for action consists of very fast processing that is predominately unconscious. The ventral stream computes 'vision-for-perception' using methods that are slower and sometimes conscious. Brogaard studied the existence of unconscious visual tasks and whether any of the ventral processing (vision for action) is conscious or is completely unconscious [45].

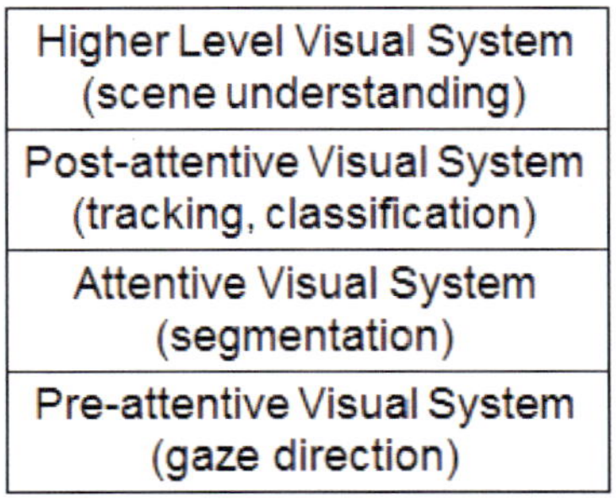

Figure 2: Conceptual architecture of a hierarchical visual system.

This type of layered parallel architecture is even further extended by Rizzolatti and Matelli and Gallese who suggest that the dorsal/ventral distinction may be too coarse-grained. They propose there is actually a tripartite organization of vision for action, vision for perception, and a third intermediate and overlapping pathway [46]. Overall Clark summarizes the various architectural models as follows: "Aspects of the dual visual systems picture are supported by a large and impressively varied body of evidence including a swath of neuroimaging experiments" [46]. These parallel structures of varying level of consciousness share common input pathways and also may interact in non-trivial ways. This parallels the well-known subsumption architecture of Brooks which is provided in Figs. **3** and **4**, where higher levels of intelligence are running in parallel, share common inputs, and can also share information between layers [47].

The interaction of these layers in performing vision tasks can be modeled both from a top-down approach and a bottom-up approach. For example, attention may be directed from bottom-up stimuli such as the sudden appearance of an object, which well matches our proposed synthetic vision system architecture provided earlier in Fig. **2**. LeMeur, *et al.,* successfully exploits the bottom-up layered artificial vision system for attentive processing [2]. Zhang, *et al.,* also have defined the lower level V1 visual cortex as providing a saliency map to focus higher level vision processing. They note that: 'that: "Because neural resources are severely limited, only a very small fraction of the visual inputs can reach all the way to perception" [48]. LeMuer notes that: "the human fixation regions present higher spatial contrast and spatial entropy regions" [2]. Likewise Park, *et al.,* proposed an attention module for a smart camera which would be responsible for a low-level attention direction function, which would then direct the video streams to higher level processing if motion is detected [49]. We will see in subsequent chapters that this model of layered functionality with shared inputs and increasing levels of both consciousness and complexity will also serve us well in developing a complete vision system based on chaos theory. Additionally, the concept of entropy and sudden change in a scene providing saliency information for fixation will map well onto the concept that chaos is a measure of information creation. Regions in the field of view where information is being created should be of interest to a biological visual system. Representations of this information can be readily shared amongst the various levels of the vision stack through the phase plots of the grayscale trajectories of the pixels in the image. We will see later in this text that the phase plot of an image or image pair captures the information generating behavior of the system and can be exploited in different ways by the lower and higher level processing functions. This approach of sharing the phase plot across various levels of processing is well-suited for an artificial vision system since it naturally maximizes the efficiency of utilization of processing resources. The mechanisms through which chaos theory can be applied to the various vision tasks associated with increasingly higher levels of processing will be the subjects of subsequent chapters. Note the highest level processing, namely Scene Understanding, will not be addressed in this text as it only peripherally involves vision-specific tasks. Additionally, it relies on much higher levels of contextual processing and knowledge representation than is required for many cognitive tasks.

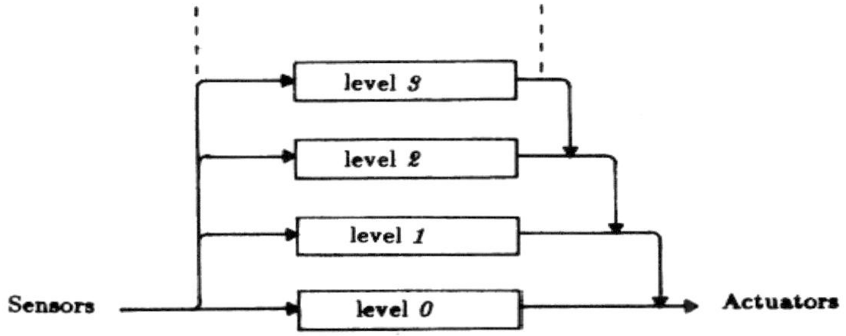

Figure 3: High level conceptual architecture of the Subsumption Architecture for Artificially Intelligent systems [47].

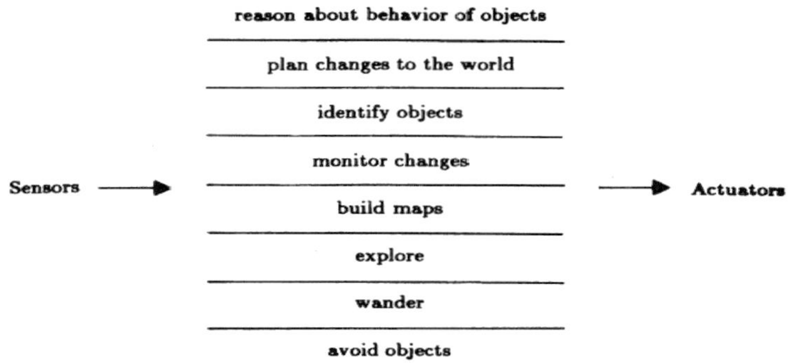

Figure 4: Proposed possible hierarchy of tasks within Subsumption Architecture for Artificially Intelligent robotic systems [47].

SIGNAL CHARACTERISTICS OF BIOLOGICAL PERCEPTIVE SYSTEMS

In addition to using the macro-architecture of the biological vision system for motivation in the design of an artificial vision system, we also use the microscopic signal characteristics as motivation for our chaos-based processing methodology.

There is considerable evidence that biological neural pathway signals exhibit a chaotic nature [4, 42, 50, 51]. Nagao, *et al.,* notes that: 'diverse types of chaos have been confirmed at several hierarchical levels in the real neural systems from single cells to cortical networks" [4]. In their work, they define a chaotic model to explain the problem of alternation in perception of ambiguous objects. They showed that switching between the classifications of two ambiguous objects can be explained by the neural signals switching between two distinct basins of attraction, each accounting for a different classification choice [4]. Additionally, Freeman proposed that biological olfactory systems exhibit chaotic behavior. He explained the ability of biological systems to recognize a single scent from a complex background of scents using chaotic basins of attraction [42]. Freeman also found evidence of chaotic behavior in visual perception systems where he observed: "the images [of Electroencephalograph (EEG) brain activity] suggest that an act of perception consists of an explosive leap of the dynamical system from the "basin" of one chaotic attractor to another' [42]. Freeman's work in pattern recognition demonstrated that the quiescent state of the brain is a state of chaos prior to decision making, but then transitions to more periodic activity when attention focusses to a single stimulus [43, 51]. Korn and Faure further reinforced these findings when they stated, "dynamical information [in sensory neurons] can be preserved when a chaotic input… is converted into a spike train" [3].

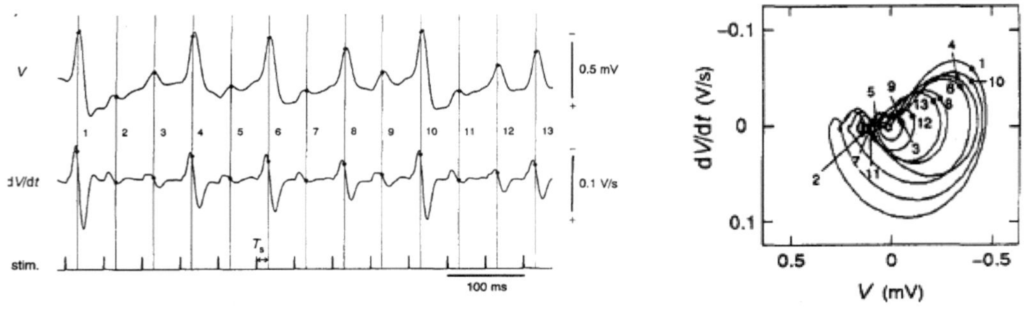

(a) (b)

Figure 5: Example neural signal in rat, (a) time series of signal, and (b) phase plot showing chaotic basin of attraction [52].

In [52, 53] Ishizuka and Hayashi demonstrate the reaction of neurons in a rat to stimulus. Fig. **5** (a) shows the time series of signals from the rat neurons and Fig.

5(b) shows the phase space representation of these signals where chaotic-appearing basins of attraction are apparent. Likewise they further demonstrated additional chaotic signal behavior in response to stimuli of the hippocampal tissue in [53] and note: "(a) chaotic signal is an effective temporal pattern to increase the synaptic efficacy". Additionally, Korn and Faure note that "there could be considerable benefits for the nervous system to choose chaotic regimes given their wide range of behaviors and their aptitude to quickly react to changing conditions" [3]. Fig. **6** (a) provides an example of a simulated brain signal developed by Korn and Faure in [3] and Fig. **6** (b) provides a companion actual brain signal with a distinct basin of attraction formed. Le Meur, *et al.*, also recognized and used nonlinear models to describe the stimulation of visual cells in biological systems [2]. Subha, *et al.*, note that "it was observed that nonlinear dynamics theory would be a better approach than traditional time domain and frequency domain methods in analyzing and characterizing the EEG signals" [20].

Researchers have also had considerable success "using fractal theory to…characterize neuronal dynamics" [50]. Zheng *et al.*, demonstrated in [50] that neural firings in the human brain "are consistent with a multi-fractal process…". We will discuss later in this text the intimate relationship between chaotic signals and fractal patterns in phase space. We will exploit this observation throughout this text as we provide an alternate non-linear dynamics foundation for many common tasks performed in computer vision.

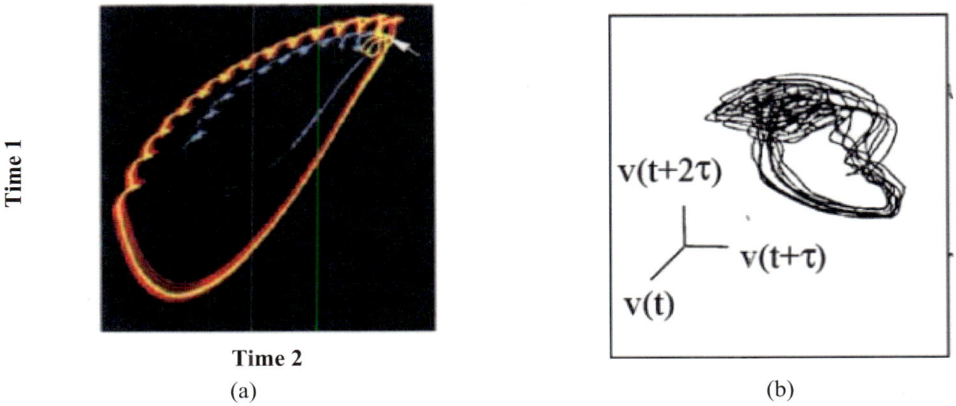

Figure 6: Additional examples of neural signals, (a) simulation of distinct basins of attraction resulting from external stimuli of neurons [3], and (b) human epileptic brainwave behavior [3].

CONCLUDING REMARKS

There is considerable evidence supporting biological neural pathways exploitation of chaotic signal behavior to ensure rapid reactions to the perception of complex changing environments. The incredible efficacy of biological visual and perceptual systems, coupled with the considerable research indicating the presence of chaotic behavior in biological neural systems, provides the motivation to explore employing approaches from chaotic signal analysis to computer vision. The remaining chapters of this text further expand on chaotic signal analysis and its application to various common tasks in computer vision.

CHAPTER 3

Foundations of Chaos and Fractals

Abstract: Chaos theory has been found to be a very effective tool for analyzing complex non-linear systems with its beginnings being traced to weather systems prediction by Lorenz. Chaotic systems have also been tied to information theory, and systems that exhibit chaotic behavior have been shown to be sources of information. Definitively identifying systems as being chaotic, however, is extremely difficult. Fortunately simply identifying a system as being chaos-like can be beneficial and even adequate for certain analysis, and this is the approach we will adopt in this text for addressing computer vision applications using chaos theoretic techniques. Chaos and fractals are interconnected because systems that behave chaotically have phase space trajectories that are fractal in nature. Thus analyzing the fractal dimension of the phase space trajectories of systems will allow us to determine how chaotic they are and more importantly for computer vision how strongly they are creating information. The strength of information generation will prove effective in developing robust motion and change detection algorithms even in the face of complex spatio-temporally varying illumination in later chapters.

Keywords: Eckmann-Ruelle conjecture, ergodicity, embedded dimension, information, fovea, phase plot, noise, thermal equilibrium.

INTRODUCING THE PHASE PLOT

Researchers have shown a tangible connection between information creation and chaos [1, 39]. Abarbanel notes: "Stable linear systems generate zero information, so selecting information generation as the critical aspect of non-linear systems assures us from the outset that the quantity we focus on is a property of non-linear dynamics not shared by linear evolution" [21]. This is a critical observation for our application of chaos theory to computer vision since the focus on information generation will provide an approach with a natural proclivity for detecting the creation and distribution of information in images. This is a dramatically different focus than that of traditional computer vision and image processing approaches such as optical flow [25]. These traditional approaches focus on the movement of grayscale values, and require an explicit assumption of image constancy. Note however, that there have been other image processing approaches in the past that have exploited the concept of information content. The most obviously of these is

Michael E. Farmer

the use by Pluim, *et al.*, of mutual information for image registration [38]. The mutual information between two images is defined by [38]:

$$I(A;B) = \sum_{a,b} p(a,b) \cdot \log\left(\frac{p(a,b)}{p(a)p(b)}\right), \tag{1}$$

where $p(a)$ and $p(b)$ are the probability distributions of images A and B, and $p(a,b)$ is the joint distribution (approximated by the joint histogram) of images A and B. Additionally a is the intensity of a pixel in image A and b is the corresponding intensity of the same pixel in image B. It is clear from Equation (1) that the joint histogram plays a key role in the estimation of the mutual information. Cho and Kim in [54] have analyzed the structure of the joint histogram for global illumination analysis. They use the joint histogram as a means for detecting and removing global illumination changes. Interestingly, they treat the non-linear effects of possible motion being present as data outliers to be ignored while computing the global illumination amplitude. In our approach we embrace these non-linear effects as manifestations of information creation [54].

The construction of a joint histogram and the construction of the phase plot for two images are very similar. Rather than using the amplitude from the first image and the amplitude from the second image directly in the joint histogram, phase plot uses the amplitude and relative delta-amplitude between each pixel in the two images. As can be seen in Fig. **7** there is a strong correlation between the structure of the phase plot (Fig. **7** (b)) and the joint histogram (Fig. **7** (a)) which is generated from the image pair in Fig. **8** of a vehicle moving through a scene. Peitgen, *et al.*, state that chaotic behavior of dynamical systems can be detected in the phase plot of the system [1]. Finally, Tel and Gruiz state: "chaotic motion is characterized (when)… a complex but regular structure appears in the position *vs.* velocity representation (*i.e.* the phase plot)" [22]. The complex structures mapped out by the trajectories of nonlinear systems in phase space are called attractors and chaotic attractors are termed 'strange attractors' [1]. Within attractors there are often basins of attraction around which the trajectories evolve, and in Fig. **7** (b) we see there are two distinct basins of attraction. Nagao, *et al.*, has noted that meta-stable perception, namely the lack of certainty between two possible explanations of a visual event can be modeled by the transitioning of the neural signals between two distinct basins of attraction [4]. As an aside, note that we do not have access to the true phase space of a system without knowing the underlying dynamics equations. Consequently we will have to reconstruct the phase space *via* methods discussed in later in this chapter. Fortunately, as Lindgren states; "Reconstructed phase spaces have been proven to be topologically equivalent to the original system and therefore are capable of recovering the nonlinear dynamics of the generating system" [36].

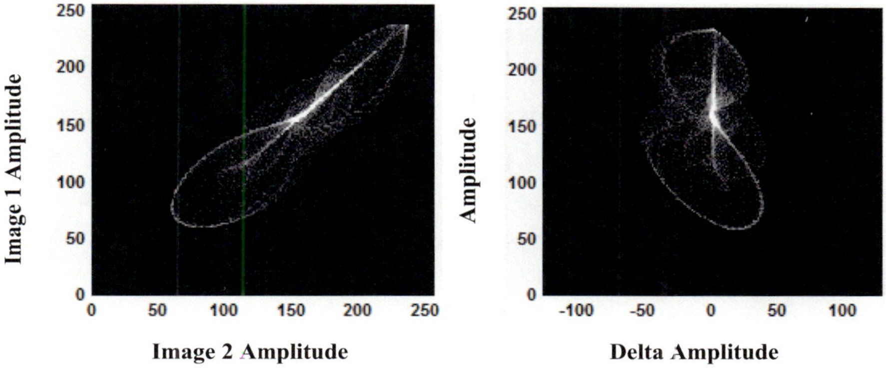

(a) (b)

Figure 7: Comparison of structure of joint histogram and phase plot of an image pair experiencing object motion, (a) joint histogram and (b) phase plot.

(a) (b) (c)

Figure 8: An image sequence experiencing object motion, (a) the original image with a highlighted region with motion, (b) the first image in the pair, and (c) the second image.

In Chapter 2 we saw some interesting examples of the analysis of complex neural time series signals in phase space. As Klonowski notes, "signal complexity can be analyzed either in time domain, frequency domain, or in the system's phase space" [57]. However, Tel and Gruiz noted that observing chaotic behavior in real space is extremely difficult and "the use of phase space is inevitable as a means of understanding the structure accompanying chaos" [22]. They also note that chaotic behavior results in complex but ordered behavior in phase space. In a very simple interpretation, the more complex and space-filling the trajectory is, the more highly chaotic the signal is. The extent to which a trajectory fills its phase space is commonly measured by the fractal dimension of the phase plot. This close inter-relationship between chaos and fractal structure in phase space can be witnessed by the fact that various researchers in neural signals use the terms fractal and chaotic somewhat interchangeably. One must actually be very careful here, however, as Klonowski notes: "(the raw signal fractal dimension) should not be confused with the fractal dimension of the… system in phase space" [57]. In particular, when we discuss texture analysis later in the text we will see that all past work has been on computing fractal dimensions of the actual grayscale images, whereas in our chaos-centric approach we will analyze the fractal behavior of textures in phase space.

We saw the potential for interesting behavior exhibiting the space-filling nature of a chaotic system in phase space in the phase plot in Fig. **7** (b) produced by the moving object in Fig. **8**. Since we will be relying on the space-filling nature of interesting image phenomena we need to define the phase plot resulting from the baseline analysis. Fig. **9** (a) provides an example of a typical street scene which will be used to compute the phase plots in Fig. **9** (b). In Fig. **9** (b) the phase plots for every grid cell of the image demonstrates a simple vertical line. This implies that for every amplitude pixel in the image there was no change, as was expected, since we compared the image with itself. Fig. **9** (c) provides a zoom of a single phase plot further clarifying the vertical phase plot. We will utilize the idea of a vertical line in phase space representing no change when we analyze the effects of global illumination changes on an image in the Chapter 4. We will see that global illumination merely changes the slope of this vertical line which implies phase space is a very natural representation for providing illumination immunity.

In conclusion, it is commonly recognized that there is a strong relationship between chaos and fractals, where Peitgen notes: "as geometrical patterns, strange attractors (in phase space) are fractals; (while) as dynamical objects, strange attractors are chaotic" [1]. We will see in Chapter 5 that there are numerous measures of dimensionality of the phase plots that can be computed to measure their fractality, and hence the underlying chaotic nature of the original signal. Throughout the remainder of the text we will concentrate on using the phase plots generated by image pairs for the various vision tasks and use measures of their fractal dimension as indicators of interesting phenomena.

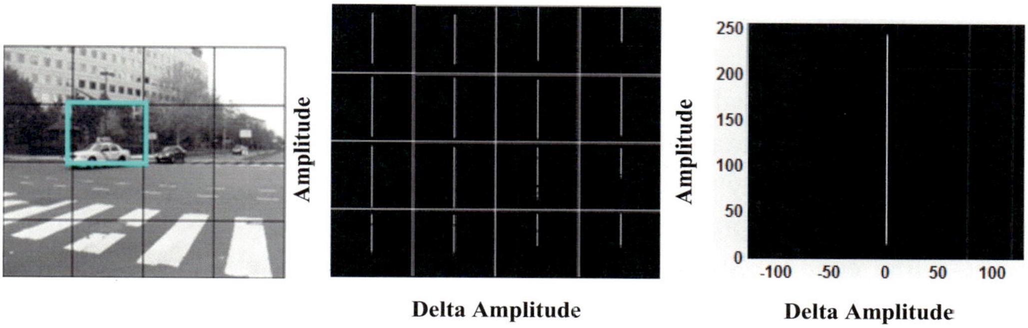

(a) (b) (c)

Figure 9: The phase plot of an image with itself: (a) image, (b) collection of all phase plots of comparing image (a) with itself, and (c) zoom of single phase plot for highlighted region in image (a) [67].

In the remainder of this chapter we will discuss how phase plots are actually constructed and how they can capture the behavior of the dynamics of an underlying system. We will explore how sequences of time lags between images can be used to construct an approximation of the actual phase space. We will then show how some dimensions of the phase space provide more descriptive views of the underlying chaotic behavior of the image sequences. We will then show, with a little book-keeping, how we can map specific locations in phase space back to the locations in the original images to allow us to determine which regions in an image are the sources of chaotic behavior.

We will explore the effects of noise in phase space and how it can mask actual chaotic signals unless properly handled. We will also explore an important concept called ergodicity which is a common assumption when analyzing many physical systems, yet is rarely able to be proven. We will show that in our imaging applications we are actually able to demonstrate the validity of ergodicity. Ergodicity will allow us to not need to follow every pixel's trajectory over time to determine whether its behavior is the result of an underlying chaotic process. Instead we can rely on the ensemble of pixels that represent the particular image, and use the ensemble behavior to replace the individual pixels' behaviors. This is essential since it will allow us to develop a system which has the potential for high speed reactions to changes in the image content.

ARE COMPUTER VISION IMAGE SEQUENCES CHAOTIC, CHAOS-LIKE, OR PSEUDO-CHAOTIC AND DOES IT MATTER?

Traditional chaotic signals generated by mathematical functions such as the Roessler function are examples of *permanent* chaotic signals [1]. Permanent chaotic signals are only one class of chaotic systems. The other important category of chaotic signals is *transient* chaotic signals. In transient signals, specific initial conditions can lead to finite time chaotic events. These transient chaotic events distinguish themselves in phase space from nonchaotic events when analyzed over their finite time interval. Biological neural signals are finite duration transient signals that last only as long as the stimulating event being perceived by the perception system. Likewise, any signals of interest in computer vision will be transient by nature [22]. The passing of a moving object through an image scene only lasts as long as it takes for the object to pass through the scene. The sudden appearance of an object in an image scene is an interesting case. While the scene may not contain an object for a very long period of time, its appearance occurs over a relatively short finite time interval. For example the duration of the chaotic signal may be while a person carries a briefcase across a scene and deposits it on the floor. It is during the appearance of this deposited object that we are most interested in the scene as it represents a possibly important event.

While these concepts of transient chaos are important for temporal analysis of image sequences, we will see that chaos can also play an important role in the analysis of texture in images as well. In the case of texture we will be employing the concept of *spatial* chaos. Spatial chaos was initially proposed by Coullet *et al.,* to model the chaotic effects of defects in solid state physics [23]. Coullet noted that chaos theory can be applied to pattern formation in extended physical systems. Spatial chaos has also been used by Peng *et al.,* to model long-range correlations within DNA sequences [59]. Texture within a scene definitely represents a distinct spatial pattern formation that is not easily characterized by traditional statistical measures [23].

Researchers have found it to be extremely difficult to prove the actual existence of chaos in finite duration signals. The neural signals shown in Chapter 2 were never confirmed to be absolutely from chaotic sources. By analyzing them in terms of chaos theory, however, researchers have been able to better understand and model their behavior. Mattfeldt notes that all the common criteria for determining if a system is chaotic can be fulfilled by systems whose underlying generating function is highly correlated, or colored, noise [60]. Qin and Oommen in [61] note that the very popular Adachi chaotic neural network model is not purely chaotic when analyzed using Lyapunov exponents. Rather the Adachi network outputs complex periodic signals whose precise periodicity cannot be anticipated. They propose that this complex periodic behavior be termed *quasi-chaotic*. Trying to definitively prove if a system is chaotic can be quite difficult, and one could argue it is not fundamentally necessary to prove given the efficacy of the quasi-chaotic models employed by these systems.

Velazquez proposes a more pragmatic approach by suggesting neural systems may possess "attractor-like" behavior rather than committing to the existence of pure chaos when analyzing neural signals [5]. He notes that for neural signals their non-predictable nature may be neither from chaos or stochastic origins but from an *aperiodic forcing phenomenon*. This concept of an aperiodic forcing function is also a very reasonable model for the interesting phase plot behavior demonstrated in Fig. **7** which was created by an object moving through a scene. Consequently, we propose that the motion of an object through an image sequence can be viewed as an aperiodic forcing function perturbing the image radiance received by the imaging sensor. As the object moves through the image field over time, the grayscale value representing the scene radiance in each pixel is the result of the object's changing normal vector and albedo within that pixel as the object moves through it. The moving object can then be considered an aperiodic forcing function resulting in a chaos-like time series of changing grayscale values. Also we will further propose that characteristics such as image texture can be modeled this way. Pentland proposed the underlying roughness of a natural scene's surface causes the resultant images of the scene to appear fractal [10]. We will extend this model one step further and propose that the underlying roughness of the surface can be considered as a hidden aperiodic forcing function within the scene that causes the resultant grayscale variations in the image. This will also allow us to distinguish the behavior of regular texture patterns such as brick walls from natural patterns which would appear more 'random', but are actually exhibiting a more chaos-like behavior. Likewise, returning to the idea of information creation, an aperiodic forcing function would convey significantly greater amounts of information than a simple periodic signal. The adoption of the concept of the aperiodic forcing function allows the chaotic approach of this text to coalesce myriad approaches to various vision tasks ranging from motion analysis to texture analysis into a unified view of computer vision. In this unified view interesting phenomena in images are the result of underlying aperiodic forcing functions that can be detected and characterized by the tools of chaos theory. These aperiodic forcing functions may be either temporal functions in the case of motion and change detection, or spatial functions in the case of texture analysis.

One additional important fact to consider is that true chaotic behavior requires real-valued signals rather than discrete signals. Computer systems in general and digital imaging systems in particular rely on data that are quantized. The significance of quantization can be seen with a typical 'toy problem' from image processing of a uniform amplitude square object moving across a uniform background of a different color as shown in Fig. **10** (a) and (b). This example can be thought of as a camera of extremely low dynamic range (*i.e.* a binary camera) where all the amplitude values across the object are the same. In this case the object moving through the scene no longer provides an aperiodic forcing function and any expectations of chaos-like behavior are lost. This is verified in its phase plot in Fig. **10** (c) which is highly degenerate and consists of only four points. Two points are at zero along the x-axis corresponding to the unchanging points on the background and the middle of the object. The two other points are shifted, either to the left or the right corresponding on the change in amplitude of the pixels that were on the object and are now on the background and *vice versa*.

Interestingly low pass filtering (see Fig. **10** (d) and (e)) can help with this degeneracy of the phase plot since intermediate amplitudes are created by the weighting process of the filter. The trajectories of the points moving between object and background amplitudes are now visible, as can be seen in the phase plot in Fig. **10** (f). Thus even if we have a very highly quantized camera system, low-pass filtering to reduce the effects of noise will also help to re-create some of the filamentary structure within the trajectory that was lost in the quantization process.

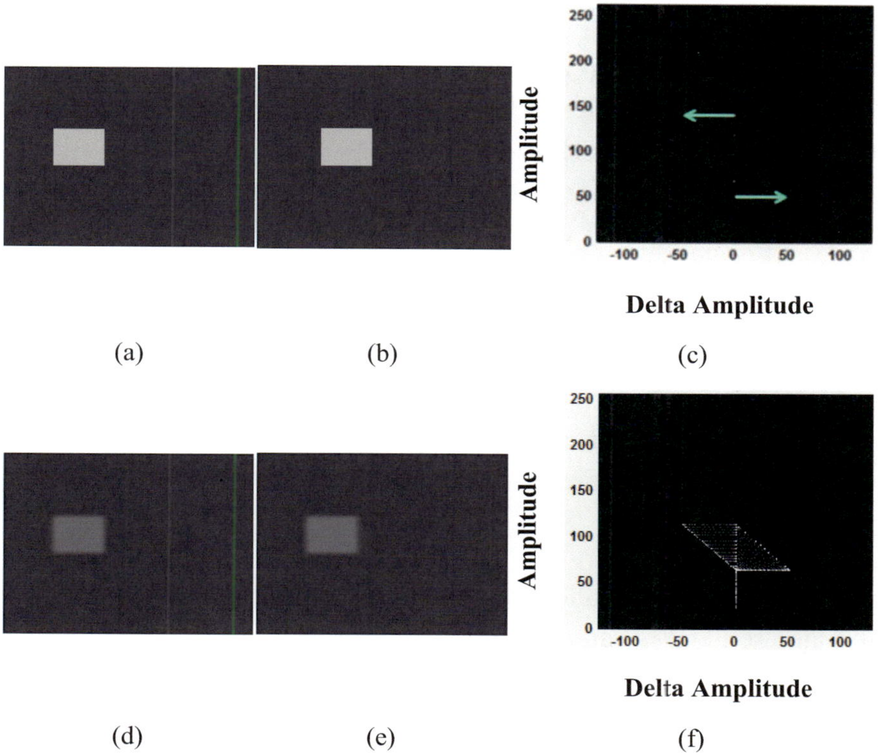

Figure 10 : Examples of degenerate phase space behavior for toy problem: (a) first image, (b) next image, (c), phase plot, (d) filtered first image, (e) filtered next image, and (f) phase plot from filtered data showing trajectory excursions.

Chirikov has proposed that for discrete systems we define the concept of *pseudo-chaos* to describe the chaos-like behavior that can often be seen in discretely valued systems [62]. Pseudo-chaos is defined as the statistical behavior of a dynamical system with discrete energy levels. The term pseudo-chaos is borrowed from computer science from pseudorandom number generation. Chirikov additionally states, "Classical chaos is impossible in finite and closed quantum systems", *i.e.,* systems where the allowable motion of the system is bounded in phase space [62]. This is clearly the case for imaging systems which often only have 8 bits of resolution, and where even high resolution systems are often limited to 16 bits. Chirikov also points out that "... the motion within a discrete spectrum may exhibit all the statistical properties of classical chaos but on some ***finite*** time scales" [62]. This is exactly the same behavior that is seen with random number generators as well; their behavior appears random until long enough time scales are used and then the sequences becomes periodic.

Unfortunately there has been very little research in discrete systems and the applications of chaotic principles to them. McDonough *et al.,* in [63] note that the effects of quantization on detection of chaos have not been widely addressed in the literature. Most research focused on using tools from chaos theory, such as research applying multi-fractal analysis of phase space trajectories have focused on continuous dynamical systems rather than quantized systems such as a digital imaging system. Continuous dynamical systems such as those defined by the Rosller equations produce trajectories that are quite effectively detected by fractal measures. The trajectory associated with the Rosller functions shown in Fig. **11**(a) never crosses the same point which results in individual trajectories being at infinitesimally close which results in the space-filling characteristic associated with fractal dimensions.

In our image processing application, the trajectories mapped out by moving objects in image sequences can *theoretically* generate arbitrarily close trajectories. The term $\rho \vec{N} \cdot \vec{I}$ in the image reflectance equation generates a continuum of values corresponding to the continuously changing surface normal of the object relative to the illumination field. However, in digital imaging systems, the image values are quantized either directly in the camera as with complementary metal-oxide semiconductor (CMOS) devices or in a subsequent analog-to-digital converter used with a charge-coupled device (CCD) camera. Fig. **11**(b) shows the phase plot of the vehicle that has been used throughout this text. When this phase plot is thresholded with a local fractal measure, regions of fractal and non-fractal behavior become apparent with the non-fractal region of the phase space provided in Fig. **11**(c). In these regions of the phase space the fractal measures produce non-fractional dimensions since the space-filling characteristic of the fractal pattern is lost as adjacent trajectories combine into a single higher amplitude trajectory. The quantization of our imaging sensor leads to ***compaction*** of the trajectories in phase space due to the discrete values which the image pixel values may attain. This compaction of the trajectories results in the otherwise fractal dimension of these signals reducing towards their more traditional (integer) dimension.

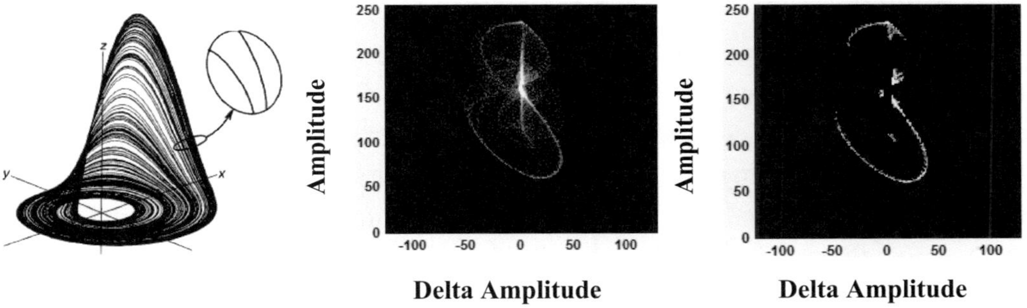

(a) (b) (c)

Figure 11: Quantized phase space trajectories, (a) Rosller trajectory showing high resolution region, (b) motion-based trajectory, and (c) regions of trajectory compaction.

Traditional methods in chaotic analysis suggest that trajectory compaction may be solved by increasing the dimensionality of the phase space *via* analyzing the signal at higher time lags [21]. This approach is not preferred for many computer vision applications for three reasons [64]: (i) the measures here fail due to signal resolution rather than due to the underlying physical process and the chaotic trajectory may still not be discernible, (ii) additional lags would impact the response time of the system, and (iii) many computer vision events are quite transient so an extended observation time may be of limited effectiveness. While these compacted regions of phase space do not have a suitably high fractal dimension, they are still significantly different in topological form from the effects due to other phenomena that the imaging sensor may encounter. In Chapter 4 we will see that the topological structure of the compacted phase space trajectory is dramatically different from the topology of the phase space trajectories of illumination. In Chapter 5 we will introduce additional measures to exploit the unique topological characteristics of compacted trajectories to overcome the effects of compaction. Specifically we will show that the algebraic curvature of the compacted orbits will allow us to differentiate them from signals that are not of interest.

THE 'THERMAL EQUILIBRIUM' STATE OF AN IMAGE – PURE NOISE

As we have discussed throughout this chapter, there is a strong connection between chaos and information creation in signals [1]. The concept of entropy plays a key role in information theory, and likewise it is strongly related to many of the fractal measures we will introduce in Chapter 5 for detecting chaotic-like behavior in images. Consequently, as Bromiley *et al.,* recommend in [65], "if you think you are computing something equivalent to entropy, (you need to understand)… the equivalent of 'thermal equilibrium' for your system". For vision systems, thermal equilibrium would be an image of pure noise. Fig. **12** (a) and (b) and Fig. **13** (a) and (b) provide images under uniform and Gaussian noise, respectively. Likewise Fig. **12** (c) and (d) and Fig. **13** (c) and (d) provide phase plots for the entire image and for a single grid cell within the images. Notice as expected the phase plot trajectory is a nearly uniform covering of phase space. The resultant fractal dimensions provided in Table **1** show the fractal dimension for the uniform and the Gaussian noise. Note the fractal dimension for the uniform noise is nearly two which represents a complete filling of the two-dimensional space. The same measures for the Gaussian noise are slightly lower based on the particular variance used.

Any objects in an image field of view can be viewed as a collection of forcing functions impacting the imaging sensor and creating an image superimposed on this state of 'thermal equilibrium'. For example, we will demonstrate in Chapter 4 that moving objects can be considered aperiodic forcing functions which will generate interesting chaos-like behaviors. Alternatively, we will show that illumination changes will create highly deterministic changes in the images. Textures within an object in an image scene are also sources of forcing functions impacting the imaging sensor. We will show that some textures are periodic and others are aperiodic depending on the type of texture being considered and the behavior in phase space of different textures can be dramatically different.

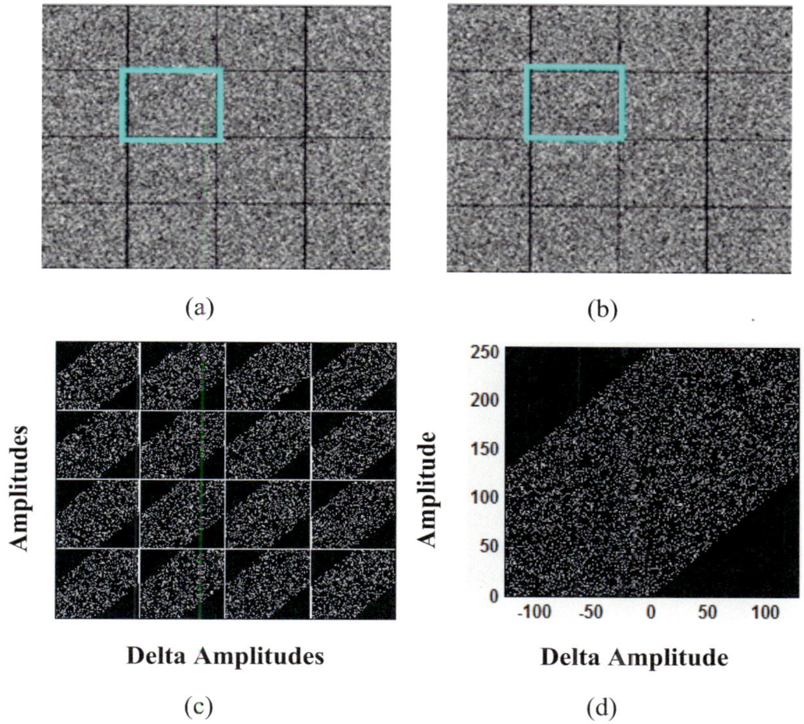

Figure 12: The thermal equilibrium state of an image under uniformly distributed noise: (a) 1st image, (b) 2nd image, (c) collection of all phase plots of (a) and (b), and (d) zoom in of single phase plot for highlighted region in image (a).

Table 1: Summary of Dimensions for Phase Plot in Figs. **12** and **13**

Fractal Dimension Measure	Value for Uniform Noise	Value for Gaussian Noise
Box Counting Dimension	1.91	1.76
Information Dimension	1.81	1.62
Correlation Dimension	1.93	1.64
Renyi Spectrum (max value)	2.2	2.2

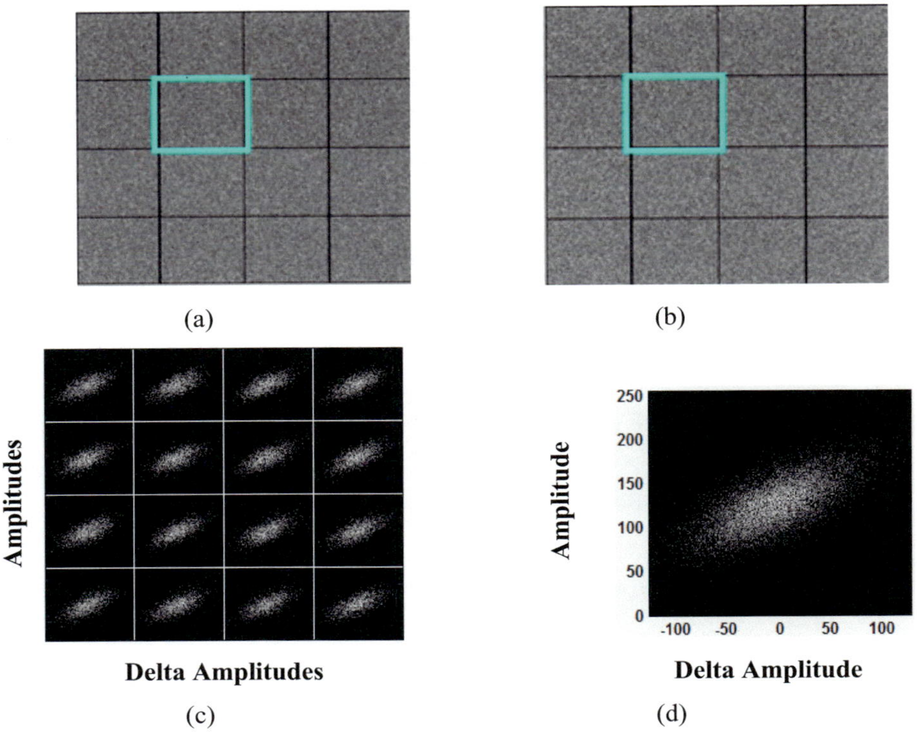

Figure 13: The thermal equilibrium state of an image under Gaussian distributed noise: (a) 1st image, (b) 2nd image, (c) collection of all phase plots of (a) and (b), and (d) zoom in of single phase plot for highlighted region in image (a).

Since the phase space trajectory of pure noise of high amplitude has a high fractal value two issues arise that must be addressed, (i) how does the presence of noise impact our ability to detect chaos, and (ii) just because a phase plot is space filling does not imply chaotic behavior. We will address this first issue later in this chapter when we directly address the effects of noise on the phase plot. We will see that to be able to analyze our image sequences in phase space we will first need to low-pass filter the images to reduce the noise. The characteristics of the low pass filter will prove important since over-filtering an image can also mask the chaotic effects. The second issue in the analysis of images using phase space methods will arise when analyzing texture. Texture can be modeled using fractional Brownian noise [10], we will see that many phase plots of texture are highly space filling with phase plot trajectories that are visually quite different yet of equal fractal dimension. Many researchers have noted that the properties and characteristics of a fractal signal are not completely determined simply by their fractal dimension [58, 66]. We will see that fractal dimension is only useful for differentiating a fractal signal from a non-fractal signal. Additional measures will be required to differentiate two fractal signals since both will have a high fractal dimension. In Chapter 5 we will address these other measures in addition to the traditional fractal measures.

BUILDING THE PHASE PLOT

As we have seen throughout the text, the phase plot is the critical analysis tool we will be using for differentiating chaotic and non-chaotic behavior in the image sequences. The purpose of developing the phase plot in chaos analysis is to develop a complete reconstruction of the actual underlying strange attractor [1, 20]. The goal is that the reconstructed phase space preserves the topological properties of the system's true phase space trajectory [20]. This is important since to completely understand the underlying dynamics of a system, one must develop this multi-dimensional phase plot. Each dimension represents an increasing derivative of the state variable of the system using the following [21]:

$$s(t)\colon \left[s(t)\ \frac{ds(t)}{dt}\ \frac{d^2s(t)}{dt^2} \dots \frac{d^ns(t)}{dt^n}\right] \tag{2}$$

Each increasing order of derivative calculation, however, becomes more and more suspect as the effects of noise become more dominant. Recall we can approximate the derivatives of the system by [21]:

$$\frac{ds(t)}{dt} \approx \frac{s(t+\tau)-s(t)}{\tau} \tag{3}$$

$$\frac{d^2s(t)}{dt^2} \approx \frac{s(t+2\tau)-2s(t+\tau)+s(t)}{2\tau^2} \tag{4}$$

Each increasing order of derivative depends on an increasing time lag based on a multiplicative factor applied to a base time lag. Thus if one considers only the source of new information for each derivative, then these higher order derivatives can be more reliably and more simply captured by simply using the collection of highest order time lags corresponding to each derivative to represent Equation (2) [21]:

$$s(n): [s(n)\ s(n+T)\ s(n+2T) \ldots s(n+kT)] \tag{5}$$

Originally Packard *et al.,* devised the approach of building a higher dimensional representational space from a time series by collecting samples of the time series at varying time lags [68]. The complete signal reconstruction is defined by the infinite series of increasing integer products of this base time lag. There is no guaranteed method for the determination of this base time lag, but we will see in subsequent chapters that there are heuristics that have proven quite reliable for its estimation.

Fig. **14** provides an example of a series of three time snaps of increasing time lag of a moving vehicle. Fig. **15** provides the three-dimensional phase plot constructed both from the sequence of direct estimation of the order zero, one, and two derivatives and the approximation of the derivatives using simply the zero, one and two multiple time lag differences. Fig. **16** provides a projection of the three-dimensional phase plot in Fig. **15** along the second-order time lag axis. Notice both in Fig. **15** and Fig. **16** the trajectory in phase space has a filamentary structure to it, where one can see recurring and slightly offset trajectory curves which create the space-filling nature of the phase plot. This filamentary structure is indicative of chaotic signals in phase space [22].

(a) (b) (c)

Figure 14: Three time snaps of a moving vehicle [67].

The relative changes in the image amplitude across the image rather than through time for an image sequence are important. The relative roughness in the image can spatially be determined by the spatial derivatives rather than the temporal derivatives according to:

$$\frac{ds(x)}{dx} = \frac{s(x+\Delta x)-s(x)}{\Delta x} \tag{6}$$

$$\frac{d^2s(x)}{dx^2} \approx \frac{s(x+2\Delta x)-2s(x+\Delta x)+s(x)}{2(\Delta x)^2} \tag{7}$$

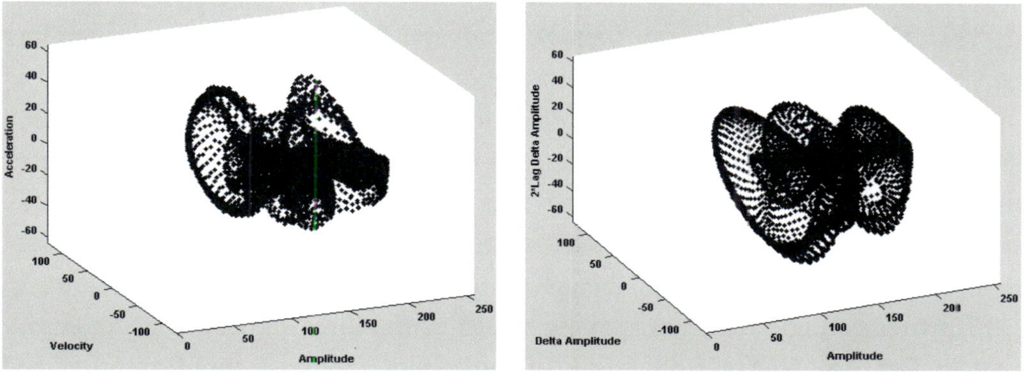

(a) (b)

Figure 15: Comparison of structure of phase space approximations: (a) the sequential approximated derivatives and (b) the sequential time lag approximation.

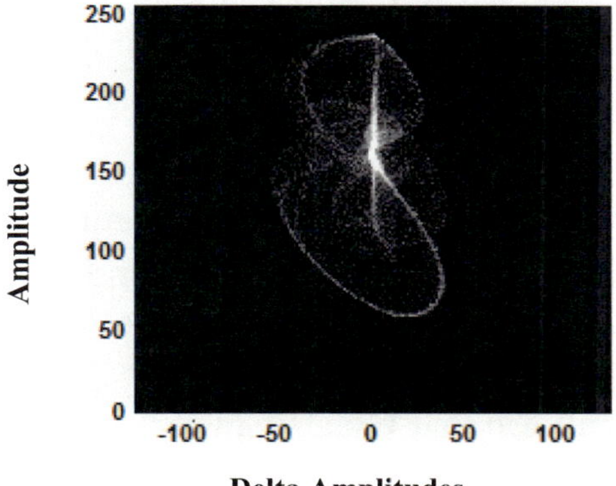

Figure 16: Zoom of the amplitude-delta amplitude projection of the phase plot from Fig. **15** showing filamentary structure of phase plot indicative of chaotic behavior.

Each increasing order of derivative depends on an increasing spatial lag rather than an increasing time lag used for temporal derivatives. Thus if one considers only the source of new information for each derivative, then these higher order derivatives can be captured by using the highest order spatial lag corresponding to each derivative to represent Equation (4) [21]:

$$s(n): [s(n)\ s(n+\Delta x)\ s(n+2\Delta x) \dots s(n+k\Delta x)] \quad (8)$$

Theiler noted: "the delay-time [(or spatial lag for texture)] embedding makes it possible for one to analyze the self-organizing behavior of a complex dynamical system without knowing the full state at any given time [(or spatial location)]" [68]. This higher dimension can then be analyzed for the underlying embedding dimension which represents the actual number of dimensions of free variables of the system. This is similar to manifold learning in pattern recognition where a collection of feature vectors are transformed into a higher dimension within which a lower dimensional subspace that provides the best separability may be found. The lower-dimensional sub-spaces used when analyzing chaotic systems represent the time lag where the chaotic behavior of the system fully manifests itself. Fig. **17** provides a collection of varying views of the three-dimensional trajectory shown in Fig. **15**. Notice how some of the views are quite uninformative and others show the actual considerable spread of the phase space trajectory.

While high dimensional analysis can be both computationally costly and error prone due to finite data sets, we will find in Chapter 4 that for most computer vision applications we are primarily interested in differentiating non-chaotic signals from chaotic signals. We will see in Chapter 4 that motion and change produce chaotic-like behavior while illumination produces a simple linear multiplicative effect. We will see that differentiating motion only requires analysis in two-dimensions since we are only looking for trajectories of fractal dimension greater than one caused by the motion [69].

For texture analysis we will see that higher dimensions are required since texture processing is a recognition task differentiating between two potentially chaotic signal families. We will remind the reader that traditional approaches to texture analysis have analyzed the texture patterns over a collection of spatial lags [14, 70]. It has been proven analytically that for a fractal set with a three-dimensional fractal dimension, D_f its projection down to a two-dimensional space yields a projected fractal dimension [69, 71]:

$$D_{proj} = min\{2, D_f\} \quad (9)$$

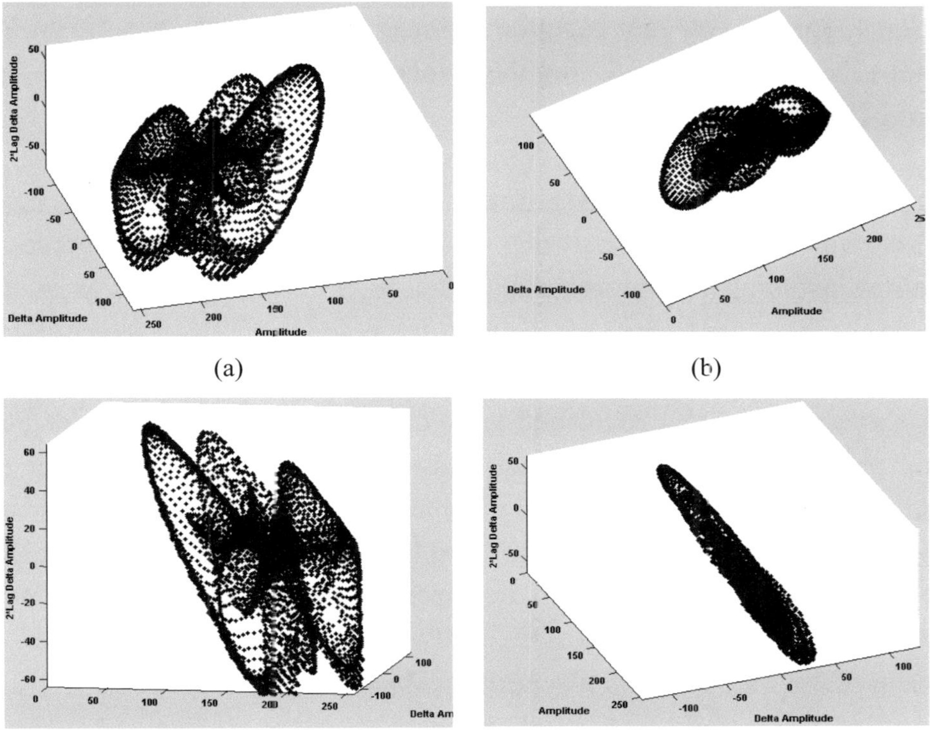

(a) (b)

(c) (d)

Figure 17: Varying views of the sequential time lags showing the dominant dimensions of the structure of the phase space.

It is important to note that Equation (9) is only valid for "indefinitely extensive fractals" [71]. It is not guaranteed for finite time extent fractal signals such as what we would generate in the computer vision applications in this text. The good news, however, is that multiple studies have shown there are strong correlations between the fractal dimensions of higher-dimensional fractal structures and their lower dimensional projections [71, 72]. Amarasinghe and Sonnadara showed that the fractal dimension of a three-dimensional electrical discharge correlated strongly with projections into the corresponding X-Y and Y-Z directions, but the calculated fractal dimension in each of these projections were different since they correspond to different aspects of the electrical discharge [72]. For texture analysis each dimension will correspond to different spatial lags and hence will be capturing different effects in the texture, but the fractal nature of these higher dimensional spaces can be captured through a series of two-dimensional projections thereby at least reducing the computational complexity of high order processing [71, 72].

One important aside worth noting is that phase plots for traditional temporal signal analysis are built by analyzing long time series. For image processing applications involving motion and change detection, however, this is impractical due to the resultant long time lags. Instead, we propose applying the concept of ergodicity which allows us to consider the behavior of the ensemble of pixels that comprise a pair of consecutive image frames rather than considering the long term temporal phase space behavior of each individual pixel [74]. Thus rather than analyzing the time series of individual pixel amplitudes over time, we are instead treating each image as an ensemble of pixels and we propose analyzing these ensembles to infer the longer term behavior of individual pixels. While this assumption initially seems impossible, we will justify our ability do this in a subsequent of this chapter when we introduce the concept of ergodicity.

DETECTION OF CHAOS IN PHASE SPACE THROUGH PROPER DATA LAG SELECTION

As the phase plots are developed by comparing two consecutive images, the next critical parameter to consider is the lag between the subsequent image frames. The inherent visibility of the trajectory is intimately connected with the selection of these lags. Abarbanel notes there are three critical considerations for selecting data lags [21]:

i. The data lag must be a multiple of the sampling rate of the incoming data stream.

ii. If the data lag is too short then the data will not be sufficiently independent.

iii. The data lags cannot be too long.

The first point is important for any real-time applications such as are often required in computer vision because resampling the incoming images to different time steps, while possible, would be computationally demanding. This point is one of implementation rather than the actual dynamics of the situation, but nonetheless is an important point to consider for computer vision applications.

The second point defined by Abarbanel is very easily understood in image processing applications related to motion detection. If an object is moving too slowly through a scene its motion is very difficult to detect using traditional methods such as optical flow, but as the rate of motion increases, the flow patterns are then distinguishable. If the frame rate of the camera was sufficiently fast then the two images would be perfectly correlated and hence as Abarbanel says not sufficiently independent [21]. Alternately, when the frame rate is sufficiently slow then the objects will be sufficiently de-correlated. Another way to understand this point is to recall the research on using mutual information for image registration was directed at determining the minimum extent of the joint histogram which would correspond to well-registered image pairs. The better the registration between the two images, the less independent the images are.

For computer vision applications there are two distinct situations when we must determine the data lags in the images, the first is for motion detection and the second is for texture analysis. We will see in Chapter 4 that the estimation of the minimum time lag selection for motion detection is relatively straightforward and is pragmatically based on whether we can detect the motion based on its speed and the corresponding frame rate. We will likewise see in Chapter 4 that the selection of data lags for texture analysis is more difficult to determine, but fortunately Abarbanel and others have devised means for determining these optimal lags based on either the auto-correlation of the signals or the average auto-mutual information [21].

The third point of Abarbanel is critically important to consider for image processing applications related to motion detection. If the time lag is so long that any moving objects are missed then the motion characteristics of the object of interest are lost. For other applications such as change detection, the concern of selecting time lags that are too long will not be important, except to note that the time lags must be selected based on the behaviors of the change being detected.

In summary, chaos theory for image analysis provides a solid mathematical foundation for understanding the importance of selection of time lags when comparing image pairs for motion detection. Most motion detection algorithms such as those based on optical flow have difficulty detecting small motion changes. They also lack a general framework for determining an adequate time lag between frames for detection. The phase plot provides a natural way of selecting time lags based on a process called unfolding where a multi-dimensional phase space is generated by creating new dimensions for successively increasing time lags. A subspace of this multi-dimensional space can then be selected where the presence of chaos can be either confirmed or refuted [21]. This can be applied to a chaos-based motion detection system that will simply monitor image sequences over an acceptable range of time lags to detect slow moving objects as well as fast moving objects in the same image sequence. If beyond a certain time lag window no motion is detected then a declaration of no motion can be made.

MANAGING COMPLEXITY WITHIN THE PHASE PLOT

Fig. **18** (a) provides the complete first image in the sequential pair where the image has been divided into regions, which we term grid cells in Fig. **18** (b) and (c). This image division is an important first step in chaos-theory based analysis since the phase plot of the entire image is the result of multiple motions, lighting effects, and noise which makes detecting motion from a phase plot of an entire image difficult. The phase plot corresponding to the entire image in Fig. **18** (a) is provided in Fig. **19** (a) where the phase plot appears to be a complex superposition of multiple effects. Fig. **19** (b) and (c) provide the phase plots of the smaller grids provided in Fig. **18** (b) and (c), respectively. These phase plots are clearly simpler in structure and presumably easier to analyze. Consequently, we propose working with the phase plots of these smaller grid cells. Cho *et al.,* and

Russakoff, *et al.*, have also previously proposed dividing the image into regions for using mutual information for image similarity analysis [57, 75].

(a) (b) (c)

Figure 18: Creation of varying number of grid cells count: (a) single cell (entire image), (b) 2x2 grid cells, (c) 4x4 grid cells [67].

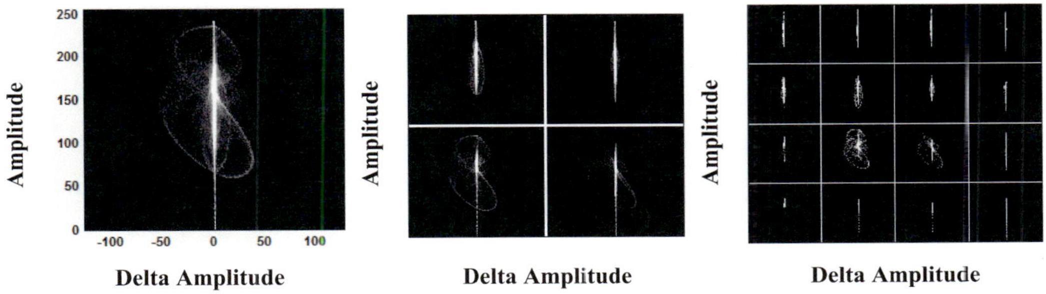

(a) (b) (c)

Figure 19: Demonstration of effect of grid cell count on phase plots: (a) phase plot for single cell, (b) phase plots for 2x2 grid cells, and (c) phase plots for 4x4 grid cells. (NOTE: the image in grid cell (4,2) will be used extensively throughout the remaining chapter).

Fig. **20** shows phase plot superposition. The region of the phase plot that is highlighted in Fig. **20** (a) is the result of the motion of the vehicle in the image sequence visible in the upper left quadrant of Fig. **18** (b) while the remainder of the phase plot is due to the moving vehicle in lower left quadrant of Fig. **18** (b). Notice the structure of this highlighted region in Fig. **20** (a) is identical to the structure of the phase plot in the upper left grid cell of Fig. **19** (b). When there are multiple moving objects within a single image the trajectories of each of these objects is superimposed on each other. This can dramatically complicate the ability to both reliably calculate the fractal measure and also limit the ability to detect or segment specific objects in the scene.

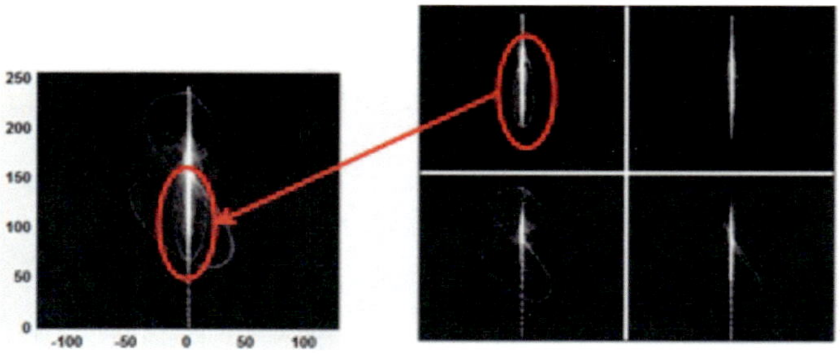

(a) (b)

Figure 20: Superposition of phase plot effects due to motion effects in different regions of image with lower grid cell count.

An alternative approach to using the multiple rectangular regions of Russakoff is to adopt a fovea approach where the center of the image is one region and then the peripheral portion of the image is divided into additional regions as shown in Fig. **21** (a) [76]. The complete adoption of fovea processing can be expensive if the rotational symmetry is to be preserved, which requires log-polar processing of the pixel field [77]. The basic concept of using the fovea division of an image field into a central region and peripheral regions can also be approximated through a simple rectangular decomposition as well as shown in Fig. **21** (b). Fig. **22** (b) shows the simpler phase plots generated using the foveal regions rather than the entire image and the phase plot of the entire image is provided in Fig. **22** (a) for comparison. Note the phase plots for the fovea show similar reduction in complexity as was shown in the phase plots for the rectangular grid regions in Fig. **19** (b) and (c).

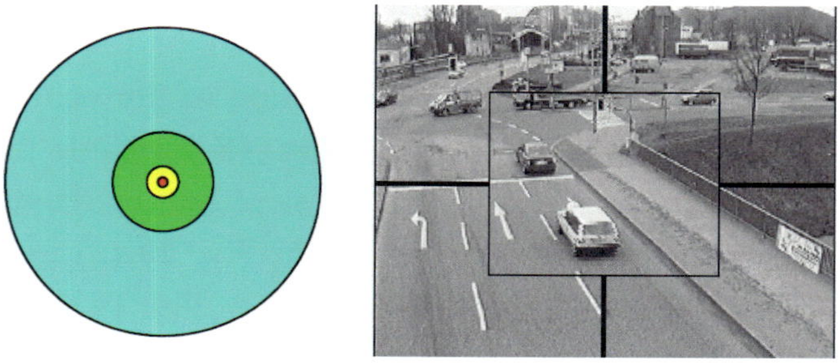

(a) (b)

Figure 21: Demonstration of fovea division of image, (a) fovea arrangement of biological retina, (b) fovea-inspired division of image into central region and peripheral regions [67].

In the human biological vision systems there is also a natural division of the optical field of view based on fovea vision, where the center of the vision field is higher resolution and the peripheral vision is lower resolution [76]. These peripheral regions can then be processed at the original resolution or these regions can be reduced in resolution to preserve processing capacity of the system. The purpose of the fovea is to reduce the field of view of the image used to create the phase plot, and thereby reduce its complexity. This approach may be of interest in certain applications such as pre-attentive vision for surveillance applications where the general area of interest within an image is desired.

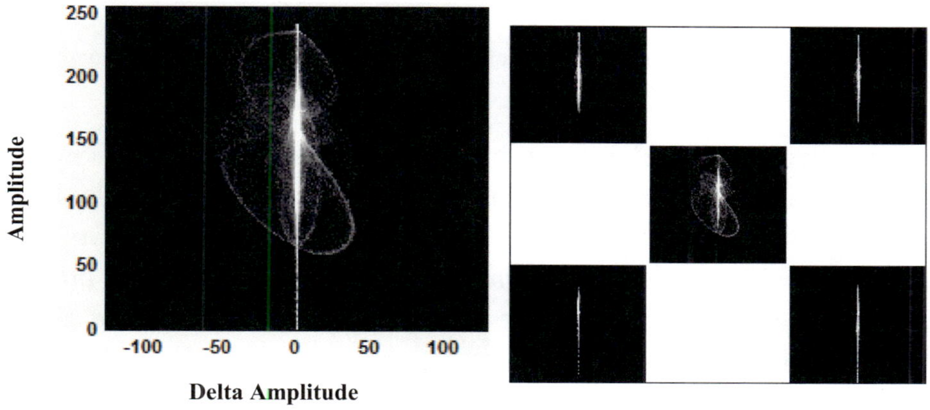

(a) (b)

Figure 22: Demonstration of fovea division of image and resultant phase plots, (a) single cell (entire image), and (b) simple fovea and peripheral regions.

To improve the attention direction accuracy it may be desirable to increase the number of regions in the foveated image. When using the foveal division of the image the choice of the number of regions is determined by the number of peripheral rings. Fig. **23** (a) shows dual-ring fovea structure with one central (fovea) region and two concentric rings of increasing peripheral vision. Fig. **23** (b) shows the resultant collection of phase plots created for each of the fovea regions defined in Fig. **23** (a). The attention directed to the outer rings can either be equal or the system can employ decreasing peripheral resolution as the biological systems employ.

(a) (b)

Figure 23: Analysis with dual-ring fovea vision, (a) fovea regions and (b) corresponding phase plots [67].

Irrespective of whether a grid or fovea-based approach is employed it is important to discuss the decision criteria for selecting the cell count. For example, for low-level attention direction, a single grid cell is not useful since it provides no information regarding to where in the image the higher level attention processing should be directed. Alternatively, the use of too fine of a collection of grid cells can be problematic due to two issues: (i) if the region selection is smaller than the objects of interest then it is possible to suffer from the aperture effect which is common in optical flow analysis, and (ii) inadequate amounts of image data may be available to develop a reliable phase plot.

Regarding the first issue, if a grid cell only covers a small region of a moving object it will be possible for there to be no change in grayscale values as the object moves. This would result in no underlying aperiodic forcing function being present which would result in a degenerate phase plot. A general rule of thumb is that the grid cells should be defined based on the expected sizes of the objects of interest. For applications with a broad varying range of object sizes, the employment of a range of grid cells may be required.

The second issue relates to the availability of enough image data to develop a reliable phase plot. We will see in Chapter 5 when we discuss various measures for estimating the fractal dimension of the phase plots that many of these measures have either explicit or implicit assumptions of large datasets. If the grid cells become too small then there is a limited amount of image data to be used to generate the phase plot, and the resultant fractal measures may no longer be either accurate or even meaningful. Thus it will be the responsibility of the computer vision practitioner to consider this tradeoff when applying chaos theoretic tools to their applications.

RECORDING TO WHERE IN THE PHASE PLOT PIXELS MAP

We add a step to the phase plot generation process to facilitate future image segmentation. In this step we record to where in the phase plot each pixel in the original image maps. This step will provide us a look-up table with which we will be able to determine where interesting regions in the phase plot correspond to in the original image. Once we determine a location in phase space of interest, we can immediately find the corresponding pixels in the grayscale images that produced that interesting behavior. We accomplish this mapping by creating an entry in a look-up table where we register which pixel location in the original image was logged into that phase plot location as shown in Fig. **24**. Each row in the table will typically have a varying number of columns corresponding to the number of pixels mapped to that particular phase plot location. Note each location in phase space may have multiple image pixels that correspond to it. This is due to the natural quantization of the image data that results in multiple regions in the image having similar amplitude and delta amplitude values.

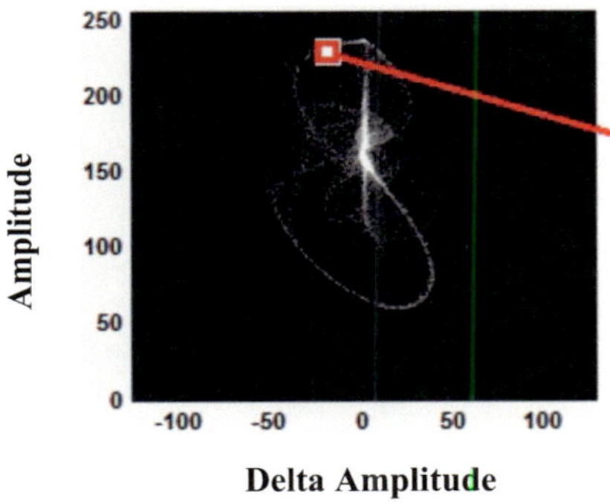

Phase Plot Amplitude	Phase Plot Delta Amplitude	Image Row	Image Column	Image Row	Image Column	...
...						
220	25	101	50	101	51	
220	26	150	21			
220	27	122	35	123	35	
220	28					
...						

Figure 24: Look-up table construction mapping each phase plot cell to each image pixel that produced that location in phase space.

EFFECTS OF NOISE ON THE PHASE PLOTS

Earlier in this chapter we demonstrated that a pure Gaussian noise signal produces a high fractal dimension in phase space. The topological structure of the noise signal trajectory however is dramatically different from the trajectory of a chaotic signal. We know however, that in real world situations our signals of interest are embedded in noise. Consequently, it is possible that the presence of noise can mask the effects of chaos in phase space [1]. Fortunately low-pass filtering is a proven method for reducing the effects of noise on signals. When implementing a low-pass filter, the size of the low-pass filter is a particularly sensitive parameter. Having too large of a filter window will introduce correlation in the signal and distort the chaotic nature of the underlying signal, thereby possibly reducing the space-filling nature of the trajectory [78]. Fig. **25** (a) and (b) show two consecutive image frames image with no change in a video. Fig. **25** (c) shows their resultant phase plot when the incoming images were not noise filtered. Fig. **25** (d) shows the phase plot for the two images after the images have been low-pass filtered to reduce noise. The straight vertical line is what is expected for an image pair with no change present. In the original, unfiltered image, the expected result of no amplitude change between pixels was masked by the noise in the image.

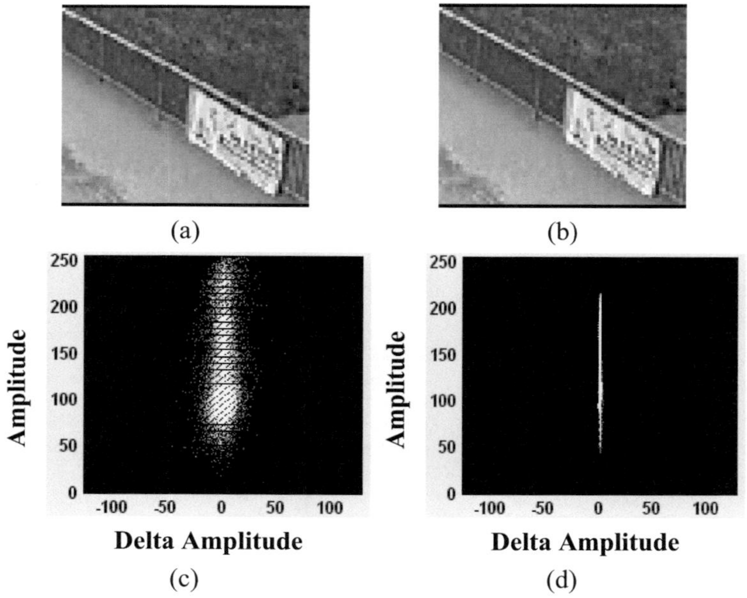

Figure 25: Effects of noise, (a) first image frame from full image in Fig. **19** (a), (b) second image frame, (c) phase plot without noise filtering and (d) phase plot after noise filtering.

Fig. **26** (a) provides the phase plot for the image pair of the moving vehicle in Fig. **18** with no filtering of the image pair for noise. Notice the significant spread of the phase plot and the lack of structure in the phase plot. The noise in the underlying signals has effectively hidden all traces of a structured trajectory, thereby hiding any evidence of chaos. Fig. **26** (b) provides the same phase plot after the incoming image pair was low pass filtered. Notice the structure of the phase plot trajectory is now clearly visible. While clearly low pass filtering of the incoming images is critical to exposing the chaotic behavior, it is important to recognize that excessive filtering can likewise introduce correlations in the signal that will also mask the effects of chaos [78].

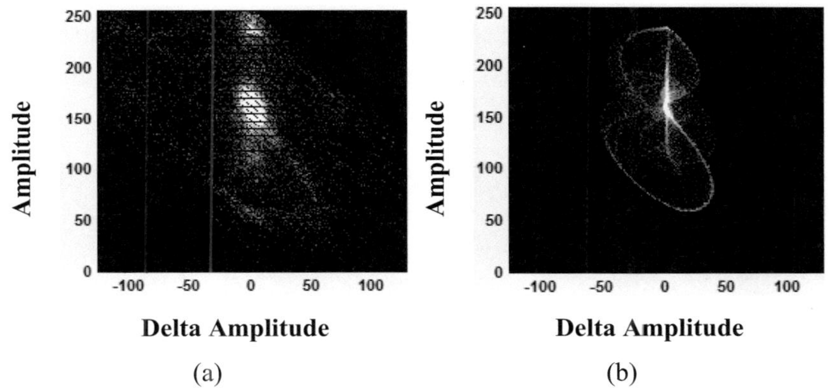

Figure 26: Effects of noise, (a) phase plot without noise filtering and (d) phase plot after noise filtering for image pair in Fig. **18**.

Fig. **27** provides an exploration into the effects of filter window size and form on the phase plot. For all of the images in this sequence, and all of the images in the remaining sections of this text, we use a Gaussian shaped filter. The Gaussian filter has many positive characteristics from a signal processing viewpoint, and as Randen and Husoy state: "Experience has taught us that the Gaussian filter is the far better choice" [79]. In the Gaussian filter there are two parameters to manage, the filter window size and the standard deviation, σ, of the Gaussian kernel. The standard deviation affects the shape of the filter while the window size affects its overall extent. A small standard deviation leads to a focused point filter, and a large standard deviation will result in a relatively flat filter which nearly serves as a uniformly weighted filter. In Fig. **27** (a) the filter is a very small *3x3* filter with a nearly flat response ($\sigma = 3$). Likewise, Fig. **27** (f) provides the phase plot for a massive *50x50* filter window ($\sigma = 20$). The details of the structure of the phase plot trajectory in Fig. **27** (f) are lost since there is now considerable correlation of the pixel values. Interestingly, the general macro-structure of the phase plot remains, but it is no longer adequately detailed to support fractal analysis. Fortunately, as can be seen by the phase plots in Fig. **27** (b) through (d) the exact filter size is not particularly important, as long as it is not either unreasonably large or small. For motion segmentation the filter size that has been found to work well throughout the chaos research in this text is the *10x10* filter with $\sigma = 5$, for which the phase plot in Fig. **27** (c) is the result. Clearly there is adequate internal structure of the phase plot trajectory visible, while the effect of the noise in the image appears mitigated. We will see in Chapter 7 where we discuss the chaotic analysis of texture that smaller Gaussian windows will often be required to ensure the filter does not destroy the structure of the texture.

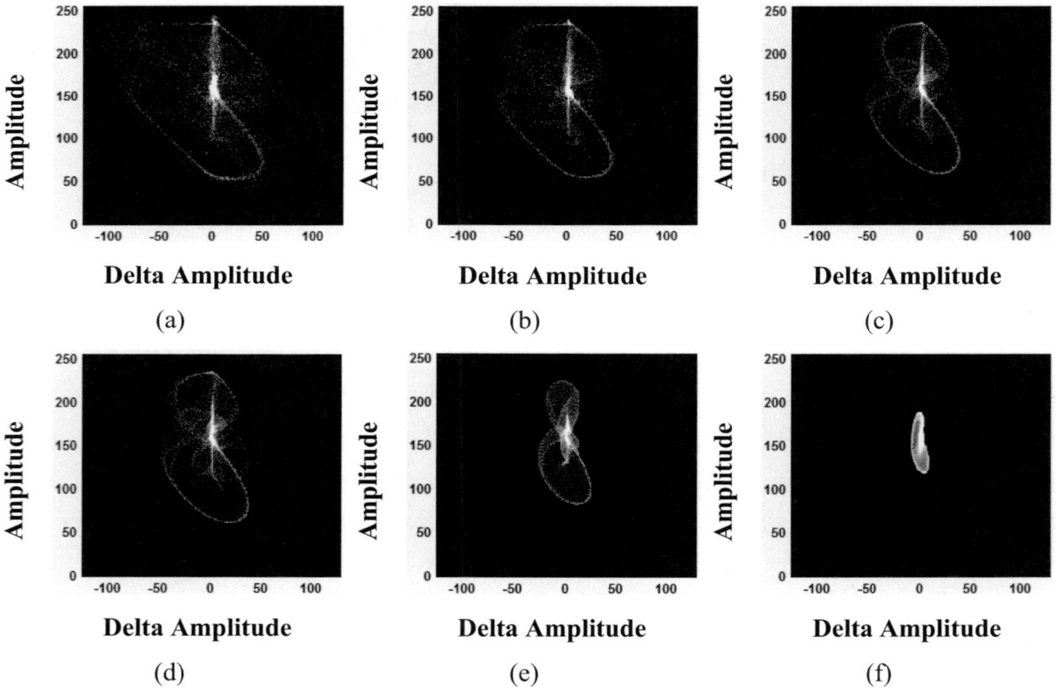

Figure 27: Exploration of filter window size: (a) window=3, sigma=2, (b) window=5, sigma=5, (c) window=10, sigma=5, (d) window=20, sigma=5, (f) window=20, sigma=10, and (f) window=50, sigma=20.

AN ASIDE ON ERGODICITY AND WHY IT IS IMPORTANT FOR COMPUTER VISION

Ergodicity is a critical concept in analyzing chaotic systems, and it can be expressed mathematically by [39]:

$$\lim_{m\to\infty} \frac{1}{m+1}\sum_{k=0}^{m} g(x_k) = \int_A g(x)d\mu(x) \tag{10}$$

where m is the size of the ensemble, $g(x)$ is the ergodic quantity being computed, x is the state space variable, and μ is the measure of integration over the region A of the phase plot. Very simply this equation states that analyzing an ensemble of particles is equivalent to analyzing the long term trajectory of a single particle over time. While ergodicity is a well-accepted assumption in many physical systems, it can rarely be visually demonstrated.

(a) (b) (c) (d)

Figure 28: Same image sequence extended over four time windows for creating temporal phase plot of the highlighted points in the image [67].

Ergodicity manifests itself when the ensemble averaged phase plot mimics the structure of the phase plots of the extended trajectories of individual pixels within the image. This implies the temporal behavior of a single particle (in our case a pixel) is equivalent to viewing the spatial average of an ensemble of particles at a single time instance (an image pair in our application) [39]. It has been demonstrated in [24] that the phase plots captured from image sequences exhibit ergodicity as can be seen by comparing the ensemble phase plot provided in Fig. **19** with the phase plots provided in Fig. **28** extended image sequence in Fig. **29**. The phase plots in Fig. **29** allow us to visualize the generation of the time series trajectory as the vehicle in Fig. **28** moves through the scene resulting in the amplitudes experienced by the pixels in the four color circles. Notice the resultant trajectory in Fig. **29** (c) is extremely similar in structure to the ensemble phase plot provided in Fig. **19** where the figure-eight shape of the two basins of attraction is clearly visible.

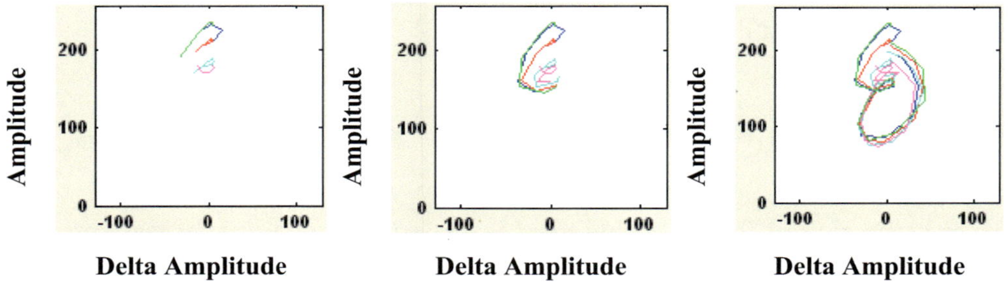

(a) (b) (c)

Figure 29: Temporal phase plot of neighborhood, (a) plot for images shown in Fig. **28** (a) through (b), (b) plot for images shown in Fig. **28** (a) through (c), and (c) plot for entire sequence shown in Fig. **28** through frame (d).

Fig. **30** (a) shows an interesting example from the CAVIAR dataset of human motion [80] in a very severe illumination condition where the humans move between regions of high amplitude background and low amplitude background. Fig. **30** (b) shows the ensemble phase plot where there are two distinct basins of attraction, one of lower amplitude background region and one of higher amplitude background region. Fig. **30** (c) through (f) then shows the original images in the sequence with the pixels being tracked over time. Fig. **31** then provides the time series-based phase space trajectories for these selected pixels as the human subjects move through the image and consequently through these highlighted pixels. Note they create two distinct basins that map directly to the basins seen in the ensemble phase plot in Fig. **30** (b).

The results provided in comparing Fig. **19** and Fig. **29** as well as the results in comparing Fig. **30** and Fig. **31** is extremely exciting since they provide a side-by-side comparison of the ensemble-based phase plot and the time series phase plots and the correspondence is strong. In most physical systems ergodicity is an assumption; however, it is an assumption for which there is no easy way to prove its validity. Our imaging application actually provides us at least anecdotal evidence that the ergodicity assumption may be valid.

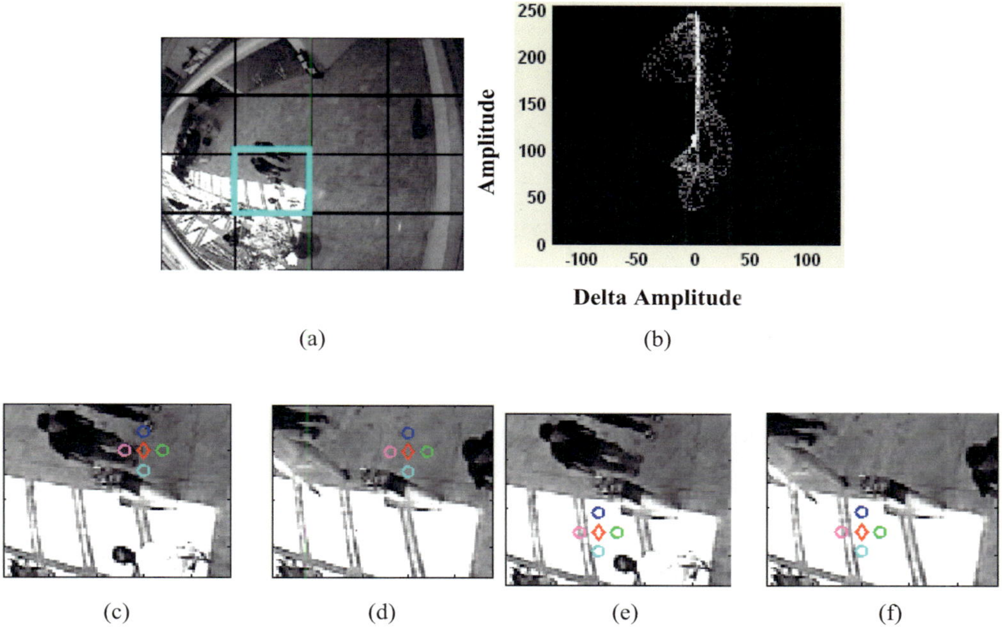

Figure 30: Demonstration of ergodicity in human sequence: (a) start image with grid cell highlighted, (b) frame-wise phase plot for mosaics, (c) 1st image in sequence, (d) 2nd image in sequence, (e) 3rd image in sequence, and (f) 4th image in sequence [80].

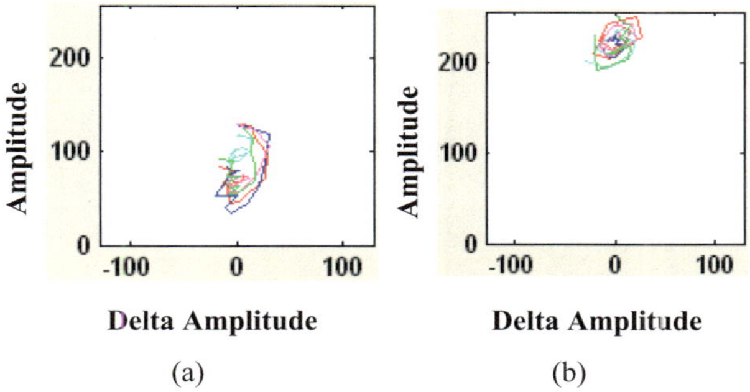

Figure 31: Ergodic behavior in two distinct basins of attraction (a) lower amplitude basin from the motions during the period between figure (c) and (d) above, and (b) higher amplitude basin from the motions during the period between figure (e) and (f) above.

In summary, ergodicity provides us the ability to analyze the behavior of the phase plots of image pairs rather than need to examine the individual trajectories of each pixel over long time sequences. As we mentioned earlier, this is critical since being limited to long term temporal analysis would make any algorithm for motion detection impractical due to the resultant long latency in detecting the motion.

One other very useful property of ergodicity is that it ensures that "sets defined by dynamical systems have locally the same (fractal) dimension everywhere", (commonly referred to as the Eckmann-Ruelle conjecture) [39]. This means that regions of phase space which are the result of common underlying chaotic forcing functions will exhibit consistent fractal behavior and hence have a consistent fractional dimensional measure. Likewise regions of phase space that are the result of non-chaotic underlying dynamics will exhibit consistent non-fractal behavior with a non-fractional dimension. In terms of computer vision, this means that regions in an image that are experiencing common phenomena will exhibit common fractal dimensions. Fig. **32** (a) and (b) show two images where an object is moving and there is also spatio-temporally varying illumination. Fig. **32** (c) shows the resultant ensemble phase plot from the region highlighted in (a) and (b). Notice within Fig. **32** (c) there are two distinct regions of behavior, the upper very dense region and the sparser higher fractal dimension region in the lower portion of the image. We will see in Chapter 4 that the structure in the upper region of the phase plot is typical for varying illumination.

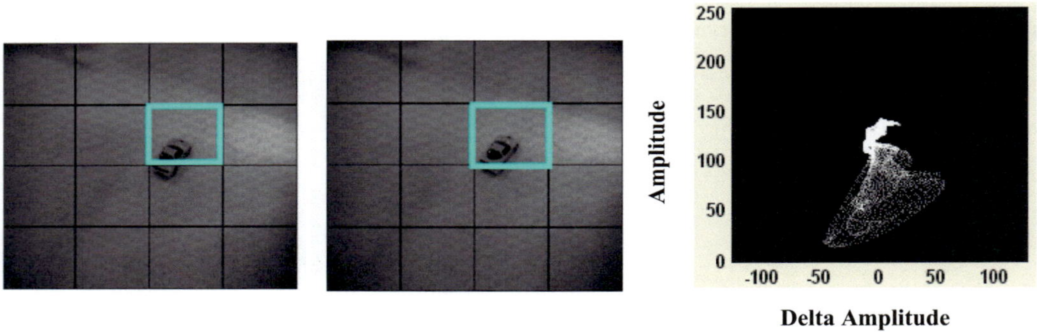

(a) (b) (c)

Figure 32: Simultaneous spatio-temporal illumination and motion, (a) 1st image, (b) 2nd image, and (c) phase plot [74].

Fig. **33** (a) provides a segmented version of the phase plot from Fig. **32** (c) based on fractal dimension. The higher fractal dimension regions were maintained and the lower fractal dimensional regions were removed. Fig. **33** (c) shows the resultant segmented image where the moving vehicle was nearly perfectly segmented while the spatio-temporal illumination changes were completely ignored. Thus the Eckmann-Ruelle conjecture allows us to use regions of phase space exhibiting common fractal behavior as a segmentation feature. We will see in Chapter 4 that this will allow us to segment regions experiencing motion and change in image sequences while ignoring the effects of complex spatio-temporally varying illumination.

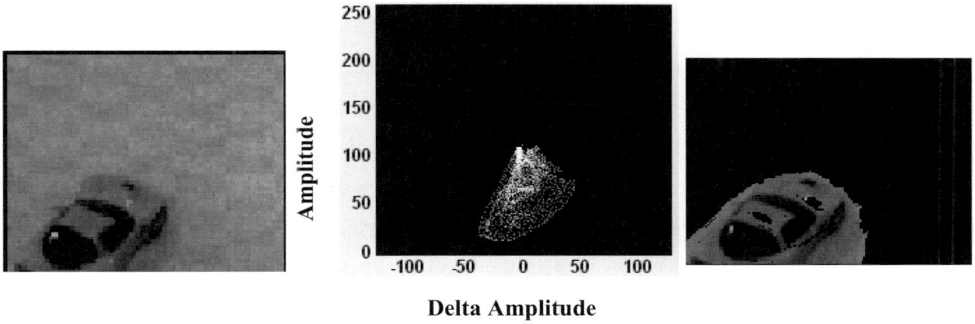

(a) (b) (c)

Figure 33: Segmentation: (a) original image, (b) segmented phase plot, and (c) regions of original image corresponding to chaotic portion of phase plot [74].

In summary, ergodicity is an essential property in applying chaos to computer vision. Firstly, it allows us to treat incoming images as ensembles of pixels which collectively will exhibit the same behavior as individual pixels over time. This will allow us to avoid long latency signal analysis. Secondly, it ensures that the behavior in phase space of either underlying chaotic or non-chaotic dynamics will be locally consistent thereby allowing us to perform image segmentation based on the fractal measure of the various regions of phase space.

CONCLUDING REMARKS

While in general it is extremely difficult to prove the actual existence of chaos in finite duration signals, Velazquez proposes a more pragmatic approach by suggesting an "attractor-like" behavior rather than committing to the existence of pure chaos when analyzing signals [5]. He also notes that the non-predictable nature of neural signals may be neither from chaos nor stochastic origins but rather from aperiodic forcing phenomena. We noted that this aperiodic forcing function concept also provides a reasonable model to explain the complex phase plot trajectories in computer vision when motion is present. The complex variation of an object's surface normal vectors and albedos as it moves through an image scene impart an aperiodic forcing function on the scene radiance. These aperiodic forcing functions result in chaos-like trajectories in phase space.

This chapter reviewed the role of the phase plot in analyzing the chaos-like behaviors and demonstrated its structural equivalence with the joint histogram which is a key tool in information theory. It then discussed critical issues associated with constructing the phase plots such as time lag selection for allowing chaotic behavior to emerge. The critical role of low-pass filtering of the images for noise reduction was demonstrated since the presence of noise can easily mask the underlying chaotic behaviors in phase space. The critical concept of ergodicity was introduced, and its role in computer vision application was demonstrated. This is a critical concept for image processing since it removes the need for us to track individual pixels over long time frames. We can equivalently process the collection of pixels within pairs of images.

Send Orders for Reprints to reprints@benthamscience.net

CHAPTER 4

Behavior of Images and Image Sequences in Phase Space

Abstract: Chaotic systems are created by an underlying non-linear dynamics. In the previous chapter we explored the characteristics of chaotic systems. Objects under motion within an image can be modeled as aperiodic forcing functions impacting the amplitude response of the imaging sensors in computer vision. Recall from the previous chapter that systems undergoing aperiodic forcing functions exhibit chaos-like behavior. Interestingly, illumination changes in image sequences do not exhibit this chaos-like behavior, but rather exhibit very deterministic behavior that has very limited excursions in phase space. Recall systems can also exhibit spatial chaotic behavior and the amplitude variations across an image under varying textures will exhibit varying behavior in phase space. Also the traditional methods of analyzing texture through grey-level co-occurrence matrices is closely related to the reconstructed phase space analysis methods defined in the previous chapter. Thus chaos theory can provide a unifying framework for describing interesting temporal and spatial behavior in computer vision while providing an inherent immunity to even complex illumination changes.

Keywords: Temporal chaos, spatial chaos, texture, global illumination, spatio-temporal illumination, Lambertian model, Sparrow-Torrance Model, grey-level co-occurrence matrices, saturation, gamma correction.

INTRODUCING TEMPORAL AND SPATIAL CHAOS

Chaotic dynamic systems generate interesting complex trajectories in phase space. Likewise many systems that are not necessarily chaotic but whose dynamics is the result of an underlying aperiodic forcing function also generate interesting and complex trajectories in phase space. In the previous chapter we provided some anecdotal evidence that moving objects through a scene produce interesting trajectories in phase space. We also saw that images with complex textures also have complex phase space trajectories resulting from spatial aperiodic forcing functions related to the roughness of the surface being imaged. This chapter will be dedicated to a more systematic and complete analysis of the imaging phenomena that can result in chaotic-like effects. Specifically we will show that the contextual or motion-based change in an image results in complex trajectories in phase space that are indicative of highly non-linear systems. This non-linear behavior is the result of the changing object surface normal and albedos serving as the aperiodic forcing function. Equally importantly, we also show that

Michael E. Farmer

illumination changes in images can be explained through a simple multiplicative process based on the changing illumination amplitude. This simple multiplicative variation for illumination is in stark contrast to the complex aperiodic forcing functions used to characterize the effects of moving objects in an image scene. These contrasting effects of illumination and motion will be manifested in phase space by dramatically different trajectories, where motion will cause complex space-filling trajectories exhibiting fractional dimensions while illumination will create very compact non-fractal trajectories.

Traditional grayscale image processing algorithms dedicated to scene change detection and motion analysis tend to perform poorly when illumination and motion are present in image sequences simultaneously. We will see that due to the distinct behaviors of the two phenomena in phase space that the simultaneous presence of both is easily handled when approached from a chaos-theoretic framework. Even complex illumination effects that are varying temporally and spatially can be differentiated from motion and contextual change. Effects as complex as moving cloud cover and the changing direction of sunlight over the extent of the day create non-chaotic patterns in phase space that are easily distinguished from the effects of motion.

While temporal chaos is the most common type of chaotic systems addressed in the literature, we saw that the effects of texture in images can also be explained in terms of the less common *spatial* chaos. Texture has traditionally been directly analyzed in amplitude space using fractals and also very commonly analyzed using grey-level co-occurrence matrices (GLCM) [10, 14]. Interestingly, we will demonstrate there is a strong parallelism between these matrices and the reconstructed phase space methods employed to analyze chaotic systems. The measures traditionally employed on GLCMs can also be applied to these reconstructed phase spaces to characterize texture in images. Likewise we will see additional measures can be exploited to analyze the phase space characteristics of texture.

THE EFFECTS OF ILLUMINATION CHANGE IN PHASE SPACE

The most basic equation describing the radiance of an image scene is defined by the Lambertian scene radiance, L_m :

$$L_m = \rho \, \vec{N} \cdot \vec{I} \, , \tag{11}$$

where ρ is the albedo of the object surface, $\vec{N}$ is the normal to the surface of the object, and $\vec{I}$ is the directional illumination. This equation assumes simple diffuse scattering of light off of the object surfaces. A more complete model that also includes specular objects is the Torrance-Sparrow model which combines specular and diffuse components of scene radiance, can be used [32]:

$$L = \left(\vec{K}_d + \vec{K}_s\right) \cdot \vec{I} \, , \tag{12}$$

where $\vec{K}_d$ is the diffuse component, and $\vec{K}_s$ is the speculative component of the surface. Note the structural similarity between the forms of these equations.

The Torrance-Sparrow model is also considered by Smith and Hancock to have two major shortcomings: (i) it does not account for micro-facets in the surface material and (ii) the concepts of diffuse and specular reflectance actually have no physical meaning which can lead to physically impossible reflectance values when blindly applied [81]. Oren and Nayar proposed a model that remedied the first issue by modeling complex surface reflectance as a combination of direct and inter-reflected radiance according to the equation [82]:

$$L_{\text{total}} = L_{\text{direct}} + \mathrm{X} \cdot L_{\text{inter-reflected}} \, , \tag{13}$$

where X is the inter-reflection parameter and $0.5 \le X \le 1$. In Equation (13) L_{direct} and $L_{inter\text{-}reflected}$ both depend on the same terms as the Lambertian or Torrance-Sparrow model, namely the angle of between the direction of the light and the surface normal vectors, and the surface albedo. They also depend on a new term, the surface variance. When the surface variance is zero, the model defaults to the Lambertian model in Equation (11). The fundamental difference between the Lambertian model and these other models is that "the Lambertian [model] assumes that all incoming light on a surface patch is scattered and hence diffusely reflected" while these other models recognize that "a portion of the light striking each micro-facet [of a surface] is reflected specularly" [81]. Smith and Hancock propose an alternate model that, rather than having surface parameters, such as K_d and K_s, related to specular and diffuse behavior of the surface, simply have specular and diffuse contributions to the surface reflectance that are based on the relative angle between the surface normal and the illumination source and the surface variance. The albedo, however, only contributes to the diffuse scattering component [81].

$$L_{\text{total}}(I,...,\rho) = L_{\text{specular}}(I,...) + L_{\text{diffuse}}(I,...,\rho), \tag{14}$$

Equation (14) can be expressed in a form that is more easily compared to the Torrance and Sparrow and Oren and Nayar models by:

$$L = |I| \cdot \left(\rho \cdot f_{diffuse}(\theta_i, \theta_r, \alpha_r, v, \eta) + f_{specular}(\theta_i, \theta_r, \alpha_r, v, \eta)\right), \tag{15}$$

where $|I|$ is the amplitude of the illumination, ρ is the albedo, θ_i is the angle of incidence of the illumination, θ_r and α_r are the spherical coordinates of the viewer, v is a measure of surface roughness and η is the refractive index of the surface. The critical point to note is that in all of these models the resultant scene radiance is a combination of the effects of diffuse and specular reflection which are dependent on the surface characteristics of the object being imaged. These surface characteristics captured by these various terms will provide the aperiodic forcing function needed to generate the complex phase space trajectories that we will see are associated with motion, scene change, and texture. In the above equations the surface characteristics define the aperiodic forcing function defined by the surfaces of interest. The interaction of these terms with the illumination, however, provides the complete behavior of the scene radiance so we must now investigate the effects of illumination.

EFFECTS OF GLOBAL ILLUMINATION CHANGE IN LABORATORY CONDITIONS

There has been considerable research on modeling the effects of global illumination change in image scenes with various researchers debating whether illumination changes are additive or multiplicative in a scene [32, 54, 74]. Using the simpler Lambertian model we see that if illumination changes are additive then the scene radiance changes enter Equation (11) as an additive factor λ to the illumination, resulting in additive scene radiance $L_{additive}$ [74]:

$$L_{additive} = \rho\,\vec{N}\cdot\left(\vec{I}+\vec{\lambda}\right) = \rho\,\vec{N}\cdot\vec{I} + \rho\,\vec{N}\cdot\vec{\lambda} = L_{original} + \Delta L. \tag{16}$$

If we analyze such an equation in phase space we see that every radiance level would have the same relative change under a global illumination change which would result in a lateral shift of the vertical line in phase space resulting from an image being compared with it. The vertical line will shift either to the left or right depending on whether the global illumination change was positive or negative. However, if illumination changes are multiplicative then the changes in scene radiance enter Equation (11) as multiplicative scale factor λ to the illumination, resulting in scene radiance L_{mult} [74]:

$$L_{mult} = \rho\,\vec{N}\cdot\left(\vec{I}\cdot\lambda\right) = \left(\rho\,\vec{N}\cdot\vec{I}\right)\cdot\lambda = L_{original}\cdot\lambda, \tag{17}$$

The more complex models proposed by Torrance-Sparrow or Smith and Hancock maintain the basic form of the illumination multiplied by a surface descriptor, which implies even specular illumination changes can be modeled multiplicatively by:

$$L_{mult} = \left(\vec{K}_d + \vec{K}_s\right)\cdot\left(\vec{I}\cdot\lambda\right) = \left[\left(\vec{K}_d+\vec{K}_s\right)\cdot\vec{I}\right]\cdot\lambda = L_{original}\cdot\lambda \tag{18}$$

and

$$L_{mult} = |\lambda\cdot I|\cdot\left(\rho\cdot f_{diffuse}(\theta_i,\theta_r,\alpha_r,v,\eta) + f_{specular}(\theta_i,\theta_r,\alpha_r,v,\eta)\right) = L_{original}\cdot\lambda \tag{19}$$

According to Equations (17) through (19) the multiplicative models will result in a change in the slope of the phase plot for a fixed illumination angle with changes only to illumination amplitude. Fig. **34** (a) and (b) provide two images with changes in illumination. In this laboratory situation, large fluorescent overhead lights were turned on between the time of the images in Fig. **34** (a) and (b) being captured. Fig. **34** (c) provides the resultant phase plot between these two images and it indeed verifies that illumination change is multiplicative. Note the slope of the line created in phase space is the value of the multiplicative illumination that is present in the scene. This is an exciting and quite visually compelling verification of the fact that illumination change in image sequences is multiplicative. This is important since even recently, many authors have discussed additive models for illumination change. This is due to the fact that many of the authors analyze the image sequences using methods that only look at changes in grayscale values rather than the definitive changes that can be witnessed when analyzing sequences in phase space [32]. Thus phase space analysis has proven useful for validating the underlying physical models of image change.

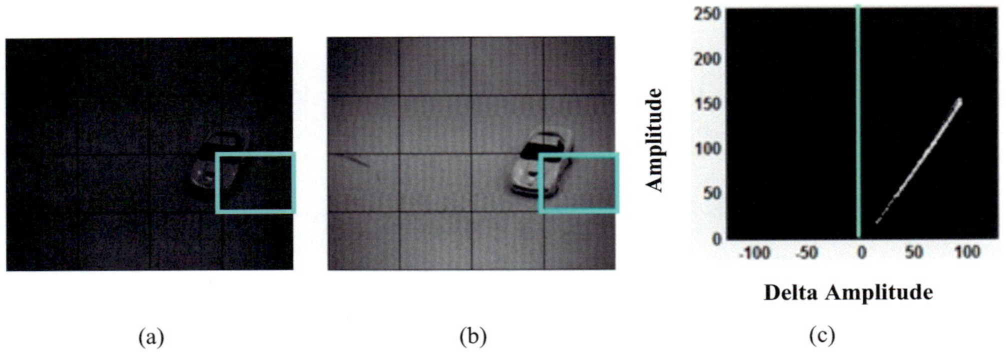

Figure 34: Effects on phase plot of global illumination : (a) first image, (b) image with global illumination change, and (c) phase plot for (a) and (b).

EFFECTS OF GLOBAL ILLUMINATION CHANGE DUE TO REAL-WORLD SUNLIGHT CONDITIONS

In the previous section we saw the well-defined multiplicative effects of laboratory controlled global illumination changes resulting from diffuse distant overhead lighting changes. While useful for validating the mathematical model of illumination, few interesting computer vision tasks take place in such controlled lighting conditions. We will now analyze the effects of natural outdoor sunlight changes in phase space. Sunlight changes are created through two distinct mechanisms:

i. Moving cloud cover on a moderately short timescale; which can cause interesting amplitude modulation, and

ii. Motion of the sun as it tracks across the sky over the length of the day; which changes the amplitude of the sunlight *and* the angle of incidence of the light.

Also in some cases we will see that the sun is not simply radiating from overhead but is reflected off of nearby objects. This makes the term $\vec{N}\cdot\vec{I}$ a complex combination of radiant sources of the form: $\sum_i \vec{N}\cdot\vec{I}_i$ where the combination of direct and reflected incident sources produce a combined illumination.

Also, while cloud cover appears relatively uniform, the density of the clouds is often quite variable. This will cause a spatio-temporally varying illumination pattern, the details of which will be discussed later in this chapter. In summary, while the effects of sunlight may appear to be global illumination to the casual observer, they are actually significantly more interesting. We will see that the resultant phase space trajectories can help us appreciate how interesting these effects are. The complexity of the phase space trajectory will depend on the changes in sunlight conditions (clouds *versus* time-based sun motion). For the case of changes in time of day the complexity of the surface upon which the sunlight is radiating will play a key role as the dot product with the surface normal plays a critical role. Fig. **35** (a) and (b) provides an example of a highly uniform surface (a tennis court) with varying cloud cover. Fig. **35** (c) shows the resultant phase plot, which exactly represents the multiplicative effects of illumination change shown previously for the controlled laboratory conditions in Fig. **34** [83].

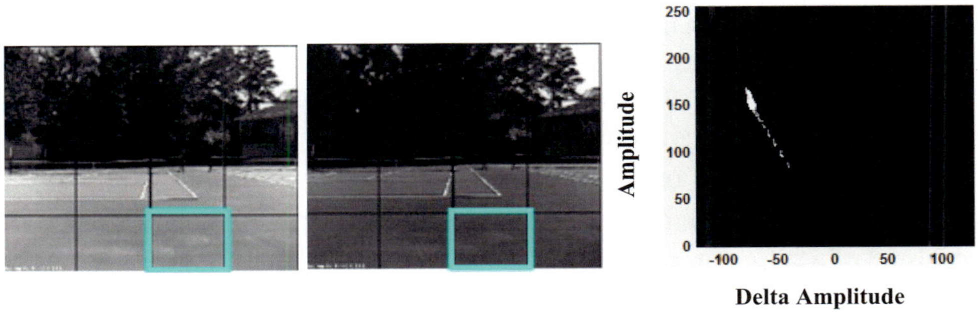

(a) (b) (c)

Figure 35: Effects on phase plot of daylight illumination across many hours over the day: (a) first image with region of highly uniform surface normal vectors highlighted, (b) image with global natural illumination change with region of highly uniform surface normal vectors highlighted, and (c) phase plot for (a) and (b) showing clear multiplicative behavior [83].

Fig. **36** (a) and (b) show another interesting region of the image where, in addition to the diffuse illumination change, there are regions of saturation (the white lines on the tennis court), and the resultant phase plot is provided in Fig. **36** (c). Notice in this phase plot the expected global illumination change is seen in the diagonal line, but there is an additional compacted region of the phase plot at the higher amplitudes due to the saturation effects. Later in this chapter we will more fully explore the effects of saturation on the resultant phase plots. From the phase plot in Fig. **36** (c), it is clear that the effects of image saturation slightly distort the expected multiplicative effects of global illumination change. Fortunately, they do not produce complex trajectories in phase space that may interfere with detecting motion and contextual change, as will be seen later in this chapter.

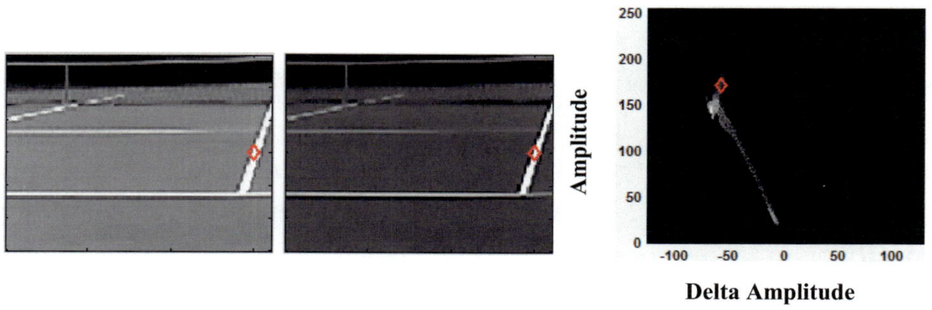

(a) (b) (c)

Figure 36: Effects on phase plot of daylight illumination across many hours over the day: (a) first image with saturation point highlighted, (b) image with global natural illumination change with saturation point highlighted, and (c) phase plot for (a) and (b) showing multiplicative behavior with additional effects from high intensity region [83].

Another excellent example of global illumination change due to cloud cover can be seen in Fig. **37**, with the highlighted region focused upon in the figure expanded in Fig. **38**. In each sub-figure of Fig. **38** we have focused on a different point in the image. Each point was selected because it posessed a very different normal vector and consisted of a different material and hence different albedo [83]. Fig. **38** (a) and (b) highlight points on the ground with a common normal vector and very different albedos. Likewise Fig. **38** (c) and (d) highlight points with orthogonal normal vectors to the first two images (points on the wall) and each of slightly different albedos. The resultant phase plot generated from the highlighted image regions in Fig. **37** (a) and (b) is provided in Fig. **39**. All of the subfigures in Fig. **39** provide the same phase plot, however the points of interest identified in the sub-figures in Fig. **38** are mapped to their respective phase space locations. Note that the phase plot is composed of a collection of linear structures where each linear structure is representative of global illumination on a particular surface with a given normal and albedo. Notice that even with these dramatic changes in illumination across multiple surfaces of varying albedo and normal vectors the phase plots maintain a compact highly localized appearance associated with global illumination change. These compact linear trajectories will result in low fractal dimension which we will see in the following sections differs dramatically from the fractal dimension of phase plot trajectories due to motion and contextual change.

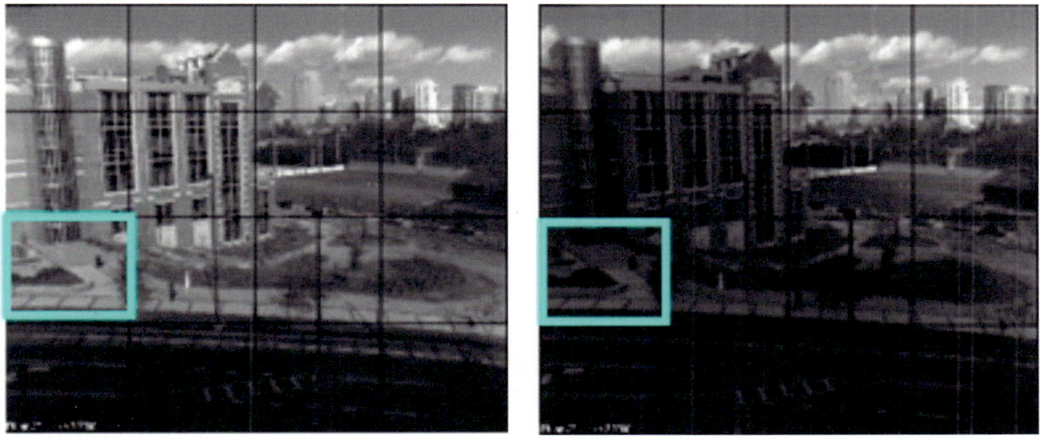

(a) (b)

Figure 37: Daylight illumination changes due to moving cloud cover: (a) first image, (b) image with 'global' natural illumination change due to a cloud moving between the sun and the scene [83].

(a) (b) (c) (d)

Figure 38: Analyzing the effects of daylight illumination changes due to moving cloud cover for regions with four differing normal vectors and albedos (see following figure for locations in phase space where these points reside) [83].

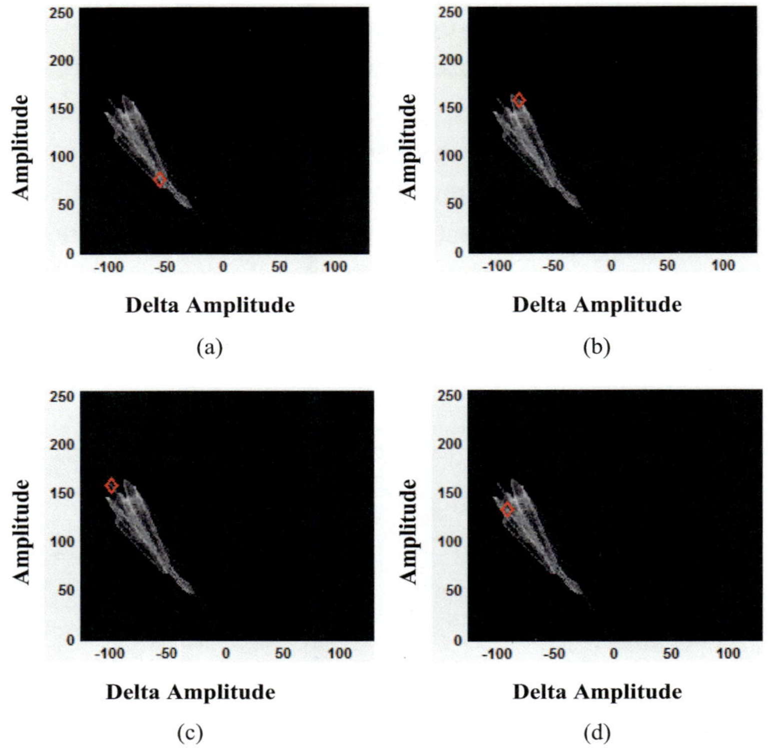

Figure 39: Effects of globally varying natural sunlight illumination: (a) phase plot with point highlighted from (a) above, (b) phase plot with point highlighted from (b) above, (c), phase plot with point highlighted from (c) above and (d) phase plot with point highlighted from (d) above.

Fig. **40** provides two interesting scenes produced by moving cloud cover which significantly darkens the image in Fig. **40** (b) [83]. In the image we have highlighted two regions where we will more closely analyze the impact of the illumination change. Fig. **41** (a) through (d) provides points of interest within these highlighted regions that have varying normal vectors and albedos. Fig. **42** (a) through (d) provides the phase plots for each of the images in Fig. **41** with each showing interesting effects from the illumination change for a variety of surface conditions. Fig. **41** (a) and (b) provide two regions of closely valued normal vectors with two different albedos, one due to natural material and one due to manmade material. Fig. **42** (a) and (b) show the respective locations in the phase plot of these two points in the image. Note the phase plot does not have a purely linear behavior we expect from global illumination change but rather has adopted a ***curvilinear*** pattern. We will show later in the chapter that the gamma compaction algorithm employed by many cameras can explain this curvature in what should be a simple linear phase plot.

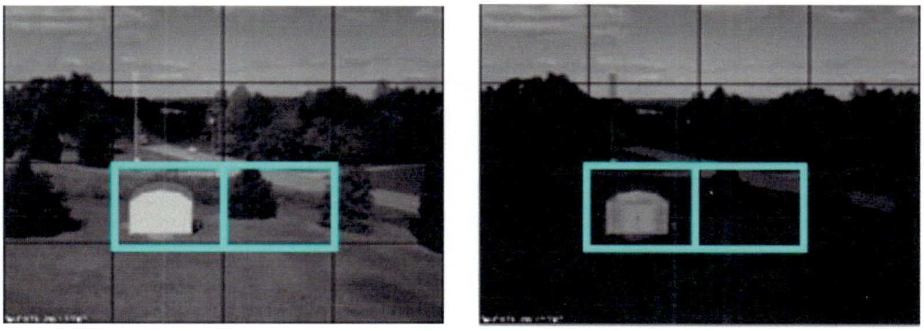

(a) (b)

Figure 40: Daylight illumination changes due to moving cloud cover: (a) first image, (b) image with 'global' natural illumination change due to a cloud moving between the sun and the scene [83].

(a) (b) (c) (d)

Figure 41: Analyzing the effects of daylight illumination changes due to moving cloud cover for regions with four differing normal vectors and albedos (see following figure for locations in phase space where these points reside) [83].

As in Fig. **38**, Fig. **41** (c) and (d) provide regions of the scene with manmade objects and Fig. **42** (c) and (d) provide the phase plot with the locations in the phase plot of the points of interest highlighted. The point highlighted in Fig. **41** (d) shows a region where there is initially camera saturation that is reduced to a non-saturation state as the cloud cover moves across the image. The resultant phase plot in Fig. **42** (d) shows the point resides along a degenerate compressed region of the phase plot trajectory. Later in this chapter we will further explore the effects of saturation. Fig. **41** (c) shows a point of interest on the roof of the structure, where the resultant phase space trajectory is provided in Fig. **42** (c) and once again the point on the phase space trajectory is part of a curvilinear trajectory associated with the change in illumination.

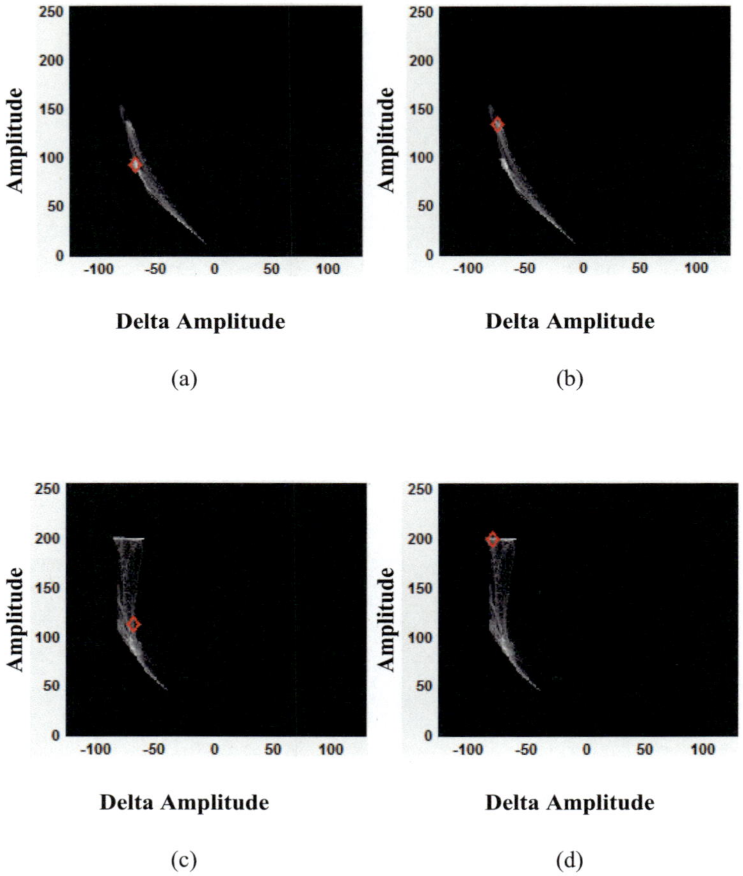

Figure 42: Effects of globally varying natural sunlight illumination: (a) phase plot with point highlighted from (a) above, (b) phase plot with point highlighted from (b) above, (c) phase plot with point highlighted from (c) above, and (d) phase plot with point highlighted from (d).

To understand the power of analyzing the effects of these natural illumination conditions in phase space Fig. **43** provides another image pair from the sequence introduced in Fig. **40** [83]. Two image segmentation processes are applied to this image pair using first a chaos-based algorithm and second the popular Gaussian Mixture Model (GMM). The results of the segmentation are provided in Fig. **44** (a) and (b) respectively. The chaos-based methods that we are discussing in this text result in modest residual segmentation effects along the upper edges of the image due to edge effects of the low pass filtering, and also along the border of the tree line and the sky. This is in stark contrast to the results of the GMM algorithm which has captured nearly the entire image except for the sky where there was very little amplitude change. This is a commonly known problem with GMM-based segmentation as is mentioned by Tian in [33]. Many researchers have attempted to develop mechanisms to make this popular technique more robust to sudden illumination change through either post processing [33] or illumination compensation processing [30, 84]. No illumination compensation is required for the chaos-based method since the changes due to illumination in phase space are dramatically different than the changes due to motion and contextual change. Throughout the subsequent chapters in this text we will demonstrate in detail the advantages of using the proposed chaos-theoretic approach as they are inherently immune to illumination change.

(a) (b)

Figure 43: Image pair with sudden illumination change due to cloud cover, (a) original image and (b) image during cloud-cover [83].

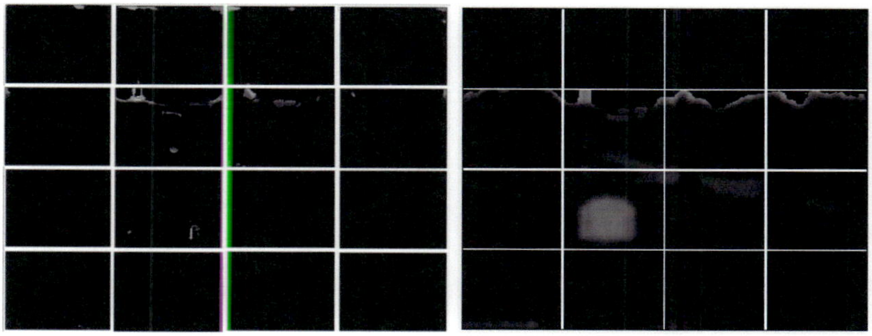

(a) (b)

Figure 44: Resultant segmentation of image with illumination change: (a) segmented grayscale image using the chaos-based techniques in this text and (b) segmented grayscale image using Gaussian Mixture Models.

EFFECTS OF SPATIO-TEMPORALLY VARYING ILLUMINATION CHANGE IN CONTROLLED LABORATORY AND INDOOR CONDITIONS

Now that we understand the effects of global illumination change on an image pair in phase space, we need to explore the more complex case of spatially varying illumination. Spatio-temporally varying illumination within image sequences experiencing other effects such as motion and contextual object change are very common in real-world imaging scenarios. Cho and Kim [54] analyzed the joint histograms as a means for detecting global illumination changes; however, they did not discuss spatio-temporally varying illumination patterns. The effects in phase space between a pair of images experiencing spatio-temporally varying illumination changes under the same controlled laboratory conditions are provided in Fig. **45** [74]. The image pair shows a light beam which is projected across the image from the right hand side moving downward as the image sequence advances. Note the locally compact conical structure in the phase plot in Fig. **45** (c) due to spatial-temporal variation in the illumination. The outer boundary of the conical structure is determined by the largest amplitude illumination change within the spatially varying illumination. Also note the manifestation of the multiplicative illumination model where the higher amplitude pixels (further up on the phase plot) are shifted by a greater amount.

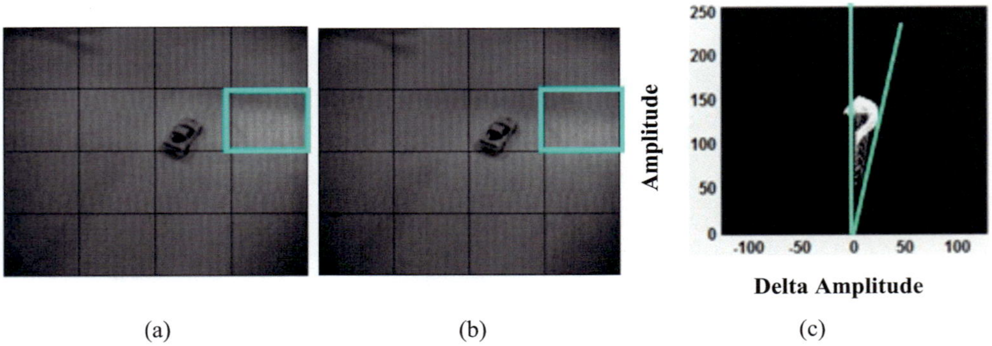

Figure 45: Effects on Phase Plot of spatio-temporally varying illumination : (a) 1st image, (b) 2nd image (note moving light band), and (c) phase plot resulting from images (a) and (b) [24].

Fig. **46** provides an interesting real-world example of an image set containing both global illumination changes and interesting spatially varying illumination changes [85]. Fig. **46** (a) provides the first image prior to the entrance of a subway car into an underground station and Fig. **46** (b) provides a subsequent image in the sequence when a subway car is entering the station. Two regions are highlighted in Fig. **46**. In the first region (row=2, column=4) we see spatially varying illumination from the lights within the car being projected out the side window directly onto the side wall. In the second region (row=4, column=4) we see a regionally global illumination change from the overall brightness due to the subway car lights at more of a distance from the wall. In Fig. **47** (a) note the angle of the phase plot is due to the increase in global illumination in that grid cell.

(a) (b)

Figure 46: Effects of spatio-temporally varying illumination and demonstration of its multiplicative nature: (a) first image, (b) second image with a subway car present and significant complex spatially varying illumination change from windows, headlights, *etc.* being projected onto wall [85].

The structure of the phase plot in Fig. **47** (b) is more interesting and is based on the underlying mathematics of the scene radiance in Equation (13) and Equation (14). The trajectory of the image pixels in this phase plot is confined to a well-defined region. This confined region is clearly not space filling and consequently non-fractal and resulting from a non-chaotic underlying process. The phase space trajectory has a conical structure, where the greatest angular extent of the cone is due to the highest amplitude illumination change within the spatially varying illumination. The phase plot has a conical structure rather than the simple linear model of global illumination because the spatially varying illumination has an amplitude pattern that has an inherent roll-off in amplitude across the beam of light illuminating the region. Thus the conical structure can be considered a superposition of a series of illumination amplitudes with each following the mathematical model of illumination defined in Equation (13).

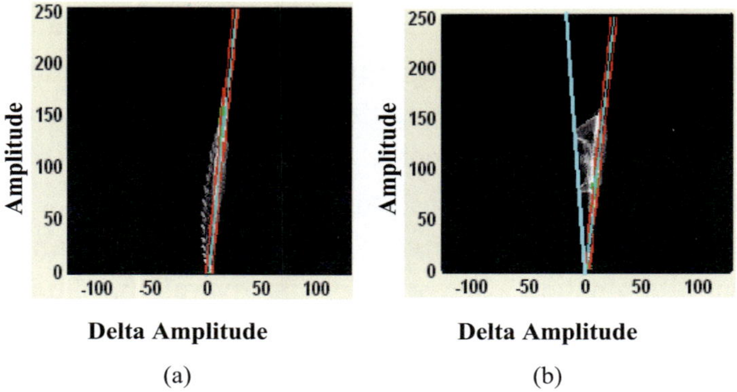

Figure 47: Effects of spatio-temporally varying illumination and demonstration of its multiplicative nature: (a) phase plot showing effect in phase space of global illumination change in region (row=4, col=4), and (b) conic structure of phase plot due to spatially varying illumination in region (row=2, col=4) [86].

EFFECTS OF SPATIO-TEMPORALLY VARYING ILLUMINATION CHANGE IN NATURAL SUNLIGHT CONDITIONS

Now that we understand the effects of spatio-temporally varying illumination change created in controlled laboratory conditions, it will be interesting to explore if these effects are also present in naturally occurring illumination conditions. The controlled laboratory conditions demonstrated that spatio-temporally varying illumination creates compact and distinct structures in phase space, with the resulting construct being pie shaped excursions of limited extent. We will see that spatio-temporal illumination variation is present when clouds are moving across the sun as well as when two images are taken many hours apart and there is considerable motion of the sun across the sky.

Fig. **48** provides an interesting example of complex spatio-temporal illumination variation due to passing cloud cover [83]. Notice in the upper portion of Fig. **48** (a) there is a series of light bands due to an overhead structure on the building partially blocking the sun in the image.

These illumination bands are gone in Fig. **48** (b), and that portion of the image is now in a shadow. The corresponding phase plot in Fig. **48** (c) shows two components: (i) the vertical line produced by the regions of the image that had no illumination change, and (ii) the diagonal region of the phase plot produced by the region in the original images with the spatio-temporal illumination change. Clearly cloud cover can produce an interesting array of global and spatio-temporal illumination effects. Fortunately, these illumination effects still yield compact well-defined phase space trajectories that contrast sharply from the effects of other contextually important image changes.

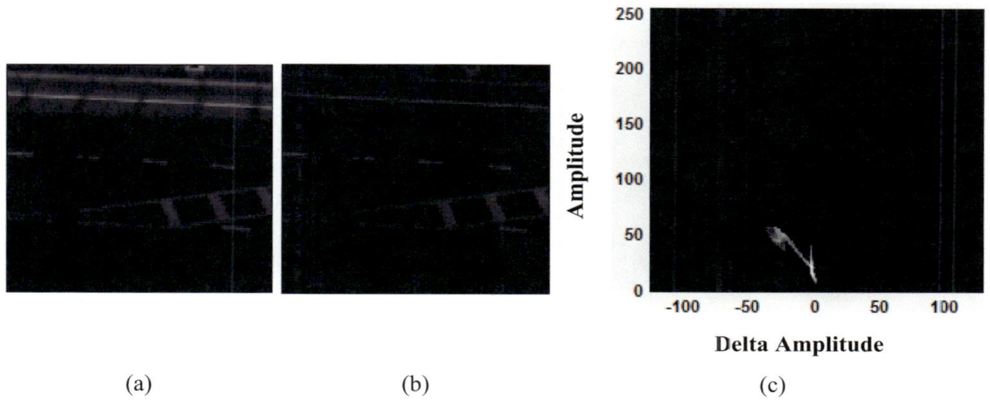

Figure 48: Effects on Phase Plot of spatio-temporally varying illumination due to sunlight: (a) first image, (b) second image, and (c) phase plot resulting from images (a) and (b) [83].

In addition to the motion of clouds across an imaging scene, the advancement of the sun across the sky during the day creates interesting variations in illumination. The motion of the sun imparts not only a multiplicative scale factor λ to the resultant scene radiance, but also imparts changes to the term $\vec{N} \cdot \vec{I}$ due to the changing angle of incidence. Consequently it is expected that the effects of the moving sun may be more complex than the effects of moving cloud cover, and we will now explore this phenomenon.

One effect that the change in incidence angle can have on the resultant image is that the directional sunlight can create shadows from other foreground structures in the image. Fig. **49** (a) and (b) provide views of a complex cityscape from the Columbia University WILD dataset [87] when the sun is initially relatively high in the sky and then when the sun is very low in the sky at dusk. This variation in sun angle produces highly focused direct illumination on the buildings and also produces shadows as foreground structures block the sun. Fig. **50** provides a series of views from the highlighted regions in Fig. **49**, and also provides points of interest that we will map into phase space in Fig. **51** to help understand the differing illumination effects. Fig. **49** (b) is interesting since in the second image in the sequence the sun is setting behind the viewer so the angle of incidence has changed dramatically to be nearly parallel to the view angle. Oren and Nayar state, "Surface radiance increases as the viewing direction approaches the source direction"[82].

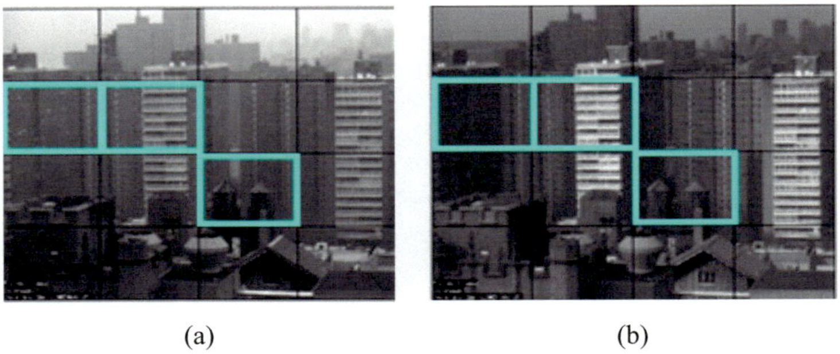

Figure 49: Daylight illumination changes due to change of day and motion of sun: (a) first image, (b) image with 'global' natural illumination change due to motion of the sun [87].

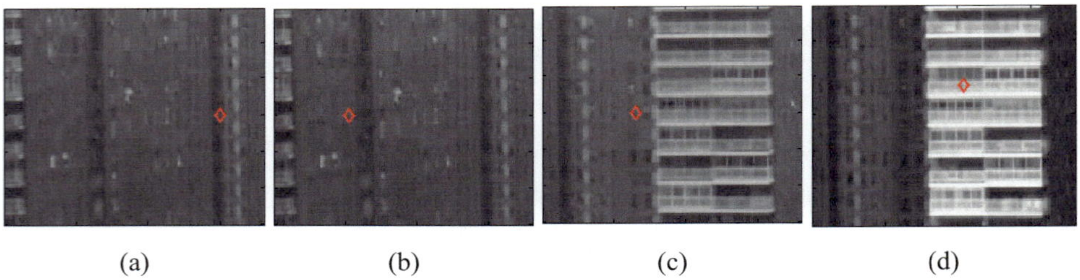

Figure 50: Zooming in on the image in Fig. **49** to show the effects of daylight illumination changes due to motion of sun across sky causing shadows and illumination highlights [87].

In Fig. **51** (a) through (e) we can see the phase space trajectories are more complex than the earlier phase plots we saw in outdoor scenes with moving cloud cover. These phase space trajectories are also more complex than the spatio-temporal illumination change phase plots derived from indoor conditions such as the moving subway car. Fig. **51** (c) and (d) provide the phase plots for the images in Fig. **50** (c) and (d) with differing points in the image being highlighted to demonstrate different illumination effects. This image is interesting because half of the image has an increase in illumination due to the more direct sunlight, and half of the image has a decrease in illumination due to shadowing. This creates triangular regions in phase space on either side of vertical, signifying an increase in illumination in one case and a decrease in illumination in the other. In chaos theory these regions are referred to as basins of attraction. The regions of the phase plot corresponding to each of the illumination effects maintain a compact topology similar to that found for more controlled laboratory and indoor scenes shown earlier. Notice also that basins of attraction are connected *via* a faint region of the phase plot between these two basins. In conventional chaotic dynamic systems the phase plot trajectory can migrate from one basin to another based on external stimuli as those of meta-stable perception seen in neural models in [4]. In the case of computer vision these connecting regions between basins correspond to the illumination transition regions in the actual grayscale image where the two illumination effects meet.

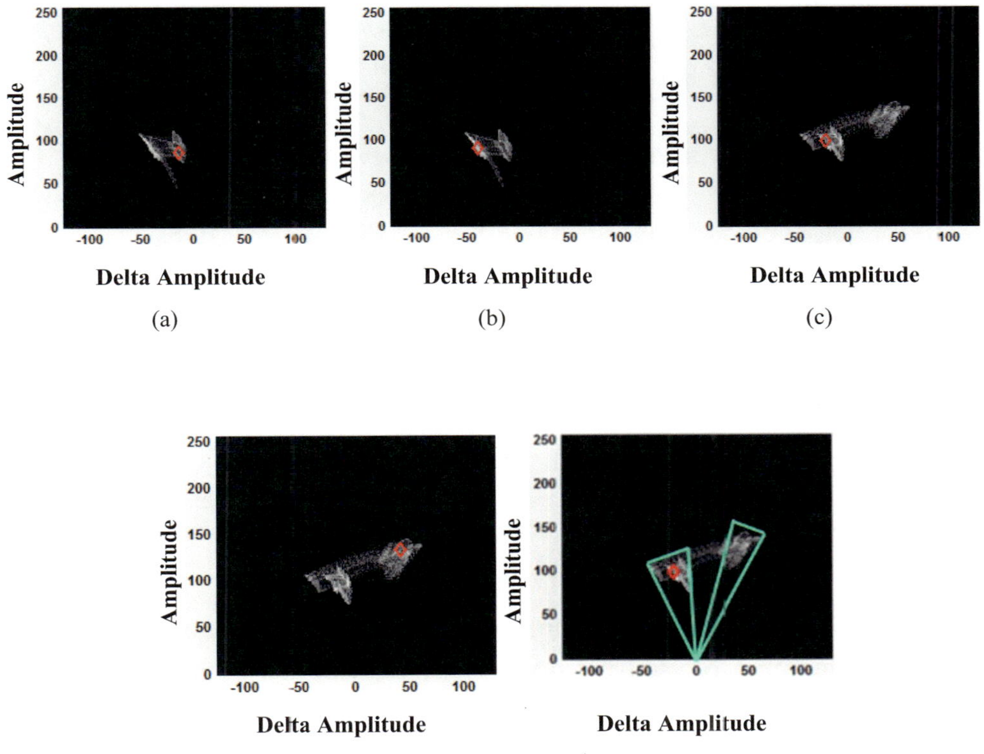

Figure 51: Effects of globally varying natural sunlight illumination: (a) phase plot with point highlighted from (a) above, (b) phase plot with point highlighted from (b) above, (c), phase plot with point highlighted from (c) above, (d) phase plot with point highlighted from (d) above, and (e) highlighting two basins of attraction for differing illumination change, one from the brightened region of the image and the other region from the shadow region of the image.

Fig. **52** provides a collection of images from the *(3, 3)* grid cell in Fig. **49**. This is an interesting cell because it has three distinct illumination effects:

(i) a decrease in illumination in part of the image due to shadows being cast by foreground structures due to the late day sun,

(ii) an increase in illumination due to the lower incidence angle of the sunlight on the building surfaces facing the setting sun, and

(iii) a foreground effect of an increase in illumination on cylindrical surfaces.

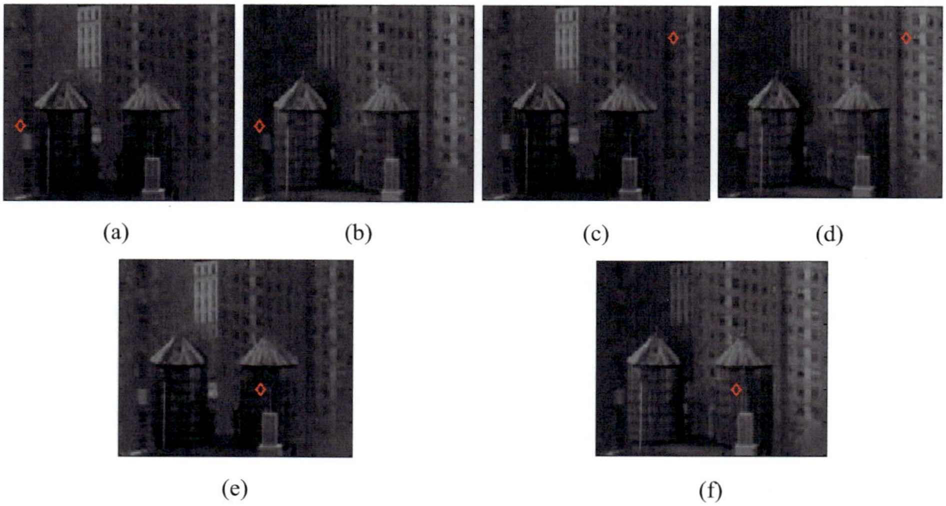

Figure 52: Image pairs with points of interest highlighted to analyze the effects of daylight illumination changes due to motion of sun across sky causing spatio-temporal illumination changes [87].

Fig. **53** (a) through (c) shows the more complex phase plot resulting from this interesting combination of sunlight conditions, with points highlighted to show the locations in phase space for each of the illumination effects that are occurring in the grayscale images. Fig. **53** (d) overlays possible basins of attraction from the three illumination change effects in the image pair. As in Fig. **51** (e), these basins of attraction are inter-connected by less dense regions of the phase space representing the transition regions between these illumination effects.

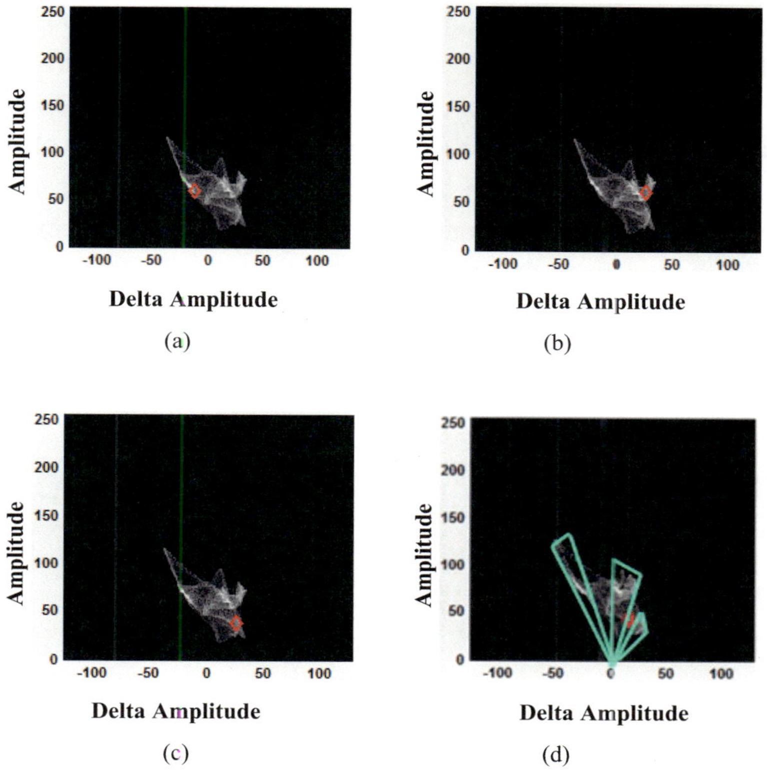

Figure 53: Effects of globally varying natural sunlight illumination: (a) phase plot with point highlighted from (a) and (b) above, (b) phase plot with point highlighted from (c) and (d) above, (c), phase plot with point highlighted from (e) and (f) above, and (d) highlighting three basins of attraction for the three differing illumination effects.

Now that we have quite fully studied the effects of illumination change, we will direct our attention to more salient changes in image sequences due to motion and contextual change due to interesting artifacts such as abandoned or removed objects.

THE EFFECTS OF MOTION OR CONTEXTUAL CHANGE IN PHASE SPACE

Recall from Equation (11) the contribution to the scene radiance by the objects within the image frame are provided *via* the term ρ, the albedo of the object surface and the term $\vec{N}$, the normal to the surface of the object in the image frame. Thus the amplitude of each pixel in the image represents a sampling of an object's albedo and surface normal within the region corresponding to the projection of that particular pixel onto the object. As objects move through an image scene, their relative motions lead to changes in the albedo and surface normal that is being mapped to each pixel. Fig. **54** shows example changes in the albedos and surface normals within a particular pixel due to either the motion of or the appearance of an object. Adopting Velazquez's model of aperiodic forcing phenomena [5], we propose that the changing sequence of normal vectors and albedos due to moving objects can be considered aperiodic forcing functions. We will show in the following sections that these aperiodic forcing functions cause interesting trajectories in phase space of the image pixel amplitudes.

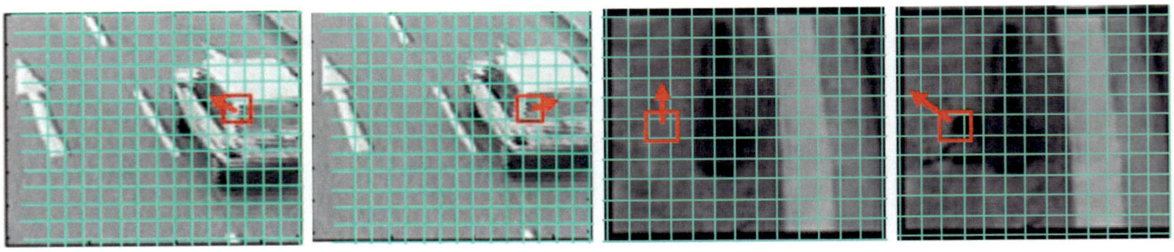

(a) (b) (c) (d)

Figure 54: Aperiodic forcing function behavior of the image normal vectors in an image sequence: (a) pixel is initially over corner of vehicle from [67], and (b) albedo and normal vector changes direction as vehicle moves through the image frame and that same pixel is now almost completely over the back window, (c) prior to bag, pixel has normal towards ceiling, and (d) normal of pixel is now at another direction due to corner of bag bow being in pixel.

PHASE PLOT TRAJECTORIES FOR VARIOUS TYPES OF MOTION AND CONTEXTUAL CHANGE

Fig. **55** (c) shows the interesting behavior in phase space that is caused by the motion of a rigid object. Likewise Fig. **56** (c) shows that the motion of a semi-rigid body creates equally interesting phase space trajectories. Fig. **57** (c) provides a very interesting non-traditional image, namely an ultra-sound of an animal heart, and the deformations of the heart during its contractions also produce the same complex phase space behaviors of the other more traditional visual imaging systems. Lastly, Fig. **58** (c) demonstrates the effects of contextual change where an object appears in one image and is not present in past images. This type of image would occur in an abandoned bag surveillance system. Note once again, the interesting behaviors in phase space. Tel and Gruiz also state, "[one difference] between chaotic and non-chaotic systems is that, in the former case, the phase space objects… trace out complicated (fractal) sets, whereas in the non-chaotic case the objects suffer weak deformations" [22]. Clearly there is a distinct difference in the behavior of the phase plots from illumination change shown in the previous sub-chapter and the behaviors of the phase plots of motion and contextual change. It is also important to note that the effects shown in these phase plots are quite distinct from the effects of noise.

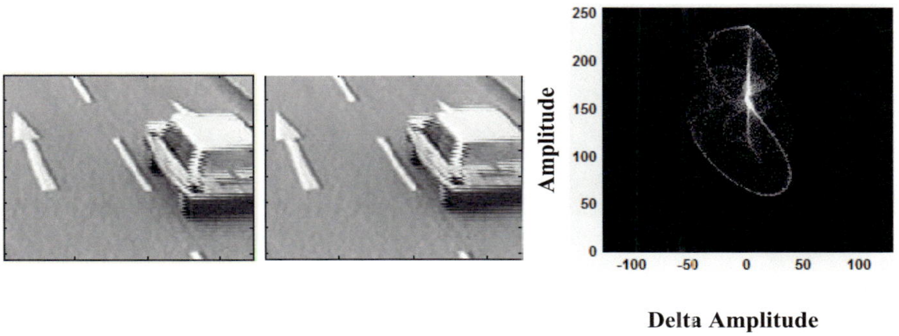

(a) (b) (c)

Figure 55: Examples of chaotic behavior due to motion: (a) first image, (b) next image, and (c) and phase plot [67].

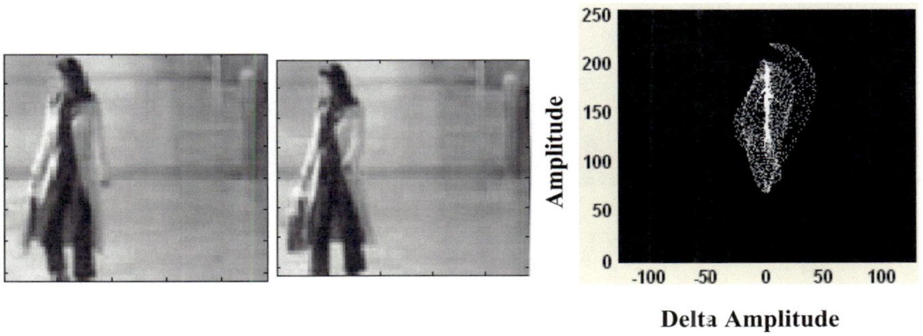

(a) (b) (c)

Figure 56: Example of chaotic behavior due to motion of a slightly deformable object (human): (a) first image, (b) next image, and (c) and phase plot [80].

One characteristic that is clearly visible in a few of the phase plots is the presence of the basins of attraction that we first introduced with the images containing complex illumination. In most of the phase plots above we again see clear regions in the phase plots that appear to have distinct sub-trajectories. Fig. **59** (c) and Fig. **60** (c) highlight the mapping of two separate regions of the vehicle into phase space. We see that each of the highlighted regions in the grayscale image map into distinct subregions of the phase space trajectory. In the case of these phase plots the basins have a structure that is quite orbit-like and each explores a different portion of phase space. These regions are different in structure from the basins shown for illumination but they again occupy a distinct dense subspace.

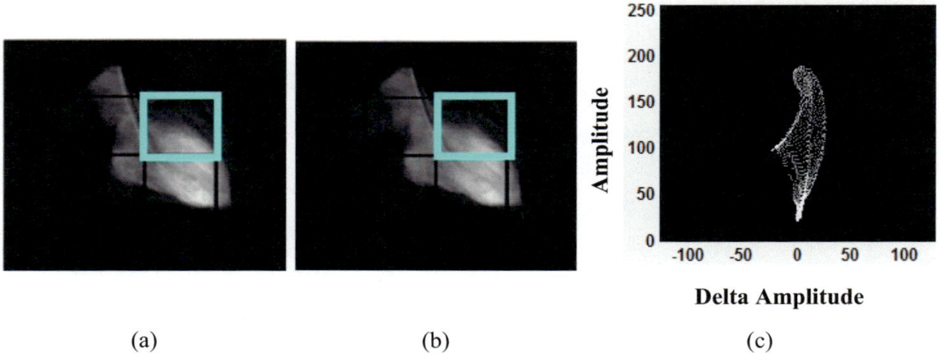

Figure 57: Example of chaotic behavior due to motion for a highly deformable object (heart) in an atypical image (ultrasound): (a) first image, (b) next image, and (c) and phase plot.

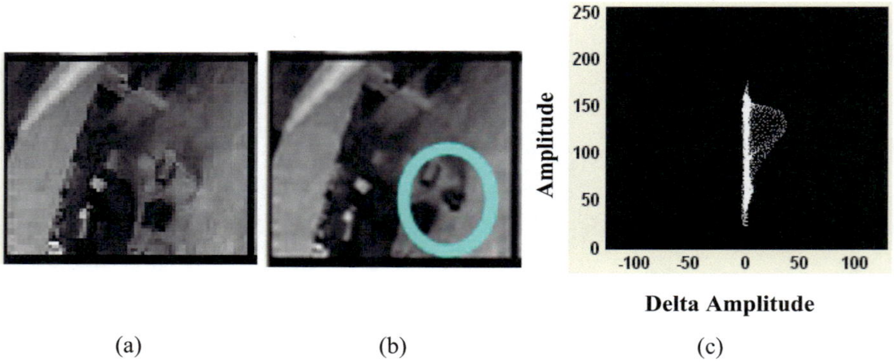

Figure 58: Example of chaotic behavior due to image change: (a) first image without bag, (b) next image where bag was left, (c) phase plot [80].

The reader is referred now to the image sequence in Fig. **61**. Note it is very similar to the image sequence in Fig. **55**, and is actually taken only a few frames after the sequence in Fig. **55**. It is interesting to compare the phase plot trajectories provided in Fig. **55** (c) with the trajectory in Fig. **61** (c). While there is some similarity we see that the overall structure of the phase plot is dramatically different. Thus only a slight change in the initial conditions of the object's location within the image results in dramatically different phase plot trajectories. We can summarize the phase plot characteristics we have seen so far in this chapter in two ways:

i. the phase plots exhibit sensitivity to the initial pixel location of the trajectory through phase space and

ii. the phase plots can be seen as being comprised of distinct regions of in phase space corresponding to basins of attraction.

iii. Both of these phenomena are critical characteristics of chaotic systems [1, 21, 22].

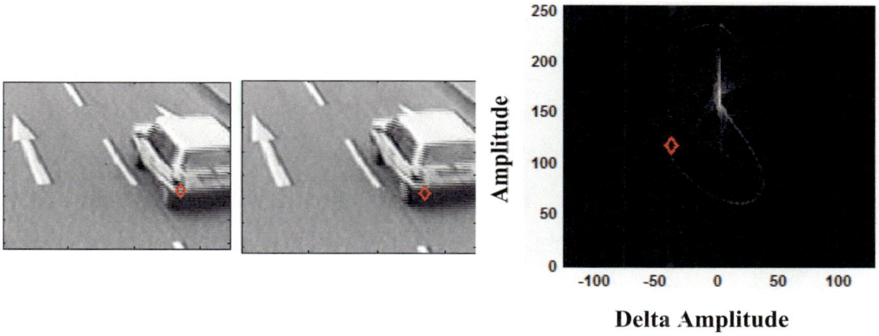

(a) (b) (c)

Figure 59: Example of basin of attraction associated with specific behaviors of the image grayscale amplitudes: (a) first image, (b) next image, (c) phase plot [67].

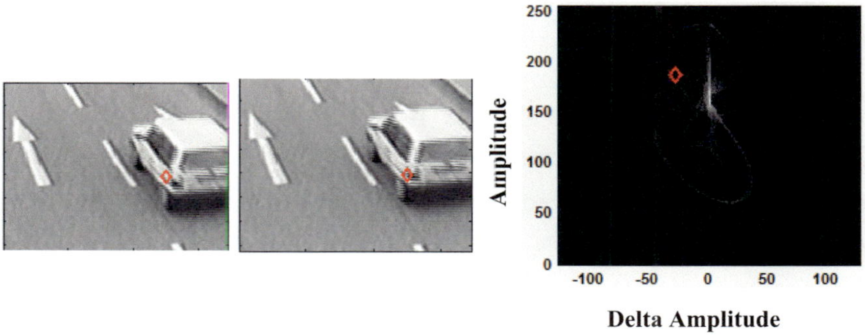

(a) (b) (c)

Figure 60: Attraction of pixels to alternate of basin of attraction: (a) first image, (b) next image, (c) phase plot [67].

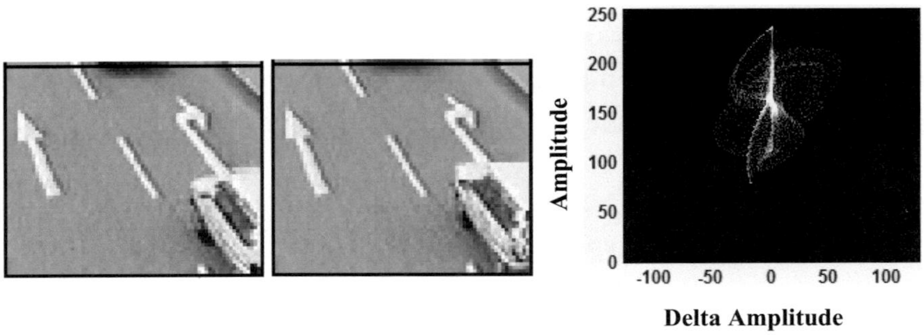

(a) (b) (c)

Figure 61: Examples of sensitivity of phase plot to initial conditions: (a) first image, (b) next image, and (c) and phase plot [67].

In summary, the phase plots of image change due to motion and contextual change showed complex interesting structure indicative of an underlying chaos-like process. This is in stark contrast to the phase plots of image change due to illumination which showed well-defined and localized structure indicative of an underlying deterministic process. The chaos-like behavior in phase space was present for a broad range of objects, from fully rigid to completely deformable. In real-world situations, however, images will not be comprised simply of motion or illumination change but by a combination of these effects. We will now address the presence of both of these effects simultaneously.

SIMULTANEOUS PRESENCE OF MOTION AND ILLUMINATION IN PHASE SPACE

Detecting motion and change in images with illumination change has been of considerable interest to researchers and is a fundamental problem in the exploitation of images for applications such as surveillance. The traditional physics-based model of motion is the optical flow model based on the Navier-Stokes equation [25]:

$$\frac{\partial I}{\partial t} + \nabla I \cdot \mathbf{v} + I\nabla \cdot \mathbf{v} = 0, \tag{20}$$

where I is the image brightness and $\mathbf{v}$ is the velocity of the object in the image plane. This equation is based on a number of assumptions which ultimately limits its effectiveness including, small changes in position and, most importantly, ***image constancy*** which assumes all changes in pixel amplitudes are due to motion and not illumination changes.

Since image constancy is clearly violated in most real-world applications, researchers have proposed a variety of approaches to address it. Cho and Kim in [54] have utilized the structure of the joint histogram to first remove global illumination and then perform motion and contextual change. This model does not address spatially varying illumination. Mester, *et al.,* exploited the multiplicative nature of illumination and developed a co-linearity model where changes in illumination are assumed constant over small regions [28]. The limitation of this model is the underlying requirement of linearity of all the changes which limits the behaviors of the objects in the scene. Black, *et al.,* were the first of an extensive collection of mixture model approaches which attempt to model all possible conditions of change, including illumination, motion, deformation, noise, *etc.* [27]. One limitation of this approach is that first one must address all the possible sources of image change. Since the approach operates in grayscale space there are often ambiguities regarding what underlying mechanism actually caused the change.

Mixture models were further extended by Tian, *et al.,* where multiple Gaussian mixtures are used to model all possible image changes without assumptions of them being due to moving objects, contextual change, illumination or shadows [33]. GMM relies on calculating images of the number of mixtures, mean (μ_t), variance (σ_t^2), and weight (ω_t) of ***every*** pixel in the image according to [33]:

$$\omega_t = \omega_{t-1} + \alpha(o_t - \omega_{t-1}) - \alpha c_T$$

$$\mu_t = \mu_{t-1} + o_t(\alpha/\omega_{t-1})\delta_t$$

$$\sigma_t^2 = \sigma_{t-1}^2 + o_t(\alpha/\omega_{t-1})(\delta_t^T \delta_t - \sigma_{t-1}^2)$$

$$D_t^2(x_t) = \delta_t^T \delta_t / \sigma_t^2 \tag{21}$$

where α is the learning rate, c_T is a mixture weight decay value, $\delta_t = x_t - \mu_{t-1}$ and x_t is the pixel amplitude for each pixel at the current image frame time, and $D_t^2(x_t)$ is a similarity measure. If the value of $D_t^2(x_t)$ exceeds a threshold then the number of mixtures in the model is changed. Note these terms are computed for each of the *K* mixture components where *K=3* is typical [29, 33]. The selection of *K* is somewhat arbitrary and for images, particularly those with complex illumination changes. Unfortunately, the user does not know ahead of time what the conditions the system will be experiencing.

The most critical limitation of the GMM approach however is stated by Tian *et al.*, "[the GMM model] cannot adapt to quick-lighting changes and cannot handle shadows well" [33]. Sung *et al.,* extended the mixture model approach using kernels rather than straight statistical mixtures to handle ***global*** illumination change, however they also acknowledge that the approach is not robust to spatially varying illumination [34]. Lastly, Pilet *et al.,* in [30] have developed a variation of GMM where they additionally insert an Expectation Maximization algorithm to select whether pixel changes are due to illumination or object change (the source of image change is the hidden variable), however, their illumination model does not address specular illumination sources.

The sensitivity of these mixture approaches to spatially varying illumination can be seen clearly in Fig. **62** where the subway data are processed using GMM. Note the significant illumination detections in these images. In particular, note the extensive illumination trail from the headlights of the train as it entered the station and also the projections of the temporally varying illumination bands from the windows of the cars being projected onto the column of the subway station. In general it is important to note that all of the approaches highlighted above focus on making the motion detection robust to illumination while the proposed chaos-theoretic approach addressed in this book is ***inherently*** robust to illumination changes due to its ability to detect the fundamentally different physics involved in changes in illumination *versus* changes due to motion and contextual change.

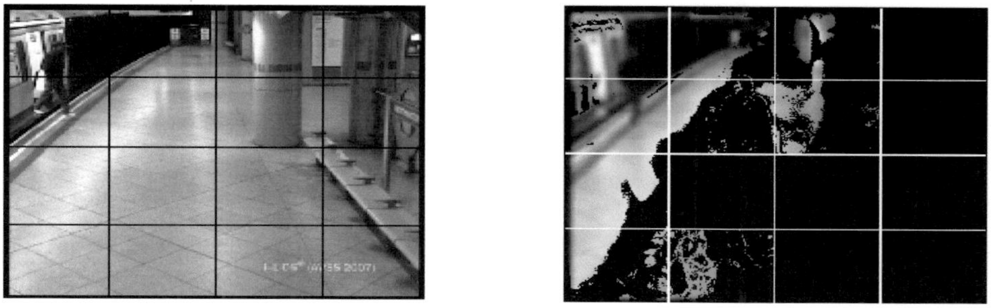

(a) (b)

Figure 62: Examples of detected changes due to illumination that is detected by GMM: (a) one of sequence of images [85] and (b) where extensive illumination is detected by GMM.

We will first address the simultaneous presence of global illumination and motion and then extend the analysis to the most difficult case of spatially varying illumination and motion. Fig. **63** (c) demonstrates the effects on the phase plot of an image sequence with both motion and globally varying illumination present. Recall the structure of global illumination change demonstrated earlier where global Illumination causes a shift in the slope of the phase plot line proportional to the amount of illumination. In Fig. **63**, (c) there is a clear line at roughly a thirty degree angle from the vertical that corresponds to the pixels in the image with only the global illumination change (*i.e.* the pixels not on the moving car). The remainder of the phase plot with the complex trajectory corresponds to the pixels in the image on the moving car. Thus we can correlate local structures in the phase plot to global illumination change or motion. Recall one useful property of ergodicity ensures that "sets defined by dynamical systems have locally the same [fractal] dimension everywhere", (commonly referred to as the Eckmann-Ruelle conjecture) [39], which is verified by the local nature of the illumination *versus* motion effects in Fig. **63** (c). This implies that the local chaotic (fractal) measures calculated within the phase plot will be consistent within regions of the phase plot corresponding to one of the three possible conditions: (i) no change, (ii) change due to moving objects (or appearance of objects), or (iii) change due to illumination.

We must now verify we will be able to extend the results of the locality of the effects of global illumination change to the more complex spatially varying illumination. Fig. **64** provides a laboratory example of spatially varying illumination bands occurring simultaneously with object motion. A light beam from the right of the image is moving downward radially while the car is moving vertically on a linear path. The resultant phase plot shown in Fig. **64** (c) for the highlighted grid cell shows a complex trajectory with a region of high density in the upper portion of the phase plot and a more dispersed and chaos-like pattern in the lower portion of the image. Fig. **65** (b) shows the same phase plot as depicted in Fig. **64** (c) with the compact region of the phase plot removed. The remaining phase plot corresponds to the more complex space-filling trajectory and the Fig. **65** (c) shows the region of the original image in Fig. **65** (a) that corresponded to this portion of the phase plot.

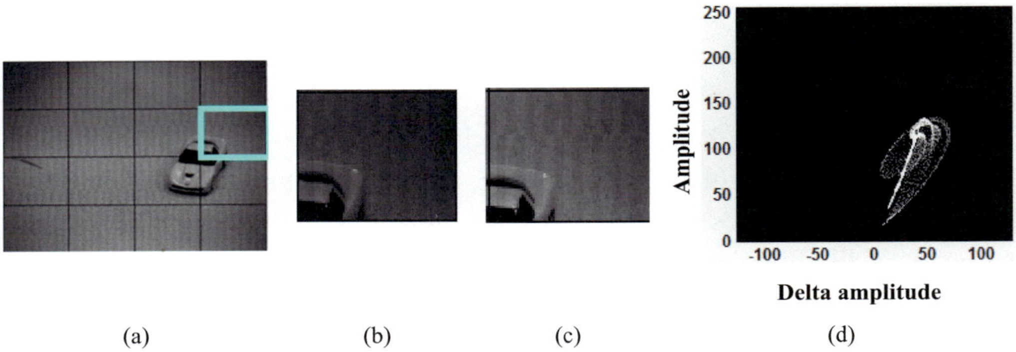

Figure 63: Example of simultaneous global illumination and motion [24]: (a) first image, (b) image with global illumination change and motion, and (c) phase plot for (a) and (b) (Note the distinct linear structure due to background global illumination superimposed onto the motion trajectory).

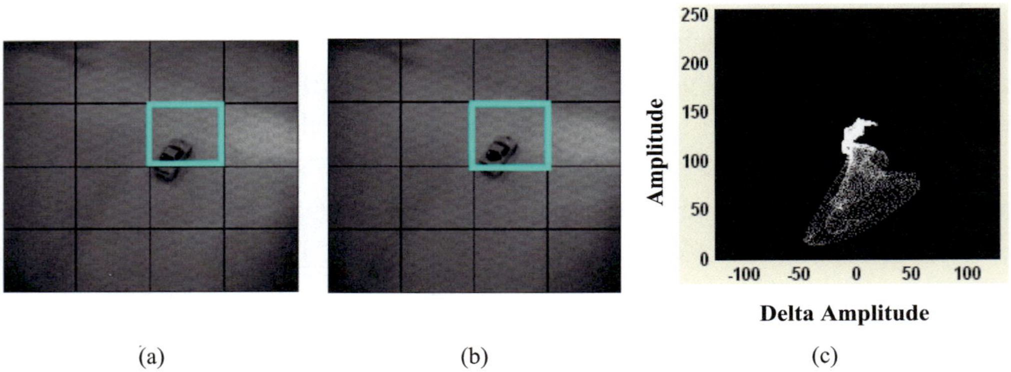

Figure 64: Example of simultaneous spatio-temporal illumination and motion, (a) 1st image, (b) 2nd image, and (c) phase plot [24].

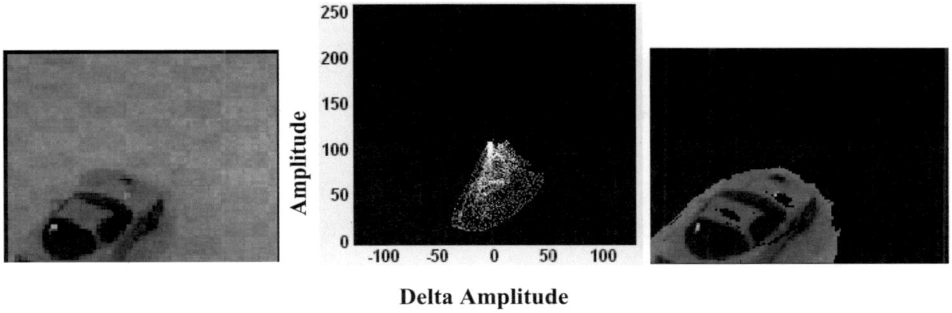

(a) (b) (c)

Figure 65: Segmentation: (a) original image, (b) segmented phase plot, and (c) regions of original image corresponding to chaotic portion of phase plot [24].

We have shown earlier in this chapter that the different underlying physics related to illumination change and motion and contextual change leads to different structures in phase space. Illumination changes results in deterministic, non-chaotic changes in the image radiance that manifest themselves in phase space as compact non-fractal and non-chaotic regions. This is in contrast to the changes due to motion which manifest themselves as space-filling complex trajectories in phase space. When motion and illumination are simultaneously present in images then each of these effects appear as locally distinct regions in phase space, as is expected by the Eckmann-Ruelle conjecture. These locally distinct regions will allow us to apply local fractal measures of dimensionality to extract regions in image sequences related to motion and contextual change while ignoring the effects of illumination.

DETERMINING TIME LAGS FOR DETECTING MOTION

Since we will use the space filling nature of motion to differentiate it in phase space from illumination, we must rely on the trajectory adequately filling phase space. The extent of the phase space trajectory will be based on the extent of the amplitude changes that result from the motion. Recall from Chapter 3 that it is important to determine the time lag, *T*, which will be used to reconstruct the underlying signal according to:

$$s(n){:}\ [s(n)\ s(n+T)\ s(n+2T)\ \ldots s(n+kT)] \quad (22)$$

From this complete space a subset of the space can then be selected based on the ideas of embedding when the chaotic nature of the underlying dynamics become well-resolved. Fig. **66** provides a set of phase plots for a moving vehicle where there is considerable motion of the vehicle so the phase plot is highly space filling even for short time lags. Fig. **67** provides an interesting case where a vehicle is slowly moving to merge into traffic at the intersection. Fig. **68** shows the set of phase plots for each of the incrementally longer time lags. Notice the emergence of the space-filling chaotic behavior as the time lag is increased. Over the longer time lags the image pairs become increasingly independent thereby causing a greater excursion in phase space. When the time lag was too short, the system did not have sufficient time to explore the phase space. Fig. **69** provides another image sequence of a pair of human subjects moving down a hallway from the CAVIAR dataset [80]. Fig. **70** provides the set of phase plots for each of the time lags, and once again, as the time lag extends to match the motion, the phase plot blooms in response to the moving objects.

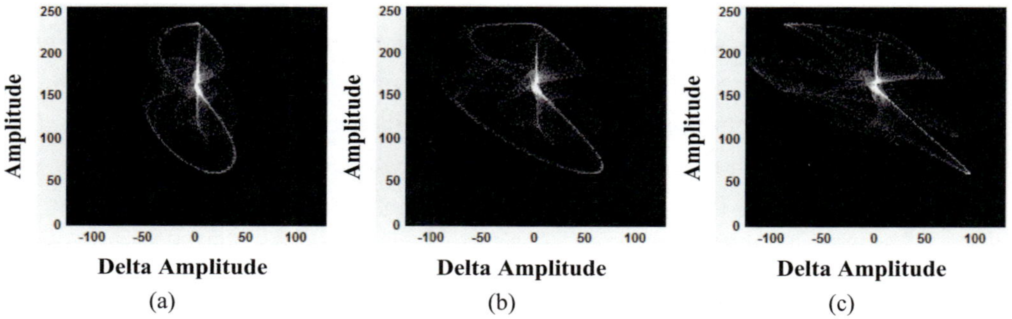

Figure 66: Exploration of time lags for image in Fig. **19**, (a) time lag of 1 image frame, (b) time lag of 2 image frames, and (c) time lag of 4 image frames.

(a) (b) (c) (d)

Figure 67: Same image sequence as in Fig. **19**, but a region with a slow moving object in grid cell (2, 3), (a) original image with grid cell highlighted, (b) time lag of 1 image frame, (c) time lag of 2 image frames, and (d) time lag of 4 image frames [67].

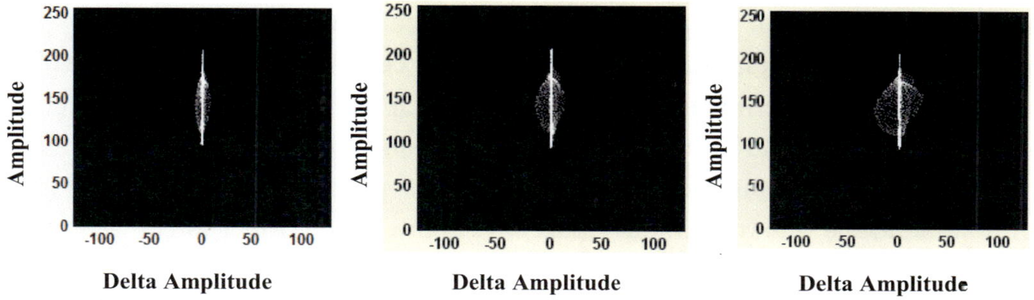

(a) (b) (c)

Figure 68: Exploration of time lags for image in Fig. **19** in grid cell (2, 3), (a) time lag of 1 image frame, (b) time lag of 2 image frames, and (c) time lag of 4 image frames.

(a) (b) (c) (d)

Figure 69: Human motion subject for time lag analysis with people moving in grid cell (2, 2), (a) original image with grid cell highlighted, (b) time lag of 2 image frame, (c) time lag of 4 image frames, and (d) time lag of 8 image frames [80].

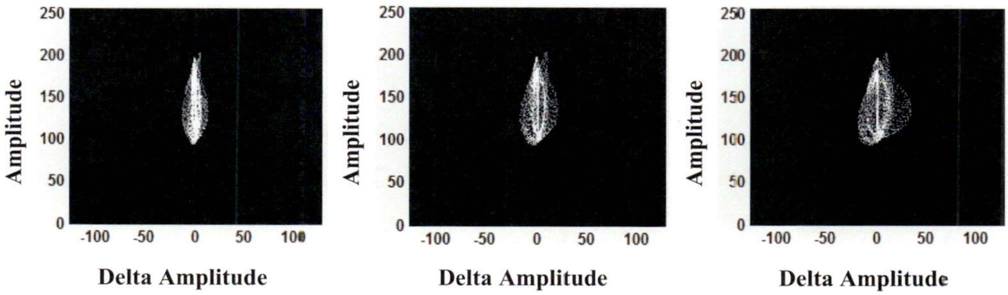

(a) (b) (c)

Figure 70: Exploration of time lags for image in Fig. **69**: (a) phase plot for time lag of 2 image frame, (b) phase plot for time lag of 4 image frames, and (c) phase plot for time lag of 8 image frames.

Thus in summary the selection of time lags for motion detection can be pragmatically based on when motion appears. Typically the minimum time lag, *T*, upon which the signal space reconstruction takes place, is determined by the frame rate of the camera. The subspace within the complete collection of possible time lags is then determined by the lag at which the motion of the object of interest becomes visible in phase space. The responsibility of the developer is to define what the slowest motion that the particular application must detect and then define this to be the maximum time lag upon which the system searches. Typically a system will begin with shorter time lags and increase them in an orderly fashion until the maximum scan time is reached. If the phase plot is still not showing adequately complex behavior then the system declares there is no motion.

EFFECTS OF TEXTURE IN PHASE SPACE

Recall that spatial chaos can be used to explain texture in images. Texture analysis has been a well-studied field for years [11]. Due to humans' apparent ease with regard to differentiating texture, it has been a common visual cue to explore for image retrieval and object segmentation. Interestingly, Mandelbrot described texture as an "elusive notion" [73] since often qualitative attributes distinguish one texture from another to humans. The challenge for researchers has been to develop quantitative measures that can be implemented in computer vision applications. The direct use of fractals for texture analysis and related tasks such as segmentation and object characterization has been well-researched [10, 11,13-15,89]. As Pentland stated many years ago that, "the fractal dimension has been shown to correspond closely to our intuitive notion of roughness…" [10]. Recalling Equation (7), $L_m = \rho \vec{N} \cdot \vec{I}$ we see that if the resultant image exhibits fractal behavior, it is due to the fractal nature of the underlying surface normal since the incoming illumination, I, is without structure. Pentland stated that the "fractal surface model offers the potential of unifying and simplifying these various 2-D texture descriptions" [10]. One key challenge, however, is that the fine or coarse roughness of a texture depends on the scale upon which it is being analyzed. This will result in requiring texture to be analyzed at a variety of scales to provide a complete description of the texture and hence the underlying surface.

Throughout this chapter that we viewed objects in the scene being imaged as imparting aperiodic forcing functions onto the imaging sensor and thereby creating the image radiance that exhibits chaos-like behavior in the final image. Since fractal behavior is often a result of underlying chaotic dynamics we propose that the texture of objects in the imaging field of view can quite possibly also be viewed as aperiodic forcing functions, and we direct the reader to Fig. **71** which contains a set of distinct texture fields. One distinction of texture is that many textures also exhibit periodic characteristics, which will produce more deterministic patterns in phase space, but their trajectories may still be of interest. Likewise Pentland in his early work stated: "the fact that fractal functions can exhibit regularities allows us to smoothly pass from random chaotic surfaces to regular patterned ones within the same conceptual framework" [10]. Here Pentland was using the term chaotic relatively loosely, however, in this section we will explore the possibilities of using our chaotic aperiodic forcing function description to explain texture in images.

(a) (b) (c) (d)

Figure 71: Example textures from standard texture library [90].

There is another advantage to considering the proposed chaos-based approaches. While direct fractal measures of the textures are related to distinguishing the roughness of the underlying surface generating the texture, a chaotic approach can provide insight into the information content in the scene. Recall from information theory that the more irregular a signal is the greater its information content (*i.e.* higher the entropy). Thus employing a chaos-based approach can provide insight into the irregularity of the textures and hence the irregularities in the underlying object creating the image.

Approaches to texture analysis are usually categorized into four categories: (i) structural, (ii) statistical, (iii) model-based, and (iv) transform-based methods [70]. The two approaches we will explore here are the statistical and the model-based approaches and demonstrate that chaos theory can be used to unify these two approaches. The statistical approach represents the texture indirectly by the non-deterministic properties that govern the distributions and relationships between the grey levels of an image. The most popular statistical features for texture analysis are derived from the co-occurrence matrix. We saw earlier in the previous chapter the structural similarity of the joint histogram and the phase plot. Consequently, it is not surprising that the co-occurrence matrix has also been found to be useful for analyzing time-dependent information, such as crowd formations in [91]. Prior to the popularization of chaos theory, Terzopoulos applied the co-occurrence matrix to the analysis of speech waveforms, where he recognized that analyzing the speech waveforms through varying time lags provided interesting information regarding the behavior of the speech waveform [92]. In a completely complementary manner, we will be applying the calculation of the phase plot over *spatial* lags rather than *time* lags and then leveraging the work on chaos theory. The chaos approach to texture analysis will treat each line in an image as a data series which will then be analyzed through a sequence of spatial lags. The collection of image lines will correspond to an ensemble of data series which can either be implicitly combined in the phase plot (as they are in the co-occurrence matrix) or analyzed as individual phase plots.

Fig. **72** (a) shows a typical non-periodic texture image from the Brodatz texture library [90]. Fig. **72** (b) shows the co-occurrence matrix for a 10 pixel stride and a 90 degree directional comparison. Fig. **72** (c) shows the resultant phase plot using these same parameters, and as expected we see there is a definite similarity in the internal structure of the co-occurrence matrix and the phase plot. Fig. **73** (a) shows a highly repetitive, regular image with relatively large texture detail, and Fig. **73** (b) provides the co-occurrence matrix and Fig. **73** (c) the phase plot, notice again the consistency in the structural similarity of the phase plots and co-occurrence matrices. This similarity between co-occurrence matrices and the phase plot is also intuitively evident when we consider Haralick 's quote: "Our initial assumption in characterizing image texture is that all the texture information is contained in the gray-tone spatial-dependence matrices" [93]. His intuitive observations are given mathematical integrity when considering the concept of reconstruction of dynamical systems *via* their complete phase space representation. Thus rather than simply assuming that all the texture information is captured by the co-occurrence matrix, chaos theory and non-linear dynamic system modeling verify that indeed the phase space representation can capture the underlying spatial dynamics that created the texture.

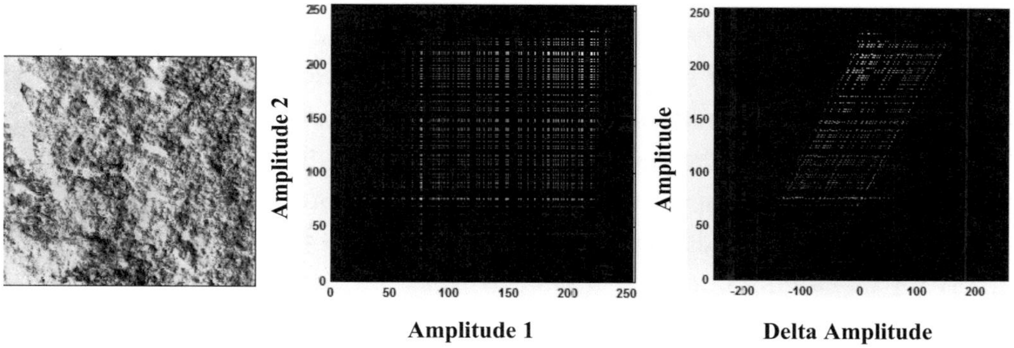

(a) (b) (c)

Figure 72: The structural relationship of co-occurrence matrix and phase plot: (a) texture image from Brodatz [90], (b) co-occurrence matrix for 10 pixel offset and 90 degree directional comparisons, and (c) corresponding phase plot.

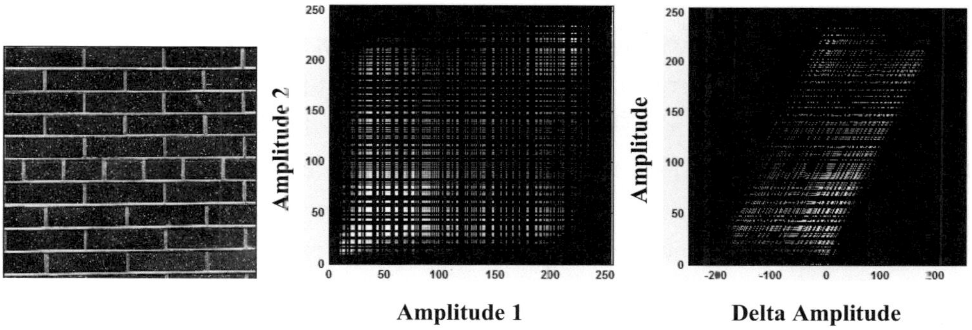

(a) (b) (c)

Figure 73: A third example of the structural relationship of co-occurrence matrix and phase plot for a texture with larger highly repetitive details: (a) texture image from Brodatz [90], (b) co-occurrence matrix for 10 pixel offset and 90 degree directional comparisons, and (c) corresponding phase plot for 10 pixel lag and 90 degree directional comparisons.

The model-based approaches to texture analysis are based on fractal and stochastic models [70]. These approaches attempt to interpret image texture by using fractal generative image models and parametric stochastic models. Fractal-based image analysis algorithms are widely used in medical applications where differing structure of tissue images provides vital information for applications such as cancer detection [11]. The direct application of the fractal dimension to images has also proven useful for remote sensing applications such as synthetic aperture radar (SAR) image analysis where the specular appearance of the images has proven to be well modeled as a fractal surface [94]. The fractal model-based approaches directly compute the fractal dimension of the actual grayscale texture images using a variety of methods, with transform methods based on wavelets being quite popular. Pentland observed that "fractal functions may be defined in terms of either the way inter-pixel differences change with distance, or the rate at which the Fourier power spectrum falls off with increasing frequency"[10]. This text, not being a thorough description of texture methods but rather an exploration of chaos for explaining computer vision, will not dedicate space to all methods equally, however given Pentland's comments this does not result in any loss of technical adequacy.

One recent popular method is the Blanket Dimension which provides a local fractal dimension of the actual grayscale image to support segmentation based on texture [95]. Unfortunately, it has been shown by various authors, and highlighted by Novianto, *et al.,* that extracting local fractal dimensions of texture images directly from the image grayscale data is not particularly accurate due to the limitation of how small of a local window can be used and still provide an accurate fractal dimension [13, 95]. The focus of this chapter, however, is not on directly exploiting the fractal dimension of the grayscale image but rather calculating the fractal dimension of phase space. For example, traditional fractal dimension estimation methods such as the Box Counting method is quite effective for computing the fractal dimension of phase plots, but has been shown to be not particularly accurate for grayscale texture images [11]. Additionally, the computation of the box counting method in phase space is quite efficient in terms of computational complexity, but it has been found to be computationally intensive in grayscale image calculations [95].

With the intimate relationship between fractals and chaos, the analysis of texture *via* phase space methods merits further study. Both the structural and model-based approaches have some elements in common with the analysis of systems experiencing chaos. Therefore it appears appropriate to investigate the analysis of texture from a more fundamental chaotic approach since it would represent a hybrid of the first two very popular approaches. By analyzing the texture of images using chaos, we will continue to embrace the central premise of this text that the underlying objects in the image field serve as aperiodic forcing functions imparting a chaos-like behavior on the output of the imaging sensor. Likewise, rather than calculating fractal dimensions directly on the image fields, we will rely on the well-accepted approach of analyzing complex dynamical systems in phase space to detect the presence of chaos and more generally chaos-like behaviors. For example, we see in the phase plots of Fig. **72** through Fig. **85** there is significantly differing structure in phase space depending on the original texture image being analyzed. We will explore in Chapter 8 potential algorithms for performing analysis of these phase plots for the purpose of texture-based recognition of images for applications such as image retrieval.

DETERMINING SPATIAL LAGS FOR TEXTURE ANALYSIS

Recall the determination of appropriate time lags for motion detection is based pragmatically on when the motion of slow moving objects become apparent and what the slowest speed objects the system must detect. Unfortunately for texture analysis there are no simple pragmatic rules. This situation of lacking pragmatic rules for time lags is actually the norm, however for many chaos applications and fortunately other researchers have devised mechanisms for estimating the maximum required data lags. As Abarbanel states, "For essentially all practical purposes one is seeking a value of [the lag] which works and is connected with the non-linear information generating properties of the dynamics" [21].

The first approach to estimating these data lags is to use the auto-correlation function. The second approach to estimating data lags is to use a measure called the average auto-mutual information, and to use the first minimum of this function as an estimate of the appropriate data lag. Both of these measures can provide an estimate for the spatial lag, Δx, upon which the signal space reconstruction is based:

$$s(n): [s(n)\ s(n+\Delta x)\ s(n+2\Delta x) \ldots s(n+k\Delta x)] \quad (23)$$

The auto-correlation is a popular measure in traditional signal processing applications. It can be used to determine the repeating structure of an underlying signal and to also serve as a basis for estimating the energy within a signal. It is also useful for estimating where the minimum information redundancy exists between a time series and a lagged copy of the time series. For the texture application the goal of the auto-correlation function is to estimate this point of minimal information redundancy. The desired measure is the first zero-crossing of the auto-correlation function which defines the least lag which minimizes the information redundancy. The auto-correlation function is defined by [21]:

$$C(\Delta) = \sum_n [s(n) - \bar{s}][(n + \Delta) - \bar{s}] \tag{24}$$

where the mean of the signal is defined to be [21]:

$$\bar{s} = \frac{1}{N} \sum_{n=1}^{N} s(n) \tag{25}$$

The lag, Δ which corresponds to the first zero-crossing, will provide the base lag upon which the signal will be reconstructed. Unfortunately this measure is based on the linear analysis of the data series, and as we have been discussing throughout this text, the model we have adopted for the creation of image content is one of an aperiodic *non-linear* forcing function. Thus using an optimal linear estimator for analyzing a fundamentally non-linear process is problematic.

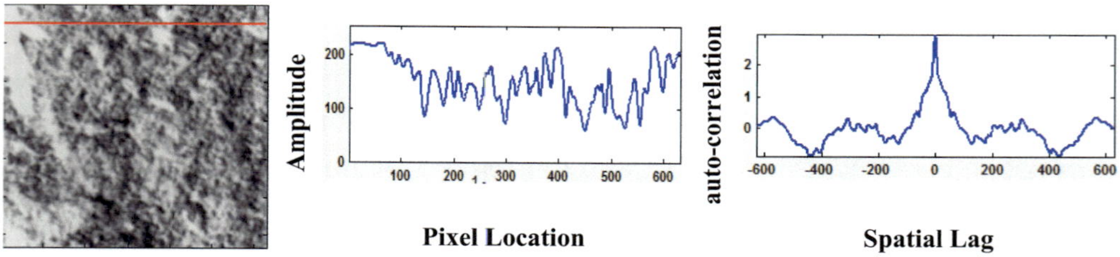

(a) (b) (c)

Figure 74: The auto-correlation function for first texture image with first zero crossing at spatial lag of 95: (a) texture image from Brodatz [90], (b) pixel amplitude spectrum for identified line, and (c) corresponding auto-correlation function.

Fig. **74** through Fig. **77** provide a collection of these auto-correlation functions and the estimates of these optimal spatial lags. Notice that in most cases these optimal lag estimates are quite large which would significantly limit our ability to reconstruct the signal of interest since it is constructed from integer multiples of this optimal lag estimate. More importantly, note in Fig. **78** the evaluation of the auto-correlation metric for all of the lines of an image of a common texture produce dramatically differing auto-correlation measures, and in all cases, the mode and mean values are both quite large, and hence not useful operationally.

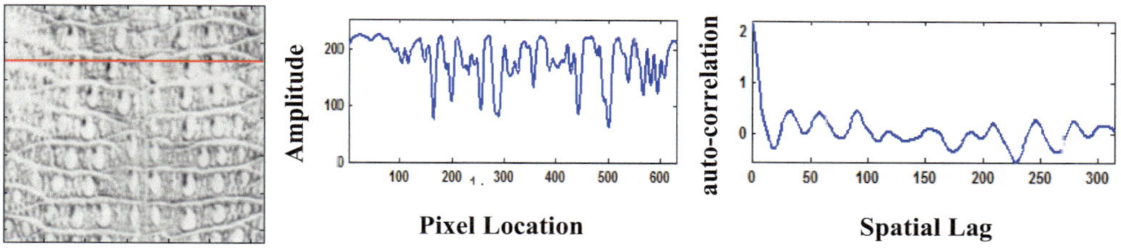

(a) (b) (c)

Figure 75: The auto-correlation function for second texture image with first zero crossing at spatial lag of 11: (a) texture image from Brodatz [90], (b) pixel amplitude spectrum for identified line, and (c) corresponding auto-correlation function.

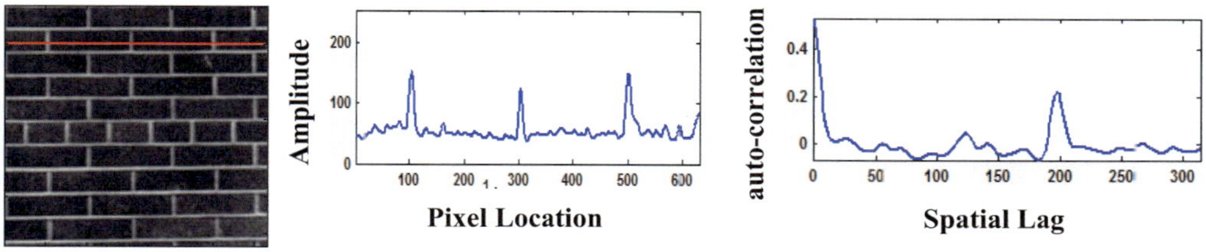

(a) (b) (c)

Figure 76: The auto-correlation function for third texture image with first zero crossing at spatial lag of 32: (a) texture image from Brodatz [90], (b) pixel amplitude spectrum for identified line, and (c) corresponding auto-correlation function.

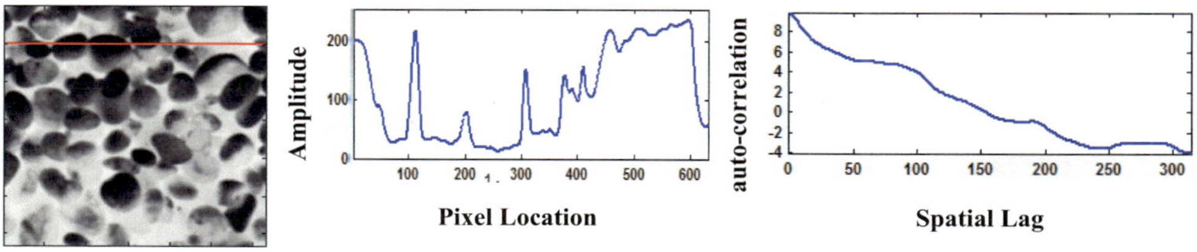

(a) (b) (c)

Figure 77: The auto-correlation function for fourth texture image with first zero crossing at spatial lag of 154: (a) texture image from Brodatz [90], (b) pixel amplitude spectrum for identified line, and (c) corresponding auto-correlation function.

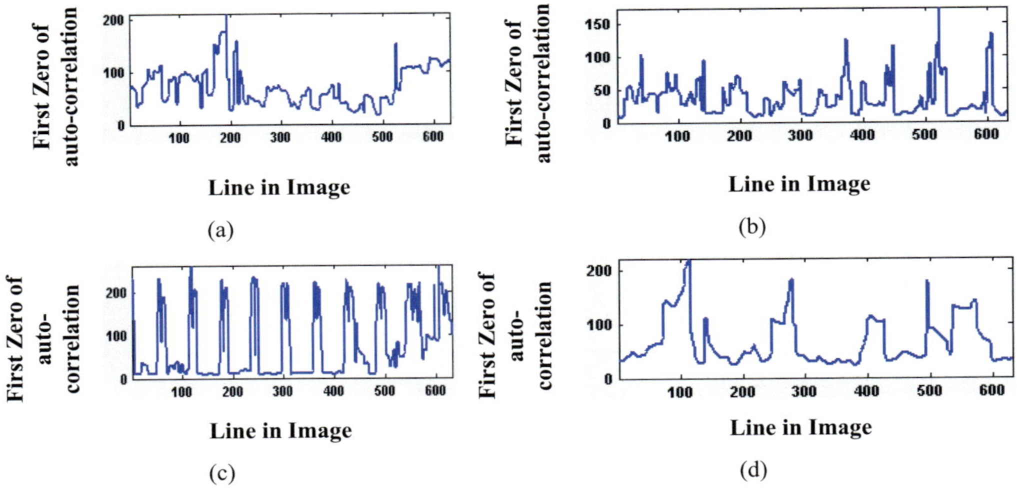

Figure 78: The variation of first zero of the auto-correlation function *versus* line in the image: (a) first zeros for first texture image, mode=107, mean=71, std. dev.=36, (b) first zeros for second texture image, mode=10, mean=35, std. dev.=26, (c) first zeros for third texture image, mode=9, mean=77, std. dev.=81, (d) first zeros for fourth texture image, mode=31, mean=65, std. dev.=42.

The preferred method for estimating the optimal base spatial lag is the Average auto-mutual information function which is a measure of the relative mutual information of a signal data series with a sequence of increasing lags [21]. The first minimum of this function provides the first data lag at which the relative mutual information content between the signal and its lagged version is minimized. The average auto-mutual information function is defined by [21]:

$$I(\Delta) = \sum_{s(n),s(n+\Delta)} P(s(n), s(n+\Delta)) \cdot log_2 \left[\frac{P(s(n),s(n+\Delta))}{P(s(n))\cdot P(s(n+\Delta))}\right] \qquad (26)$$

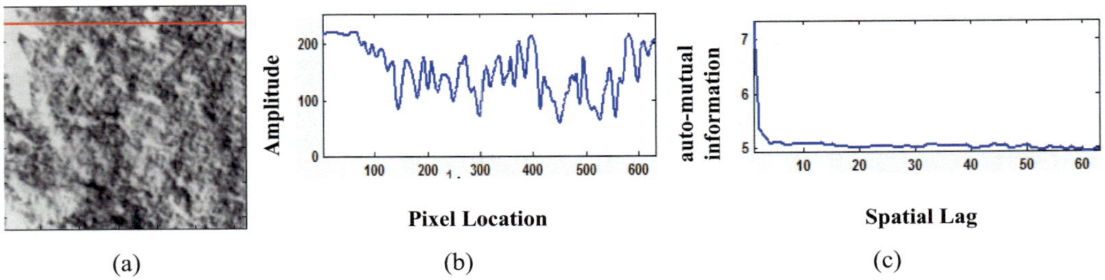

Figure 79: The auto-mutual information function for first texture image with first minimum at spatial lag of 4: (a) texture image from Brodatz [90], (b) pixel amplitude spectrum for identified line, and (c) corresponding auto-correlation function.

Fig. **79** through Fig. **82** provide a collection of these auto-mutual information functions and the estimates of these optimal spatial lags. Notice that in all cases these optimal lag estimates are in general reasonable, ranging from four to seven pixel lags. Even the last image which recall had an auto-correlation measure of *154* has an auto-mutual information measure of only *5*.

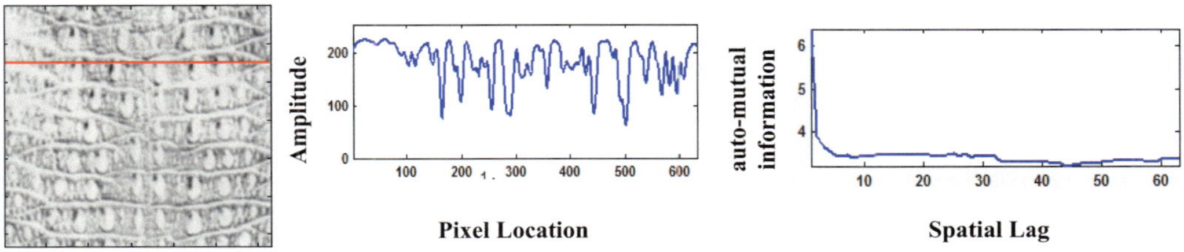

Figure 80: The auto-mutual information function for second texture image with first minimum at spatial lag of 6: (a) texture image from Brodatz [90], (b) pixel amplitude spectrum for identified line, and (c) corresponding auto-correlation function.

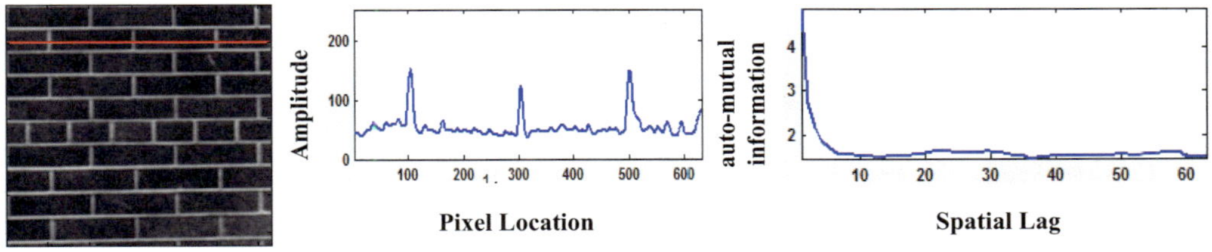

Figure 81: The auto-mutual information function for third texture image with first minimum at spatial lag of 7: (a) texture image from Brodatz [90], (b) pixel amplitude spectrum for identified line, and (c) corresponding auto-correlation function.

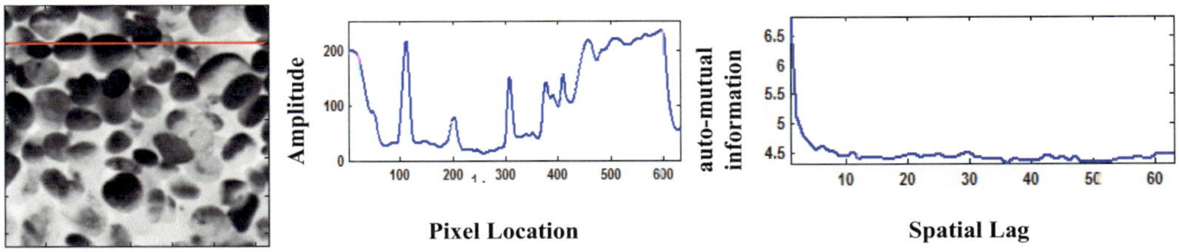

Figure 82: The auto-mutual information function for fourth texture image with first zero crossing at spatial lag of 5: (a) texture image from Brodatz [90], (b) pixel amplitude spectrum for identified line, and (c) corresponding auto-correlation function.

Additionally, note in Fig. **83** the evaluation of the auto-mutual information metric for all of the lines of an image of a common texture produce extremely similar values which is in marked contrast to the measures calculated using the auto-correlation measures. In all cases, the mode and mean values are of reasonable size and more importantly have a very small variation across the entire image being considered which is extremely important since we do not want the lags used for the phase plot to be highly line-dependent. Thus for processing texture using our chaos-theoretic approach we will first employ the auto-mutual information measure to establish the base time lag that will be used for generating the phase space reconstruction.

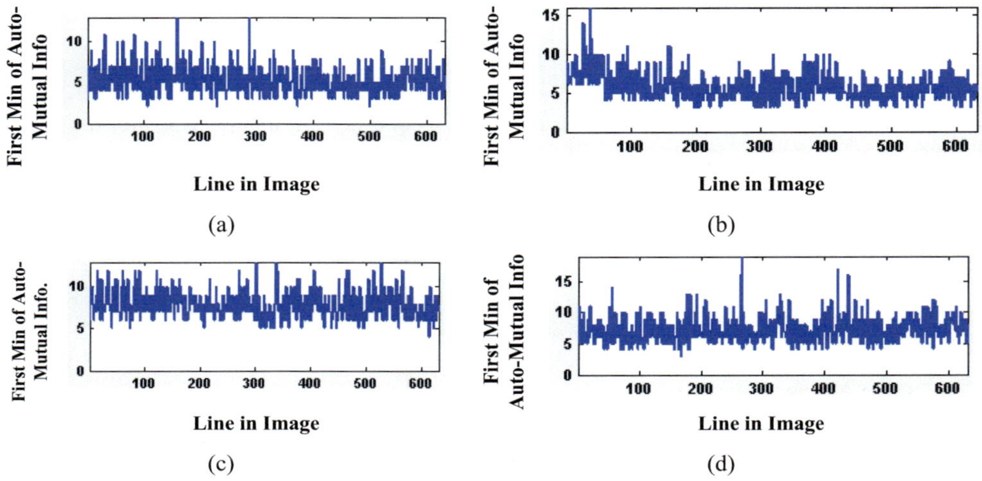

Figure 83: The variation of first zero of the auto-mutual information function *versus* line in the image: (a) first zeros for first texture image, mode=4, mean=5, std. dev.=1.7, (b) first zeros for second texture image, mode=5, mean=6, std. dev.=1.8, (c) first zeros for third texture image, mode=7, mean=8, std. dev.=1.6, (d) first zeros for fourth texture image, mode=6, mean=7, std. dev.=2.

EFFECTS OF NOISE ON TEXTURE IN PHASE SPACE

As we saw earlier in this chapter, in Fig. **25** and Fig. **26** we showed the importance of low-pass filtering the images in order to allow the interesting chaos-like behavior in phase space to become visible. Varma and Garg likewise state: "Filters can smooth over image noise and lead to more robust features" [13]. In Fig. **84** (a) we see the texture image from Fig. **71** (b) after a small *3x3* Gaussian kernel low-pass filter, and Fig. **84** (b) shows the co-occurrence matrix and Fig. **84** (c) shows the resultant phase plot for this filtered image. This filter is significantly smaller than the filters used for motion analysis since we do not want to risk losing fine texture details. Likewise, Fig. **85** (a) through (c) show the effects of the same *3x3* low pass Gaussian kernel filter on the co-occurrence and phase plot of the second texture image from Fig. **71** (c). The difference in structure of the phase plots from these two distinct images is still quite apparent. Notice in Fig. **86** (a) and its corresponding phase plot in Fig. **86** (c) even modest low-pass filtering results in the appearance of significant structure in the phase plots of the two images. The remaining images in Fig. **86** will be used to explore the effects of increasing filter size on texture analysis.

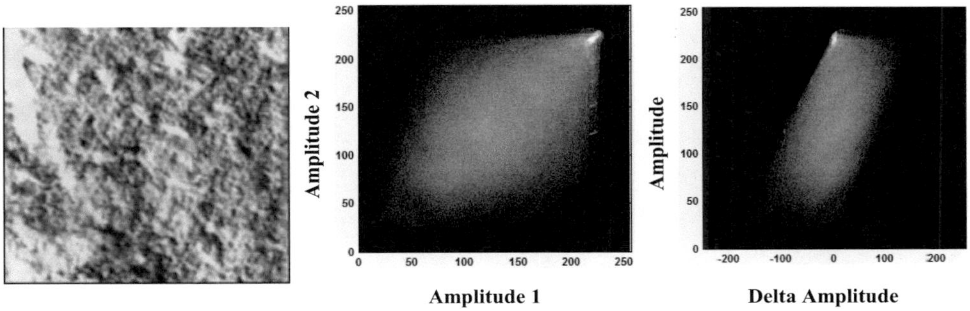

(a) (b) (c)

Figure 84: Examination of the effects of filtering on the structural relationship of co-occurrence matrix and phase plot: (a) *filtered* texture image from Brodatz [90], (b) log of the co-occurrence matrix for 10 pixel offset and 90 degree directional comparisons, and (c) corresponding log of the phase plot.

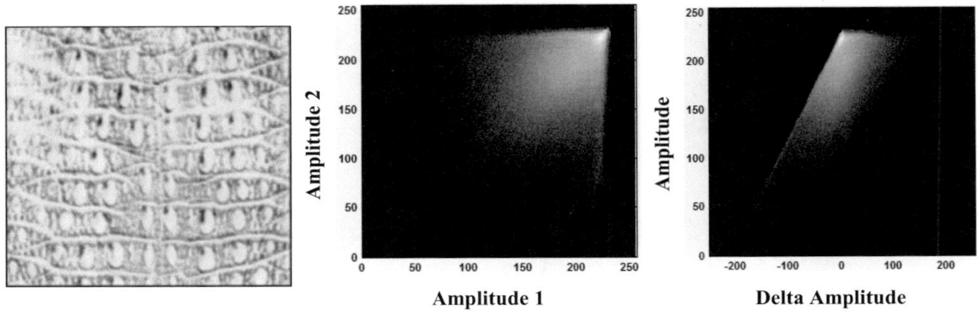

(a) (b) (c)

Figure 85: The second examination of the effects of filtering on the structural relationship of co-occurrence matrix and phase plot: (a) *filtered* texture image from Brodatz [90], (b) log of the co-occurrence matrix for 10 pixel offset, and (c) corresponding log phase plot.

Fig. **86** (a) through (c) provides the results of low-pass filtering a texture image with very large macro-features and repetition. Fig. **86** (d) through (f) provides the phase plots of each of these images. We see for the largest filter of size *15x15* there are still interesting subtle features in the phase plot. Correspondingly, Fig. **87** (a) through (c) shows the results of low-pass filtering a texture image with finer scale features. We see that particularly in Fig. **87** (f) the phase plot shows very little structure remaining as the texture has been overwhelmed by the filter window. Thus the larger window filters that are required for motion analysis are not recommended for texture in order to ensure the smaller features of the texture are not lost. Smaller kernels are still effective for texture analysis in reducing the effects of noise while ensuring the micro-structures of the textures are still preserved.

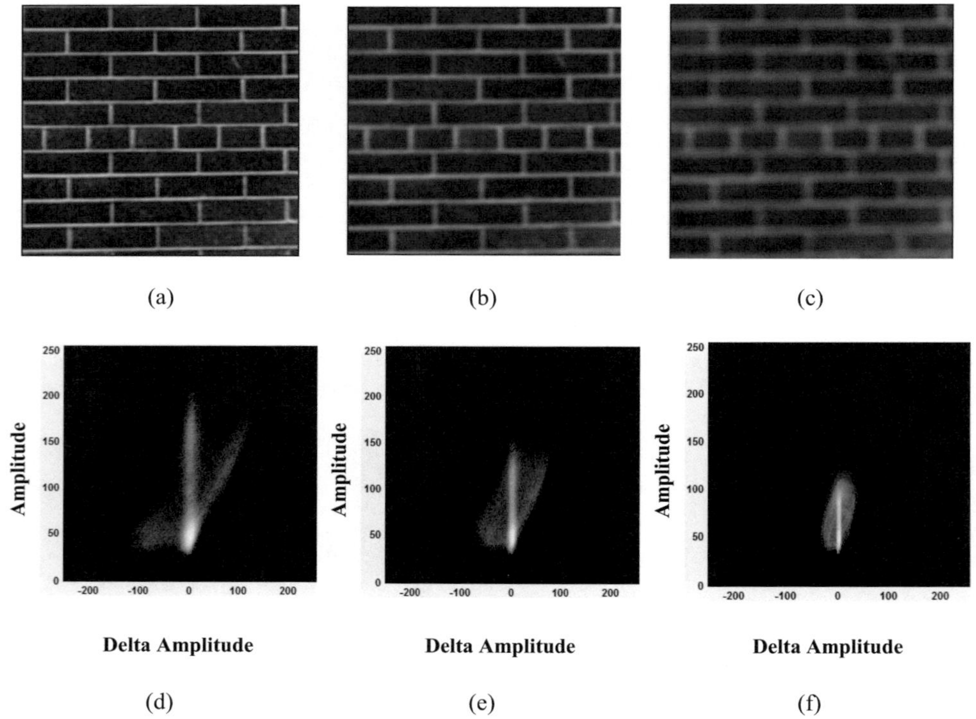

Figure 86: An examination of the effects of filter size on texture image phase plot second further examination of the structural relationship of co-occurrence matrix and phase plot: (a) texture image from Brodatz [90] filtered with *3x3* filter, (b) texture image from Brodatz filtered with *10x10* filter, (c) texture image from Brodatz filtered with *15x15* filter, (d) phase plot for image (a), (e) phase plot for image (b), and (f) phase plot for image (c).

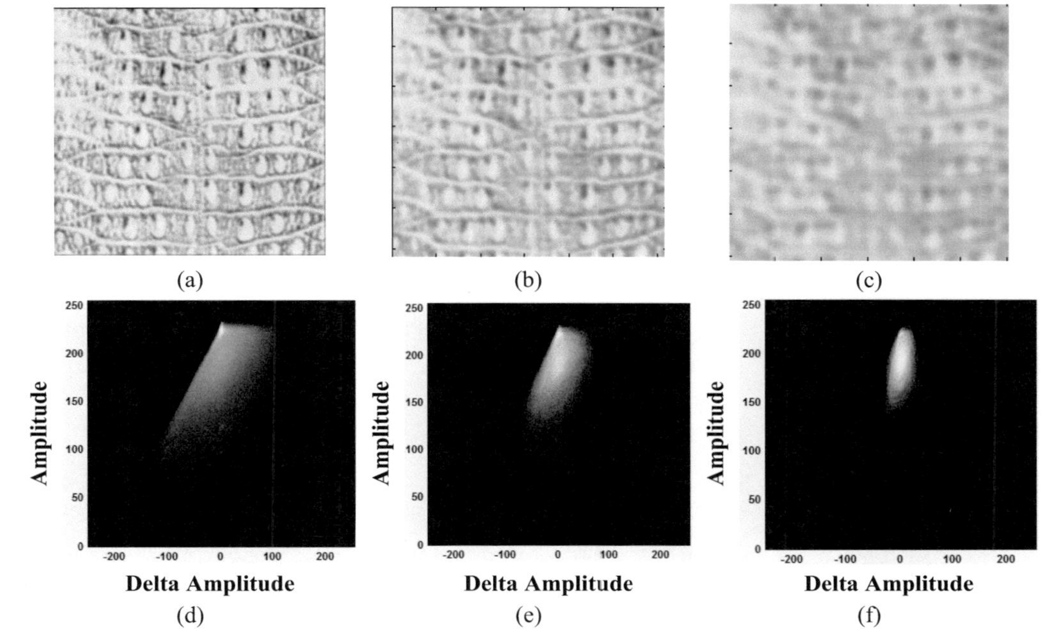

Figure 87: Additional examination of the effects of filter size on texture image phase plot second further examination of the structural relationship of co-occurrence matrix and phase plot: (a) texture image from Brodatz [90] filtered with *5x5* filter (identical appearance to *3x3*), (b) texture image from Brodatz filtered with *10x10* filter, (c) texture image from Brodatz filtered with *15x15* filter, (d) phase plot for image (a), (e) phase plot for image (b), and (f) phase plot for image (c).

MANAGING COMPLEXITY IN PHASE PLOTS FOR TEXTURE ANALYSIS

Recall that the phase plot of an entire image often becomes very complex due to the superposition of many effects present within the image. In the case of analyzing images for motion, the presence of multiple moving objects, illumination, and noise all contributed to the complexity. We proposed earlier that to more effectively identify the various underlying chaotic and deterministic sources in the image we reduce the problem by performing a grid-cell sampling of the image into a collection of smaller images. Likewise for texture -based image query Kim, *et al.,* proposed dividing images into a collection of windows similar to the grid-cell approach we advocated for motion [96].

Fig. **88** shows two phase plots of smaller regions in the complex small-scale texture and Fig. **89** shows two regions of an image with larger scale texture. In

Fig. **88** note the highly random structure of the texture is still reflected in the phase plots of the smaller image grid cells whose structure very closely resembles that of the original full image shown earlier in Fig. **84** (c) except the current phase plot is less dense due to the fewer pixels being integrated. This reduced density allows us to see some internal structure in the phase plots as can be seen in Fig. **88** (b) and (c). Likewise the internal structure is clearly visible in Fig. **89** (b) and (c) and is significantly different than the internal structure in Fig. **88** (b) and (c).

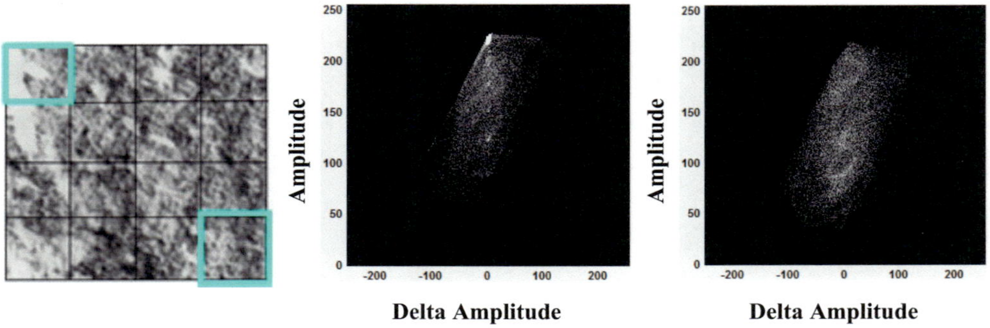

(a) (b) (c)

Figure 88: Phase plots of regional analysis of texture image with fine scale and large scale features, (a) *filtered* texture image from Brodatz [90] with two regions highlights, (b) log phase plot for *10* pixel offset of grid cell *(1, 1)*, and (c) log phase plot for *10* pixel offset of grid cell *(4, 4)*.

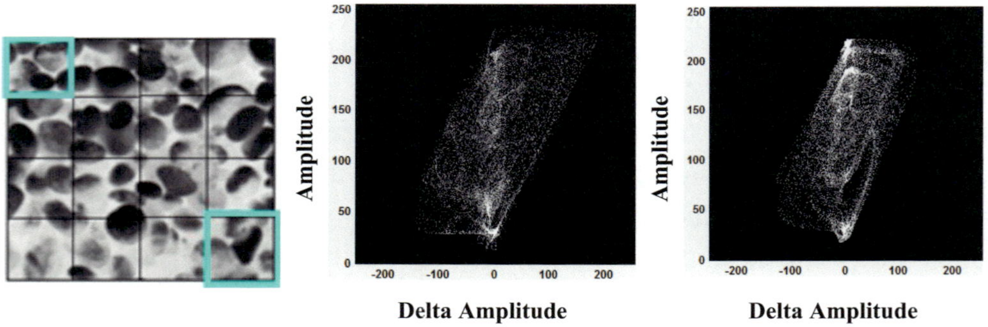

(a) (b) (c)

Figure 89: Phase plots of regional analysis of texture image with large scale features, (a) *filtered* texture image from Brodatz with two regions highlights [90], (b) log phase plot for 10 pixel offset of grid cell (1, 1), and (c) log phase plot for 10 pixel offset of grid cell (4, 4).

An alternative approach for reducing the quantity of data to process and the complexity of phase space may be to analyze individual lines in the image since texture analysis naturally uses directional analysis. Kim, Kim and Tang adopted a similar approach to estimating the fractal dimension of amplitude lines in the image and then computing the co-occurrence matrix of these fractal dimensions with some success [97]. Fig. **90** (a) shows a typical Brodatz texture image and the amplitude spectrum of a single line in the image in Fig. **90** (b). Fig. **90** (c) shows the resultant phase plot of this amplitude profile which would then provide a fractal measure to describe its space-filling nature. Likewise, Fig. **91** (a) shows a second dramatically different texture image with an amplitude profile in Fig. **91** (b) and its corresponding phase plot in Fig. **91** (c). Another interesting amplitude profile and resultant phase plot may be seen in Fig. **92**. In this texture the highly repetitive structure can clearly be seen in the amplitude profile due to the mortar sections of the bricks *versus* non-mortar sections. Note the significant differences in phase space structure of the three phase plots is more dramatic than when considering the phase plots of the entire image that were shown in Fig. **72** through Fig. **85**.

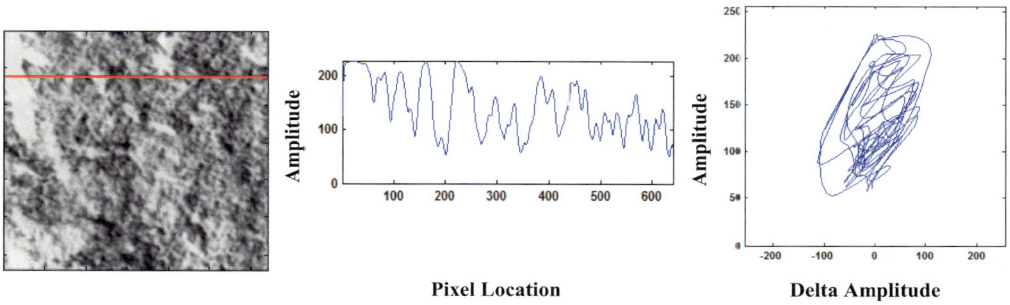

(a) (b) (c)

Figure 90: Analysis of phase plot for a single line image [90], (a) identified line, (b) amplitude profile, and (c) phase plot for *10* pixel lag.

Since texture is by nature a two-dimensional characteristic of an image it is not enough to merely consider the phase plots of individual lines in the image, but rather the interrelationships between these lines as well. Kim, Kim and Tang captured these interrelationships by computing the co-occurrence matrix of the fractal values of each of the actual amplitude profiles and determined the relative frequency of occurrence of fractal dimensions for differing spatial offsets [97]. This captures any repetitive information in the images. Fig. **93** provides the sequences of fractal dimensions of the phase plots of each line in the images as the sampling line is swept across the image for each of the texture images in Fig.

90, Fig. **91**, and Fig. **92**. Notice the differing behaviors of each of these fractal profiles of the images.

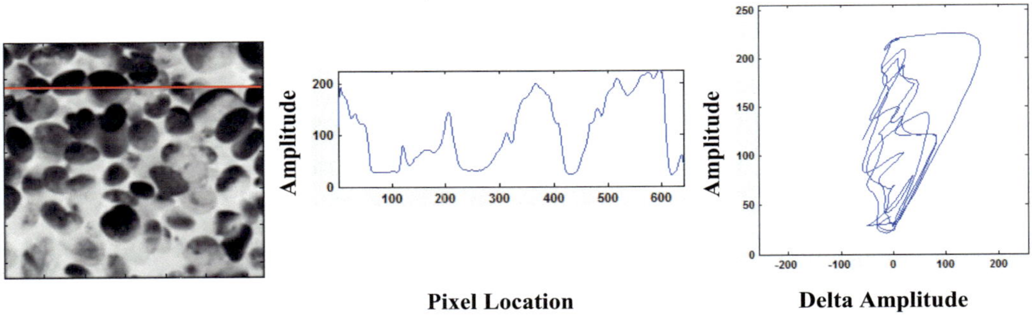

(a) (b) (c)

Figure 91: Analysis of the second texture image phase plot for a single line image, (a) identified line [90], (b) amplitude profile, and (c) phase plot for 10 pixel lag.

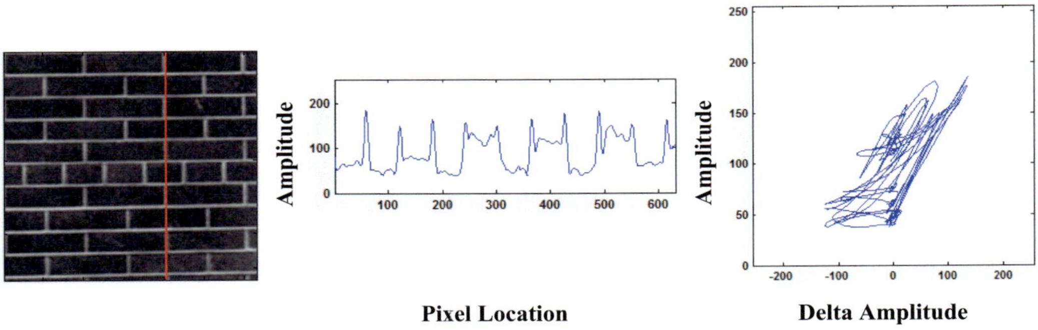

(a) (b) (c)

Figure 92: Analysis of the second texture image phase plot for a single line image [90], (a) identified line [90], (b) amplitude profile, and (c) phase plot for 10 pixel lag.

There is one interesting difference when analyzing the motion and illumination image sequences using the proposed chaos-theoretic models compared with using the models for texture analysis. When differentiating motion from illumination a single fractal measure of the phase plots was quite effective, however, the objective was simply to detect a chaotic-like effect from a non-chaotic effect. With the analysis of texture, the problem becomes one of attempting to differentiate the effects of the aperiodic forcing function of one texture from the aperiodic forcing function of a different texture. This will require additional measures due to the more difficult task of recognizing the existence of different underlying aperiodic forcing functions rather than detecting the existence of an aperiodic forcing function *versus* a deterministic source function. In Chapter 5 we will explore a broad variety of measures for understanding and characterizing the phase plots and hence the underlying dynamics of the pixel amplitudes. In addition to the traditional measures of fractality we will see that additional measures from the characterization of the co-occurrence matrix will also be proposed as being suitable due to the similarity of the co-occurrence matrix with the phase plot.

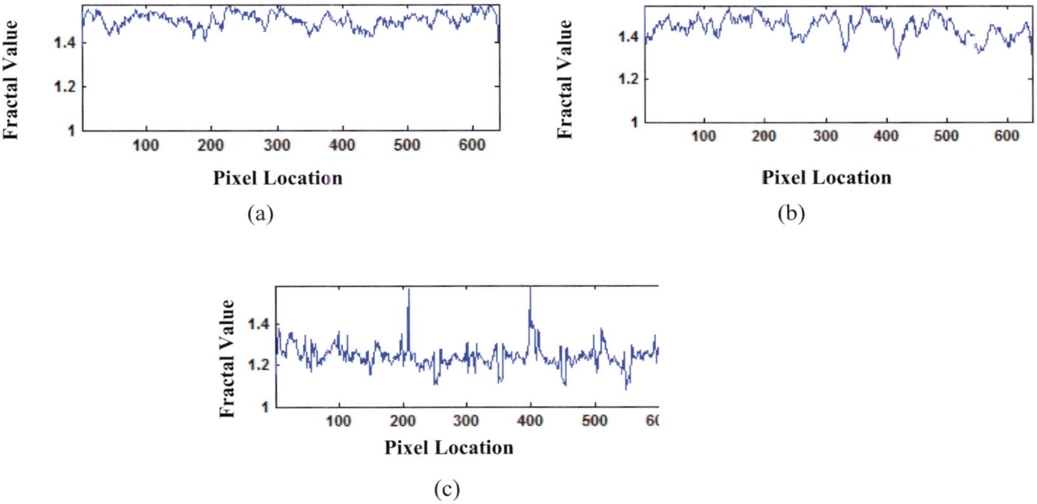

Figure 93: Comparison of sequence of Box Counting fractal dimensions of the phase plot for each line of the image, (a) sequence of fractal dimensions for image in Fig. **90**, (b) sequence for image in Fig. **91**, and (c) sequence of fractal dimensions for image in Fig. **92**.

In summary the interesting trajectories that texture produces in phase space validates the model adopted by this book that objects in images can be modeled as aperiodic forcing functions impacting the imaging sensor and producing chaos-like behaviors. One significant aspect of our proposed approach to modeling images in computer vision is that it provides a *unification* of the two distinct approaches to texture analysis, namely statistical analysis using co-occurrence matrices and model-based analysis using image-domain fractal analysis. We showed the structural equivalency of the co-occurrence matrix from the statistical approach and the phase plot. Likewise, the model-based approach which employs a fractional Brownian motion model to the underlying dynamics of the amplitude values of image texture is a special case of the chaotic model proposed in this text which only requires an aperiodic forcing function model, of which a fractional Brownian model is a special case.

AN ASIDE ON THE EFFECTS OF IMAGE QUALITY ON CHAOTIC MEASURES

Throughout this chapter we have demonstrated that the non-linear effects that are imposed on our imaging sensor by interesting image phenomena modeled by aperiodic forcing functions can be detected easily in phase space. Likewise the immunity of the proposed chaos-based approach to illumination change is due to its ability to ignore linear effects as they result in non-chaotic trajectories in phase space. We must ensure, however, that the only-linear effects in the image are due to the aperiodic forcing functions of the objects in the image and not due to an underlying non-linear physical process of the imaging sensor. This requirement of linearity results in limitations on two fronts, firstly on the linearity of the imaging device with which the images are captured, and secondly on the image file formats that can be used when performing chaos-based image analysis. We will see in the following two sections that the proposed chaos approach is actually quite robust against common non-linearities in image capture such as saturation, image compression, and gamma corrections, all of which will be discussed in the following sections.

IMPACT OF SATURATION ON PHASE PLOTS

One of the common issues with computer vision is the effects of image quality on the performance of image processing algorithms and the systems within which they are embedded. One of the most common issues in digital image capture is that of image saturation. In this section we will discuss the effects of saturation on the phase plot to understand its potential impact on the chaos-based computer vision algorithms being investigated in this text. Its impact on the phase plot of an image sequence is important because saturation is a non-linear effect, and we are relying on the non-linear nature of motion and contextual change in phase space to differentiate it from the linear effects of illumination. Saturation has the most significant impact when it is temporally varying, due to temporally varying illumination, as opposed to saturation that is common between two image frames in a sequence.

Thus we will specifically investigate the effects of saturation on phase plots with illumination change, where for the first image in a pair there is no saturation and then in the subsequent image frame saturation is present. In Fig. **94 (a)** we see saturation on the front of the shed due to bright sunlight and the non-saturated image in Fig. **94 (b)** when cloud cover is present. We see in the phase plot in Fig. **94** (c) that the saturated region results in all the grayscale values converging to a single value in the original image. The horizontal line in the phase plot shows that these common grayscale values underwent a varying degree of amplitude change, ranging from a reduction of roughly ten grayscale values to fifty grayscale values. This non-linearity certainly does not follow the multiplicative illumination change model. Fortunately, however, this region of phase space has a very non-fractal nature and hence would never be misconstrued as being due to the non-linear effects of motion or contextual change.

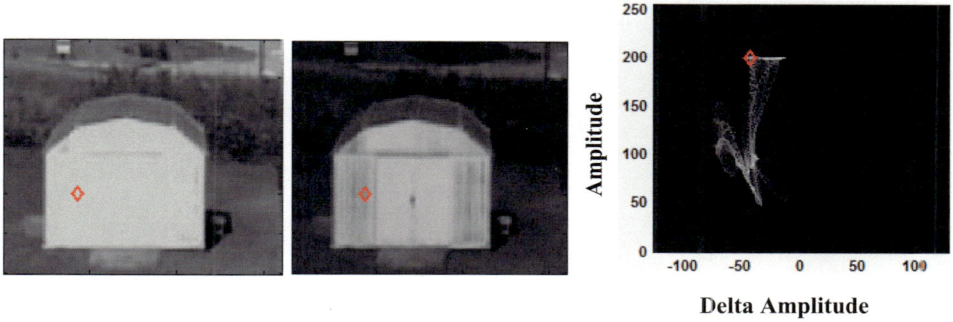

(a) (b) (c)

Figure 94: Effects on phase plot of daylight illumination due to moving cloud cover: (a) first image with region of interest highlighted [83], (b) image with global natural illumination change with region of interest highlighted [83], and (c) phase plot for (a) and (b) showing clear multiplicative behavior.

To more carefully analyze the effects of saturation we created a set of artificially increased amplitude images using the standard multiplicative illumination model with a hard threshold at a grayscale value of *250* to simulate imaging sensor saturation. Fig. **95** provides an example image pair that is designed to mimic the effects shown in the real-world cloud cover images in Fig. **94**. Notice that the naturally occurring cloud cover-based phase plot in Fig. **94** (c) has the same horizontal artifact as the artificially generated phase plot in Fig. **95** (c). We then invert the order of the illumination effect to be a darker image turning lighter in Fig. **96** (a) and (b), and the corresponding phase plot is provided in Fig. **96** (c).

(a) (b) (c)

Figure 95: Artificially generated effects of saturation : (a) first image with saturation [67], (b) image with global illumination *decrease* to remove saturation, and (c) resultant phase plot showing clear multiplicative behavior as well as effect of saturation and behavior compares to that due to cloud cover effects in Fig. **94**.

(a) (b) (c)

Figure 96: Artificially generated effects of saturation on phase plot: (a) first image [67], (b) image with global illumination *increase* resulting in saturation, and (c) resultant phase plot showing clear multiplicative behavior as well as effect of saturation.

(a) (b) (c)

Figure 97: Artificially generated effects of saturation on phase plot *with* low pass filtering of images: (a) first image with saturation [67], (b) image with global illumination *decrease* to remove saturation, and (c) phase plot showing regionally constrained effects in phase plot.

In Fig. **97** we apply low-pass filtering and the phase plot now has a triangular effect that is filled in rather than a simple line as before and provides the conic section structure that we saw earlier in Fig. **45** (c) and Fig. **47** (c). Notice the outer limit of the trajectory is identical to the non-filtered phase plot in Fig. **95** (c). To investigate whether this spread in the phase plot trajectory may negatively impact us, we perform a fractal dimension-based segmentation based on the Mass Dimension which we will define in Chapter 5. Fig. **98** (b) provides the segmentation of the phase plot based on keeping regions only of high fractal value and then Fig. **98** (a) provides the resultant grayscale image segmentation. Note that only edge artifacts remain in the image, and the illumination change is effectively ignored.

(a)

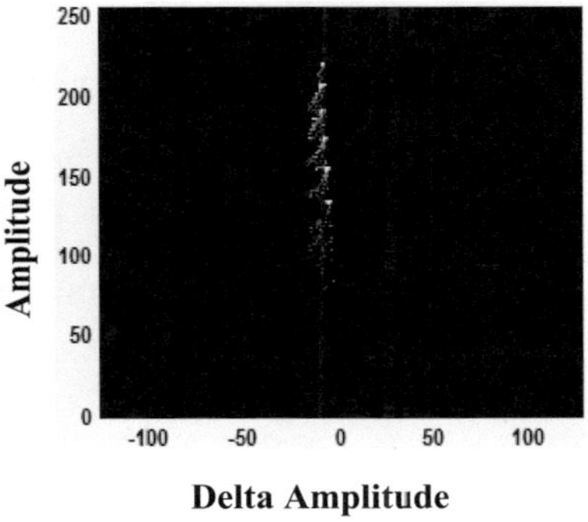

(b)

Figure 98: Resultant segmentation of image with illumination change: (a) segmented grayscale image and (b) segmented phase plot from Fig. **97** with only higher fractal regions preserved.

IMPACT OF CAMERA GAMMA CORRECTIONS ON PHASE PLOTS

Computer-based vision techniques clearly depend on the behavior of the imaging sensor. We already demonstrated that the non-linear effects of a saturated camera sensor have minimal impact on the phase plots as it does not create a space-filling trajectory. Another common non-linear effect is gamma correction or gamma encoding. Gamma encoding compensates for how the human eye perceives light and the unfortunate fact that: "The nonlinearity of a CRT is very nearly the inverse of the lightness sensitivity of human vision" [98]. While the use of actual CRT screens is becoming obsolete, the need for correcting the displays to best match the human eye remains for LCD screens as well, because "the human eye naturally has a non-linear sensitivity to luminance intensity (perceived brightness), which is referred to as "lightness" [99]. Additionally, "the relationship between applied voltage and transmittance of the TFT-LCD … is inherently non-linear due to the nature of the transmittance capability of liquid crystal cells" [99]. Fig. **99** provides a set of curves of perceived luminance versus actual input grayscale value for matching LCD displays to the human visual system.

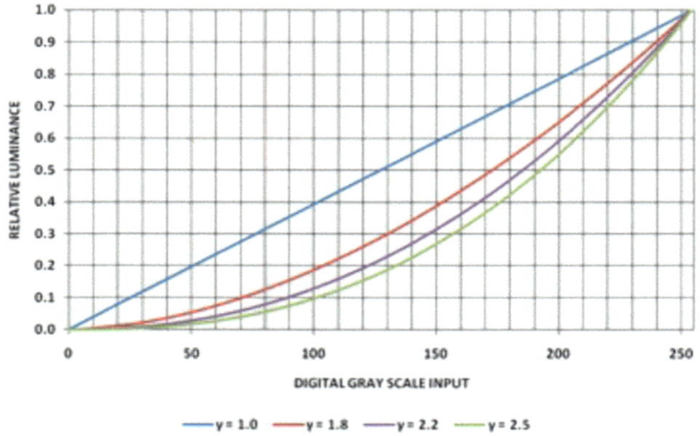

Figure 99: Gamma correction of LCD for varying gamma coefficients [99].

(a) (b) (c)

Figure 100: Artificially generated effects of gamma correction of a dimmed image on phase plot *without* low pass filtering of images: (a) first image [67], (b) image with global illumination *decrease*, and (c) phase plot showing gamma encoding effect in phase plot.

To understand the effect of gamma encoding the reader is referred to Fig. **100** where we artificially decreased the amplitude between the two images and then hand applied a gamma encoding to the image. Note the curvature of the phase plot in Fig. **100** (c) as opposed to the theoretical straight line that was demonstrated in earlier global illumination change phase plots. In Fig. **101** we apply low pass filtering to the two images prior to the generation of the phase plot, as we do normally with incoming image pairs to understand the effects of low pass filtering. We see the phase plot in Fig. **101** (c) maintains the curvature with a slight broadening of the trajectory space as is expected from previous results.

(a) (b) (c)

Figure 101: Artificially generated effects of gamma correction of a dimmed image on phase plot *with* low pass filtering of images: (a) first image [67], (b) image with global illumination *decrease*, and (c) phase plot showing gamma encoding effect in phase plot.

Notice that the shape of the trajectory in Fig. **101**(c) exhibits similar curvature to real-world images, such as the phase plots in Fig. **42** that were generated from the grayscale images in Fig. **41**. In the images in Fig. **41** a low cost webcam was used to collect the data and the gamma curvature can be seen [83]. Clearly this trajectory curvature, while deviating from the simple theoretical straight line, does not exhibit any significant excursions throughout phase space that may be misinterpreted as moving or changing objects. Consequently, the effects of gamma encoding in digital cameras will not negatively impact the ability of the chaos-based methods defined in this text to differentiate motion and contextual change in image sequences from illumination effects.

IMPACT OF IMAGE FORMATS AND COMPRESSION ON PHASE PLOTS

There is a plethora of available image formats from which the computer vision and image processing practitioners may select, including: .bmp, .jpg, .png, .tif, *etc.* Likewise for video sequence capture there is a comparable list of video file formats, including: .mpg, .avi, .mov, *etc.* Some of these file formats, specifically,

.jpg and .mpg have sophisticated lossy image compression algorithms embedded in their formats. The fact that these compression formats are lossy implies that the stored image is no longer completely representative of the original image format. Approaches such as .mpg implement significant spatial and temporal compression algorithms which are highly non-linear in nature and are known to sometimes produce annoying artifacts that are perceptible to the human eye. Similarly, these approaches can induce non-linear effects in the images that may then be detected by the chaos-based approach, leading to reduced performance of the algorithms and to the false detection of perceived contextual change. The effects of compression are dependent on how aggressive the original user was in terms of driving the compression of the images in the file format conversions.

Fortunately, due to the initial low-pass filtering that is recommended for the chaos-based analysis the resulting fractal nature of the phase plots are only minimally affected even with relatively aggressive compression. Fig. **102** provides examples of three images from a range of jpeg compression image quality settings. Notice in Fig. **102** (c) the obvious compression artifacts, particularly in the background around the vehicle. Fig. **104** provides the phase plots for each of these levels of compression quality for the images in Fig. **102**. Notice that the overall structure of the phase plot is maintained even down to the lowest quality settings. Note in particular the main effects in this phase plot are the spreading of the periphery of the phase plot trajectory where there was compaction of the phase plot trajectory due to quantization.

(a) (b) (c)

Figure 102: Comparison of various image file formats, (a) 50% quality JPEG, (b) 10% quality JPEG, and (c) 1% quality JPEG [67].

Alternately, Fig. **103** provides three images of decreasing compression quality for a more interesting indoor elevator scene which is much more complicated in content. Due to the complexity of the image, Fig. **103** (c) shows very dramatic artifacts due to the severe degradations in image quality. Fig. **105** provides the phase plots for each of these images which unlike the phase plots in Fig. **104**, Fig. **105** (c) now show some more macroscopic structural differences due to the compression artifacts. These artifacts in Fig. **105** (c) are predominantly within the central portion of the phase plot and as in the other phase plot in Fig. **104**, the overall space-filling nature of the phase plot has not changed dramatically.

(a) (b) (c)

Figure 103: Comparison of various image file formats, (a) 50% quality JPEG, (b) 10% quality JPEG, and (c) 1% quality JPEG [100].

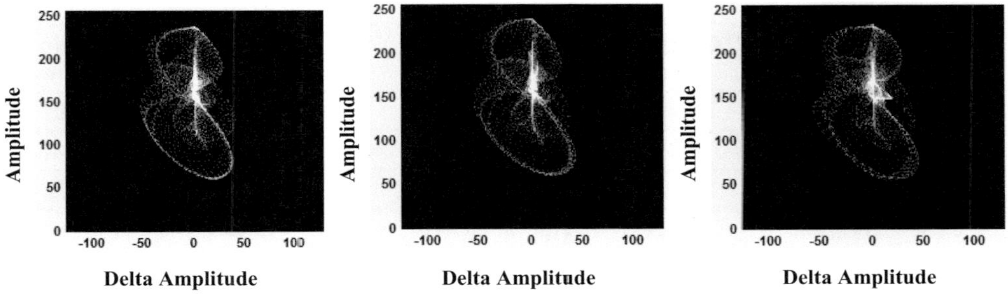

(a) (b) (c)

Figure 104: Comparison of the resultant phase plots for the various image compression qualities for grayscale images in Fig. 102, (a) 50% quality JPEG, (b) 10% quality JPEG, and (c) 1% quality JPEG.

It is important to analyze these phase plots from more than a superficial qualitative level and Table **2** provides some quantitative measures of the phase plots from Fig. **104** for each of these compression qualities. Notice again that since the overall space-filling nature of the phase plot is still maintained, the values of the fractal measures of the phase plots are only changed by roughly 1%. The measure of joint entropy between the images has changed by roughly 5%. Table **3** provides the same collection of quantitative measures for the phase plots in Fig. **105**. Once again the changes in the fractal measures were quite modest as for this set of images; the space-filling nature of the phase plot has also not changed dramatically.

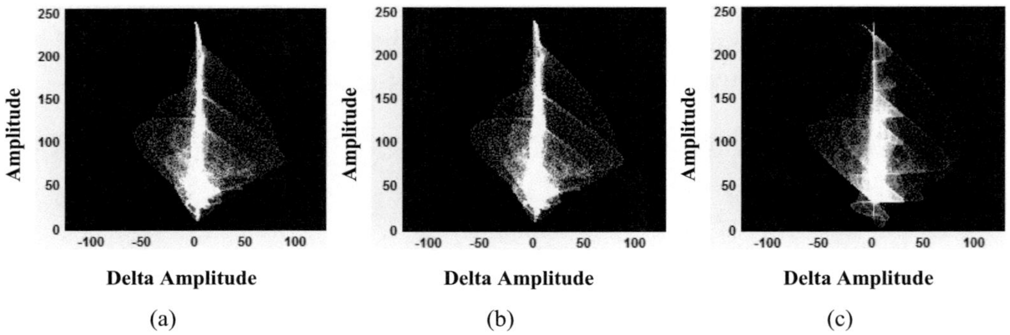

Figure 105: Comparison of the resultant phase plots for the various image compression qualities for images in Fig. **103**, (a) 50% quality JPEG, (b) 10% quality JPEG, and (c) 1% quality JPEG.

Table 2: Summary of Fractal Measures of Phase Plots in Fig. **104** for a Variety of JPEG Compression Qualities

Computed Measure	Original .bmp Format	50% .jpg Quality	10% .jpg Quality	1% .jpg Quality
Joint Entropy	6.383	6.398	5.974	6.007
Mutual Information	2.127	2.091	2.033	1.741
Information Dimension	1.304	1.309	1.301	1.338
Box Counting Dimension	1.477	1.476	1.490	1.492

Table 3: Summary of Fractal Measures of Phase Plots in Fig. **105** for a Variety of JPEG Compression Qualities

Computed Measure	Original .bmp Format	50% .jpg Quality	10% .jpg Quality	1% .jpg Quality
Joint Entropy	7.10	7.13	7.36	6.91
Mutual Information	2.66	2.63	2.39	2.38
Information Dimension	1.41	1.41	1.41	1.48
Box Counting Dimension	1.54	1.54	1.54	1.55

The results of this subsection are quite encouraging in terms of the preservation of the effects of moving objects within image scenes under even relatively severe compression quality degradation. The lower quality image phase plots preserved the important space-filling structure of the higher quality images and the resultant fractal measures were not dramatically affected. There were visually distinguishable internal changes to the phase plots in the cases of the most severe quality degradation, however for even 90% quality reduction, there were very few artifacts. It was only at the highest 99% quality reductions where these internal effects were present; however, since they did not have a dramatic effect on the outer extents of the trajectories, the fractal dimensions were not dramatically affected.

CONCLUDING REMARKS

A chaos-theoretic analysis of simultaneous changes due to motion and illumination in images has demonstrated that the effects of illumination and motion can be detected in the phase plot based on the deterministic (non-chaotic) nature of illumination *versus* the chaotic nature of motion. In this chapter we demonstrated the effects of both global and spatially varying illumination changes in phase space. We then demonstrated the effects of motion and contextual change and showed that the dramatic differences in their phase space trajectories can be explained by the fundamentally different physical processes that cause them. Both the traditional Lambertian model and more complex models such as the Torrance-Sparrow and the Oren and Nayar models of image radiance provided clear mathematical models for the differences between illumination change and motion and these were empirically verified. We explored the effects of illumination on the phase space trajectories of image sequences, using a spectrum of images from laboratory collected images, to indoor images, and finally to outdoor images with moving cloud cover and changing positions of the sun. We then demonstrated that the effects of motion and contextual change in image sequences and the resultant phase space trajectories that these image sequences generate. We explored the phase space trajectories of objects undergoing rigid motion, semi-rigid motion and deformable motion. The distinctly different underlying physical and mathematical models associated with illumination and motion was shown to result in significantly different phase space trajectories. Motion and change caused complex space filling excursions while illumination produced excursions that remained within well-defined conical regions.

We also explored the effects of texture within an image. We demonstrated that the phase space representation is structurally equivalent to the traditional grayscale co-occurrence matrix that is quite popular for texture analysis. The equivalence of these constructs is important since it allows us to provide the chaos-based computer vision techniques proposed in this text as a unifying theory for the broad array of computer vision techniques, based on the fact that computer vision processing can now be interpreted as a process of understanding the distribution and creation of information in images and image sequences. This provides a more meaningful interpretation of computer vision processing than methods that simply rely on grayscale processing, where artificial interpretations such as optical flow are common, which while often effective, have no real theoretical meaning in analyzing image sequences.

Since the effects of motion, contextual change, and texture can be explained by our aperiodic forcing function model which causes non-linear behaviors, we also explored the effects of other common non-linear effects in image sequences. These effects were saturation, gamma encoding, and image compression. We demonstrated that while these effects do affect the phase space trajectories of the image sequences, they do not affect them in a manner that would confuse them with any underlying motion or contextual change within the image sequence.

We also introduced the concept of thermal equilibrium in images as the case of pure noise and demonstrated its appearance in phase space to serve as an upper limit for the space-filling trajectories of objects of interest in image sequences.

In the following chapter we will now explore measures for evaluating the degree with which a particular phase space trajectory is chaotic based on its fractal dimension. We will present a number of existing fractal dimensions that are candidates for quantifying the fractal nature of the phase plots. We will explore both global and local fractal measures. Global measures will prove suitable for determining the overall chaotic nature of a phase plot, and local measures will allow us to determine exactly which portions of a phase plot are chaotic and which are deterministic. This will prove critical for computer vision tasks such as object segmentation.

CHAPTER 5

Mathematical Measures for Analyzing Phase Space

Abstract: To be able to differentiate image sequences exhibiting the complex behavior of moving objects and contextual change from image sequences simply experiencing changes in illumination we must be able to characterize the trajectories of these systems in phase space. The Hausdorff dimension provides a theoretical estimate of the fractional dimension of any curve in space; however it is quite difficult to calculate. Fortunately there are a number of approximations to the Hausdorff dimension that will be defined in this chapter, with one of the most common being the Box Counting dimension. The Hausdorff dimension is a global measure of the fractional dimension of a space. One of the goals of many computer vision applications is image segmentation which will require an estimate of the fractal behavior of each pixel in the image. This will require local measures of the fractality of the phase space Fortunately there are a number of local measures that will be available to us. Lastly, fractal dimensional measures will only differentiate between chaotic and non-chaotic trajectories to characterize and differentiate various textures we need measures that will be able to also differentiate between different fractal behaviors. We propose adapting measures used to analyze the Grey-level Co-occurrence Matrix for this purpose due to the structural similarity between the GLCM and the phase plot.

Keywords: Box counting measure, correlation dimension, Hausdorff dimension, global dimensions, local dimensions, Lyapunov exponent, Renyi spectrum, Lacunarity, multi-fractal.

OVERVIEW OF MEASURES OF FRACTALITY

According to Peitgen [1]: “as geometrical patterns, strange attractors are fractals; [while] as dynamical objects, strange attractors are chaotic”. This implies that measures of fractality may be suitable indicators of possible chaotic behavior in systems [1]. Mandlebrot originally described a fractal set as one whose Hausdorff dimension strictly exceeds the topological dimension [73]. We will see throughout the remainder of this text that interesting chaotic patterns exhibit phase space trajectories whose measured dimension indeed exceeds its topological dimension. When analyzed as time series, the most common measure for detecting chaos is the Lyapunov exponents. These measures provide a “useful bounds on the dimensions of the [the underlying chaotic] attractors” of the time series [39]. Unfortunately for many computer vision applications, time series analysis is not

Michael E. Farmer

feasible due to the resultant delays required to collect a sufficiently long time series. Fortunately, Eckmann and Ruelle state, "the Lyapunov exponents, the entropy, and the Hausdorff dimension associated with an attractor …all are related to how excited and how chaotic a system is" [39]. These other measures can be applied directly to the phase plot of the signal rather than the raw time series. In this chapter we will investigate a collection of measures for analyzing the phase space trajectories that result from analyzing either image sequences temporally for computer vision activities such as motion and change detection or single image frames individually for activities such as texture analysis. We will introduce traditional fractal measures suitable for global analysis of a phase space trajectory as well as for local analysis of a phase space trajectory to identify fractal regions within the space. Traditional fractal dimensional measures will be adequate for problems where we need to discriminate chaotic behavior from nonchaotic behaviors such as differentiating change due to motion from change due to illumination.

For other applications such as texture recognition, however, determining if the signal is chaotic due to an underlying aperiodic forcing function is not adequate since recall we showed that all textures can be modeled as resulting from varying forcing functions. Consequently, we will also, investigate non-traditional measures that do not directly measure the fractality but instead measure more subtle internal structures within trajectories. Klonowski states in [58], "the properties and characteristics of a fractal set are not completely determined by its fractal dimension". Specifically he notes that many fractal patterns have the same fractal dimension but very different internal structure. These differing internal structures must be analyzed using additional tools beyond multi-fractal analysis. This internal structure is referred to as the lacunarity of the fractal set, or in our case the phase plot. In the latter sections of the chapter we will introduce a collection of measures that use lacunarity to measure internal structure as well as a number of measures from traditional co-occurrence matrix analysis for texture that are equally suited for phase space analysis.

In this chapter we will also review the Lyapunov exponents since these measures may prove useful for analyzing either long time series of images or spatially analyzing texture in images. In particular we will explore a common method for calculating the largest Lyapunov exponent and how it relates to other fractional dimensional measures.

Additionally recall we discussed the issue of pseudo-chaos and the effects of imaging sensor quantization on the phase space trajectories. We demonstrated that these quantization effects can result in ***compaction*** of portions of the phase plot into what would appear to be more traditional highly deterministic orbit-like trajectories. For some applications, such as object segmentation, simply relying on the local fractal dimension can result in segmentations that are missing portions of the object of interest since the original image pixels fell on a compacted orbit in phase space. Since these orbits are still dramatically different in topological structure from illumination changes, we will propose alternate measures for detecting these compacted structures in phase space.

MEASURES OF FRACTALITY IN PHASE SPACE

As we present a number of different measures for estimating fractal dimension, it is important to note that these techniques only provide *estimates* of the dimension of the fractal curve since the true underlying dynamical model of the output from a vision system cannot be known. As Theiler notes in [68], "practical estimation of dimension begins with a finite description of the fractal object". We will explore the variability of these estimates of dimensionality of our phase space trajectories using various dimensional measures.

To determine fractality of the chaotic attractor one must measure the dimension of that attractor. There are three classes of measures of dimensionality that can be used for computing fractal dimensions [101]:

(i) Morphological

(ii) Entropy

(iii) Transform.

Throughout this book we will concentrate on using the morphological dimension for estimating the fractality of the phase plots of the image amplitudes within the image sequences. The reasons for this choice are twofold. Firstly, we are interested in the geometrical patterns of the trajectories of the system in phase space, and morphological measures are the most direct measures of the shape of these patterns. Secondly, there are very fast algorithms for calculating these morphological dimensions, and we will take advantage of the efficiency of these calculations to propose feasible approaches to real-time computer vision processing.

One method of determining dimension is to view the attractor as a set of points [103]. The Hausdorff dimension is a common general morphological measure suitable for analyzing sets of points to determine their dimension. Consequently, most morphological-based dimension measures are either directly related to, or motivated by, the Hausdorff dimension, $h_{\varepsilon}^{S}(A)$ is defined as [1]:

$$h_{\varepsilon}^{S}(A) = \lim_{\varepsilon \to 0} \left\{ \inf \left[\sum_{i=0}^{\infty} diam(U_i)^S \right] \right\}, \tag{27}$$

where $\{U_i\}$ is the set of hyper-spheres of dimension s providing an open cover of space A where the hyper-spheres are of $diam(U_i) < \varepsilon$. Not Note the following inequality generally holds for any given fractal set, S [69]:

$$dim_{Topological}(S) \leq dim_{Hausdorff}(S), \tag{28}$$

Qualitatively we can see this from the simple example of a line, where a simple straight line has a topological dimension of one, yet as the line becomes increasingly fractal and winding throughout a two-dimensional space, the line approaches filling the space, and hence its fractal dimension approaches two. While the Hausdorff dimension is a member of the morphological dimensions; it is not easily calculated due to the limit of $\varepsilon \to 0$ and the resultant summation over an infinite number of hyper-spheres. Fortunately, there are numerous dimensions, such as the Box Counting dimension, which are closely related to the Hausdorff dimension and are quite easily calculated. It is also important to note that the Box Counting dimension is also provably an upper bound to the Hausdorff dimension. It is these related dimensions that will serve as the basis for the calculations in the remaining chapters of this book.

Recall earlier we introduced the notion of two types of measures that can be applied to phase space analysis, *global* and *local*. Global measures provide a single measure of the fractality of the entire phase space trajectory, while local measures provide a measure of the fractality of the trajectory at every location in phase space. These types of measures are suitable for different applications of computer vision. Global measures are suitable for tasks such as attention direction which identify phase plots where some interesting behavior is occurring and image registration. A large global fractal measure will allow us to quickly detect possible non-linear dynamics manifested in complex trajectories in phase space to identify frames of an image sequence where interesting change has been detected. Local measures are required for applications such as object segmentation where the user must identify which portion of the phase space trajectory is associated with the behavior of a particular object in the scene.

The notion of a local measure of fractality implies that differing regions of the phase plot will have differing fractal measures. Additionally some regions may be exhibiting fractal behavior while other regions are exhibiting deterministic behavior. Applications for which the fractal measures are not the same for all points are referred to as ***multi-fractal***. Fig. **32** provides a phase plot that is multi-fractal. In this phase plot the non-fractal the portion of the phase plot corresponds to illumination and the fractal portion of the phase plot corresponds to the object motion [1, 102].

GLOBAL MORPHOLOGICAL MEASURES OF FRACTALITY

Global measures of the fractality of a phase plot provide a single value, or small collection of values, to describe the 'space-filling' nature of the trajectory. For an n-dimensional phase space, the more the trajectory fills the phase space, the closer the fractal dimension approaches the value n. When the fractal dimension equals n the trajectory has completely filled the phase space. For computer vision applications we will focus predominantly on two-dimensional phase spaces, so the upper limit of the global fractal measures will be two. Likewise a lower limit is either zero, where the trajectory is so compact it is basically a single point, or the value one where the trajectory in phase space is reduced to a single line.

Box Counting Dimension

The Box Counting method is probably the most popular dimensional measure that approximates the Hausdorff dimension [1]. The Box Counting dimension, $\dim_B(A)$, which is defined as [1]:

$$\dim_B(A) = \lim_{\delta \to 0} \frac{\log N_\delta(A)}{-\log \delta}, \tag{29}$$

where $N_\delta(A)$ is the number of boxes of size δ that cover the space trajectory over the phase space *A*. Recall the Box Counting dimension serves as an upper bound to the Hausdorff dimension, which implies the measure will be a conservative estimate and never report a phase plot to be more fractal, and hence a system to be more chaotic than it actually is [67]. Mathematically this can be defined for a given set, *S* as [69]:

$$dim_{Topological}(S) \leq dim_{Hausdorff}(S) \leq dim_{Box}(S), \tag{30}$$

This characteristic of the Box Counting Dimension will prove extremely useful for computer vision since we use the fractal dimension to differentiate phenomena such as moving objects and contextual change (high fractal dimension) from the phenomena related to illumination change (low fractal dimension). If there was a chance our measures could underestimate the fractal dimension then it would be possible for us to mistake change due to motion with illumination change.

The Box Counting algorithm begins with a single box covering the entire phase space and then recursively decreases the box size by factors of two. The value $N_\delta(A)$ is then computed by summing all of the boxes at a particular resolution δ that contain *any* portion of the trajectory within the boxes. Fig. **106** shows the sequential covering of the phase plot from Fig. **7** (b) for three different box sizes. Notice the covering has finer resolution at each pass as the size of the box element is reduced. The Box Counting measure is a good measure for understanding the behavior of the fractal measures in phase space as it is relatively simple to calculate and it is also relatively intuitive to understand.

The Box Counting dimension is computed by fitting a straight line to the log-log plot of the number of boxes required for the cover *versus* the size of the boxes used. The most common method for this line fitting is the simple Least Squares fit. Fig. **107** shows the resultant least squares line fit that is used to compute the Box Counting dimension for the original phase plot in Fig. **7** (b). Typically at both extremes of the calculation (*i.e.* a single box and boxes of size one), the data deviates from a straight line. This is a well-known effect, and it is recommended that the end points of the line fit corresponding to these extreme box sizes be ignored when calculating the slope [1].

(a) (b) (c)

Figure 106: Calculation of box counting for phase plot showing recursively smaller boxes overlaid on regions containing trajectory

The Box Counting dimension will prove useful for problems requiring rapid calculations of a global dimensional measure such as for attention direction in early vision, texture characterization for attentive vision, or image registration for higher level vision functions such as tracking. In all of these applications the behavior of the entire phase plot is important for the analysis. For example, for attention direction in pre-attentive vision, a highly complex phase space trajectory would infer the creation of information which would be indicative of the sudden appearance of an object of interest subsequent higher order perceptual functions. One potential limitation of the Box Counting dimension, however, is as Theiler states: "the geometrical structure of the fractal set is analyzed [by the Box Counting dimension] but the underlying measure is ignored" [67]. We will next introduce the Information Dimension which will address this issue by also considering the ***density*** of the possibly fractal structure within each box.

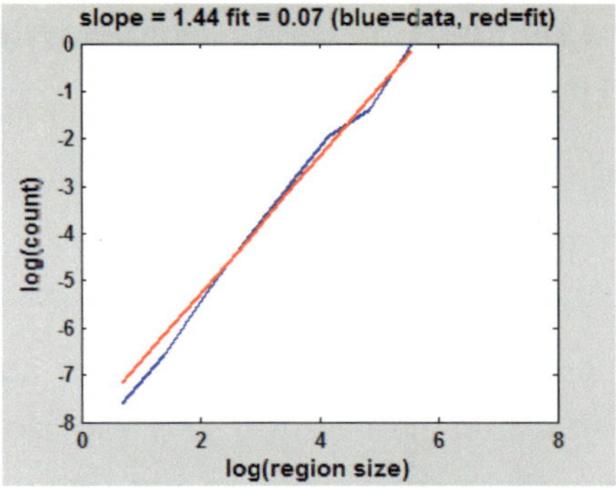

Figure 107: Calculation of box counting for box counting calculation shown in Fig. **106**.

Information Dimension

The Box Counting method treats the phase plot simply as a set of points, however as Hunt and Kaloshin point out, " it is often useful to consider other notions of dimension that take into account the distribution of points…on the attractor" [103]. The Information Dimension is one such dimension. It is closely related to the Box Counting dimension yet provides information regarding the density of points throughout the phase plot. It is also quite popular and in some cases believed to be more effective, but slightly more complicated to compute compared to the Box Counting method [104]. The concept of the Information Dimension is that it provides a weight to the box covering based on the density of the trajectory within each box. This is a measure of how ***often*** the trajectory can be found in the box rather than the simple binary decision of whether or not ***any*** portion of the trajectory was within the box as in the Box Counting method.

Mathematically the Information Dimension is based on Shannon's definition of the information content in a signal and measures the sum of the information across all boxes at a given resolution [104]:

$$S(\delta) = -\sum_i P_i log P_i \text{ where } P_i = \frac{\mu(B_i)}{\mu(A)}, \tag{31}$$

where $\mu(A)$ is the total mass of the trajectory within the entire phase space, and $\mu(B_i)$ is the mass of the trajectory within a box B_i. The Information Dimension is then defined to be the ratio of the information content with respect to box size rather than simply the number of boxes needed to cover the trajectory *versus* box size as with the Box Counting method. Mathematically the Information Dimension is defined by [104]:

$$\dim_{\inf o}(A) = \lim_{\delta \to 0} \frac{-S(\delta)}{\log \delta} \tag{32}$$

The management of the box sizes and their overlay upon the phase plot is identical between the Information Dimension and the Box Counting method as was shown Fig. **106**. Also once again a slope of the line generated by the log-log plot of the entropy measure for a given box size *versus* the size of the boxes used provides the final Information Dimension measure.

In summary, the fact that the Box Counting dimension is binary in the sense of the trajectory being contained within a box means it can be sensitive to outlier points in phase space due to noise [104]. The measure of the frequency of occurrence of the trajectory within a box makes the Information Dimension more robust to these outlier events since a single point will be very lightly weighted and hence not have a dramatic effect on the overall fractal dimension calculation. Additionally, the Box Counting measure can be inaccurate for small datasets since the phase space trajectory may not have been allowed to completely manifest itself. Roberts notes that "it is impossible to tell the difference between truly empty space and space which is visited so rarely that no data point happens to fall within it" [104]. In conclusion, Roberts states that the Information Dimension "is most representative of the fractal as a whole" based on the issues associated with small datasets [104]. Still there are advantages to the Box Counting dimension's binary characteristic related to its ability to compute the measure using very simplistic algorithms using potentially very simplistic embedded hardware. One advantage of computer vision applications is that we are data rich. As camera resolutions have increased we have been burdened by increasing processing needs, but we also benefit from an adequate number of data points for phase space-based analyses.

Correlation Dimension

Another popular global measure is the Correlation Dimension. Rather than being based on analyzing the presence of a phase space trajectory within a box as in Box

Counting and Information dimension, the Correlation Dimension measures the pairwise closeness of all points on the trajectory in phase space. The motivation for the Correlation Dimension can be seen by recalling that chaotic signals generate more space-filling trajectories. This measure basically characterizes how smoothly the density of the trajectory is distributed across the attractor. The idea of the Correlation Dimension is that trajectories that are more smoothly distributed across the space fill it more completely. It is based on the correlation integral which is defined to be [105]:

$$C(r) = P\{(X,Y): \|X - Y\| \leq r\} \tag{33}$$

Thus the term can be approximated for large data sets by [106]:

$$C(\varepsilon) = \lim_{N\to\infty} \sum_{i,j}^{N} \theta\left(\varepsilon - \left|\vec{x}_i - \vec{x}_j\right|\right) \tag{34}$$

where θ is the unit step function, or Heaviside function. Note Equation (34) is simply the detailed form of Equation (33) where the assumptions of large N needed to make *Pr{}* in Equation (33) valid is explicitly shown. Once again for the applications of computer vision, where we usually have very large datasets (*i.e.* a large number of pixels) the assumption of this limit is usually valid.

The Correlation Dimension is then calculated by reducing r to zero according to [105]:

$$\dim_{correl}(A) = \lim_{r\to 0} \frac{\log(C(r))}{\log r} \tag{35}$$

The Correlation Dimension can also be calculated *via* [1]:

$$\dim_{correl}(A) = \lim_{\varepsilon\to 0} \lim_{M\to\infty} \frac{\log\left(N_\varepsilon / M^2\right)}{\log \varepsilon} \tag{36}$$

where N_ε is the number of pairs of points within distance ε of each other and M is the total number of points sampled on the trajectory. While not directly based on the box-based calculations, the Correlation Dimension can be simplified for numeric calculations to use box-like regions similar to the Box Counting and Information Dimensions [106]:

$$\dim_{correl}(A) = \lim_{\varepsilon \to 0} \frac{\log\left(\sum_i p_i^2\right)}{\log \varepsilon} \tag{37}$$

The numerator term $\sum_i p_i^2$ is the probability that two points lie within cells in the phase plot of size ϵ, and as Cross points out: "scales in the same way as the probability that two points in the dataset are separated by a distance less than ϵ" [106].

In all of these versions of the Correlation Dimension, the slope of the line of the log-log plot of the numerator *versus* the denominator provides the final Correlation Dimension value. Note the limit on M to infinity in Equation (36) is problematic in many applications and thereby limits the accuracy of the measure, but is has not been seen to be a problem in most computer vision applications due to the large number of pixels in images.

Mattfeldt notes that the Correlation Dimension is one of the most popular quantities for estimating the fractal dimension because of the following three properties [60]:

(i) $\dim_{correl}(A)$ is a lower bound for the theoretical Hausdorff dimension which makes it a reliable estimator for the fractal dimension,

(ii) The above algorithm based on the Grassberger-Procaccia algorithm is easy to implement, and

(iii) The number of data points required for a reliable estimate is roughly the square root of the number of points needed to get a reliable estimate using the Lyapunov exponents.

The Grassberger-Procaccia algorithm defined in Equation (36) for calculating the Correlation Dimension does not require the processing to overlay boxes (or hyper-cubes in higher dimensions) onto the phase plot as is required by the Box

Counting and Information dimensions but only requires us to generate a pair-wise calculation of all the points on the trajectory. Thus only non-zero points in phase space need be considered when using the Correlation Dimension, rather than developing boxes across the entire phase space even when no trajectory points are present. One issue that arises with using the Correlation Dimension measure also arose with the Box Counting measure, namely the distance between points in our phase space cannot approach zero since we have quantized image data. Likewise, the distance cannot grow arbitrarily large either since the phase space is limited by the maximum pixel amplitude value. These two issues lead to a bias when estimating the Correlation Dimension measure. One common solution was proposed by Ellner to limit the allowed ranges of measures. This can be accomplished by once again ignoring the end points of the log-log linear plot defined by Equations (36) or (37) [105].

Generalized Dimension

While it seems there are a number of distinct measures for estimating the fractal dimension of a space, in reality all of the dimensions we discussed so far are actually special cases of the Generalized Dimension [1]. The Generalized Dimension is based on the Renyi Generalized Information Measure which rather than producing a single value, produces a feature vector of dimensional measures. It is a generalization of all of the above measures, where each of the above measures is actually a special case of a single of the values. The concept of the generalized dimension arose from practitioners in fractal analysis trying to reconcile why the various measures gave differing results for the same fractal image. The Renyi Dimension is defined by [1]:

$$\dim_{\mathrm{Renyi}(\alpha)}(A) = \lim_{\varepsilon \to 0} \frac{-R(\alpha)}{\log \varepsilon} \tag{38}$$

where $R(\alpha)$ is Renyi's generalization of Shannon's entropy in Equation (31) and is defined to be [1]:

$$R(\alpha) = \frac{-1}{1-\alpha} \log_2 \left(\sum_i p_i^{\alpha} \right) \tag{39}$$

where a unique dimensional value is computed for each value of α. Thus, rather than using a single measure for quantifying a fractal curve the full spectrum of generalized dimensions can be computed, from $D_{-\infty}$ to D_{∞} [1]. Clearly an infinite number of measures in impractical but a collection from -5 to 5 have been proven quite effective for our computer vision applications.

Notice that the Box Counting dimension in Equation (29) is the order-zero ($\alpha = 0$) element in the Renyi spectrum or Generalized Dimension vector. When the order is zero then the summation in Equation (39) reduces to simply the number of non-zero boxes. Likewise the Information Dimension defined in Equation (32) is the first order ($\alpha = 1$) dimension, and the Correlation Dimension in Equation (37) is clearly the second order ($\alpha = 2$) dimension.

The values for each of the dimensions computed by the various generalized dimensions should in theory be the same since they are all estimating fractal dimension of the same set, however for various reasons they rarely are the same value. This is not necessarily a problem as Theiler points out: "the subtle distinction between the Information Dimension at $\alpha = 1$ and the Correlation Dimension at $\alpha = 2$ may not be as important as the basic issues that arise from experimental noise, finite samples or even computational efficiency" [68].

If a structure has significantly varying values of $\dim_{\mathrm{Renyi}(\alpha)}(A)$ for each α then the underlying fractal structure is said to be multi-fractal. We saw an example of a multi-fractal phase plot in Fig. **32** where both illumination and motion were present. In general for most computer vision applications, there is not a need to detect whether or not a phase plot is multi-fractal. Multi-fractality plays a role in two important ways. First, multi-fractality will be used for image segmentation where we are only interested in the fractal regions of the phase plot. Secondly, multi-fractal phase plots can produce global measures of the phase plot dimension that incorrectly estimate the fractal content due to the bias caused by the non-fractal regions. We will explore this bias effect in the following sub-section.

Aside from the underlying set being multi-fractal, the various measures within the Renyi spectrum may not be equal due to practical issues related to the impact of finite datasets and noise in the phase plot. Recall these factors can cause sensitivities in the calculation of the various dimensional measures. Roberts notes that there are other issues with this generalized dimensional measure [104]. For large negative values of α he states that the measure is effectively meaningless. Likewise for large positive values of α, the Renyi dimension is "determined only by [the most densely populated regions] of the multi-fractal and so is not representative of the whole fractal" [104].

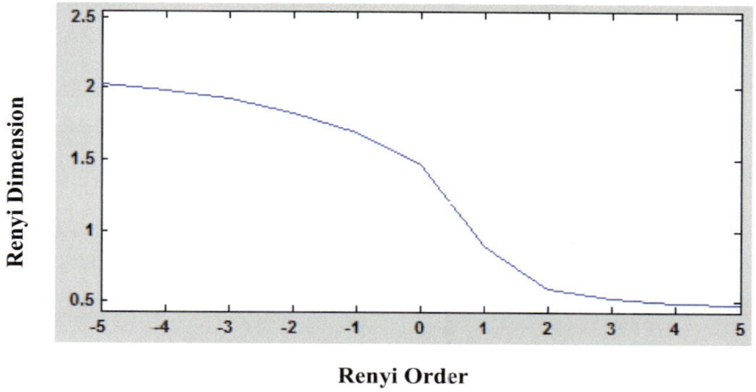

Figure 108: Renyi Spectrum for phase plot in Fig. 7 (b).

Fig. **108** provides the Renyi spectrum for the phase plot in Fig. **7** (b) which resulted from the moving vehicle shown in Fig. **19** (c). Note the relatively close values for the zeroth-order and first-order measures with the strongly decaying values for both very large negative and very large positive values. Fig. **109** shows an interesting image from a moving camera where the building is now closer to the camera in subsequent frames and the resulting phase plot in Fig. **109** (c). Fig. **110** provides the Renyi spectrum for this phase plot. Lastly, Fig. **111** shows a very simple image where there is only illumination change resulting in the rotation of the linear phase plot line in Fig. **111** (c) corresponding to the global illumination change. The Renyi spectrum for this phase plot is provided in Fig. **112** where the order zero measure correctly captures the linear nature of the trajectory, however, the large negative values have yet a third behavior which is again dramatically different from the other two spectra shown in Figs. **108** and **110**.

Fig. **113** provides an interesting example of a texture -related phase plot. The phase plot in Fig. **113** (b) is based on the amplitude changes across the line highlighted in Fig. **113** (a). Fig. **114** provides the Renyi spectrum for this phase plot. Note the form of the Renyi spectrum is much more uniform in amplitudes, which would be indicative of a more uniformly fractal space rather than a multi-fractal space.

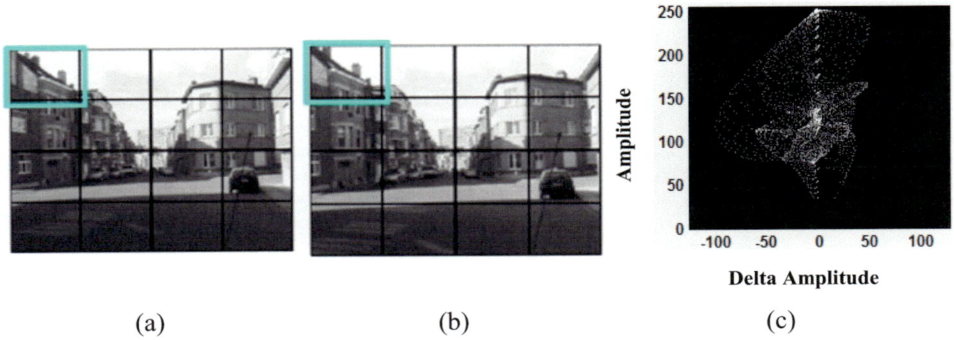

Figure 109: Image with camera motion causing large amounts of change, (a) first image frame, (b) second image frame, and (c) phase plot for highlighted grid cell with Box Counting measure of 1.62, Information Dimension of 1.98, Correlation Dimension of 1.46.

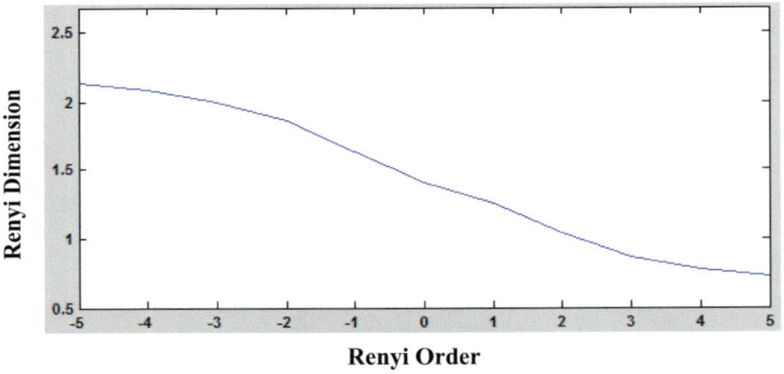

Figure 110: Renyi Spectrum for phase plot in Fig. **109**.

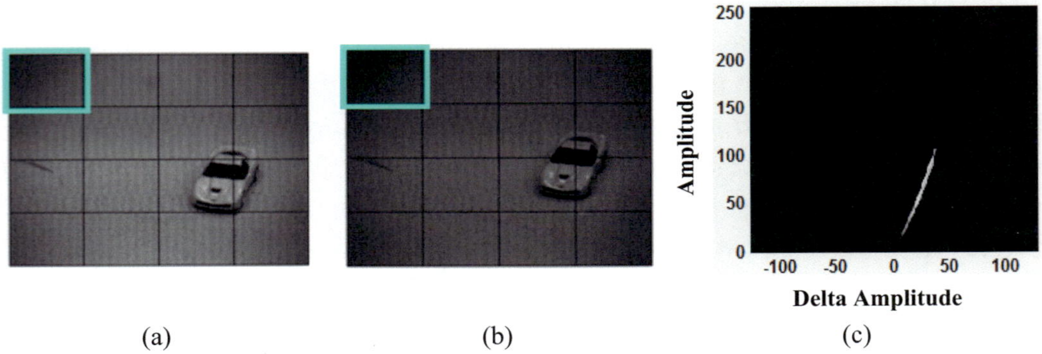

Figure 111: Image with camera motion causing large amounts of change, (a) First image frame [24], (b) Second image frame [24], and (c) phase plot for highlighted grid cell with Box Counting measure of 1.08, Information Dimension of 1.29, Correlation Dimension of 0.95.

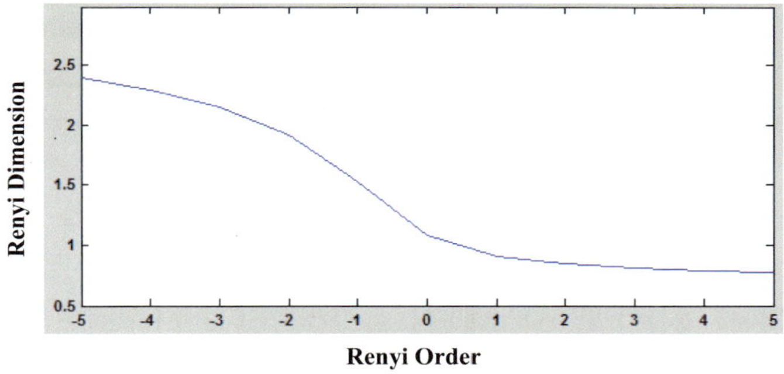

Figure 112: Renyi Spectrum for phase plot in Fig. **111**.

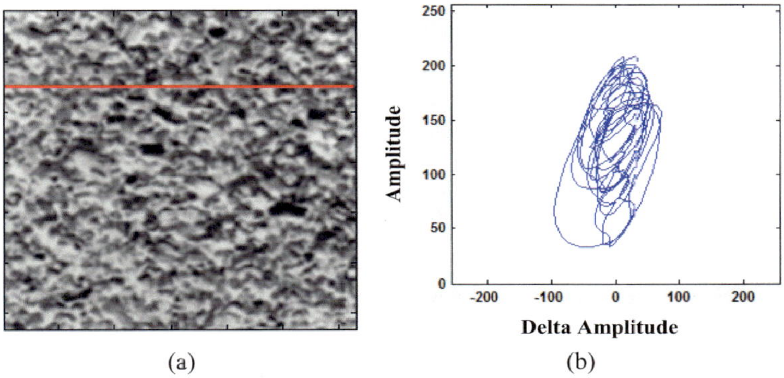

Figure 113: Image with texture : (a) Texture image showing line of interest [90] and (b) phase plot for highlighted line in image with Box Counting measure of 1.43, Information Dimension of 1.40, and Correlation Dimension of 1.33.

Thus from this disparate collection of images it appears Roberts recommendations can be extended slightly to propose that either the Box Counting (zeroth-order), the Information dimension (first-order), or the Correlation Dimension (second-order) measures are the most reliable global measures for estimating the fractal nature of phase plots for the variety of computer vision applications discussed in this text.

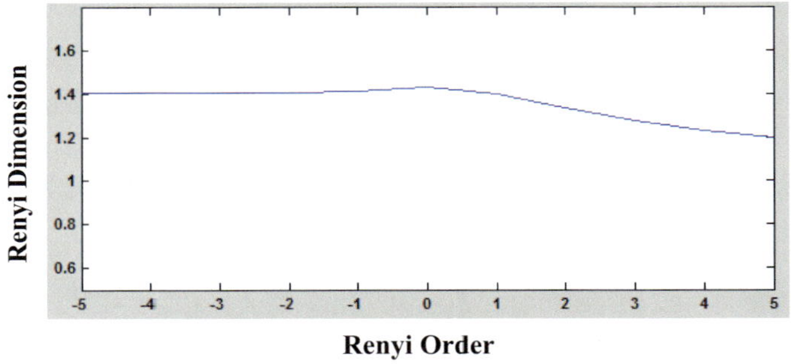

Figure 114: Renyi Spectrum for phase plot in Fig. **113**.

Since we know all of these global measures often give differing values it is advisable in any given application to test the performance using each of these measures. We see in Table **4** that for the phase plot provided originally in Fig. **7** (b) the various dimensional measures provide a relatively broad range of values. The developer may find that one measure may be more reliable than others for a particular application since each application tends to have differing underlying dynamical structures at work. For example, we will see later in this text that the simplest Box Counting dimension outperformed the Information Dimension in detecting chaos for pre-attentive vision despite the fact that Information Dimension is often regarded as more reliable.

Table 4: Summary of Dimensions for Phase Plot in Fig. **7** (b)

Fractal Dimension Measure	Value
Box Counting Dimension	1.47
Information Dimension	0.90
Correlation Dimension	0.60
Renyi Spectrum (Vector)	[2.03 1.98 1.92 1.83 1.69 1.47 0.90 0.60 0.53 0.50 0.48]

The global measures provided in this sub-chapter allow us to estimate the fractal dimension of a complete phase plot. Due to their global nature, however, they are not able to determine which portions of the phase space correspond to fractal behavior and which do not. To perform the type of image segmentation provided in Fig. **32** we will need a local measure of fractality that can provide us the fractal measure for every region in the phase plot. Then we will be able to extract the regions of the phase plot which are high in fractal value and correspond to regions in the original images where motion is present. Consequently, in a subsequent sub-chapter we will introduce local measures of fractality, but first we will discuss some issues that multi-fractality can have on global dimensional measures.

Issues Arising with Global Fractal Measures of Multi-fractal Phase Plots

These global measures provide a single value to attempt to capture the fractal nature of the phase plots of interest. As we saw in Chapter 4 the phase plots that are produced in various computer vision applications are rarely generated from a single underlying mathematical forcing function. Portions of the phase plot are created by motion effects which exhibit fractal behavior. Other portions of the phase plot, however, may be generated by spatio-temporal illumination effects, and these effects are deterministic in nature. Additionally, since computer vision systems rely on digital image processing, the images are quantized, often to only eight bits, which we saw resulted in orbital compaction of normally highly fractal phase plot trajectories.

Thus for most interesting computer vision applications, the phase plots we encounter will be multi-fractal, namely consisting of a complex intermixing of fractal and non-fractal elements. Thus it is equally important to explore the impact of multi-fractal phase plots on calculation of global fractal measures. Fig. **115** provides an example of a multi-fractal phase plot generated by an image sequence with simultaneous motion and spatio-temporally varying illumination. Note in Fig. **115** (c) the region in the phase plot of a fractal trajectory and the compact region due to the illumination effects.

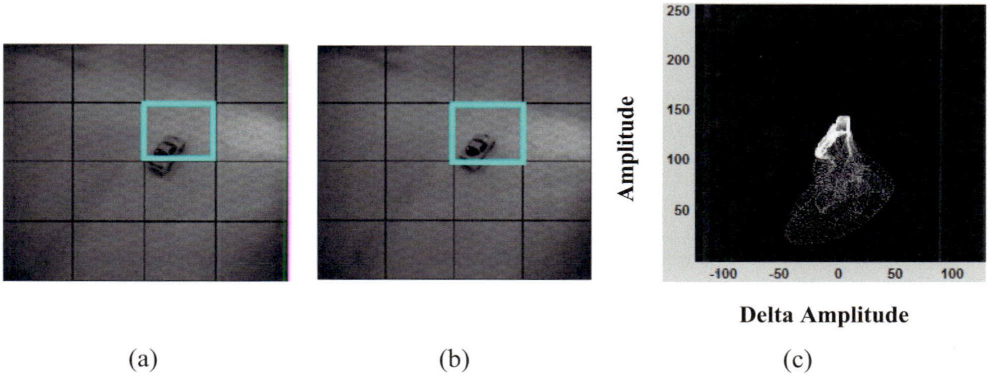

Figure 115: A multi-fractal phase plot produced by simultaneous spatio-temporal illumination and motion, (a) 1st image [24], (b) 2nd image [24], and (c) phase plot from highlighted region in image in (a) and (b).

In order to analyze the effects of multi-fractal phase plot trajectories on the calculation of the fractal dimension, we utilized a local fractal measure called the Mass Dimension which will be defined in the following sub-chapter to segment the phase plot in Fig. **115** (c) into purely fractal and purely non-fractal regions. The fractal-only region can be found in Fig. **116** (a) and the purely non-fractal region is provided in Fig. **116** (b). The fractal dimensions for the original phase plot and the fractal-only and non-fractal phase plot regions were calculated for the Box Counting, Information Dimension and Correlation Dimension measures and these results are summarized in Table **5**. The results show that while the Box Counting method is relatively immune to the presence of both fractal and non-fractal components in the phase plot trajectory, the Information Dimension and Correlation Dimension are both quite sensitive to the presence of non-fractal components.

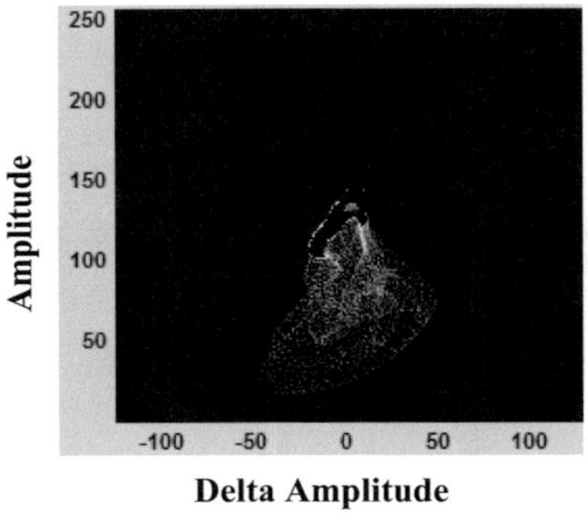

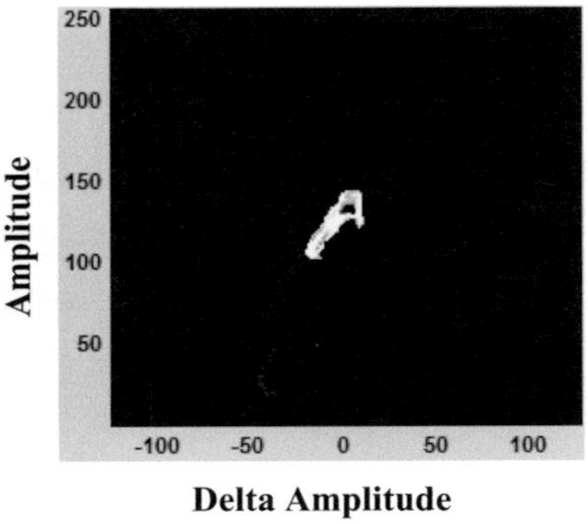

Figure 116: Reduction of multi-fractal phase plot to components, (a) Fractal-only portion of phase plot, (b) non-fractal portion of phase plot.

Table 5: Summary of Changes in Fractal Dimension due to multi-fractal regions in the phase plot in Fig. **115** (c) and Fig. **116**

Fractal Dimension Measure	**Fractal Dimension of Multi-fractal Phase Plot (Figure 115 (c))**	**Fractal Dimension Fractal-only Phase Plot (Figure 116 (a))**	**Fractal Dimension non-Fractal Phase Plot (Figure 116 (b))**
Box Counting Dimension	1.61	1.59	1.03
Information Dimension	0.91	1.35	0.57
Correlation Dimension	1.16	1.57	1.06

We further explore these findings with the image sequence from the traffic scene in Fig. **55**. Fig. **117** (a) shows the fractal-only portion of the phase plot which was segmented using a local fractal measure, and Fig. **117** (b) shows the remaining non-fractal components. In this non-fractal phase plot we see we have contributions due to the common background in both images mapping to the vertical line in the phase plot, as well as the compacted phase plot trajectory along the outer boundary of the phase plot. Table **6** provides the summary of the calculated fractal dimensions for the three common global fractal measures for the original phase plot, the fractal-only phase plot contribution and the non-fractal phase plot contribution. Once again we see the Box Counting method is relatively immune to the presence of both fractal and non-fractal components in the phase plot trajectory. However, the Information Dimension and Correlation Dimensions are both quite sensitive to the presence of non-fractal regions in phase space and are heavily biased by these non-fractal regions.

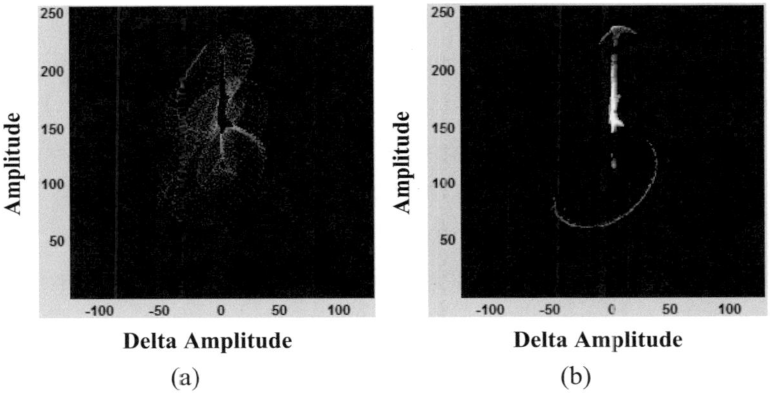

Figure 117: Reduction of multi-fractal phase plot to components, (a) Fractal-only portion of phase plot, (b) non-fractal portion of phase plot.

Table 6: Summary of Changes in Fractal Dimension due to multi-fractal regions in the phase plot in Fig. **55** (c) and Fig. **117**

Fractal Dimension Measure	Fractal Dimension of Multi-fractal Phase Plot (Figure 55 (c))	Fractal Dimension of Fractal-only Phase Plot (Figure 117 (a))	Fractal Dimension of non-Fractal Phase Plot (Figure 117 (b))
Box Counting Dimension	1.67	1.67	1.09
Information Dimension	0.7	1.37	0.27
Correlation Dimension	0.83	1.58	0.75

Notice in all cases the estimated fractal dimension of the complete phase plot is lower than the fractal dimension of the fractal-only phase plot. This can be understood by analyzing the third column in Tables **5** and **6** which provides the fractal dimension of the non-fractal contributions. These non-fractal contributions lower the actual fractal dimension in the cases of the Information Dimension and the Correlation Dimension. We can understand their sensitivity when we recall that in both of these dimensional measures, the value captures the relative frequency the phase plot trajectory is located either within a box (Information Dimension) or is located within some radius of other portions of the phase plot. Thus they rely on the amplitude of the phase plot within a particular region of space while the Box Counting dimension only relies on the overall structural shape of the phase plot. Since the non-fractal components occupy very limited regions in phase space they do not appreciably change the overall space-filling nature of the trajectory, and therefore have very little impact on the Box Counting dimensional measure. Since they are confined to a small region of phase space, however, the non-fractal regions tend to be very dense. This density is what leads to a bias in the Information and Correlation dimensions. Likewise, this reliance only on the structural nature of the phase plot trajectory contributes to the robustness of the Box Counting measure against the corrupting influences of the non-fractal regions of the phase plot.

To minimize the potential impact of these non-fractal contributions which are common occurrences in our computer vision application on these amplitude-based measures, there are three options to consider:

(i) Only rely on the Box Counting measure when computing global measures,

(ii) Compute the local fractal dimension and segment the non-fractal components from the phase plot before computing the global dimension, or

(iii) Remove these non-fractal regions by other methods based on the knowledge of their causes (background, global illumination change, spatio-temporal illumination change, and compaction).

We will see in the following chapters that discuss applications of chaos-based methods to a variety of computer vision applications that a common early stage in the processing will be to remove the known background and global illumination artifacts and then compute the fractal dimension. While this approach does not remove all of the known non-fractal components, it will remove a large portion of them thereby allowing any of the fractal dimensional measures to better estimate the purely fractal dimensional value more accurately.

LOCAL MORPHOLOGICAL MEASURES OF FRACTALITY

While in general images can often contain millions of pixels, the regions of the images actually containing objects of interest can be relatively small. Consequently, different regions of phase space may correspond to significantly different underlying dynamical processes, namely motion/change *versus* illumination in computer vision applications. A local fractal measure is needed to identify the regions of interest in the phase plot and then a mapping is required to map these phase plot regions back into the original image space to extract the object from the background. This section will discuss the local fractal measures that will be required. Recall in Chapter 3 we discussed the mechanism for developing the mapping from phase space to image space.

Holder Exponent Dimension

The Holder exponent is a local variant of the Box Counting dimension that incorporates features of the Information Dimension. It is also referred to as the point-wise dimension since it determines the fractal dimension for every point in phase space. It is defined according to [1, 101]:

$$\alpha(x) = \lim_{\delta \to 0} \frac{\log \mu\left(B_x(\delta)\right)}{\log \delta} \tag{40}$$

where $B_x(\delta)$ is a ball of size δ located about the point x, and $\mu\left(B_x(\delta)\right)$ is the sum of the probability density contained within the ball $B_x(\delta)$. As with the Box Counting method this measure is then evaluated by computing the slope of the log-log plot mapping the radius of the ball, δ to the sum of the probability density contained within each ball, $\mu\left(B_x(\delta)\right)$. If the line does not adequately fit a straight line then the measure is not meaningful. A non-straight line implies that the region of the phase plot is non-fractal, and likewise assumed to be non-chaotic [1].

Fig. **118** (a) shows the mechanics of the placement of the concentric regions, $B_X(\delta)$ used to compute the Holder exponent of the phase shown in Fig. **7** (b). Fig. **118** (b) provides the corresponding line fit at a single point within the phase plot. The high value for the Holder exponent implies that this point on the phase plot may be due to chaotic behavior. As an aside note that the lines rarely fit for the largest radii, just as the largest boxes were not meaningful for the Box Counting method. Consequently, the point for the largest radius region is ignored for the line fit. [1]. The fractal dimension from the Holder exponent serves as the measure for estimating the *local* fractality of each point in the phase space. The phase plot points with a fractal dimension above a particular threshold can then be used with the look up table defined in Fig. **24** to identify each pixel of interest in the original grayscale image.

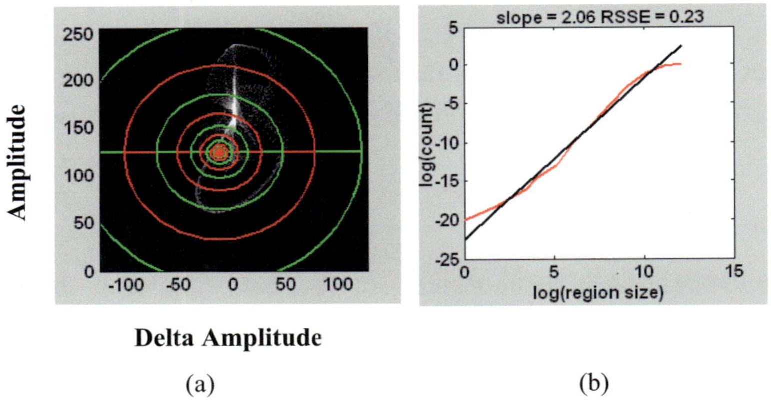

Figure 118: Holder exponent: (a) construction of circles of increasing radii around point in phase plot shown in Fig. **7** (b) and (b) line fit of location in phase plot due to motion.

While for motion segmentation, it appears that the Holder exponent (point-wise dimension) provides the required features, Eckmann and Ruelle ask a critical question: "is there any chance that the dimensions, exponents, and entropies [for chaotic measures] are finite numbers" [39]. Since optical flow calculations in image sequences is restricted to two-dimensions, two key ergodic quantities: (i) the rate of entropy creation and (ii) the Hausdorff dimension, are ensured to remain finite. Since the Holder dimension is closely related to the Hausdorff dimension, with cell counting replaced with a weighted cell counting, where the weight of each cell being the density measure, μ with $\mu < 1$, we can be reasonably confident that the Holder dimension should also remain finite in the presence of the chaotic dynamics we are hoping to detect.

In addition to the measures being ensured to be finite, the ergodic nature of the phase plots ensures the local consistency of the fractal dimension across the phase space. In other words, regions of common fractal dimension in the phase plot will correspond to regions of common pixel amplitude dynamics in the original images. This is a crucial fact since it enables the segmentation of the object from the original image based on the identification of the high fractal dimension regions of phase space.

Local Fractal or Blanket Dimension

One other possible multi-fractal measure is the more recently developed Local Fractal Dimension [95]. Rather than using point-based measures to detect the presence of the phase plot in regions over a range of sizes, it is based on treating the phase plot as a *surface* and covering the surface with planes of varying sizes. It performs grayscale morphology operations to compute the blanket surfaces of the image at varying resolutions. A blanket is defined as a surface below or above which all the image amplitudes within a local neighborhood are contained [95]. The blanket dimension was originally developed to directly calculate the fractal dimension of texture images. The blankets are determined within a window, *W*, where the goal for texture analysis is to use as small a blanket as possible to avoid masking fine micro-features in the texture. The algorithm works by defining a bounding set of blankets above and below the maximum and minimum pixel amplitudes, respectively, within the window, *W*. These upper and lower bounding blankets are defined by [95]:

$$u_\epsilon(i,j) = max\{u_{\epsilon-1}(i,j) + 1, \max_{|(m,n)-(i,j)\leq W|}(u_{\epsilon-1}(m,n))\} \quad (41)$$

and

$$b_\epsilon(i,j) = min\{b_{\epsilon-1}(i,j) - 1, \min_{|(m,n)-(i,j)\leq W|}(b_{\epsilon-1}(m,n))\} \quad (42)$$

The area of the blanket is then determined by [95]:

$$A(\epsilon) = \frac{\sum_{i,j}(u_\epsilon(i,j) - b_\epsilon(i,j))}{2\epsilon} \quad (43)$$

The fractal value of the surface is determined from the slope of the line of $log(A(\epsilon))$ *versus* $log(\epsilon)$ as was done for the Hausdorff-based approaches such as Box Counting. While the local fractal dimension was shown to be suitable for texture images, we found it was not well-behaved for the phase plots. We believe this is due to the sparse nature of the phase plot image in comparison to a conventional grayscale texture image. For most of a phase plot, the trajectory produces curvilinear effects of unit amplitude from the trajectory of the image pixel amplitude changes through phase space. Recall a chaotic trajectory is one where the trajectory never visits the same point in phase space but rather visits regions arbitrarily close. Thus the phase plots are not sensibly represented by a sequence of blankets since the first low amplitude blanket covers them.

ADDITIONAL MEASURES FOR CHARACTERIZING VISION-RELATED PHASE PLOTS

Recall the issue related to texture processing is that rather than simply detecting the presence of a chaos-like signal caused by our aperiodic forcing function model we are actually trying to differentiate multiple forcing functions that create the different textures. There are two main sub-applications related to texture analysis: (i) texture-based segmentation and (ii) texture recognition. In texture-based segmentation we need to differentiate the presence of multiple textures but not specifically identify them. In texture recognition the goal is to actually identify the specific texture being analyzed from a database of possible texture candidates. Both of these tasks are common in computer vision and both require that we do not simply *detect* chaotic signals from non-chaotic signals, but rather we *differentiate* one class of chaotic signal from another. The goal of differentiating between chaotic signals is 'equivalent to differentiating between the underlying aperiodic forcing functions that produce the different textures. Thus it would be foolhardy to expect a single value such as fractal dimension to be able to differentiate one such complex underlying process from another. To be able to differentiate one texture from another the details of the internal structure of the phase plot must be inferred. Indeed, originally Mandlebrot and more recently

Klonowski noted that "fractal dimensions cannot alone provide a complete characterization of the texture of an image and that fractals that have the same dimension may look very different" [58, 73].

There are various studies [107-110] where the authors employed additional measures such as the lacunarity measure which characterizes the amount of gaps or holes in an image. In reality we will see there is actually a multitude of measures that we can borrow from traditional texture analysis to provide insight into the internal structure of the phase space trajectories. Recall from our earlier discussions of the phase space characteristics of texture we demonstrated the structural similarity of the phase plot and the greylevel co-occurrence matrix. This implies that the wealth of measures applied originally by Haralick and various other authors to the greylevel co-occurrence matrix may also be candidates for developing detailed measures of the internal topology of the phase plot trajectories [14, 15, 89, 93].

MEASURES OF LACUNARITY OF THE PHASE PLOT

One common measure of detailed internal structure of an image is referred to as the lacunarity of the image whose literal Latin meaning is a measure of the amounts of gaps that are present [73]. It was first defined by Mandlebrot as an additional measure of the complexity of fractal patterns and was proposed by Mandlebrot to quantify the texture or spatial arrangements of the internal features of a set [73, 111]. Kilic and Abiyev note, "fractal dimension only measures how much space is filled and lacunarity complements fractal dimension by measuring how the data fills the space" [109]. Just as fractal dimensional measures have been commonly applied to the image, lacunarity has also been directly applied to the images for texture analysis in the well-known study by Dubuisson and Dubes as well as other more recent studies [107-110]. One interesting feature of lacunarity is that, unlike the fractal dimension, it is ***dependent*** on the scale being analyzed. Therefore at one scale a set will have a different measure of lacunarity than at a more coarse scale. This makes sense since the concept of gaps in an image are clearly scale dependent based on the sizes of the gaps. The fact that lacunarity is scale dependent makes it an interesting complementary feature to the fractal dimension.

While lacunarity was originally proposed for analyzing texture in images, it is a particularly interesting candidate for analyzing the phase plots as well. Recall the complex trajectories of the phase plots can result in unevenness in how the trajectory explores the phase space. Feagin recognized this when he stated: "Lacunarity and [Hurst parameter] can also be computed on attractors in phase space" [110]. Recall we also explored the variations in phase plots earlier in this chapter when we recognized that most real-world phase plots will actually be multi-fractal due to the variety of phenomena influencing the image. Consequently, it is important to ask if lacunarity is simply related to multi-fractality. Feagin noted that "at first glance lacunarity … seems similar to the concept of multi-fractals" [110]. Multi-fractal measures such as the mass dimension computed local variations in the set as they scale outward from each particular locality, while lacunarity measures the variation between localities across the set [110]. It is exactly this quantification of the variance in density of the phase plot between locations that is the phenomena quantified by lacunarity [110].

As lacunarity measures the local variations of varying scale across the phase plot, it reasons that the lacunarity can be measured by comparing a statistic within local regions of varying sizes across the image. Thus it is common to define these local regions by boxes of a particular size, *r*, as we did in the Box Counting dimension. Unlike the Box Counting method, where we were defining a mathematical cover of the phase plot, here we are interested in local variation so the boxes must be slid across the image rather than simply overlaid in a grid pattern. More similar to the Information Dimension than the Box Counting dimension, however, we are interested in measuring the density of the phase plot within these boxes. Consequently, we define the probability of these sliding boxes in the image having a measure of mass, *S*, as [108]:

$$P(S,r) = \frac{n(S,r)}{N(r)} \tag{44}$$

where $n(S,r)$ is the number of boxes of size *r*, having mass *S* within them and $N(r)$ is the total number of boxes of dimension *r* that are slid across the image. Since we are interested in the local variation, we must calculate a second order statistic to capture the variability. Therefore we calculate the first and second order statistics of this measure of mass of these sliding boxes for a given box size, *r*, by [108]:

$$E_r(S) = \sum_{all\ boxes} SP(S,r) \tag{45}$$

and

$$E_r(S^2) = \sum_{all\ boxes} S^2P(S,r) \tag{46}$$

The lacunarity for this box scale, *r*, is then computed by [108]:

$$\Lambda(r) = \frac{E_r(S^2)}{E_r(S)} \tag{47}$$

Note that the lacunarity can be computed either on the actual grayscale phase plot or on a binarized phase plot. In the study by Myint and Lam they used a collection of binarized images derived by setting a sequence of thresholds on the original grayscale images [108]. Either way, note that like the generalized fractal dimension, or Renyi spectrum, the lacunarity measure is now a vector metric rather than a scalar metric. Each element of the vector metric is a measure on a different scale. This vector can either be treated as a feature vector, or as in the study by Kilic and Abiyev, the vector metric can be plotted on a log-log plot and fit to an exponential curve, and then the coefficients of this exponential curve can serve as the features for performing subsequent classification [109].

Fig. **119** (c) and (f), and Fig. **120** (c) show the log-log plots of the lacunarity measure for a range of box sizes for two phase plots due to motion or contextual change in an image sequence. Notice the dramatic difference in shape between the three lacunarity plots for the phase plots that were provided in Fig. **119** and Fig. **120**. Additionally, Fig. **120** (f) shows the log-log plots of the lacunarity measure for an image with only complex spatially varying illumination from the subway car sequence with its corresponding phase plot in Fig. **120** (e). Notice once again the different structure of the lacunarity measure compared with the other lacunarity measures shown for chaos-like changes and in particular the measure for the motion-based changes shown in Fig. **119**.

Fig. **121** (c) and (f) and Fig. **122** (c) provide the log-log plots of the lacunarity for the phase plots of three different texture images shown in Fig. **121** (a) and (d) Fig. **122** (b). Once again notice the differences in shape and values of the lacunarity measures across these three textures. Thus from these sets of phase plots and their corresponding lacunarity measures, it appears that there exists significant differences in the lacunarity measures for different phase plots. We will rely on the actual analysis of these for the attentive vision task of texture segmentation in Chapter 8 to determine the actual efficacy of these measures.

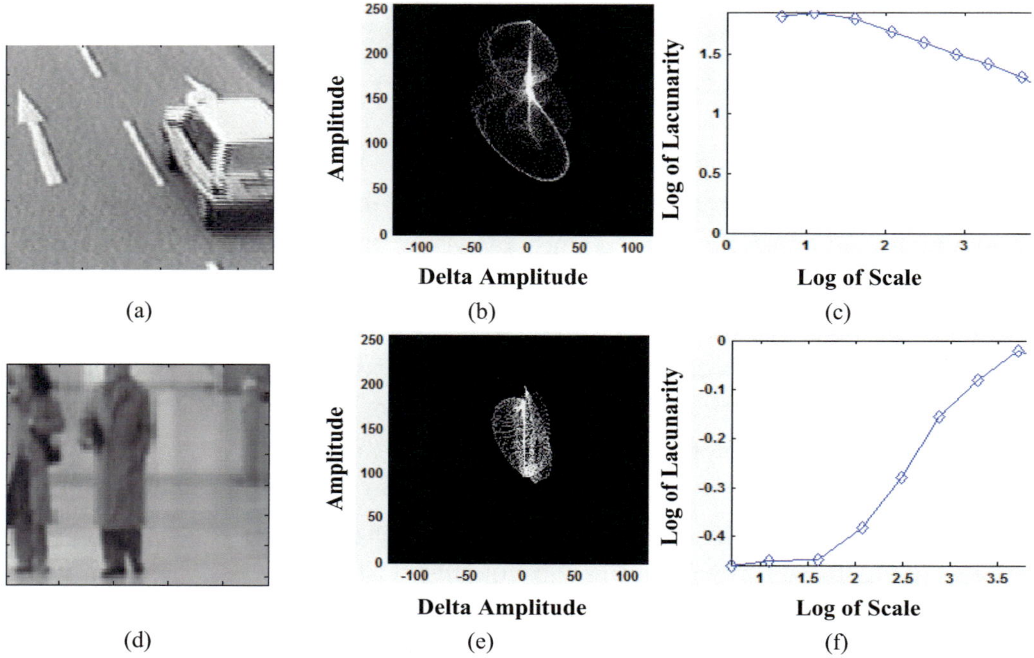

Figure 119: Examples of Lacunarity measure for contextual change (moving and appearing objects): (a) vehicle image from earlier [67], (b) phase plot, (c) lacunarity measure, (d) moving humans' image [80], (e) phase plot, and (f) lacunarity measure, (g) contextual change image from earlier, (h) phase plot, (i) lacunarity measure, (j) image with illumination change from earlier, (k) phase plot, and (l) lacunarity measure.

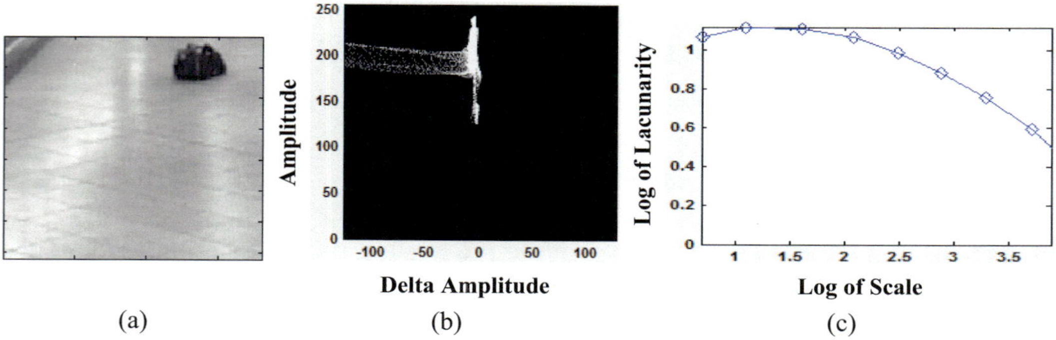

Fig. 120: contd….

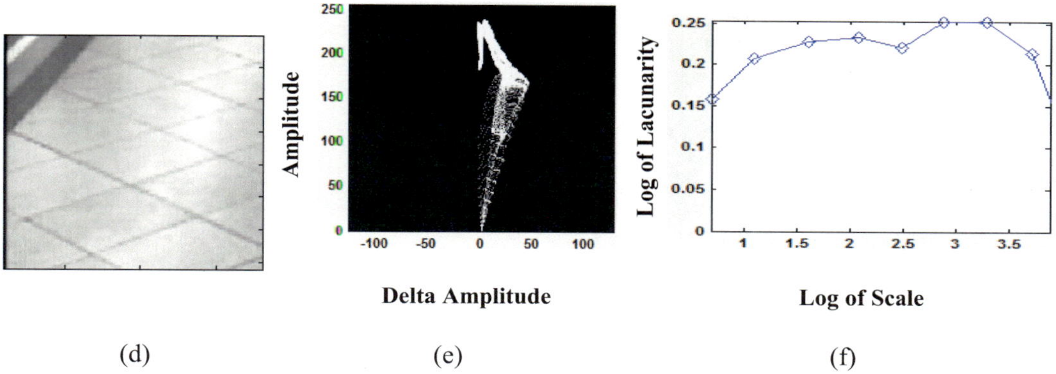

Figure 120: Examples of Lacunarity measure for contextual change (moving and appearing objects): (a) contextual change image from earlier, (b) phase plot, (c) lacunarity measure, (d) image with illumination change from earlier, (e) phase plot, and (f) lacunarity measure.

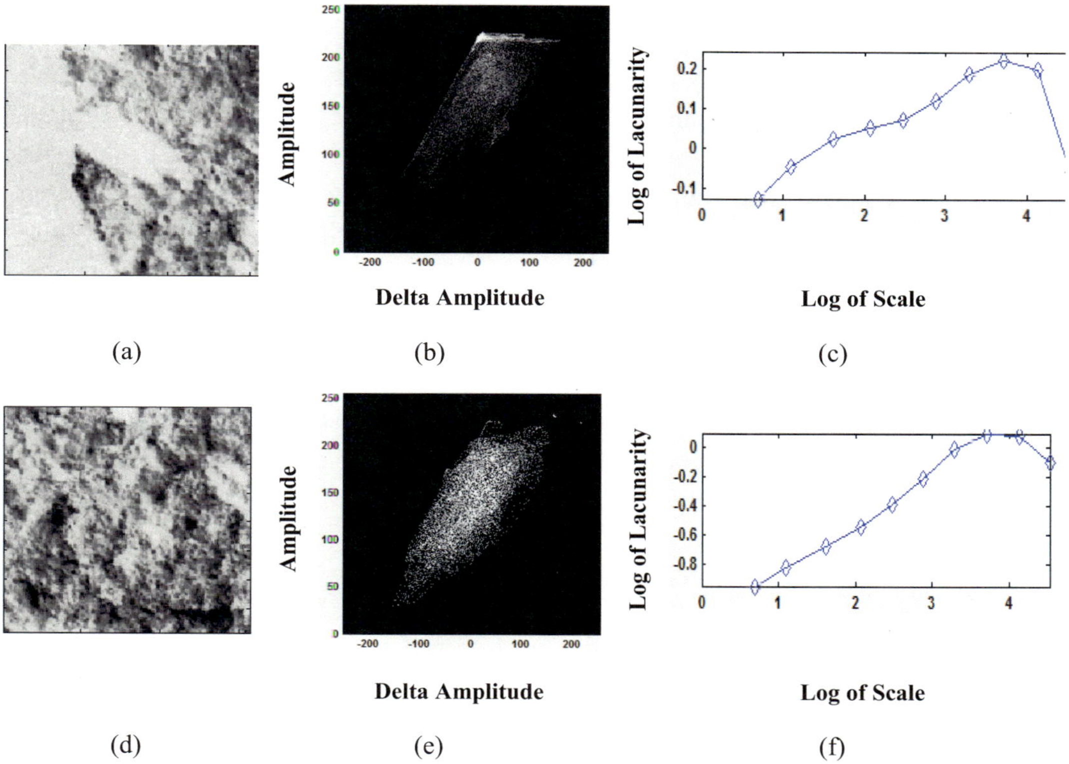

Figure 121: Examples of Lacunarity measure for texture images: (a) texture image from earlier [90], (b) phase plot, (c) lacunarity measure, (d) texture image from earlier [90], (e) phase plot, (f) lacunarity measure.

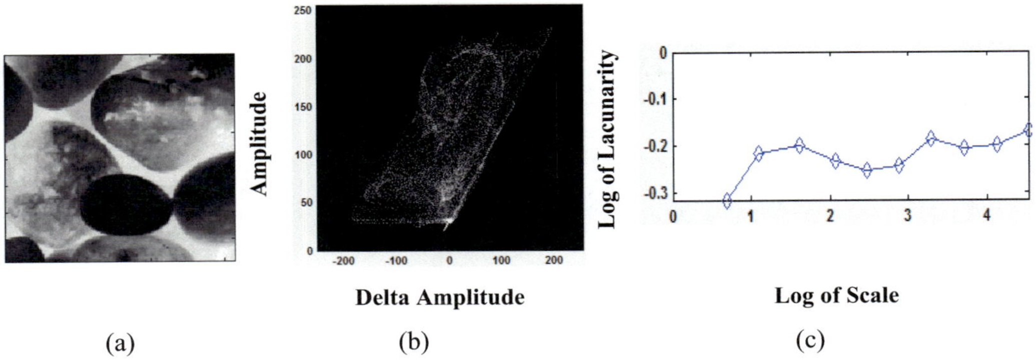

Figure 122: Examples of Lacunarity measure for texture images: (a) texture image from earlier [90], (b) phase plot, and (c) lacunarity measure.

MEASURES ADOPTED FROM CO-OCCURRENCE MATRIX ANALYSES

The texture features originally defined by Haralick in his seminal paper [93] and adopted by numerous researchers [11, 14, 15, 89] can be grouped into two main categories, (i) a set of measures related to texture characteristics such as homogeneity, contrast, and the presence of organized structures, and (ii) measures related to the complexity and nature of the grayscale transitions in the images. While these features are proposed for detecting these characteristics in the co-occurrence matrix, they are equally applicable for the characterizing the phase plots due to the structural equivalence of the two constructs as discussed in Chapter 4.

The first set of measures is related to the overall structure or orderliness of the co-occurrence matrix. The simplest measure is a first-order measure, the Maximum Probability which is defined by [96, 112]:

$$Maximum\ Probability = \max_{i,j}\left(p(i,j)\right) \tag{48}$$

where $p(i,j)$ is the co-occurrence matrix normalized to sum to one as if it were a probability distribution. The measure can be directly applied to the phase plot if it is also normalized to sum to one.

The next measure is a second-order measure of the overall distribution called the Angular Second Moment which is also often referred to as the Distribution Uniformity is defined as [14, 93]:

$$ASM = \sum_i \sum_j [p(i,j)]^2 \tag{49}$$

A closely related term is the Energy of the textural image which is defined to be [93]:

$$Energy = \sum_i i^2 \cdot \sum_j [p(i,j)]^2 \tag{50}$$

The i^2 term provides the squared sum of the actual image amplitude values that provides the energy. Since the y-axis of the phase plot captures the actual pixel amplitude the Energy measure can be used directly in its current form.

Another measure of the overall co-occurrence matrix that also can directly be applied to the phase plot is the Entropy [93]:

$$Entropy = H = -\sum_{i=1}^{nbins} \sum_{j=1}^{nbins} p(i,j) \cdot log_2\big(p(i,j)\big) \tag{51}$$

Likewise another common measure related to Entropy is the Mutual Information (MI), which is computed by [93]:

$$MI = -\sum_{i=1}^{nbins} \sum_{j=1}^{nbins} p(i,j) \cdot log_2\left(\frac{p(i,j)}{p_{row}(i) \cdot p_{col}(j)}\right) \tag{52}$$

where

$$p_{row}(i) = \sum_{j=1}^{nbins} p(i,j) \tag{53}$$

and

$$p_{col}(j) = \sum_{i=1}^{nbins} p(i,j) \tag{54}$$

Note that the Maximum Probability, Angular Second Moment, and Entropy will produce identical values for either the co-occurrence matrix or the spatial phase plot. However, due to the marginal probability distributions of the Mutual Information, the equation for Mutual Information computes a significantly different measure for the co-occurrence matrix *versus* the spatial phase plot. For the case of the co-occurrence matrix the equation measures the relative mutual information between the original image and the spatially lagging image. For the spatial phase plot the equation computes the relative mutual information between the image and the difference image corresponding to a particular spatial lag. While different, this measure may still be useful for characterizing various textures in phase space, however, it is important to note its meaning is now different.

There is also a collection of measures proposed by Haralick and others for analyzing the co-occurrence matrices that are dependent on terms of the form $|i\text{-}j|$, where i and j are the indices for the grayscale amplitudes for each of the images corresponding to each axis. They measure the symmetry of the co-occurrence matrix about the diagonal. The first is the Contrast which is defined in its original form as [93]:

$$Contrast = \sum_{n=0}^{nbins-1} n^2 \cdot \left\{\sum_i \sum_j [p(i,j)]_{|i-j|=n}\right\} \tag{55}$$

Other features with this $|i\text{-}j|$ structure are homogeneity, dissimilarity, and inverse difference moment which are defined as [93]:

$$Homogeneity = \sum_i \sum_j \frac{1}{1+|i-j|} \cdot p(i,j) \tag{56}$$

and

$$Dissimilarity = \sum_i \sum_j |i-j| \cdot p(i,j) \tag{57}$$

and finally [93]:

$$Inverse\ Difference\ Moment = \sum_i \sum_j \frac{1}{1+(i-j)^2} \cdot p(i,j) \tag{58}$$

Note that in the phase plots, the delta amplitude axis (the x-axis) is by definition the difference axis so the term $|i\text{-}j|$ is implicit in the values of that axis. These three measures should be redefined as follows for phase plots to ensure the same information is captured when using phase plots or co-occurrence matrices:

$$Contrast_{phase\ plot} = \sum_{n=0}^{nbins-1} \left(n - \frac{nbins}{2} - 1\right)^2 \cdot \left\{\sum_i p_{phase}(i,n)\right\} \tag{59}$$

and

$$Homogeneity_{phase\ plot} = \sum_i \sum_j \frac{1}{1+\left|i-j-\frac{nbins}{2}-1\right|} \cdot p_{phase}(i,j) \qquad (60)$$

and

$$Dissimilarity_{phase\ plot} = \sum_i \sum_j \left|i-j-\frac{nbins}{2}-1\right| \cdot p_{phase}(i,j) \qquad (61)$$

and

$$Inverse\ Difference\ Moment_{phase\ plot} =$$

$$\sum_i \sum_j \frac{1}{1+\left(i-j-\frac{nbins}{2}-1\right)^2} \cdot p(i,j) \qquad (62)$$

where in these equations $p_{phase}(i,j)$ is the phase plot normalized to sum to one.

There is an additional collection of second order measures related to the correlation of the two images and the variance of the co-occurrence matrix. The Correlation is defined by [93]:

$$Correlation = \frac{\sum_i \sum_j (i-\mu_{row}) \cdot (j-\mu_{col}) \cdot p(i,j)}{\sigma_{row}\sigma_{col}} \qquad (63)$$

where μ_{row} μ_{col} σ_{row} σ_{col} are the means and standard deviations in the row and column directions, respectively, of the co-occurrence matrix. Likewise, the Variance measures are defined by [93, 112]:

$$Variance_{rows} = \sigma_{rows}^2 = \sum_i \sum_j (i-\mu_{row})^2 \cdot p(i,j) \qquad (64)$$

and

$$Variance_{cols} = \sigma_{rows}^2 = \sum_i \sum_j (j-\mu_{col})^2 \cdot p(i,j) \qquad (65)$$

Notice that these measures, like the Mutual Information measure, contain information which is specific to the row or column variables of the co-occurrence matrix. This means the measure compares the original image and the spatially lagged image. When applied to the spatial phase plot, these measures compare the original image with the difference image. As with the Mutual Information, these measures may still be useful for characterizing various textures; however the measures are significantly different in meaning than when applied to the co-occurrence matrix. By measuring correlations and mutual information between the amplitude of the image and its difference image, the measures are basically testing if there is a dependence on the difference values and the amplitudes. Recall the phase plot for global illumination changes results in a linear relationship (or curvilinear relationship due to gamma correction) so a strong correlation between amplitude and delta amplitude could be an indicator of illumination changes for the temporal phase plots. For the spatial phase plots used in texture, the measure might capture textures with varying amplitude across them due to spatio-temporal illumination.

There is another collection of measures proposed by Haralick that are related to the probability distribution of the sum and difference values between the two images, namely $p(k)_{x+y}$ and $p(k)_{x-y}$. They are defined by [93]:

$$p(k)_{x+y} = \sum_{i=1}^{nbins} \sum_{j=1}^{nbins} p(i,j), \text{ where i+j=k} \quad (66)$$

and

$$p(k)_{x-y} = \sum_{i=1}^{nbins} \sum_{j=1}^{nbins} p(i,j), \text{ where |i-j|=k} \quad (67)$$

These densities are then used to compute the Sum, Variance, and Entropy of the sum and difference distributions. Note there is no corollary to the first equation for $p(k)_{x+y}$ for spatial phase plots since the amplitudes of the lagged image are lost. Likewise, the second term $p(k)_{x-y}$ is simply the marginal density of the normalized phase plot since recall the x-axis is the delta amplitude between the two images. For the phase plots, the difference distribution term is simply calculated by:

$$p_{phase\ plot}(k)_{x-y} = \sum_{i=1}^{nbins} p_{phase\ plot}(i,k) \quad (68)$$

The sum, variance, and entropy measures the spatial phase plot then results in a similar equation originally proposed by Haralick [93]:

$$Difference\ Average = \langle D \rangle_{phase\ plot} = \sum_{k=2}^{2 \cdot nbins} k \cdot p_{phase\ plot}(k)_{x-y} \quad (69)$$

$$Difference\ Variance = \sum_{k=2}^{2\cdot nbins}\left(k - \langle D\rangle_{phase\ plot}\right)^2 \cdot p_{phase\ plot}(k)_{x-y} \quad (70)$$

$$Difference\ Entropy = -\sum_{k=2}^{2\cdot nbins} p_{phase\ plot}(k)_{x-y} \cdot log\left(p_{phase\ plot}(k)_{x-y}\right) \quad (71)$$

These measures as they have been redefined above will provide the identical values as they did for the co-occurrence matrix.

There are also a set of measures related to the marginalized probability distributions that capture the correlation of the marginalized entropies. The first of these is [93]:

$$Info\ Measure\ 1 = \frac{H - HXY1}{\max\{HX, HY\}} \quad (72)$$

$$Info\ Measure\ 2 = [1 - 2 \cdot exp(HXY2 - H)]^{1/2} \quad (73)$$

Where *HX* and *HY* are the entropies of the marginal probability functions p_x and p_y and *HXY1* and *HXY2* are defined by [93]:

$$HXY1 = -\sum_{i=1}^{nbins}\sum_{j=1}^{nbins} p(i,j) \cdot log\{p_x(i) \cdot p_y(j)\} \quad (74)$$

$$HXY2 = -\sum_{i=1}^{nbins}\sum_{j=1}^{nbins} p_x(i) \cdot p_y(j) \cdot log\{p_x(i) \cdot p_y(j)\} \quad (75)$$

and *H* is simply the entropy measure defined earlier. Again these measures will compute a significantly different measure when applied to the spatial phase plot rather than to the co-occurrence matrix. They also are not commonly adopted measures and will not be considered further here [14, 15, 89].

Haralick originally proposed this complete set of measures be computed over a set of co-occurrence matrices corresponding to four directions and a set of spatial lags. When adopting these measures to our chaos-theoretic approach, we compute the phase plot of the texture images over a range of spatial lags based on the given information content in the images using our reconstruction concepts from Chapter 3. This is one of the powers of the chaos-based interpretation of texture. There are now clear rules defined for understanding the range of lags required to best reconstruct the spatial phase space of the texture image. When directly applying co-occurrence theory, however, there are no such rules for determining the spatial lags.

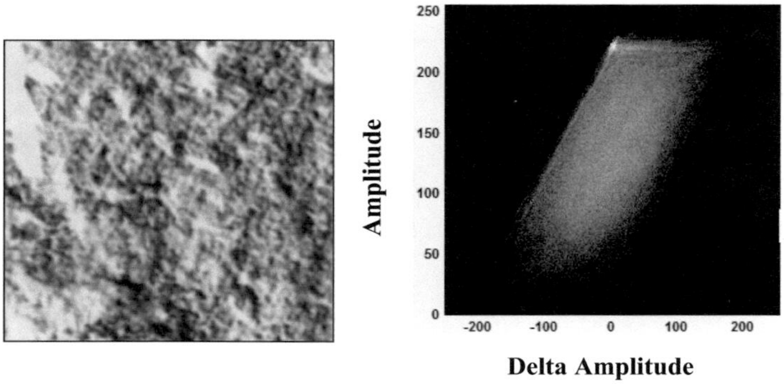

(a) (b)

Figure 123: One texture image used for calculating measures of phase plot for texture using multiples of a base lag of 5 pixels, (a) Original texture image [90] and (b) phase plot.

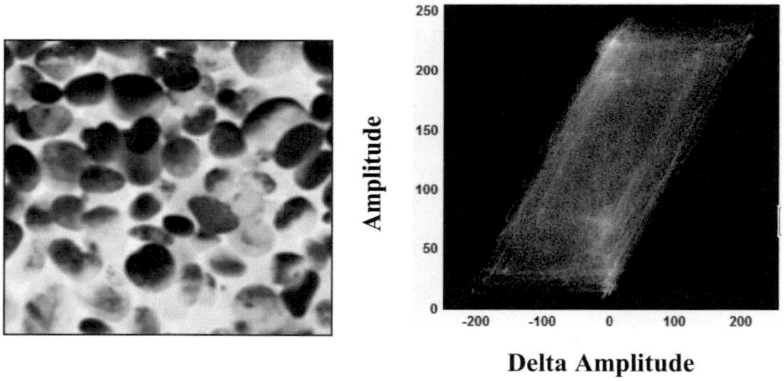

(a) (b)

Figure 124: Second texture image used for calculating measures of phase plot for texture using multiples of a base lag of 5 pixels, (a) Original texture image [90] and (b) phase plot.

We then apply a collection of these measures to the two different textures found in Fig. **123** and Fig. **124**. These two textures are significantly different with one containing highly random small-scale features while the other contains large macro-features. The curves resulting from applying them over a range of lags are provided in Fig. **125** and Fig. **126**. The measures were computed over five different time lags which were multiples of a base lag of five pixels.

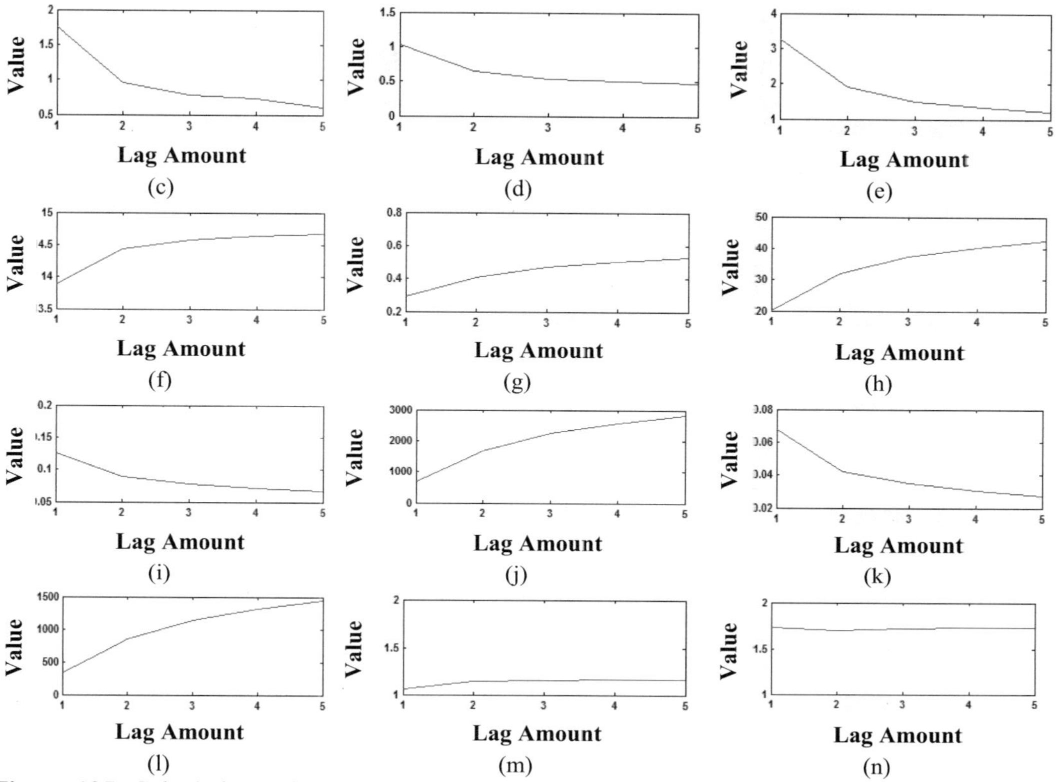

Figure 125: Calculations of measures for texture in Fig. **123**: (a) Maximum Probability (x10E-3), (b) Angular Second Moment (x10E-4), (c) Energy, (d) Entropy, (e) Mutual Information, (f) Dissimilarity, (g) Homogeneity, (h) Contrast, (i) Inverse Difference Moment, (j) Sum of Squares Variance, (k) Information Dimension, and (l) Box Counting Dimension.

DIRECTLY CALCULATING THE FRACTAL DIMENSION FROM THE IMAGE DATA - THE LYAPOUNOV EXPONENTS

While Lyapunov exponents are most often used when the equations of motion are available to provide direct calculation of the exponents, they are also used for time series analysis where the closed form equations are not available. Two issues that must be addressed when using Lyapunov exponents are: (i) they require long time series to provide accurate estimates of the fractional dimension and (ii) many of the algorithms do not provide reliable estimates of fractional dimension for noisy datasets. For most image processing applications long time sequences of images provide unacceptable time delays in processing. Recall for motion and change detection we only use pairs of images which mean Lyapunov exponents will not be useful for these applications. However, for texture analysis we can utilize lines within an image or even a rasterized collection of lines in the image to create relatively long series of pixel amplitudes. Other researchers have successfully applied Lyapunov exponents to identifying spatial texture. Specifically, Mattfeldt used the Lyapunov exponents to differentiate chaotic textures from non-chaotic textures for tumor recognition [60]. He found tumorous tissue has chaotic textures while healthy tissue has non-chaotic texture structure.

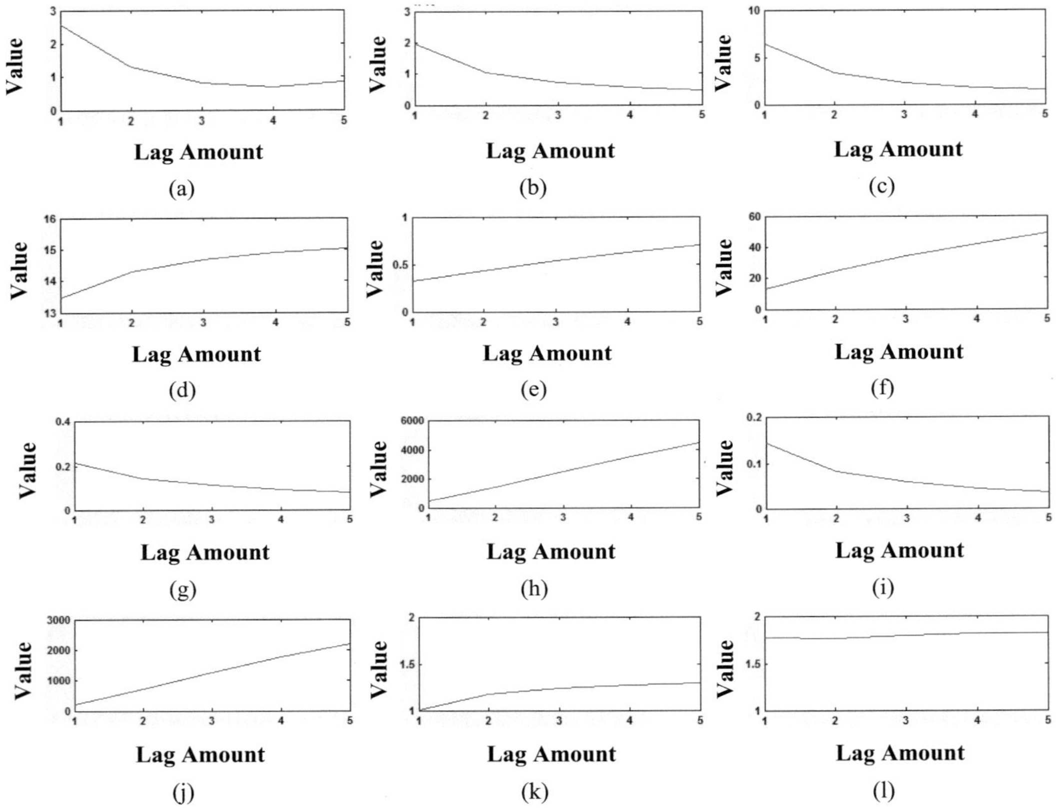

Figure 126: Calculations of measures of texture in Fig. **124**: (a) Maximum Probability (x10E-3), (b) Angular Second Moment (x10E-4), (c) Energy, (d) Entropy, (e) Mutual Information, (f) Dissimilarity, (g) Homogeneity, (h) Contrast, (i) Inverse Difference Moment, (j) Sum of Squares Variance, (k) Information Dimension, and (l) Box Counting Dimension.

With regards to the second concern, most computer vision applications require camera systems that are low cost and consequently quite noisy. Many interesting real-world applications of computer vision are also in uncontrolled environments which can cause higher noise conditions due to sensor temperature. Fortunately various authors have developed algorithms for computing the Lyapunov exponents that are better suited to shorter time series, and also more robust to series with noise.

Fig. **127** (a) and Fig. **128** (a) show two dramatically different textures, one being highly random looking and the other highly deterministic. Notice the amplitude series corresponding to the particular lines identified in the image are provided in Fig. **127** (b) and Fig. **128** (b) and these series could just as easily have been generated by a dynamical system over time. The Lyapunov exponents can capture the chaotic nature of these amplitude series, and the higher the value of the Lyapunov exponents, the more complex the excursions of the trajectory in phase space will be. This can be seen by the phase plots in Fig. **127** (c) and Fig. **128** (c). Notice the dramatically different trajectory excursions in phase space that each of these textures create. The chaotic nature of the first image in Fig. **127** (a) is characterized by all of the fractal dimensional measures and the Lyapunov exponent being large. Likewise the deterministic nature of the image in Fig. **128** (a) is shown by its relatively low fractal dimensions and correspondingly low Lyapunov exponent.

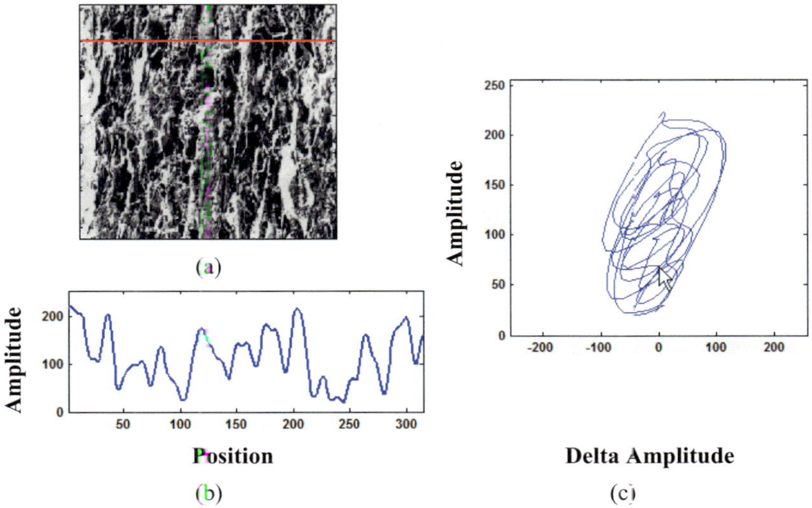

Figure 127: Example trajectory of individual line in texture image: (a) original texture image [90], (b) amplitude profile of texture line, and (c) phase plot calculated along single line highlighted in (a). Lyapunov exponent = 2.04 Information Dimension = 1.12, Correlation Dimension =1.43, and Box Counting = 1.41.

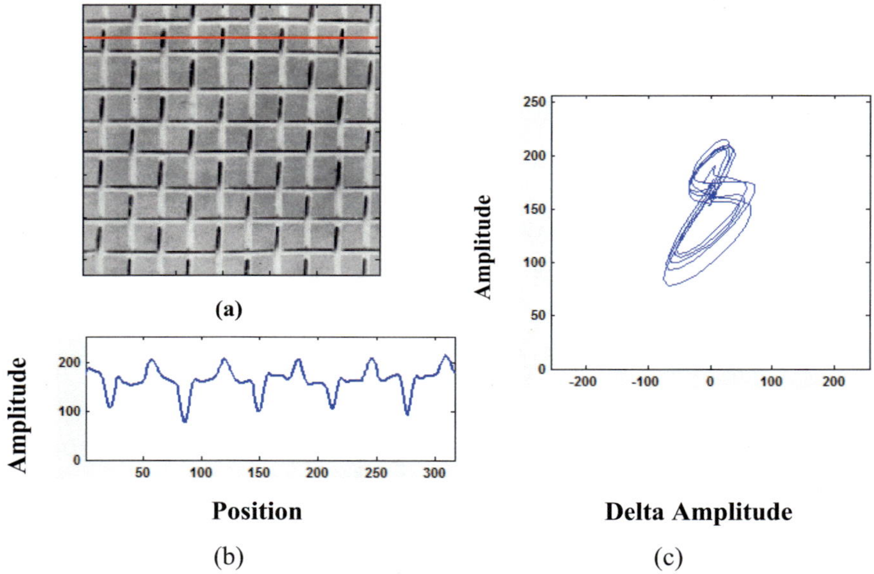

Figure 128: Example trajectory of individual line in texture image: (a) original texture image [90], (b) amplitude profile of texture line, and (c) phase plot calculated along single line highlighted in (a). Lyapunov exponent = 1.64, Information Dimension = 0.72, Correlation Dimension =0.87, and Box Counting = 1.18.

Wolf *et al.,* describes Lyapunov exponents as measures of: "the average exponential rates of divergence or convergence of nearby orbits in phase space" [113] based on the equation [114]:

$$d(t) = Ce^{\lambda_1 t}, \tag{76}$$

where *d(t)* is the distance between adjacent trajectory orbits over time, and *C* is a constant that normalizes initial distances. Positive exponents clearly lead to divergence of the trajectories in phase space, therefore any system with at least one positive Lyapunov exponent is by definition chaotic. Since the greater the positive exponents, the more rapidly adjacent orbits within a trajectory will diverge, the amplitude of the exponents are measures of how chaotic a dynamical system is. The Lyapunov exponents are conjectured to be related to the Information Dimension by Yorke, according to the equation [113]:

$$d_{information} = j + \frac{\sum_{i=1}^{j} \lambda_i}{|\lambda_{j+1}|}, \tag{77}$$

where the following condition defines j:

$$\sum_{i=1}^{j} \lambda_i > 0 \text{ and } \sum_{i=1}^{j+1} \lambda_i < 0 \tag{78}$$

In reality, it is extremely difficult to calculate the complete spectrum of Lyapunov exponents and hence derive the information dimension from the exponents. Fortunately the algorithms developed by Wolf in [113] or Rosenstein *et al.,* in [114] provide estimates for at least the largest positive Lyapunov exponent which is a useful measure of the presence of chaos and its intensity.

The Lyapunov exponents are calculated using the concept of attractor reconstruction similar to that used for our previous morphological measures. A d-dimensional space is created by building a vector space of increasing time lags, as was discussed in Chapter 3. We construct a space of the form:

$$\begin{Bmatrix} x(1)x(1+\tau)\cdots x(1+(d-1)\tau) \\ \vdots \quad\quad \vdots \quad\quad \vdots \quad\quad\quad \vdots \\ x(n)x(n+\tau)\cdots x(n+(d-1)\tau) \end{Bmatrix}, \tag{79}$$

where each column vector is created from increasing spatial lags $k \cdot \tau$ across the image to create a *dxn*-dimensional space which reconstructs the phase space.

Unlike the earlier dimensional measures which treat the phase space in its entirety, the Lyapunov exponents are computed by walking along the trajectory and measuring at each point how closely spaced is the nearest neighboring trajectory orbit. In both the Wolf algorithm and the Rosenstein algorithm the distances between various points on the trajectory are calculated and then their relative changes over time are measured to estimate the rate of divergence of adjacent orbits within trajectory [113, 114]. Examples of adjacent orbits within the phase space trajectory from Fig. **128** (c) are provided in Fig. **129**. In these algorithms the distance between the trajectory and the nearest adjacent trajectory orbits are recorded as shown in Fig. **130**. As one advances along these orbits, the distances between the orbits will increase if the system is chaotic. When the distance exceeds a threshold, this distance and the original distance between the trajectories are recorded to capture the rate of divergence.

$$\sum_{i=1}^{j} \lambda_i > 0 \text{ and } \sum_{i=1}^{j+1} \lambda_i < 0 \tag{80}$$

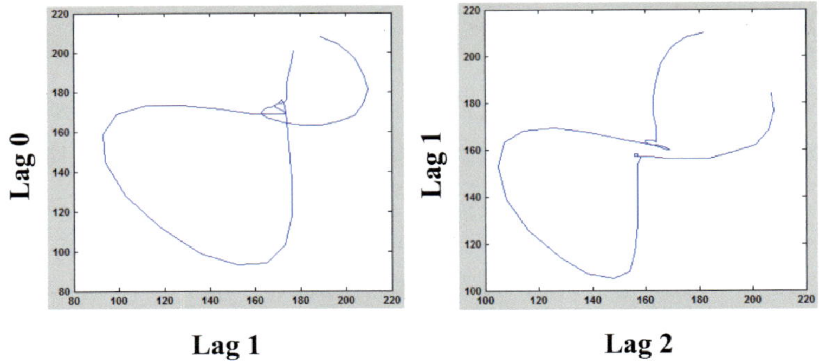

(a) (b)

Figure 129: Extraction of two orbits of the phase space trajectory provided in Fig. **128** (c).

The Wolf algorithm for computing the largest positive Lyapunov exponent is implemented using the following equation [113]:

$$\lambda_1 = \frac{1}{t_m - t_0} \cdot \sum_{k=1}^{M} log_2 \frac{L'(t_k)}{L(t_{k-1})}, \tag{81}$$

where $L(t_{k-1})$ is the distance between the current location on the orbit and the nearest adjacent orbit and $L'(t_k)$ is the distance at the time at which the trajectory orbits have spread apart. Note the time lag cannot be too great or the orbit may have entered a folding region where the distance would begin to shrink. The algorithm marches along a fiducial trajectory and collects the *M* points where the trajectories parted. A new nearest neighbor orbit is also selected as can be seen in Fig. **130**. The fiducial trajectory is a pieced-together path through the complete trajectory based on hopping from one orbit to another when the distance between orbits gets too large. The algorithm is, unfortunately, quite time consuming since at each time point where the distances exceed the threshold the distances to every trajectory point and the current point must be re-calculated and the minimum selected.

The Rosenstein algorithm also computes the largest positive Lyapunov exponent and is based on the following equation [114]:

$$y(i) = \frac{1}{\Delta t} \langle ln\left(d_j(i)\right)\rangle, \tag{82}$$

where $d_j(i)$ is the distance between the jth point on the trajectory and its nearest neighbor point on an adjacent trajectory orbit after the trajectories evolve over i time lags. The average function here is computed over all the points in the trajectory rather than over only a fiducial trajectory as in the Wolf algorithm. The Lyapunov exponent is equal to the slope of the line created by Equation (82) as the time lag i is incremented.

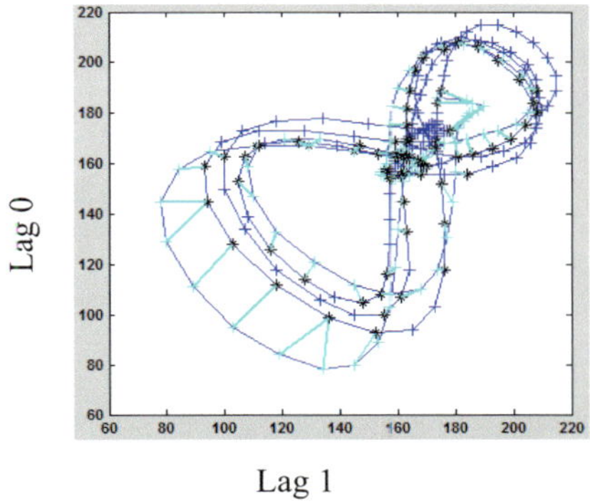

Figure 130: Distances computed between sequences of points on the trajectory with the nearest neighbors on adjacent orbits.

For the remainder of this text however, due to their computational complexity, we will forego using Lyapunov exponents for characterizing spatial chaos in images, and we will rely on the morphological measures of the phase space defined in the earlier sections of this chapter.

TECHNIQUES FOR DETECTING COMPACTED ORBITS IN PHASE PLOTS

Reviewing our discussions of pseudo-chaos and trajectory compaction in Chapter 4. Quantization is naturally present in any digital imaging device (or analog device fed through a frame digitizer) in computer vision. This causes the trajectories in phase space to suffer from compaction as was shown in Fig. **11** (b) and (c). Fig. **131** and Fig. **132** also provide comprehensive collections of image pairs with motion present whose respective phase plots show varying degrees of compaction. It is interesting to note that phase space orbits resulting from man-made structures tend to exhibit more compaction than phase space orbits from human subjects. This may be due to the ordered nature of the surface normal vectors of man-made objects. Manmade objects tend to be composed of large surfaces of constant normal and albedo such as the sides of buildings, streets and sidewalks, *etc.* Even objects such as motor vehicles have surfaces that, while not having equal normal vectors, contain families of normal vectors of constant albedo whose directions vary smoothly and often within a small range over reasonable distances. This can be seen in vehicle roofs, hoods, and doors. Human subjects, however, tend to have more aperiodic underlying structures caused by a broader range of surface normal vectors and albedos distributed across the body due to characteristics like the natural contours of the body, folds in clothing, and varying clothing material.

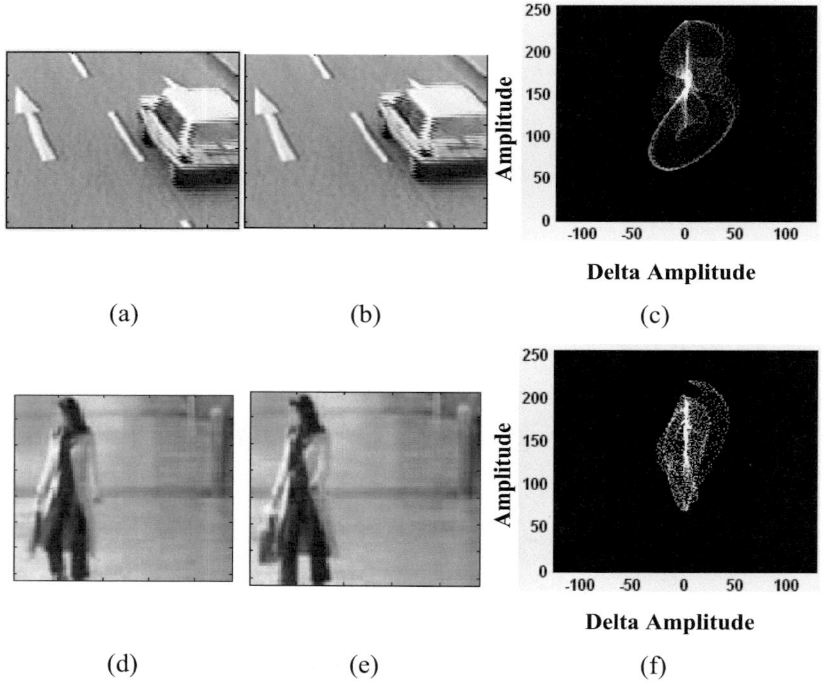

Figure 131: Examples of phase space behavior due to motion: (a) first image [67], (b) next image, (c), phase plot, (d) first image [80], (e) next image, and (f) phase plot.

Notice how the compacted regions of phase space are embedded within the chaos-like fractal structures of the remaining regions of phase space. These compacted regions are fundamentally non-chaotic in nature. Rather than exhibiting the space filling nature of the underlying aperiodic forcing function these compacted trajectories actually resemble the trajectories of *periodic* signals. For reference

Fig. **133** (a) provides an example of a purely deterministic sinusoidal time series and Fig. **133** (b) provides its resultant phase plot. Note the orbital structure of the phase plot with none of the space-filling characteristics and none of the filamentary structure we saw in the phase plots from the chaos-like signals. The chaos-like signals are modelled as resulting from an aperiodic forcing function rather than this periodic forcing function.

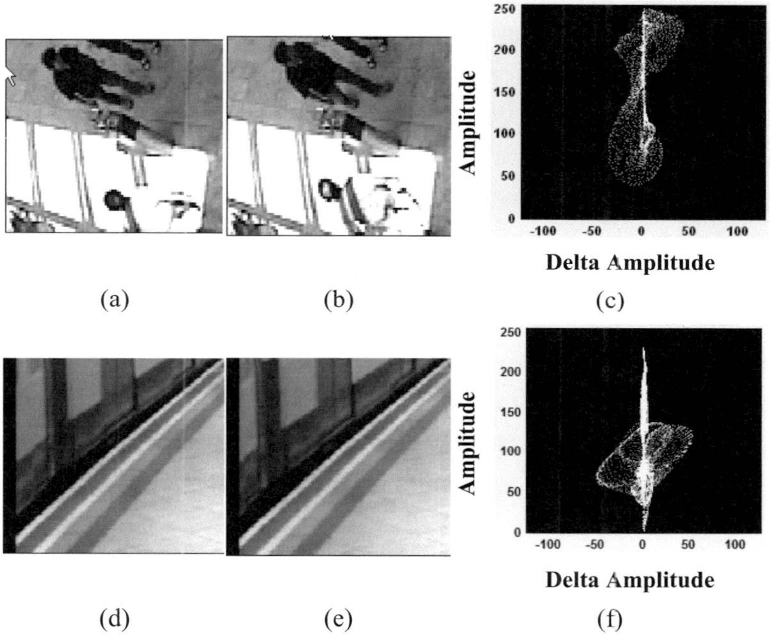

Figure 132: Examples of phase space behavior due to motion: (a) first image [80], (b) next image, and (c) phase plot, (d) first image [85], (e) next image, and (f) phase plot.

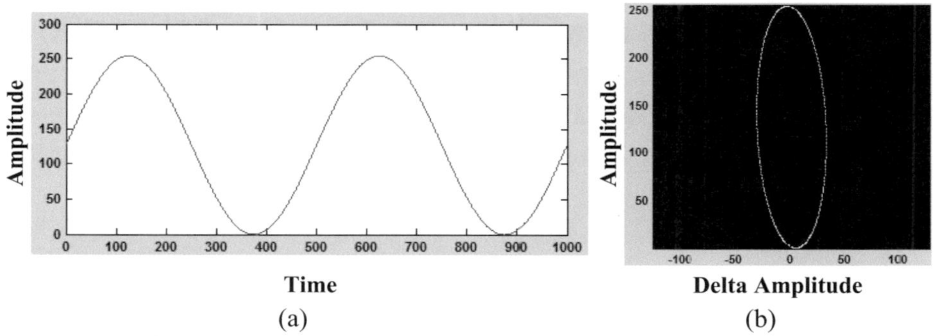

Figure 133: Example of sinusoidal signal phase space behavior: (a) time series, (b) phase plot for 20 sample lag.

The fact that the filamentary fractal structure reduces to a periodic structure could be quite problematic if we needed to distinguish all classes of non-chaotic signals from chaotic signals in our various computer vision applications (*i.e.* rigorously differentiate any periodic forcing functions from any aperiodic forcing functions). Fortunately, the computer vision applications where we need to differentiate chaotic from non-chaotic signals are those applications where we are differentiating motion and contextual change from illumination. Chapter 4 provided numerous examples of phase plots resulting from effects of simple global illumination changes as well as complex spatially varying illumination changes. In all of these cases, the multiplicative nature of illumination created distinct triangular structures (recall Fig. **45** (c) or Fig. **46** (d) for examples). This means that, even with the compaction causing some regions of the phase plot to reduce to trajectories that appear periodic, motion or contextual change-based trajectories are still significantly different in ***topological*** structure than trajectories due to temporally varying illumination. We will need to develop a means for analyzing these compacted phase plots directly using a measure other than the fractal dimension since as Tricot observed in [66], "The measure of a set does not determine its topological properties". The exploitation of topological measures rather than simple dimensional measures will be the focus of the following two sub-chapters.

While it appears that we should be able to exploit topological measures rather than simply fractal dimension measures to differentiate regions due to motion from regions due to illumination in phase space, we must also ask the additional key question of will these compacted trajectories cause us to miss detections of chaotic events. This may occur when applying global fractal dimensional measures to computer vision applications such as pre-attentive vision where we are trying to determine if there are any aperiodic forcing function events in the image scene. If compaction causes a significant reduction in the fractal dimension of the phase plot for the scene then we may miss important chaotic events.

To answer this question we need to analyze the underlying mathematics of the imaging process. Regions of compaction result from areas of the objects having radiance values that are so closely spaced together that they fall within the same quantized grayscale value of the imaging sensor. If we imagine we had infinite resolution cameras, we would then be able to distinguish the amplitude values within the compacted trajectory. The set of adjacent pixels with very small amplitude variations would result in a set of closely spaced phase space trajectories rather than a compacted trajectory. Since the global measures of fractal dimension measure the space filling nature of the trajectory we propose that their compaction may result in only modest changes in the space-filling nature of the trajectory. When we discussed global measures we did see that multi-fractal phase plots with significant non-fractal regions do bias the fractal dimension for measures that employ trajectory density. Thus if we use the Box Counting measure which simply looks for the trajectory being within a particular box we should still be able to compute a reasonable estimate of the fractal dimension if there were no compaction.

We can validate this hypothesis as follows. When computing global measures of fractality of a phase plot containing compacted regions we will derive a particular value. If we compare the space filling nature of the high resolution phase plot with the compacted phase plot, we will see that the trajectory does not explore significantly more regions of the phase space. This is because the amplitude and hence delta-amplitude values of the high resolution phase plot are by definition not appreciably different in value (they do not extend beyond the least significant bit of the original compacted phase plot). Thus the overall space filling nature of the compacted phase plot will not be appreciably different from one of high resolution, which means the global measures of fractal dimension will not be appreciably different. It is only when we are applying ***local*** measures of fractality for image segmentation that these compacted regions become significant since clearly these compacted regions of the phase plot are no longer locally fractal. Thus if the local fractal dimension was computed on these trajectories, these compacted regions would clearly not be detected. To address this, when we are applying local measures of fractal dimension we may then also need to apply supplemental topological measures to detect compacted orbital trajectories. We therefore propose a two stage process when applying local fractal measures to phase plots for the purpose of object segmentation. First traditional local measures of fractal dimension are applied and the fractal portions of the phase space trajectory are removed. Then the remaining non-chaotic, non-fractal portions of the phase space will be analyzed using a topological measure to identify any compacted trajectories.

In the first stage we apply the local Holder exponent measure to identify regions that are behaving in a conventionally chaos-like manner. In the second stage, we remove these fractally detected regions and then analyze the residual phase space for orbits which may be indicative of attractor-like behavior that has been compacted due to system quantization. For a simple model we will seek motivation from orbital mechanics where orbits can generally be of three classes of curves, parabolas, hyperbolas, and ellipses. Since ellipses are the only bounded trajectories, we will limit our search to ellipses in the residual phase plot. We require bounded trajectories since we know we have bounded systems with a finite range of allowable grayscale values being produced by the imaging device. While an ellipse is quite simple compared to the common phase space trajectories, we will see that these more complex patterns can be built of collections of these simpler orbits. This is acceptable since our goal is orbit segment detection rather than full orbital characterization. Also the compacted regions of the phase space trajectory are rarely complete elliptical orbits. The common condition is that the quantized regions of the phase plot trajectory create segments of ellipses as can be seen in the phase plots in Fig. **134**. Thus the goal of ellipse detection will be to detect the presence of segments of ellipses in the phase plot.

There are three well defined methods for detecting ellipses in an image [115]:

i. Hough transform

ii. Euclidean-based curve fitting

iii. Algebraic curve fitting

While Hough transforms are highly effective at detecting general curves, the dimensionality of the search space makes it computationally infeasible for most real-time applications. Euclidean curve fitting only provides an approximation to an elliptical curve fit; therefore we will use the algebraic curve fit to provide a more direct linear solution based on solving the generalized eigenvalue problem [115]:

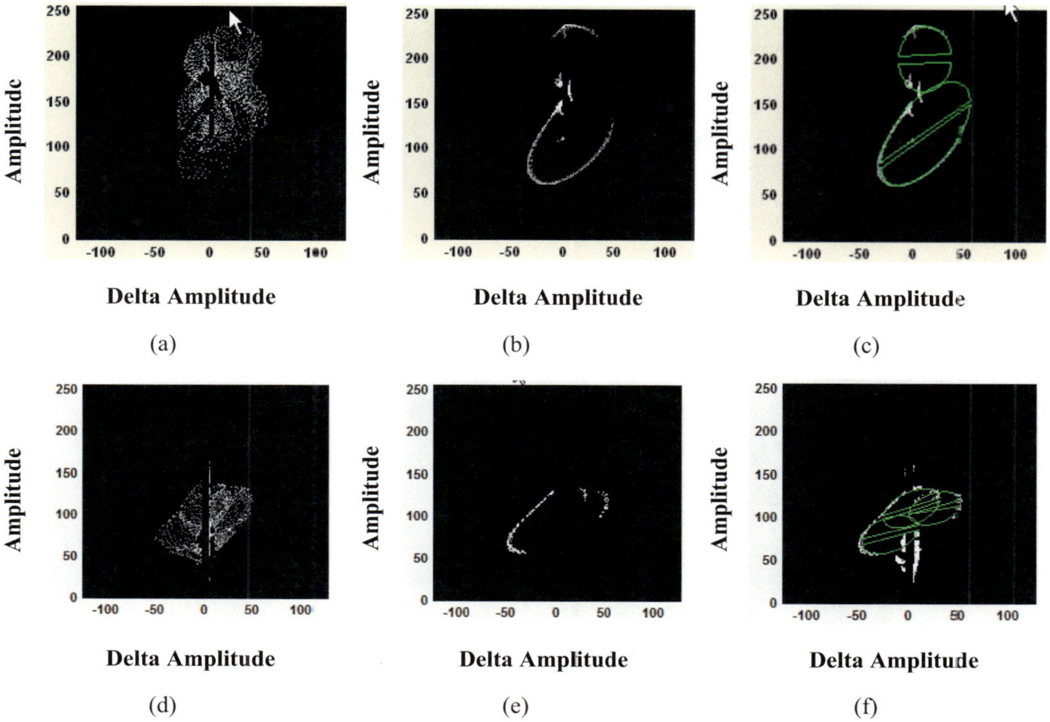

Figure 134: Chaos-like behavior in a quantized phase space, (a) fractally detected phase plot regions for Fig. **131** (a) images, (b) difference phase plot showing trajectory compaction, and (c) resultant elliptical orbits of these compacted regions, (d) fractally detected phase plot regions for Fig. **132** (a) images, (e) difference phase plot showing trajectory compaction, and (f) resultant elliptical orbits of these compacted regions.

$$Sa = \lambda Ca, \tag{83}$$

where S is scatter matrix, C is a constraint matrix to force the result to be an ellipse [115]:

$$C = \begin{bmatrix} 0 & 0 & -2 \\ 0 & 1 & 0 \\ -2 & 0 & 0 \end{bmatrix}, \tag{84}$$

and a is the vector of the coefficients of the general quadratic [115]:

$$ax^2 + bxy + cy^2 + dx + ey + f = 0. \tag{85}$$

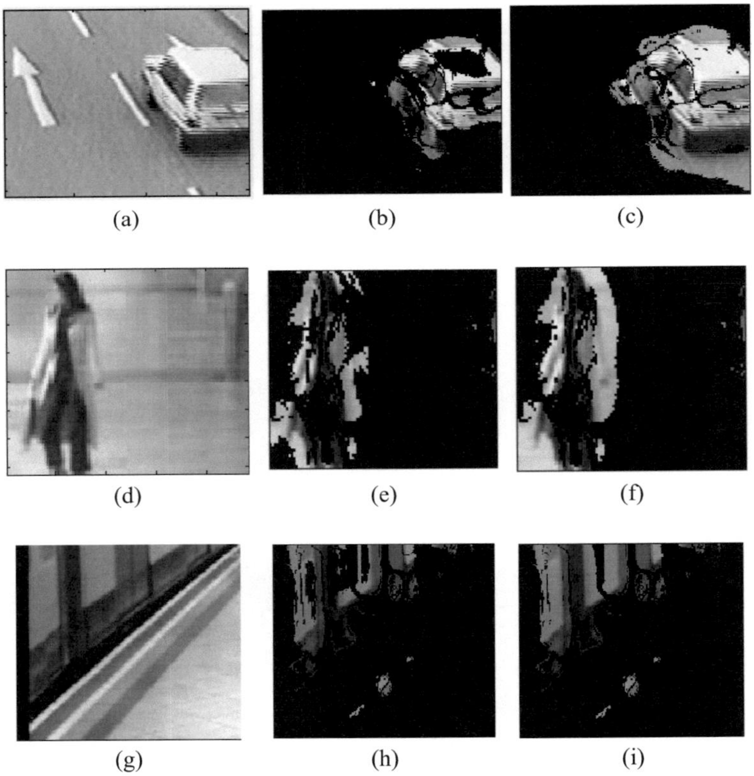

Figure 135: Demonstration of improved motion segmentation using compacted trajectory detection, (a) original image from motion sequence of car [67], (b) multi-fractal -only motion segmentation, (c) fractal/algebraic motion segmentation, (d) original image from motion sequence of human [80], (e) multi-fractal-only motion segmentation, fractal/algebraic motion segmentation, (f) fractal/algebraic segmentation, (g) original image from motion sequence of subway car, (h) multi-fractal-only motion segmentation, and (i) fractal/algebraic motion segmentation.

The S matrix is constructed by: $S = X^T X$ where [115]:

$$X(i,:) = \left[x^2,\ xy,\ y^2,\ x,\ y,\ 1\right], \tag{86}$$

for each *(x, y)* point on the candidate region of the phase space within which an ellipse may reside. Fig. **134** (c) and (f) shows the ellipses detected from the residual phase plot segments and it can be clearly seen they follow the orbits of the phase plot. Fig. **135** (c), (f) and (i) provide corrected motion segmentations where the pixels located on the compacted orbits are added back into the final segmentation. Clearly the segmentations are dramatically improved.

In summary, we demonstrated the compaction of the phase plot trajectories due to the finite quantization of the camera sensor. We recognized that a measure other than the fractal dimension was required to detect these regions since they were no longer fractal. We showed that these regions did, however, produce interesting orbital trajectories that were still structurally different from other effects such as illumination. We then introduced an algebraic approach to detect these elliptical orbits.

CONCLUDING REMARKS

In this chapter we introduced a collection of measures to characterize the complex phase plot trajectories that are present in a variety of computer vision applications. We began by introducing the conventional local and global measures of fractality which are based on the Hausdorff dimension. We then introduced the Renyi spectrum, or also called the Generalized Dimension which unifies all the various measures as special cases for this dimensional vector measure.

We then introduced the measure of lacunarity which was originally proposed by Mandelbrot as a means for measuring the fractal characteristics of an image. We showed it can equally be applied to characterize the uniformity of the phase plot trajectory across the phase space. We continued with other measures that have been used in texture analysis for analyzing the co-occurrence matrix, but have not been explored for analyzing the behavior of phase plot trajectories.

We completed the chapter with the proposal of measures to be applied to phase plots for applications where there is considerable data quantization, as is common in computer vision applications. These measures were used to detect compacted orbits in phase space, and they were demonstrated to be useful for improving motion-based image segmentation applications where the camera quantization created well-defined orbits within phase space.

 Application of Chaos and Fractals to Computer Vision, 2014, 166-185

CHAPTER 6

Applications to Pre-attentive Vision – Using the Presence of Chaos for Attention Direction

Abstract: Pre-attentive vision systems are responsible for directing the attention of higher order vision functions to regions of the field of view that may be of interest to the system. Regions may be of interest due to motion or due to a contextual change in the image that may be due to a sudden appearance or disappearance of an object. Since the outcome of the pre-attentive system is a notification of interest to the higher order vision functions, maintaining a low false alarm rate is critical. One key cause of false alarms can be either sudden or slow changes in illumination of the field of interest of the imaging system. Another key issue is the detection rate of the system. In particular the sensitivity of the system to small changes must be maintained while its immunity to non-interesting change such as illumination is preserved. Thus the use of the proposed chaos-based methods which are inherently immune to illumination change have great promise for these types of systems. In this chapter we will first define the problem of pre-attentive vision in chaos-theoretic terms, and then propose an algorithm that utilizes the chaos-based methods of phase space analysis using global fractal measures. The chaos-based system performance is compared to traditional methods such as Mutual Information, sum of absolute differences, and Gaussian mixture models. The chaos-based methods outperform all of these traditional methods.

Keywords: Pre-attentive vision, receiver operating characteristics (ROC) curve, change detection, Gaussian Mixture Models (GMM), sum of absolute differences (SAD), mutual information.

THE ATTENTION DIRECTION PROBLEM

The mechanisms for directing attention in the human visual system have been the objective of significant research in the psychology and physiology communities, and a number of computer science researchers have defined systems based on models of the human perception system [2, 40, 49]. Researchers agree that one of the 'undoubtable' low level features that direct attention is motion [40]. Park *et al.,* note "temporal saliency has high priority over spatial saliency" and Le Meur *et al.,* note "salient parts consist of abrupt onsets" and "the appearance of new perceptual object consistent or not with the context of the scene could also attract our attention" [2, 49]. Unfortunately, "a mechanism that wanted to direct attention to any visual transient would be less useful since many uninteresting events in the

Michael E. Farmer

world can produce such transients" [41]. One example of uninteresting transients is the spatio-temporally varying illumination (*i.e.* moving/suddenly appearing light bands) that was introduced in Chapter 4. An effective pre-attentive system should detect motion and contextual change, while remaining relatively immune to spatio-temporal changes in illumination. Likewise a pre-attentive system should be able to differentiate between motion and long term contextual change to allow the system to be designed for differing applications.

Two interesting datasets where subjects abandoned suspicious bags in public areas are provided in the CAVIAR and the AVSS datasets [80, 85]. Fig. **136** (a) shows an empty image frame for the CAVIAR 2 set and Fig. **143** (b) shows an image with the abandoned bag shown in the far right of the image. Fig. **137** (a) shows an empty image frame for the AVSS abandoned bag dataset and Fig. **137** (b) shows the image with a bag abandoned in the background and people moving through the terminal, and in and out of a subway car which had previously been moving. Thus this dataset contains interesting collections of large and small moving objects, passengers that sit along the bench and the abandoned bags. The goal of pre-attentive vision is to identify which frames have change and then to direct the system to the general area where the change occurs. Subsequent higher level vision tasks would then perform the operation of object segmentation and recognition and these higher level functions will be addressed in Chapter 7.

(a) (b)

Figure 136: Contextual change detection for left bag detection, (a) empty scenes for the AVSS dataset [85], and (b) scene with an abandoned bag and people moving through the scene [85].

(a) (b)

Figure 137: Contextual change detection for left bag detection, (a) empty scenes for the CAVIAR dataset [80], and (b) scene with an abandoned bag and a single person moving through the scene [80].

Radke *et al.,* provided an extensive survey of change detection algorithms in [116] and that is not the purpose of this text, however, we will highlight a few of the approaches to provide a reference point for the reader to understand the advantages of the proposed chaos-based approach. Canus and Vehel proposed a multi-fractal approach for the detection of change in image sequences [17]; however, their analysis was on the original grayscale images rather than in phase space as proposed in this text. Their approach was also not tested against any illumination variability, and their use of the grayscale domain does not provide the inherent immunity to illumination change as provided by the proposed chaos approach.

Another very popular approach to change detection employs Gaussian mixture models to model contextual change *versus* illumination in grayscale space [27, 30, 33]. These approaches employ background subtraction algorithms where a background image is managed over time using the mixture models to adapt to changes in global illumination and the motive and contextual change of objects in the scene. In all of these algorithms, however, due to the slow changing nature of the mixture model approach, the authors admit the approach cannot differentiate rapidly changing illumination from contextually interesting change [30, 33]. Also the processing burden of mixture model based approaches dramatically exceeds that of the proposed chaos-theoretic approaches in this text. The processing burden increases as the number of mixtures in the model increase to handle the various changes witnessed in images. Also the mixture models tend to be adequate at detecting motion but they do not do well at providing any natural distinction between motion and long term change events such as suspicious bags left in train stations. We will see in this chapter that the GMM approaches are less suitable for a true pre-attentive vision system than the proposed chaos-based approach.

Another common approach to change detection is to model illumination and motion effects as separate processes, and then through linearization techniques attempt to differentiate the effects of the two processes [28]. This approach requires small changes in illumination and motion, thereby setting practical limits to the rate of detectable motion and the rate of illumination change. The chaos-based approach embraces the non-linearities in the image changes due to motion instead of attempting to linearize them which leads to a simpler and more accurate approach. Thus compared to all of the above possible change detection algorithms, there is an advantage to applying a chaos-theoretic approach to pre-attentive vision.

A CHAOS-BASED ALGORITHM FOR ATTENTION DIRECTION

The processing flow for the proposed system is provided in Fig. **138** [117]. The initial step, of ***low-pass filter,*** reduces the effects of noise and can also support down-sampling to reduce the sizes of the images for even higher performance. For attention direction, we are interested in focusing attention to the region in the image where the change occurs. Consequently, rather than applying this measure to the entire image, the image is divided into a *4x4* set of grid cells and the measures are computed within these smaller regions. The specific number of grid cells is somewhat arbitrary, and is typically determined based on the possible sizes of the objects of interest as well as the available processing of subsequent computer tasks. Smaller grid cells require more processing in the pre-attentive processing but provide smaller more focused images for the higher level vision tasks.

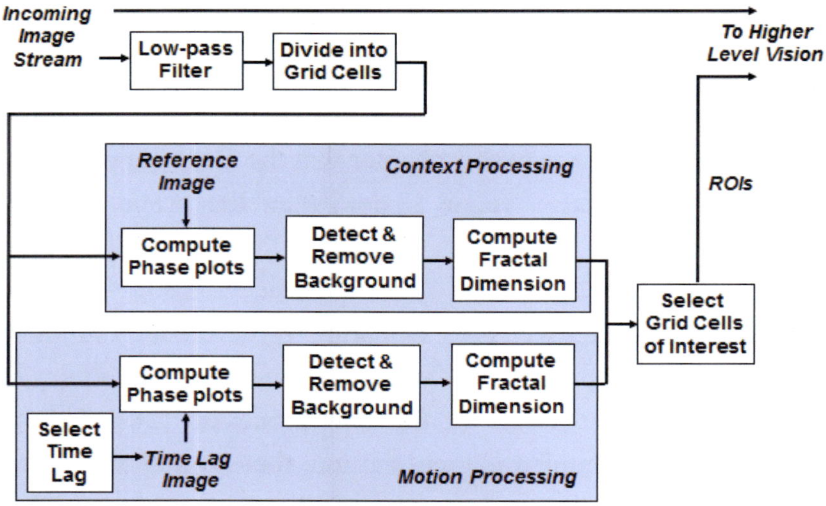

Figure 138: Processing flow for chaos-based pre-attentive change and motion detection processing [117].

There are two nearly identical parallel paths within this processing, one for motion detection and one for contextual change detection. Depending on the application of the system, the goal is usually either motion detection at the exclusion of contextual change, or in the case of suspicious bag surveillance, the detection of contextual change while ignoring the effects of moving objects in the scene. The only difference between the two paths is that in the motion processing there is a determination of time lag to be used between images while in the context path; the reference image is always used. For selecting time lags, the system currently uses one to eight image frame time lags for motion depending on the type of scene and objects (human *versus* automobile for example), and uses an original template image taken potentially days or hours earlier as the contextual change reference image. The proposed chaos-based approach does not require an updated background image when there is illumination change, as illumination change is inherently ignored by its unique behavior in phase space relative to substantive contextual change. The background images in this study were actually pieced together from sections of multiple images across all of the CAVIAR and AVSS datasets [80, 85], with the regions selected solely on their lack of objects, irrespective of the overall illumination. This provides a significant advantage for the chaos-based approach over grayscale-based methods.

The next processing task is ***Compute Phase Plots*** where each pixel in one image is paired with the same pixel location in the second image. The amplitude of the pixel determines the y-axis location in phase space and the difference between the two pixels determines the x-axis location. For each pair of pixels, the corresponding phase plot (amplitude, delta-amplitude) cell is incremented. Recall the construction of the phase plot was discussed in detail in Chapter 3.

The processing for ***Detect and Remove Background*** is provided in Fig. **139**. This stage is usually only required if the objects of interest are quite small relative to the size of the grid cell. For relatively large objects any contribution of the background and spatio-temporal illumination change will be small in phase space relative to the contribution of the object of interest. The first step thresholds the phase plot to remove trajectories corresponding to motion and spatially varying illumination. Since all of the background pixels are commonly affected by the global illumination, the diagonal line corresponding to the background tends to have relatively high amplitude. Likewise spatially varying illumination produces a compact dense conic section that is also of high amplitude. The remaining phase plot corresponds to the background with possible illumination changes and all motion and change removed. This approach is similar to that of Cho and Kim in [54]. This dense conic structure of illumination change provides the mechanism for ***Remove Outlier Points*** to ignore any compacted trajectories of moving objects since they will lie in the periphery of phase space and not within conic regions. The pseudo-code for the background removal processing is below.

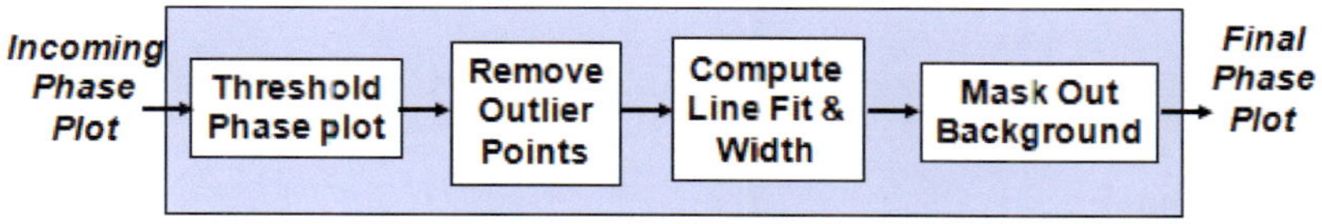

Figure 139: Processing flow for chaos-based background removal processing [117].

The remaining points in phase space are then used by a simple least squares algorithm to compute the angle of the background line in phase space and the goodness of fit is used as a measure of the line width. A simple linear mask is then created to remove the regions of phase space due to the background. Fig. **140** shows the results of the background removal process where after the line and width are computed (highlighted in Fig. **140** (a)), the background is masked and the resultant phase plot (Fig. **140** (b)) is then used to compute the fractal dimension.

Pseudo Code 1: Background Removal Algorithm

1. Set initial threshold to 1/10 max amplitude of phase plot;
2. Find all points in phase plot of amplitude above threshold;
3. If no points found then reduce threshold and try again;
4. Purge out the points in phase plot that are far from center line of image;
5. Compute the least squares fit line for remaining points in phase plot to compute slope;
6. Set base of mask line at center line of phase plot (no change line);
7. Generate global illumination line with slope computed from step 5;
8. For each remaining point in phase plot compute distance from global illumination line;
9. Histogram these distances;
10. Set mask width to first zero points in histogram about main peak;
11. Generate mask;
12. Overlay on phase plot and remove;

The processing now returns to the second step in Fig. **138**, namely ***Compute Fractal Dimension***. Since the goal of attention direction is simply to identify regions of possible interesting fractal behavior a ***global*** fractal measure is employed. Since performance is a critical constraint on a pre-attentive vision system a simple fractal measure should be employed such as Box Counting or

Information Dimension. The results provided in the following sub-chapter will show that the Box Counting dimension is actually the better of the two measures in terms of performance, and fortunately also in terms of processing burden.

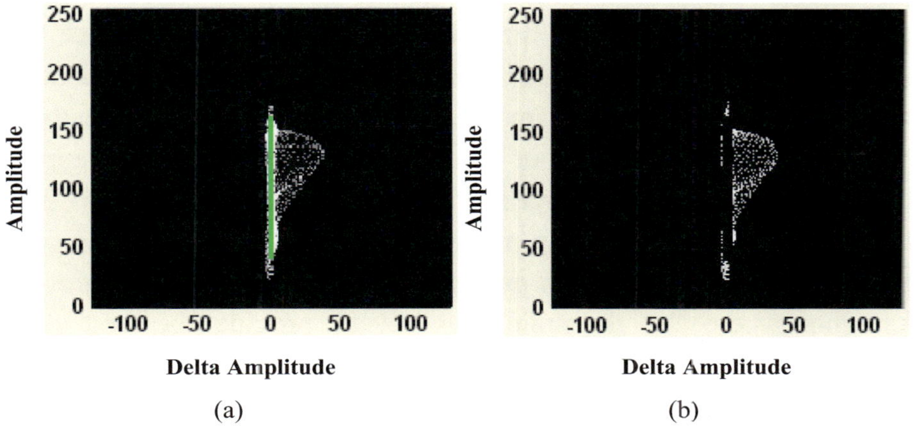

Figure 140: Results from removal of background contribution to joint histogram prior to computation of the fractal dimension, (a) phase plot with background line highlighted, and (b) phase plot with background portion of phase plot removed.

The final stage of the pre-attentive processing is the ***Select Grid Cells of Interest***, where the goal of the system is either identifying regions with motion or identifying regions with contextual change. If the goal of the system is contextual change, then any moving objects will be discovered in both paths of the processing but the moving objects will be removed from consideration in order to only detect the longer term contextual changes.

TRADITIONAL APPROACHES TO PRE-ATTENTIVE VISION

Two traditional grayscale methods for general background subtraction are the sum of absolute differences (SAD) and Gaussian mixture models (GMM). SAD is the simplest change detection algorithm. For the given image it merely calculates the following term [116]:

$$SAD = \sum_{rows} \sum_{cols} \left| I_{ref}(i,j) - I_{curr}(i,j) \right| \quad (87)$$

where I_{ref} is the reference image which is used for the basis of detecting change and I_{curr} is the current image of interest.

Note the SAD algorithm clearly has an implicit assumption of image constancy since it is simply comparing the amplitudes of each pixel between the two images. Once the SAD value is computed for each grid cell in the image, its value is compared with a pre-defined threshold and if the SAD value exceeds the threshold then change is declared for that region in the image. Notice that the threshold is nearly impossible to estimate a priori since it is dependent on the actual grayscale values within the image and these can vary dramatically across not only imaging applications, but also over time for a given application depending on the illumination sources of the scene of interest. Fig. **141** provides the histograms of the Box Counting metric and the SAD metric for the complete image sequences whose example is provided in Fig. **136**. In both figures the red line highlights where the threshold was set to provide the best detection performance *versus* false alarm performance. Notice that if an automated threshold detection was to be employed it would be relatively simple to set a threshold for the Box Counting metric as there is a clear 'double-hump' shape to the histogram with the trough between the two distributions of background and objects of interest being relatively broad. In contrast, the SAD metric histogram shows no clear separation of background *versus* objects of interest.

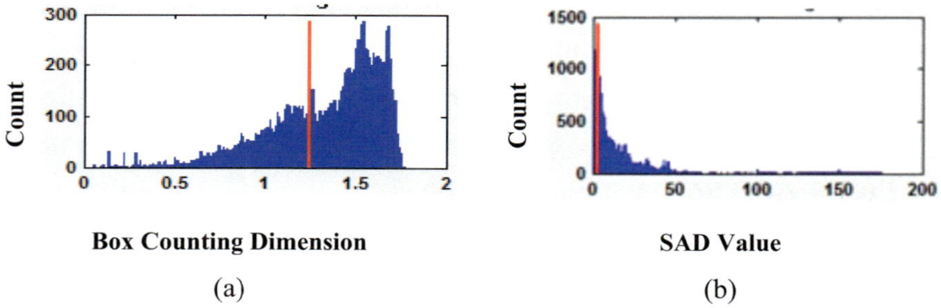

Figure 141: Histograms of measures for contextual change for the AVSS sequence in Fig. **136**, (a) chaos measure and (b) SAD measure [117].

The second traditional algorithm with which the chaos-based method is compared is the GMM algorithm. The GMM algorithm is based on the Expectation Maximization (EM) algorithm updating the Gaussian parameters (mean and variance) and the mixture weight coefficient. For an assumed mixture of Gaussians, the EM processing is based on the idea that the image is comprised of a weighted-sum of Gaussian densities, according to [118]:

$$p(x \mid \Theta) = \sum_{i=1}^{M} \alpha_i \cdot p_i(x \mid \vartheta_i) \tag{88}$$

where the α_i are the weighting factors, and ϑ_i are parameter estimates for each of the underlying Gaussians. GMM relies on calculating three data arrays corresponding to the number of mixtures being used to model the scene. These data arrays consist of the mean (μ_t), the variance (σ_t^2), and the weight of each mixture contribution (ω_t) for *every* pixel in the image and are calculated in an iterative manner according to [29]:

$$\omega_t = \omega_{t-1} + \alpha(o_t - \omega_{t-1}) - \alpha c_T \tag{89}$$

$$\mu_t = \mu_{t-1} + o_t(\alpha/\omega_{t-1})\delta_t \tag{90}$$

$$\sigma_t^2 = \sigma_{t-1}^2 + o_t(\alpha/\omega_{t-1})(\delta_t^T \delta_t - \sigma_{t-1}^2) \tag{91}$$

$$D_t^2(x_t) = \delta_t^T \delta_t / \sigma_t^2. \tag{92}$$

In these equations α is the learning rate, c_T is a mixture weight decay value, $\delta_t = x_t - \mu_{t-1}$ and x_t is the pixel amplitude for each pixel at the current image frame time. $D_t^2(x_t)$ is the similarity measure which controls the number of mixtures used. If the value of $D_t^2(x_t)$ exceeds a threshold then another mixture is added. Note these terms are computed for each of the K mixture components where $K=3$ is typical [29, 33]. The use of mixture models is further extended in Tian *et al.*, where multiple Gaussian mixtures are used to model all possible image changes without assumptions of them being due to moving objects, contextual change, illumination or shadows [33].

GMM relies on thresholding at a pre-defined percentage of detected pixels in the image grid cell. This clearly has two issues: first it requires a priori knowledge of the size of the object of interest and second, in scenes where a small object must be found amongst large moving objects a large threshold would be required to control false alarms. This large threshold means the system is now too insensitive to detect the smaller objects of interest. In the example scenes shown in this chapter, this exact problem arises because the abandoned bags were left by a human moving through the scene and the humans are quite large relative to the object of interest. The humans' image remains in the GMM image as the decay rate of the GMM algorithm leaves ghosts of moving objects. Additionally, GMM is difficult to implement since there is a variety of parameters that must be set, namely the initial variance, the learning rate, the number of mixtures, the fraction of region with change, and the decay rate of the mixture weight [29, 33].

The limitations of thresholding and the other magic parameters associated with traditional linear-processing based methods are in sharp contrast to the simplicity of the chaos-based method. The chaos-based method has a detection threshold that is set based on the fractal dimension of change and has one parameter, the time lags for motion processing. In the chaos approach the threshold is based on how fractal the phase plot should appear for the desired change detection sensitivity. The fractal value of the phase plot is directly related to the space filling nature of the phase space trajectory which is a measure of the amount of information created in the image sequence. As we saw in Fig. **143** (b) and (d) even relatively small objects can have relatively complex phase space trajectories that are independent of the amount of background image, and thus is relatively immune to the exact size of the object of interest, within reason. The time lag is directly related to the anticipated motion characteristics of the object which is commonly known for the desired application.

TYPICAL RESULTS OF APPLYING CHAOS TO ATTENTION DIRECTION

A collection of interesting abandoned-bag scenarios from the CAVIAR and AVSS-2007 datasets [80, 85] are used to demonstrate the benefits of the proposed chaos-based approach. The full scenes where bags may be abandoned are provided in Fig. **142** and the regions containing the bags are zoomed-in in Fig. **143** (a) and (c). Fig. **143** (b) and (d) provide the phase plots of the abandoned bags relative to the empty background image and provide the fractal measures for each of these bags. As can be seen in Fig. **142** these bags are quite small relative to other background and moving objects within the image.

(a) (b)

Figure 142: Complete image frames containing abandoned bags, (a) CAVIAR dataset [80] and (b) AVSS dataset [85].

As we mentioned in the beginning of this when performing pre-attentive processing we are analyzing images for either motion or contextual change, such as abandoned bags. As shown earlier, contextual change detection requires either a reference image or significant higher-level post-processing to differentiate moving objects from long-term stationary objects. As we are limiting the processing to only low-level pre-attentive vision, GMM is not capable of differentiating contextual change from motion-based change. Therefore we do not provide any context specific performance curves for contextual change for GMM.

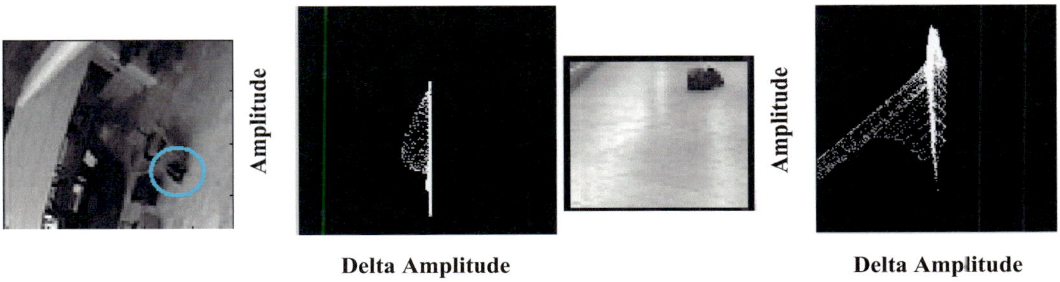

(a) (b) (c) (d)

Figure 143: Fractal measure *versus* object of interest size:, (a) grayscale region showing bag from CAVIAR -2 [80], (b) phase plot of region with fractal measure 1.21, (c) grayscale region showing bag from AVSS Medium [85], and (d) phase plot of region with fractal measure 1.62 [117].

Chapter, when performing pre-attentive processing we measure the performance of the pre-attentive processing system with the Receiver Operating Characteristics

(ROC) curve. The ROC curve provides a measure of detection probability *versus* false alarm probability which is an ideal measure for pre-attentive vision since high levels of false alarms will overwhelm the higher level vision system. We will present two sets of ROC curves, one set for the detection of moving objects and the other set for the detection of contextual change (abandoned bags). The image sequences selected are particularly interesting because they not only have abandoned bags representing contextual objects of interest but they also have moving objects of varying size, from relatively small objects representing people in the far field of view to the subway car which is quite massive. Additionally, the lights of the subway car (headlights and cabin lighting) provide very interesting spatio-temporal illumination variation which must be suppressed in a pre-attentive vision system. This data set is particularly challenging for both SAD and GMM since the developers of the GMM approach acknowledge that "it cannot adapt to quick-lighting changes and cannot handle shadows well" [33]. The issue of rapidly changing illumination causing GMM approaches to fail is particularly problematic for a pre-attentive vision system since it would cause high numbers of false alarms.

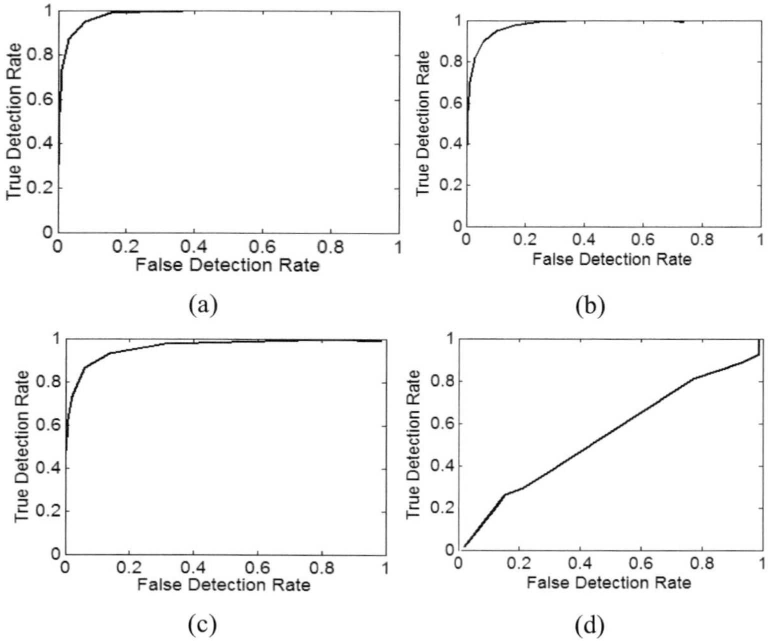

Figure 144: Motion (delta t = 8 frames) ROC Curves for AVSS Medium, (a) Box Counting dimension, (b) Information Dimension, (c) SAD, and (d) GMM [117].

Fig. **144** and Fig. **145** provide the ROC curves for detecting motion in both the AVSS and the CAVIAR II datasets. In Fig. **144** and Fig. **145** (a) and (b) we provide the ROC curves for the chaos-based approach using the Box Counting and Information Dimension as fractal measures of the phase plot trajectories. Fig. **144** and Fig. **145** (c) and (d) provide the ROC curves for the traditional approaches of SAD and GMM. Note the high false alarm rate of the GMM is due to the ghosting caused by the rapidly moving people through the scene. Both of the chaos-based approaches have superior performance in both data sets over these traditional measures.

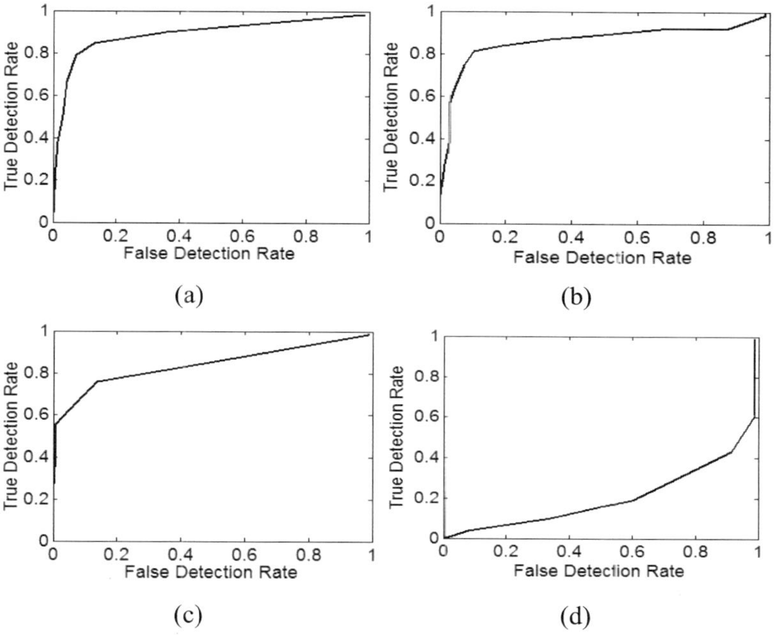

Figure 145: Motion (delta t = 8 frames) ROC Curves for CAVIAR II, (a) Box Counting dimension, (b) Information Dimension, (c) SAD, and (d) GMM [117].

Fig. **146** and Fig. **147** provide the ROC curves for the performance against detection of contextual change in the scenes, namely the detection of the abandoned bags. In this case we do not compare GMM since it does not have the ability to use a reference image, but rather it is used with extensive post-processing to extract the long term changed objects from the short term motion. Fig. **146** and Fig. **147** (a) and (b) again show the performance of the Box

Counting and the Information Dimension measures for the chaos-based approach against the traditional SAD method. Once again, the chaos-based approaches demonstrate better performance by having higher detection probabilities at lower false alarm rates.

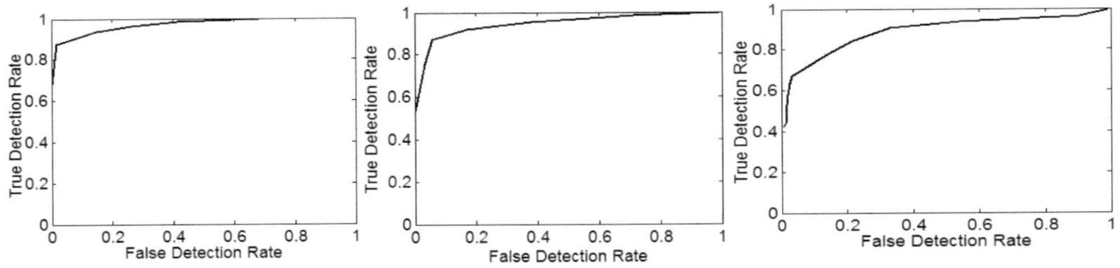

(a) (b) (c)

Figure 146: Context ROC Curves for AVSS Medium, (a) Box Counting dimension, (b) Information Dimension, and (c) SAD [117].

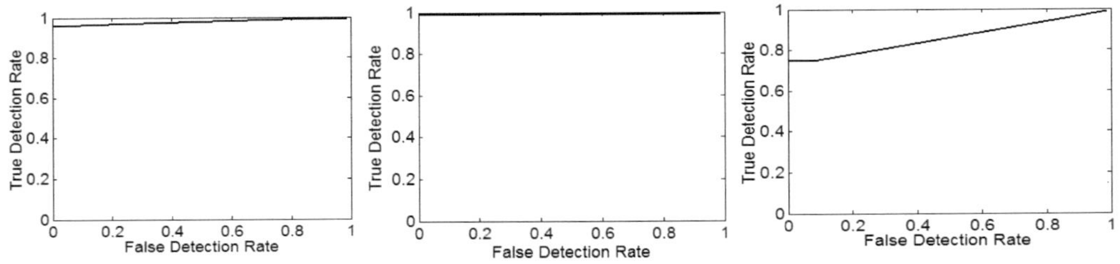

(a) (b) (c)

Figure 147: Context ROC Curves for CAVIAR II, (a) Box Counting dimension, (b) Information Dimension, and (c) SAD [117].

Fig. **148** shows an example of motion-based attention direction for an image pair within the complete sequence using the Box Counting method. The resultant phase plots shown in Fig. **148** (a) and the regions of attention direction for the left bag scenario of the CAVIAR dataset is provided in Fig. **148** (b) [80]. This is a relatively simple dataset with a single person moving through the scene depositing the bag in front of a set of furniture. Likewise Fig. **149** shows an example of motion-based attention direction for an image pair within the complete sequence for the more complex AVSS subway scene [85]. Fig. **149** (a) shows the phase plots for all of the grid cells and Fig. **149** (b) shows the regions of attention direction caused by people exiting the subway car.

Fig. **150** shows example detected regions for the Box Counting method with the resultant phase plots shown in Fig. **150** (a) and the regions of attention direction provided in Fig. **150** (b) for the very difficult and interesting subway scene. Notice in Fig. **150** (a) the phase plot in grid-cell (3,1) has a slightly elevated fractal dimension since the illumination change is due to very complex moving illumination patterns caused by passengers moving in the subway car and their shadows being cast through the car window onto the platform. While this region was detected by the Box Counting method due to its relative complexity, it is interesting to note that this spatio-temporal illumination still appears as trajectories bound within pie-shaped regions due to the multiplicative nature of illumination. Thus subsequent post-processing associated with higher level vision processing could be employed that would utilize some additional topological measures other than fractal dimension.

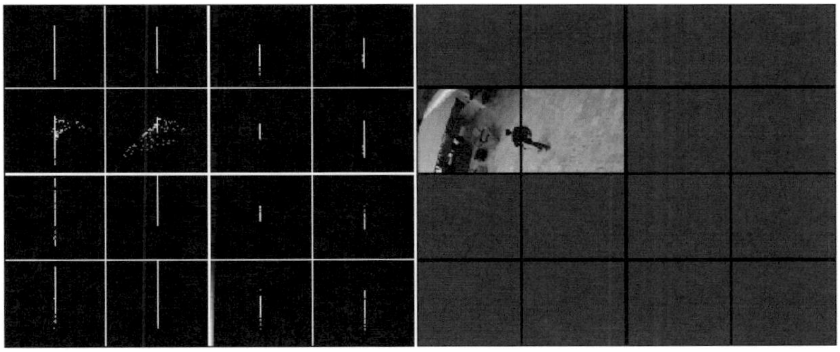

(a) (b)

Figure 148: Examples of motion-based attention direction for the CAVIAR dataset: (a) Phase plots and (b) resultant detections from Box Counting Method for a single set of frames.

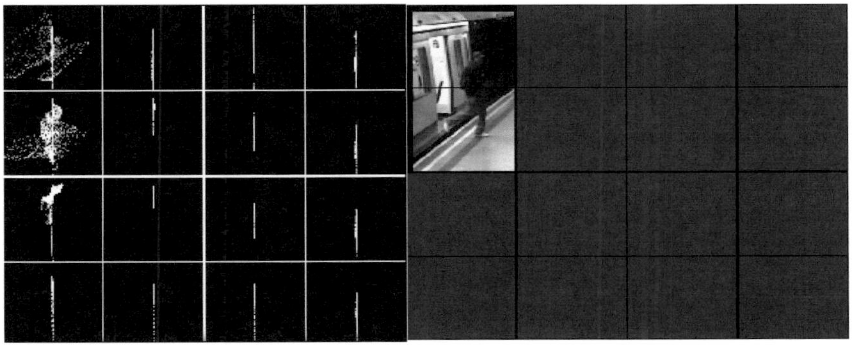

(a) (b)

Figure 149: Examples of motion-based attention direction for the more complex AVSS subway sequence: (a) Phase plots and (b) resultant detections from the Box Counting Method.

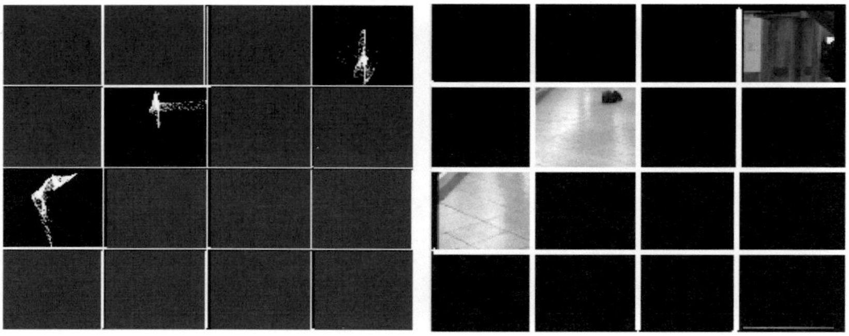

(a) (b)

Figure 150: Examples of contextual-based change detections and false alarm regions for the complex subway scene: (a) Phase plots from Box Counting Method, and (b) resultant detections from the chaos-based processing [117].

The relative merits of the chaos-based approach can only be fully appreciated when compared with the attention detections provided by the traditional SAD and the GMM approaches. First Fig. **151** (a) shows the regions of interest for motion-based attention direction for the simpler CAVIAR dataset using the SAD detection method and Fig. **151** (b) shows the regions of detection for this sequence for the GMM method. Likewise, Fig. **152** (a) shows the regions of interest for motion-based attention direction for the simpler CAVIAR dataset using the SAD detection method and Fig. **152** (b) shows the regions of detection for this sequence for the GMM method. As can be seen in both of these examples of the GMM method, the long decay rate of the GMM approach leads to a ghost of the target subject that must be removed with subsequent higher level processing functions.

Likewise Fig. **153** (a) shows all the regions of interest for contextual change detected by SAD in the more interesting subway scene. The extensive detections throughout the subway terminal are due to the elevated illumination levels projected across the platform region by the subway car with its doors open and its windows. Clearly a higher threshold for the SAD detection is required, however due to the small size of the object of interest, a higher detection threshold results in the object being lost. Likewise, the results for the subway scene using GMM are provided in Fig. **153** (b) where there are numerous regions where the GMM algorithm detect false alarms due to its sensitivity to illumination change (grid cells (*(1,2), (2,3), (2,4), (3,1)* and *(4,1)*) as well as the slow decay nature of the GMM (remaining grid cells). These limitations of the algorithm result in a high false alarm rate which either results in higher data recording requirements for commercial security systems or results in the need for significant post processing for smarter object detection systems as described, for example, by Tian *et al.,* in [33].

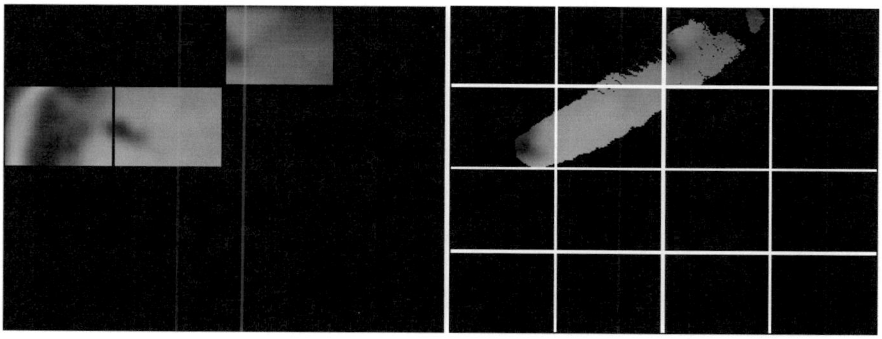

(a) (b)

Figure 151: Examples of motion-based attention direction for the CAVIAR dataset: (a) results for SAD and (b) results for GMM.

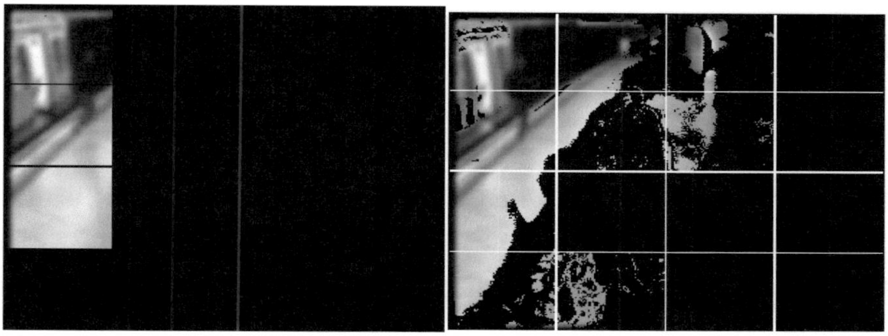

(a) (b)

Figure 152: Examples of motion-based attention direction and false alarm regions for an AVSS sequence: (a) detections from SAD and (b) detections from GMM [117].

The enhanced performance of the chaos-based algorithms is due to the fact that the fractality of the phase space trajectories is a direct measure of the *information content* within the trajectory, thereby serving as a direct measure of pre-attentive interest. This is in stark contrast to other common approaches such as SAD or

GMM which only directly measure change in grayscale space. The power of using the mathematical structure of illumination change is in the fact that both SAD and GMM methods treat all grayscale differences the same while our proposed chaos-based approach takes advantage of the structural differences in phase space between illumination change and motion/contextual change. This makes the traditional algorithms inherently highly susceptible to illumination changes, particularly the rapidly changing types of illumination that existed in the AVSS subway datasets.

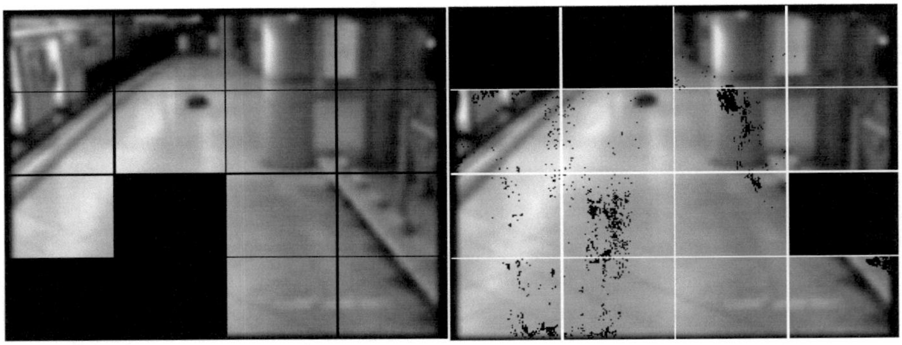

(a) (b)

Figure 153: Examples of contextual change detections and false alarm regions for: (a) sum of absolute difference processing, and (b) Gaussian mixture model processing.

CONCLUDING REMARKS

In this chapter we introduced the interesting application of pre-attentive vision, also referred to as attention direction. The goal of this type of processing in biological vision systems is to quickly alert the agent to possible changes in their environment that may be of concern. Because of the low-level nature of the processing, pre-attentive vision has three critical requirements: (i) it must have a high detection rate, (ii) it must have a very low false alarm rate, and (iii) it must be extremely fast. The processing flow required for a chaos-based approach to pre-attentive vision was provided which exhibited two parallel paths of processing, one for motion detection and one for contextual change detection. Depending on the goals of the system to detect motion or contextual change, either the motion path is used directly or it is used as a mask to remove moving objects from the contextual change path. The processing uses a global measure of fractality of the phase plot.

The algorithm was applied to two interesting datasets where suspicious bags were abandoned in public places. The performance of the algorithm was analyzing through ROC curves for the detection of motion and the detection of contextual change, two key goals of pre-attentive vision. The chaos-based approach was compared to two traditional grayscale approaches, SAD and GMM. The chaos-based approach outperformed both of these measures in terms of maximizing the detection probability while minimizing the false alarm rate.

 Application of Chaos and Fractals to Computer Vision, 2014, 186-201

CHAPTER 7

Applications to Attentive Vision – Chaotic Basins of Attraction for Motion and Contextual Change Segmentation

Abstract: Attentive vision relates to the isolation of objects of interest to be able to advance them to yet higher level vision systems such as object tracking and object recognition. Since the task is related to object segmentation from the background it will require the application of local measures of fractality in phase space. These local measures will be used to identify the regions of phase space that correspond to interesting behavior such as a moving object or contextual change. Once these regions in phase space are identified the vision system will use the mapping from phase space to the original image space to identify the pixels that correspond to the object of interest. This is markedly different from traditional methods such as Optical Flow and Gaussian Mixture Models where the decisions of important change are made in the grayscale space of the original images, yet this space is corrupted by spatio-temporal illumination changes. The performance of the chaos-based approach is demonstrated both for motion-based segmentation and also contextual change-based segmentation.

Keywords: Attentive vision, motion segmentation, change-based segmentation, optical flow, orbit compaction.

SEGMENTING CHANGING OBJECTS IN SCENES

Detection and segmentation of objects of interest from their background have been an area of intensive research in computer vision for decades. The goal of these algorithms is to utilize some feature of the grayscale images to differentiate the object of interest from the background or to partition an image into regions of common characteristics. This chapter will focus on using motion and change cues to differentiate the objects of interest from the background, and Chapter 8 will focus on using the textural characteristics of the image to divide it into regions of common texture. In both of these chapters we will apply chaos-based *features* to provide the cues for segmentation. There have also been a few authors that have applied the concepts of chaos to the segmentation *algorithms* rather than to the features for segmentation. For example, Melkemi *et al.,* applied chaotic agents to the classic Markov Random Field algorithm in [119]. Jin-Yu *et al.,* applied the concepts of chaos theory to augment the behavior of a genetic algorithm for Infrared image segmentation in [120] and Ma *et al.,* applied a chaotic

Michael E. Farmer

optimization algorithm to the segmentation task in [121]. We will address chaotic optimization in Chapter 10 when we discuss chaotic approaches to classification and recognition.

Detection and segmentation of objects based on their motion in images, including in the presence of spatio-temporally varying illumination have been the subject of intensive research for many years, with two more recent examples provided in [26] and [54]. To date none of these motion segmentation algorithms have been shown to be generally superior. Interestingly, the outputs of many of these algorithms can vary dramatically, particularly in the presence of complex spatio-temporally varying illumination patterns. Fusing the outputs of multiple segmentation algorithms proved effective in reducing these effects [123]; however there are two resulting drawbacks, (i) the fusion of multiple algorithm outputs is computationally prohibitive in most applications, and (ii) fusion addresses a solution to the problem of differing results for each algorithm but does not provide an understanding of the reasons for these differences. In addition to motion-based segmentation, the detection and segmentation of contextual change is also of great interest. This process is made significantly more difficult when spatio-temporally varying illumination is present in the image sequence. Various background subtraction algorithms develop models which attempt to identify regions of illumination change from regions of contextual change [27, 28, 30, 34, 116]. As with motion segmentation, none of these approaches have proven universally more successful, however.

One interesting observation here is that all of these methods, both for motion and contextual change, operate on the grayscale imagery. However, the grayscale image space is the result of a complex interaction of: (i) the motion of object of interest, (ii) its surface characteristics, and (iii) the external illumination pattern, which makes it difficult to separate the effects of illumination and motion [55]. The human visual system is capable of ignoring relatively complex spatio-temporally changing illumination due to the spatial organization of the optical receptive fields [2]. Unfortunately, manmade systems have been more limited in their ability to detect motion and change in the presence of spatio-temporally varying illumination [26, 55, 56, 116].

A CHAOS-BASED ALGORITHM FOR IMAGE SEGMENTATION USING MOTION OR CONTEXTUAL CHANGE

The processing flow for the proposed system for motion and change detection is provided in Fig. **154**. Note there is a strong similarity to the processing for the pre-attentive vision processing introduced in the last chapter, as the initial steps are identical, and only the later ***Segment Phase Plots*** and ***Segment Grayscale Grid Cells*** are new processing steps. There is, however, a distinct difference in the ***Compute Fractal Dimension*** as we will see below due to the fact that for attention direction we are only concerned with change within a grid cell and hence we can use a global measure of fractal dimension. However, for motion and change segmentation we must apply a *local* measure of fractal dimension to be able to segment the actual object of interest from the scene.

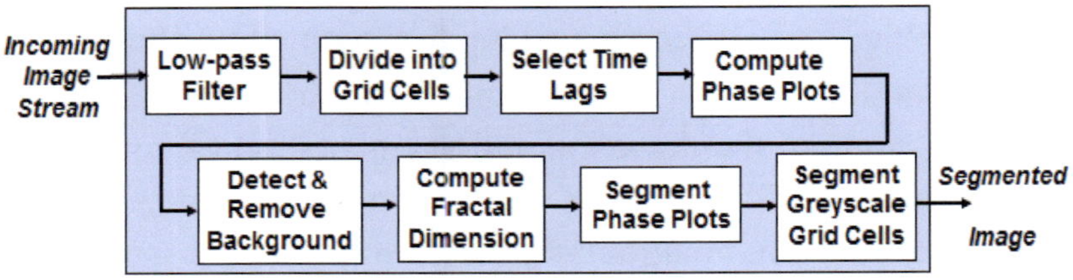

Figure 154: Processing flow for chaos-based motion and contextual change segmentation [124].

The step ***Compute Fractal Dimension*** requires that for each pixel in the original image, we assign a fractal dimension to the change in amplitude of that pixel. This requires two things:

(i) a local measure of the fractal dimension so that for each point in the phase plot we can compute the fractal dimension of that point, and

(ii) a mapping of each point in the phase plot back to the original grayscale image so we can identify the original pixels that are to be segmented as being part of the object of interest.

Recall in Chapter 3 we described developing a look-up table for the phase plot that would record where each point in the grayscale domain mapped onto the phase trajectory. This look-up table is now used to provide the grayscale image segmentation as we will describe below.

The Holder exponent was shown in Chapter 5 to be an effective local measure of fractal dimension. The Holder exponent is computed for each location in phase space and a histogram of the values is created. Regions of the phase plot that correspond the more chaotic (*i.e.* space filling) behavior will have a higher Holder dimension. Fig. **155** shows a moving object and its resultant phase plot and Fig. **156** provides an example of illumination change and its resultant phase plot. Fig. **157** (a) provides a pseudo-color image of the Holder exponent for each location of the phase plot in Fig. **155** (c). Likewise, Fig. **157** (b) provides a pseudo-color image of the Holder exponent for each location of the phase plot in Fig. **156** (c). Notice that just as the two phase plots show distinctly different structures, the perceived spread in values of the Holder exponents in these two images appears quite different. This is expected since the local behavior of each phase plot is very different, with the motion-based phase plot showing significant space-filling nature, and the illumination-based phase plot showing the compact structure.

(a) (b) (c)

Figure 155: Recall phase plot behavior for moving object: (a) first image with motion [67], (b) next image with motion, (c), phase plot.

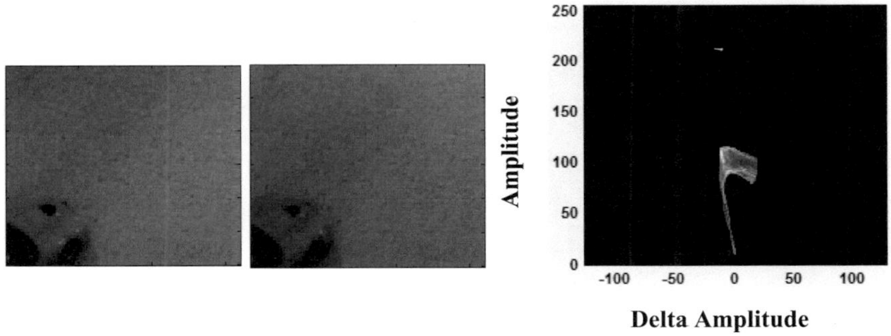

(a) (b) (c)

Figure 156: Recall phase plot behavior for illumination-only change: (a) first image with moving illumination [74], (b) next image with moving illumination, (c), phase plot.

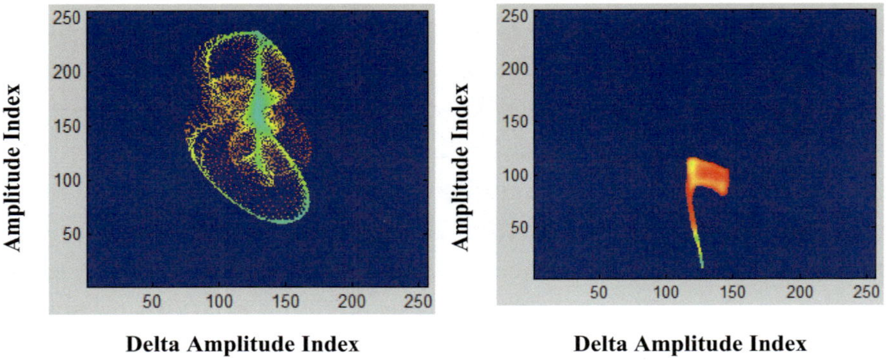

(a) (b)

Figure 157: Pseudo-color Holder exponent images for (a) phase plot in Fig. **155** (c) and (b) phase plot in Fig. **156** (c).

The processing in ***Segment Phase Plots*** segments the Holder exponent image of the phase plot to determine the regions in the phase plot that may be due to motion and contextual change in the original grayscale image sequence. The Holder exponent image and the original phase plot have a one-to-one correspondence so by segmenting the Holder exponent image we are effectively identifying (*i.e.* segmenting) the regions in the phase plot that have fractal behavior. By performing the segmentation in phase space, the chaos-based approach is provided its inherent immunity to illumination change. The first step in this processing is to generate the histogram of the Holder exponent image from the Holder dimension images. The details for the processing are in the pseudo-code below. Note the characteristics of these histograms are distinct for images where there is motion or contextual change *versus* for images with only illumination based change. For the phase plots in Fig. **155** (c) and Fig. **156** (c) the histograms are provided in Fig. **158** (a) and Fig. **158** (b) respectively. The histogram in Fig. **158** (a) shows a typical 'double-hump' behavior of a phase plot with motion. The region of the histogram with higher Holder exponent corresponds to the regions of the image where there is motion or contextual change. As illumination change does not exhibit fractal behavior in phase space, regions with illumination change should have low Holder dimension as can be seen in Fig. **158** (b).

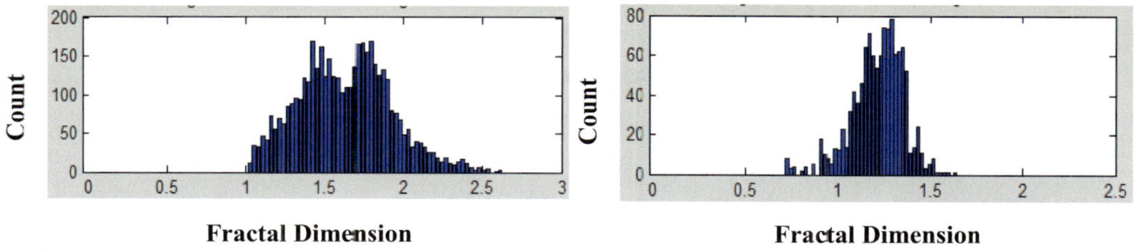

(a) (b)

Figure 158: Measures of fractality: (a) histogram of Holder exponent for phase plot in Fig. **155** (c) (motion), and (b) histogram of Holder exponent for phase plot in Fig. **156** (c) (illumination only) [124].

The next step in the processing is to threshold the Holder image. The goal of this thresholding is to identify the regions of the phase space trajectory that are exhibiting fractal behavior and are hence regions of chaos-like behavior that we have identified with an object moving through an image scene. While in many algorithms, threshold values are extremely image dependent (as in optical flow) we have found that a threshold equal to *1.4* has worked for all of the variety of images ranging from indoor to outdoor images, and for images captured from both CCD and CMOS cameras under both controlled and natural lighting. Its robustness results from the fact that the fractal dimension measures information change in the image sequence rather than the actual image grayscale values.

Pseudo Code 2: Segment Phase Plot Algorithm

1. Histogram Holder Exponent image of phase plot;
2. Find minima in Holder histogram closest to 1.4;
3. For each cell in Holder Exponent image, remove if less than threshold found in 2;
4. Set same cells as in Holder Exponent image in original phase plot to zero;
5. Use phase plot look-up table to only keep pixels in original image that have non-zero phase plot values;
6. Pixels remaining in original image are the motion segmented regions.

Fig. **159** provides an example image of a moving toy car with an illumination band moving across the image and the resultant phase plot. Notice the structure of the phase plot in Fig. **159** (c) contains both interesting chaos-like behavior and structurally dense behavior that corresponds to the motion and illumination change respectively. Fig. **160** (a) provides the pseudo-color image of the Holder exponent values for the phase plot and notice different regions are clearly discernable. Fig. **160** (b) provides the histogram of this Holder exponent image and notice the clear structure in the histogram of the regions due to illumination and the regions due to motion. The segmented fractal-only phase plot image is provided in Fig. **161** (a).

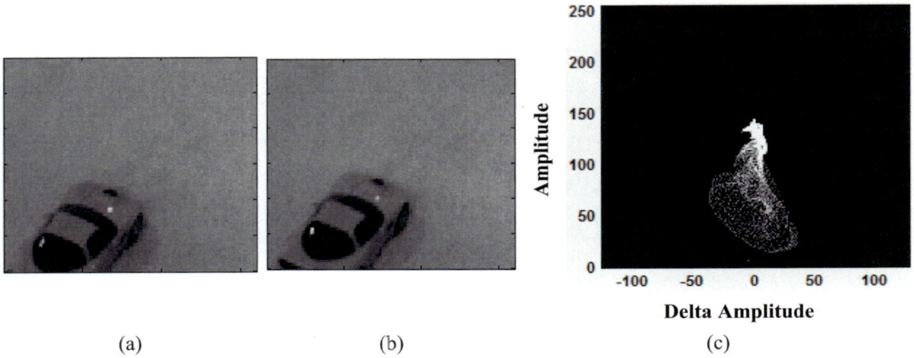

Figure 159: Recall phase plot behavior for moving object with illumination change across image: (a) first image, (b) next image with motion and moving illumination band, (c), phase plot [74].

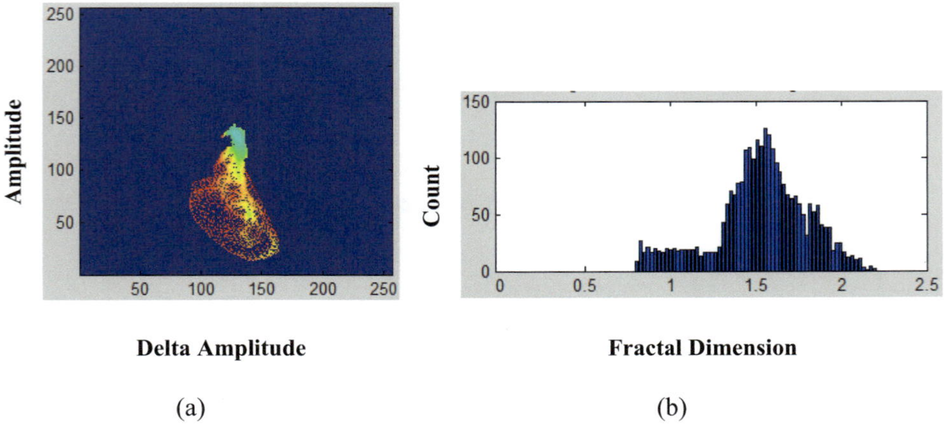

Figure 160: Holder exponent image and histogram, (a) Holder exponent image for phase plot in Fig. **159** (c) and (b) histogram of Holder exponent.

Once the fractal regions of the phase plot are identified the segmented phase plot is then sent to the ***Segment Grayscale Grid Cell*** processing. Here the algorithm uses the look-up-table that was developed during the construction of the phase plot (recall Chapter 3) to map each region of the remaining fractal phase plot to pixels in the original image. The resultant grayscale segmented image is provided in Fig. **161** (b) where we note the vehicle and some of its shadow region is retained. The shadow region around the vehicle is retained due to the fact that the local Holder exponent is computed by using increasing radius circles and is thus not purely local in nature. If precise segmentation is required then additional higher-level processing of the segmented object would be required. Also there are regions within the segmented image in Fig. **161** (b) that are missing within the image. These regions are due to the common aperture effect where the grayscale values within these regions were all identical so there was effectively no detectable change within these regions. Fig. **162** provides an example of segmentation for the image sequence in Fig. **155** where there are considerable aperture effects due to quantization of the camera pixel data in the image that resulted in the orbital compaction that we introduced in Chapter 5. While the chaos-based segmentation shown in Fig. **162** (b) has significant missing internal components, the optical flow based segmentation shown in Fig. **162** (c) has even larger missing sections.

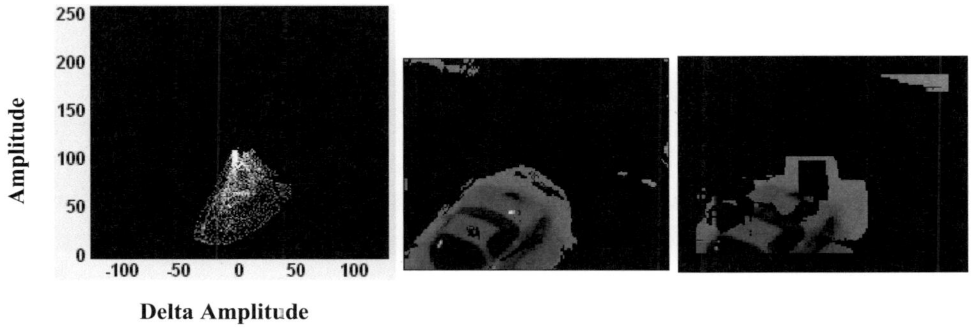

(a) (b) (c)

Figure 161: Example of segmentation: (a) segmentation of the phase plot based on the Holder exponent, (b) resultant chaos-based segmentation of original grayscale image [124], and (c) optical-flow based segmentation.

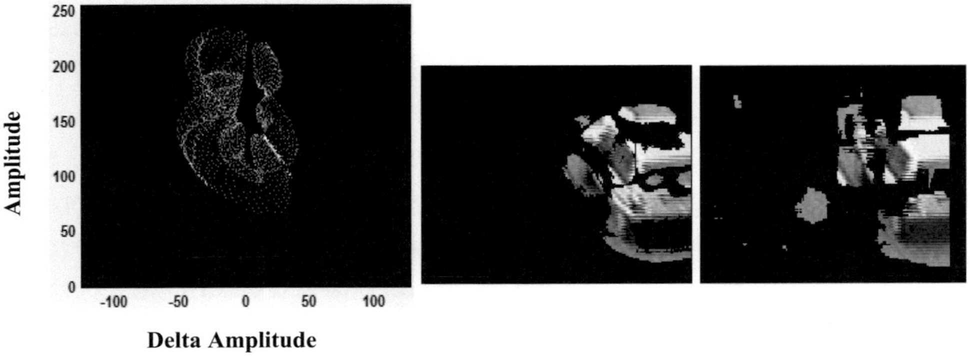

(a) (b) (c)

Figure 162: Example of segmentation (from Fig. **155**) with considerable aperture effects: (a) segmentation of the phase plot based on the Holder exponent, (b) resultant chaos-based segmentation of original grayscale image, and (c) optical-flow based segmentation.

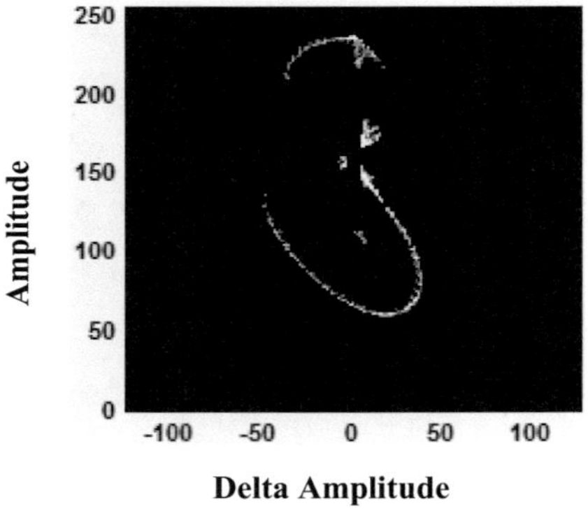

Figure 163: Remaining low fractal dimension trajectory in phase space that is clearly not due to illumination effects but rather due to trajectory compaction due to quantization [64].

While both the optical flow and the chaos-based approaches have missing regions within the segmentation caused by the aperture effect the proposed chaos-based approach has a mathematically sound mechanism for fixing them. Chapter 5 provided an approach to dealing with compacted regions of phase space using orbital trajectory analysis that is only available to the chaos-based approach. Fig. **163** shows the compacted areas in the phase plot trajectory that were not included in the fractal-based grayscale segmentation provided in Fig. **162**. Notice that the regions of the trajectory were clearly not due to illumination effects as the structure does not resemble the conic sections that are generated by the multiplicative nature of the illumination. Thus for applications that require higher quality segmentations, additional chaos-based processing may be performed to exploit these compacted phase space regions. The original processing flow defined in Fig. **154** can be augmented with the addition of an orbital processing stage as shown in Fig. **164**. For optical flow there is no equivalent concept and any additional improvements of the segmentation must rely on alternative image processing techniques such as morphology, edge following, *etc.* which are all quite computationally intensive.

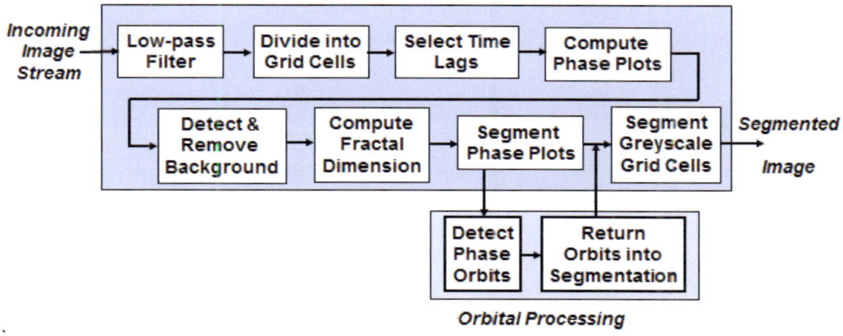

Figure 164: Augmented processing flow using orbital processing to reduce aperture effects [64].

The first stage of the Orbital Processing is the ***Detect Phase Orbits*** processing. This processing begins with the original phase plot being divided into two clusters using a simple 2-means clustering algorithm using two features: (i) the location in phase space and (ii) the original grayscale value of the original image. This is done since there is often a natural creation of two primary basins of attraction. This is typically due to one of two effects, first there are two basins corresponding to the object and its reflected/shadow region or, second due to natural grayscale distribution of the objects into generally light and darker regions. Separating the phase plot into two basins of attraction simplifies the ellipse detection since each basin often has a single distinct ellipse. The summary of the pseudo-code for this algorithm is below.

Pseudo Code 3: Detect Phase Orbits Algorithm

1. Use 2-means clustering algorithm to assign phase plot cells to one of two clusters;

2. For each cluster compute the Histogram Holder Exponent image of phase plot cluster;

3. Find minima in Holder histogram closest to 1.4;
4. For each cell in Holder Exponent image, ***keep*** if less than threshold found in Step 2;
5. These remaining phase plot cells represent dense non-fractal regions;
6. Feed all points into algebraic ellipse fit algorithm;
7. If eccentricity > threshold then dense region due to illumination and not compacted orbit so discard;
8. If eccentricity < threshold then keep ellipse fit parameters;
9. Re-insert phase plot locations that generated this ellipse back into the segmented phase plot;
10. Use phase plot look-up table to find motion segmented pixels in original grayscale image;

The pixels that may correspond to elliptical trajectories within each cluster are analyzed using the equations for algebraic ellipse fitting defined in Equation (83) through Equation (86) in Chapter 5. For each ellipse three quality measures are computed:

(i) The fraction of populated phase plot cells that lie on orbit *versus* number of populated phase plot cells that do not lie on orbit

(ii) Eccentricity of orbit (highly eccentric ellipses can be avoided by selecting appropriate time lags if the underling non-linear process is indeed motion)

(iii) Proximity of the center of the orbit to one of the two cluster centers of the phase plot (ellipses far from cluster centers are not likely related to a basin of attraction).

The phase plot cells that correspond to ellipses that pass the above three criteria are then passed on to the next stage of processing, ***Return Orbits into Segmentation***. In this stage, the phase plot cells corresponding to high quality elliptical orbits are returned to the segmented phase plot and considered cells of interest due to motion or contextual change. This combined phase plot is then used to identify pixels in the original grayscale image using the original look-up table that was generated in the original phase plot creation.

(a) (b) (c)

Figure 165: Recall example from Chapter 5 of the orbit-based segmentation enhancement, (a) original image in motion sequence [67], (b) segmentation from simply applying Holder exponent, and (c) resultant segmentation with pixels returned that resided on compacted elliptical orbits [64].

TYPICAL RESULTS FROM APPLYING CHAOS TO IMAGE SEGMENTATION USING MOTION AND CONTEXTUAL CHANGE

Fig. **166** (a) shows the complete processing for a series of image frames from the Reinhafen traffic flow sequence [67]. Fig. **166** (b) shows the phase plots for each mosaic computed. It also shows the regions in the image where higher lags are needed as a staggered stack of phase plots. The segmentation processing automatically increments the time lag and re-computes the phase plot when the resultant global fractal dimension is below a fractal threshold (usually fractal dimension=*1.4*). To prevent infinite cycling through increasing time lags, the system stops at a pre-determined maximum time lag. In this example, the system begins at a time lag of one and increments by factors of two to a maximum time lag of *16*. If the global fractal dimension is still low at this maximum lag then that grid cell is declared as having no moving objects of interest. This is in stark contrast to an optical flow approach where there is really no clear definition of when there is an adequate time lag between image frames until the final processing detects no object of interest.

Fig. **166** (c) shows the resultant motion segmentation from thresholding the Holder exponent histograms. All of the moving vehicles are detected, including the very slowly moving vehicles in grid cells (2, 1) and (2, 3) which are slowly advancing through the stoplight. For comparison, the result of motion segmentation processing this image using conventional optical flow is shown in Fig. **167** (b) and the image of the computed motion vectors in Fig. **167** (a). Note in particular the false low motion estimations along the fence boundaries and the various spurious effects in the roadway, while none of these false motions are found in Fig. **166** (c) from the chaos-based motion segmentation.

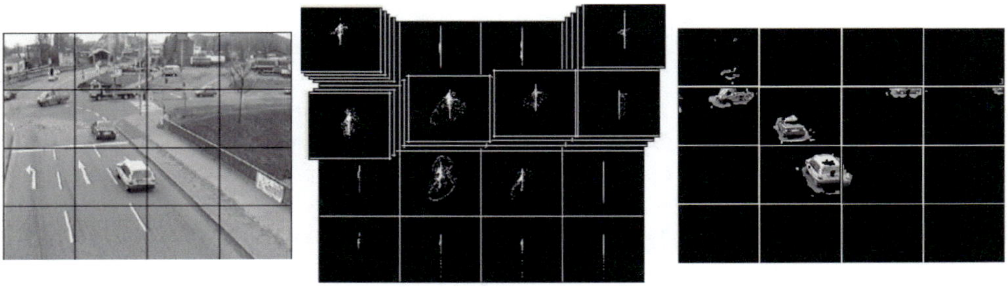

(a) (b) (c)

Figure 166: Motion segmentation using chaos: (a) mosaic of image [67], (b) phase plots of varying lags, and (c) final chaos-based segmentation [124].

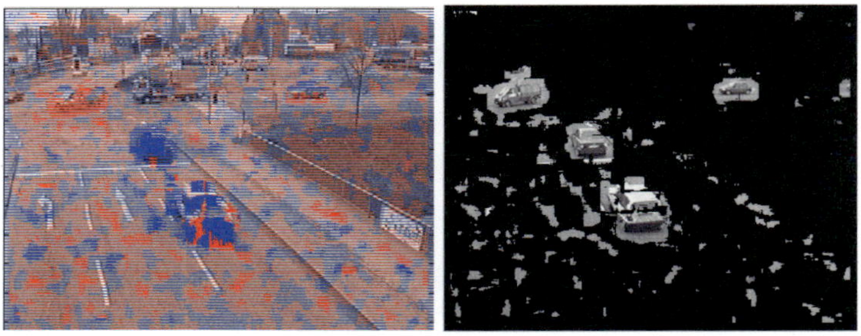

(a) (b)

Figure 167: Motion segmentation using optical flow : (a) resultant optical flow image with detected vectors and (b) segmented optical flow [124].

Recall that in addition to motion detection and segmentation, this chaos-based software can also perform contextual change detection using the identical processing in Fig. **154**. For contextual change analysis there is no time lag selection as the incoming image is compared with an a priori background image. The processing of the CAVIAR image [80] set is provided below in Fig. **168**.

Notice as with the pre-attentive vision processing the same grid cell concept is used to divide the image into manageable pieces. Then rather than a global fractal dimension being calculated, the local Holder exponent fractal dimension is used. The resultant Holder exponent image is thresholded at the same *1.4* threshold as used for motion since we are interested in a common change in information content irrespective of the grayscale values or even the application. Examples of the region where a left bag is deposited are provided in Fig. **168** (b) and (c), the phase plots for each grid cell are provided in Fig. **168** (d) and the final object segmentation is provided in Fig. **168** (e).

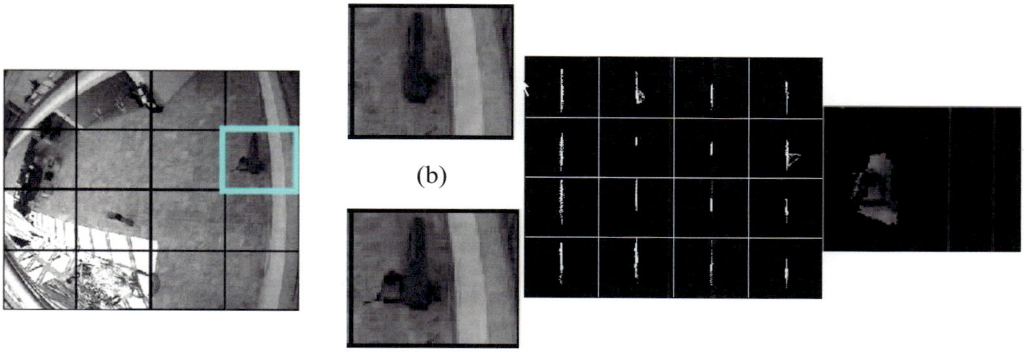

(a) (b) (c) (d) (e)

Figure 168: Contextual change segmentation using chaos: (a) second image [80], (b) grid cell from first image frame, (c) grid cell from second image frame, (d) grid cell of phase plots, and (e) final chaos-based segmentation showing left bag [124].

The chaos-based contextual change detection has also been proposed as an analysis tool for understanding human performance in contextual change. As can be seen in Fig. **169** (b) the change in the image is quite subtle and the color changes of the object of interest are also quite close to the background. Despite these difficulties the object change results in a significant bloom in the trajectory in the phase plot in Fig. **169** (c) and has a fractal-like space filling nature. The resultant object segmentation is provided in Fig. **169** (d) and the object of interest is well-captured. While there is no confounding illumination change in this image, the resulting segmentation is representative of the object of interest, even for an object that is relatively small compared to the field of view and not dramatically different in color or texture from the surrounding background.

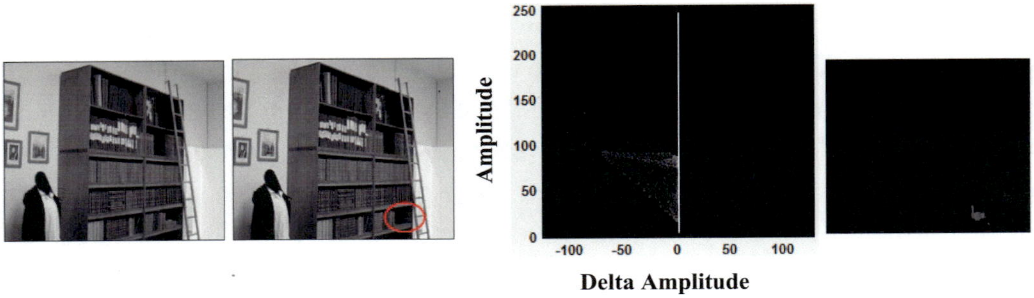

(a) (b) (c) (d)

Figure 169: Contextual change segmentation using chaos: (a) original image, (b) changed image, (c) phase plot of entire image, and (d) final chaos-based segmentation showing missing object.

CONCLUDING REMARKS

This chapter introduced the use of chaos-based techniques for the attentive vision processing task of motion and contextual change segmentation. We introduced the basic algorithm for motion and change segmentation and demonstrated its performance relative to optical flow techniques for comparing motion processing. We also introduced an enhanced motion segmentation algorithm that employs an algebraic analysis of the phase space as well as a fractal analysis to support the improved performance of the algorithm against the common aperture effect that troubles optical flow algorithms. In chaos theory the aperture effect manifests itself as a problem of trajectory compaction due in part to the quantized nature of the camera images. It results in interesting elliptical trajectories that, while not being fractal, are significantly different in algebraic structure from the conic sections associated with illumination change.

We demonstrated the improved motion segmentation performance of this enhanced phase space-based method. One of the key advantages of the chaos-based approach over the optical flow approach is the ease of selection of thresholds for motion and contextual change segmentation using chaos. The threshold values for the chaos-based approach are based on the effective change in information content in the image rather than the change in grayscale values.

The effectiveness of the algorithm on contextual change -based segmentation was also demonstrated on interesting images that contained combinations of contextual change, motion, and spatio-temporal illumination change. The resulting segmentations were highly representative of the original object and ignored changes due to illumination.

Application of Chaos and Fractals to Computer Vision, 2014, 202-232

CHAPTER 8

Applications to Attentive Vision – Chaotic Analysis of Texture for Segmentation and Classification

Abstract: The analysis of texture in computer vision has been of interest to researchers for many decades. The early work in texture by researchers such as Haralick discovered the utility of the greylevel co-occurrence matrix (GLCM) as a means for exploring the spatially varying affects present in various textures. Other means such as Gabor filters arose as being highly effective as well due to their ability to readily handle varying angles and varying spatial extents. The research in texture evolved distinctly from research in other areas of computer vision such as motion segmentation, non-textured grayscale segmentation, *etc.* This text is the first discussion of an approach to computer vision which can provide a unifying framework within which many computer vision problems can be solved using a common toolset, namely the analysis of images in phase space using tools from chaos theory. This chapter will further explore the role of spatial chaos in serving as a possible framework within which texture can be analyzed. The use of temporal chaos has proven useful throughout the text in approaching computer vision problems such as motion segmentation and image registration. Thus a common set of tools can now be used for solving the general computer vision problem.

Keywords: Texture, spatial chaos, GLCM, image segmentation, Lacunarity, homogeneity, Renyi spectrum, Kolmogorov-Smirnov measure, classification.

OVERVIEW OF TEXTURE PROCESSING

Texture analysis and the use of texture for image analysis functions such as image segmentation, object classification, and image retrieval have been a well-studied field for years. Texture has been proven useful for a variety of computer vision applications including remote sensing, face detection, document segmentation and even fruit detection in trees [125-130]. Due to humans apparent ease with regard to differentiating texture, it has been a common visual cue for tasks such as image segmentation with the idea being that objects will not only have different grayscale values from the background but also different textures from the background [107, 125, 126]. Simple grayscale-based segmentation, for static objects relies on the grayscale value of each pixel and often information of the neighborhoods of the pixels. Neighborhood algorithms include approaches such the Markov Random Fields algorithms [88] and the more recent variation of this by Melkemi *et al.,* in [119] where an initial chaotic map of the labels of various

Michael E. Farmer

segmented regions in the image and chaotic genetic algorithms are used with the MRF approach for determining the optimal segmentation. Another common neighborhood approach is the two-dimensional entropy-based algorithms used in [120, 121]. Ma *et al.,* in [121] have extended this concept by applying concepts from chaos theory to the grayscale-based segmentation of images; however they applied chaos to the process of threshold estimation *via* a chaotic optimization algorithm rather than employing the concepts of chaos for actual image features as done in this text. Likewise Jin-Yu *et al.,* in [120] applied the same entropy-based grayscale feature but determined the optimal threshold through a chaos-based genetic algorithm. These various segmentation approaches are based on general optimization theory which will be discussed in detail in Chapter 10. In this chapter we will focus on the chaos-based features of image texture to support scene segmentation and also texture recognition.

Texture-based image analysis also employs pixel neighborhoods, but examines the relative change in pixel amplitudes across varying neighborhoods rather than simply the probability distributions of pixels in the neighborhoods [14, 70] and in this chapter we will be using the concepts from spatial chaos theory to analyze these amplitude variations. The behavior of these amplitude variations not only can be used to differentiate textures but also to dictate whether what the image represents is really a texture. As Dixit and Hedge note: “If intensity variation appears to be perfectly periodic, it is call [a] periodic pattern not texture… [and] any completely random pattern would probably be called a ‘noise pattern’ rather than a texture [130]”. This distinction maps nicely into the application of the concepts of spatial chaos as a model for texture as these are also extremes for which systems are either purely deterministic or else purely random and not able to be modeled by chaotic principles. Likewise, interesting textures have complex, non-random variations in pixel amplitudes that result in interesting trajectories in phase space as is expected of chaotic systems. Fig. **170** provides a small collection of different textures from the Brodatz library, and the varying spatial extents and the varying behaviors across these spatial extents are clearly visible for the different textures [90]. Throughout the text we have seen that chaotic measures, particularly multi-fractal measures, can differentiate chaotic from non-chaotic signals. One interesting study by Yap *et al.,* employed multi-fractal analysis to pre-process face images to remove the amplitude variations due to skin texture to more easily identify the structural features of the mouth, eyes, and nose [131].

(a) (b) (c) (d)

Figure 170: Example textures from the standard Brodatz texture library [90].

The approaches to texture processing are as varied as the applications of texture with the mathematical methodologies falling into four basic categories:

(i) Statistical.

(ii) Geometrical.

(iii) Model-based.

(iv) Signal processing based.

As Dixit and Hedge note: "Because texture has so many different dimensions, there is no single method of texture representation that is adequate for a variety of textures [130]". Consequently, researchers use a variety of methods distributed across these four fundamental categories including: measures of grey-level co-occurrence matrices [70, 93, 125], local binary patterns [107, 126], fractal measures of grey-level co-occurrence matrices [97], direct fractal measures of the grayscale surface [10, 11, 13, 94, 95], Gabor filters [128, 132], wavelets[126], and most recently a fully illumination invariant approach using bi-directional texture functions [129].

By looking at the small collection of images from the Brodatz library in Fig. **170** it is clear that the resolution at which we view an image will dictate the texture that is visible in that image. This is reminiscent of the definition of a fractal boundary, where the measure of the length of the boundary will depend on the resolution at which the boundary is measured. It is not surprising then that one class of analysis methods for texture involve calculating the fractal dimension of the surfaces defined by the grayscale image using techniques such as the Blanket Dimension discussed in Chapter 5 [10, 13, 107]. Recall Pentland's observation that, "the fractal dimension has been shown to correspond closely to our intuitive notion of roughness…" [10]. Clearly the fractal dimension of textures will not be an adequate description since many textures, such as that shown in Fig. **170** (a) are not fractal patterns but rather are regular periodic patterns which was an issue addressed by Dubuisson and Dubes in [107]. Originally Mandlebrot and more recently Klonowski noted that "fractal dimensions cannot alone provide a complete characterization of the texture of an image and that fractals that have the same dimension may look very different" [58, 73]. Additionally, recall Tricot observed in [66], "The measure of a set does not determine its topological properties".

The most common traditional method for texture analysis is from the statistical family of mathematical techniques and uses the grey-level co-occurrence matrix (GLCM) originally proposed by Haralick [93]. Recall from Chapter 4 we demonstrated that the phase space representation of the spatial lags across an image and the GLCM representation are structurally and mathematically similar, The past effectiveness of GLCM-based analysis is not surprising given Klonowski's observation that, "signal complexity can be analyzed either in time domain, frequency domain, or in the system's phase space" [57]. Since the GLCM is structurally similar to the phase space representation these traditional methods were actually analyzing texture within a phase space framework, even though until now this observation was never made. The existence of spatial chaos has also been demonstrated in physical systems such as defects in solid state physics by Coullet *et al.,* [23]. The concept of spatial chaos provides a natural mechanism for modeling the variations in the pixel amplitudes across an image with texture. By analyzing the texture of images using chaos, we will continue to embrace the central premise of this text that the underlying objects in the image field serve as aperiodic forcing functions imparting chaos-like behavior on the output of the imaging sensor. In the case of texture the surface being imaged will impart aperiodic changes *via* the variation in the surface normal vectors across the scene. This observation is well matched to the previous discussions of texture being both non-random and non-periodic.

It is important to compare the traditional fractal analysis of textures with the chaos-based methods proposed in this text. Recall Klonowski noted: "[the raw signal fractal dimension] should not be confused with the fractal dimension of the… system in phase space" [57]. Thus while many authors such as Pentland had used fractal dimensions of the actual grayscale images to describe texture, the approach advocated in this text is one of defining the fractal dimension of the phase space that the textured surface produces. One common benefit throughout the text of using the phase space representation is the inherent immunity to illumination change and this benefit will be explored for texture analysis as well.

A CHAOS-BASED APPROACH TO THE ANALYSIS OF TEXTURE

Texture analysis requires analysis of the image amplitudes within a region of the image over a range of directions and spatial distances to capture the varying behaviors of the textures encountered. There are two types of processing for texture analysis: (i) image segmentation based on the partitioning of the image into regions of common texture, and (ii) texture classification based on a comparing an incoming texture with a library of textures. A typical processing flow for each of these applications is provided in Fig. **171**, where we note that the initial processing is identical for either segmentation or classification. In both cases the phase plots are computed for regions convolved across the image and the measures defined in Chapter 5 are computed for these phase plots. The processing defined also closely mimics the processing for GLCM-based texture processing which has been proven effective for texture analysis [130, 133]. A variety of the measures defined in Chapter 5 can be used to construct the feature vectors to capture the texture characteristics. The measures will either be stored locally for each pixel or for small neighborhood of pixels, for segmentation or aggregated into a global measure for classification.

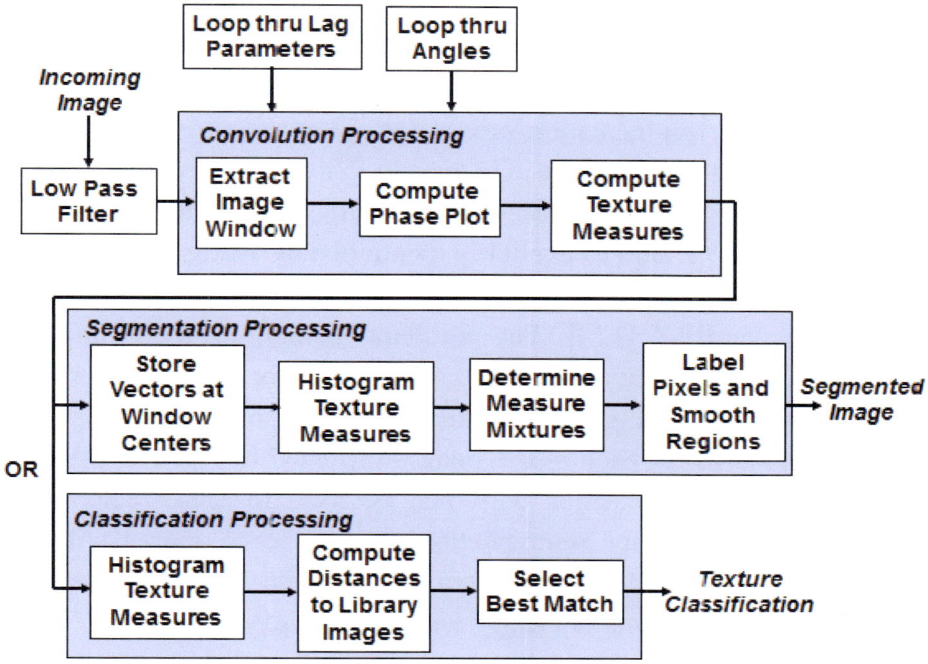

Figure 171: Processing flow for chaos-based texture segmentation or classification with common processing elements highlighted.

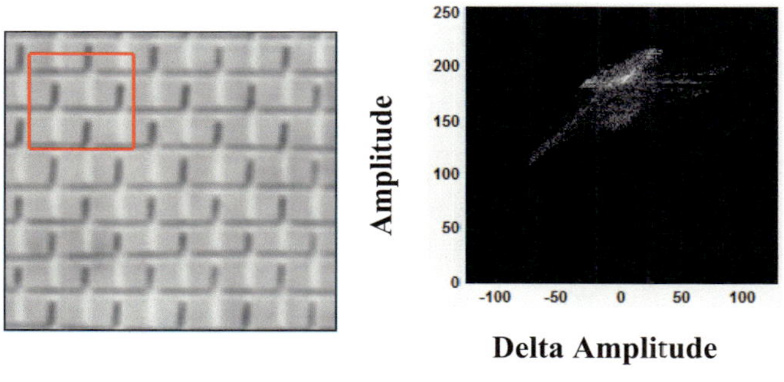

Figure 172: (a) Convolutional window for texture processing [90] and (b) the resultant phase plot.

The processing flow begins with the convolutional processing operations which require the bulk of the processing resources. In the convolutional processing for each spatial lag and each angle, the ***Extract Image Window*** step convolves a window of interest across the image and extracts the pixels within that window and advances them to the ***Compute Phase Plot*** processing where the phase plot for that window is generated as shown in Fig. **172**. The texture measures will be captured for each phase plot in the ***Compute Texture Measures*** process and stored at the pixel center of each window for segmentation in the ***Store Vectors*** stage of processing for segmentation processing. These feature vectors are also integrated into histograms in the ***Histogram Texture Measures*** for both segmentation and classification processing. Histogram generation of the texture measures is a common method as explicitly mentioned by Wang and Xie "…put a window on a pixel. Then the texture feature of the pixel is described by the histogram of the window" [126]. The resultant histograms for both the Box Counting and the Homogeneity measures are provided for two different textures in Fig. **173** (c) through (f). Fig. **174** provides additional histograms for some of the Lacunarity measures for each of the images provided in Fig. **173** (a) and (b). These histograms of the measures will then be used to either determine the mixtures within the image for segmentation or will be compared with stored histograms of the measures captured from the classifier training images. The complexity of these histograms is clearly visible, particularly in Fig. **173** (f) and Fig. **174** (d). We will see in the segmentation processing that the complexity of the histograms can cause problems with model fitting for segmentation; however these same complex histograms will provide added discrimination capability in the classification processing. The complexity of these histograms will encourage us to employ more complex classification methods which will utilize the entire histogram rather than more traditional methods that use feature vectors composed of estimates of means and variances.

(a)

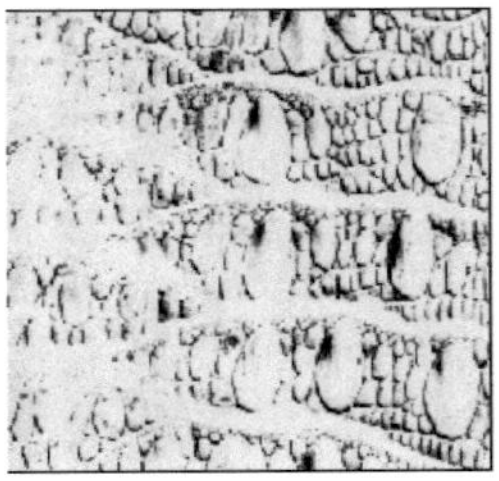

(b)

Fig. 173: contd….

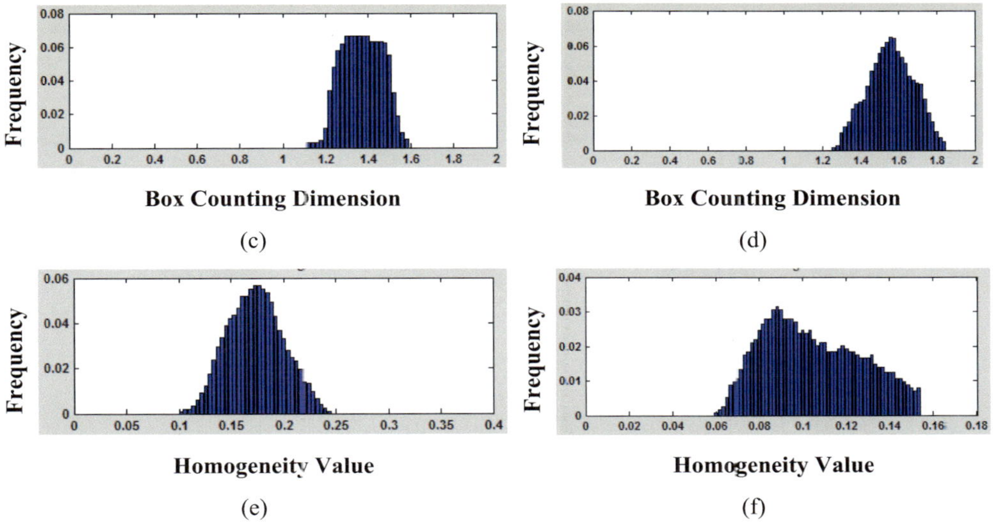

Figure 173: Histograms for images from the Brodatz texture library [90]: (a) Brodatz image D1 [90], (b) Brodatz image D10 [90], (c) histogram of Box Counting measure for D1 (d) histogram of Box Counting measure for D10, and (e) histogram of Homogeneity for D1, and (f) histogram of Homogeneity for D10.

A CHAOS-BASED APPROACH TO TEXTURE SEGMENTATION

For segmentation, the image is considered to be composed of multiple regions of differing textures and the goal is to partition the image into a collection of iso-texture regions. An example test image consisting of three different textures in four quadrants is provided in Fig. **175**. In this image two opposing quadrants are from the same Brodatz texture image but from different portions of the image and the other two quadrants are from two other Brodatz texture images. In Fig. **175** (b) through Fig. **177**(b) the phase plot for each identified window in the image is provided to demonstrate the differing structure of the phase plots for varying textures. Since none of these phase plots clearly resemble non-chaotic trajectories, there is a need for measures beyond simply estimating the fractal dimension. As a baseline we will employ the measures adapted from the original GLCM measures that were discussed in Chapter 5 to differentiate these various trajectories. We will also employ additional measures such as Lacunarity to create a more complete description of the distribution of the phase plot trajectory and we will show their improved efficacy over the traditional GLCM measures. The Renyi spectrum will also be shown to provide a strong differentiator between the various chaotic trajectories.

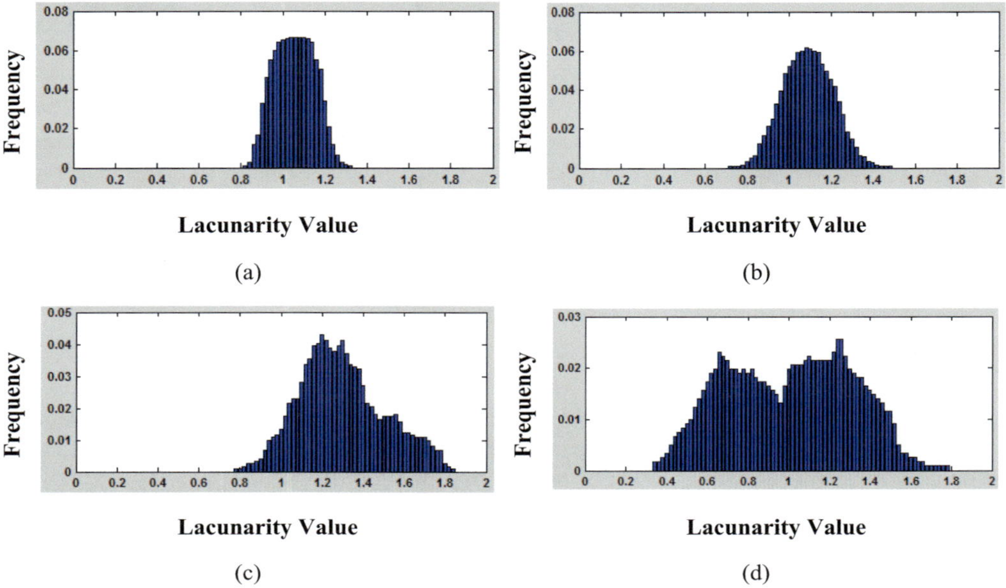

Figure 174: Histograms of Lacunarity measures for images from the Brodatz texture images in Fig. **173**: (a) histogram of 10th Lacunarity measure for lag=5 for D1 (b) histogram of 10th Lacunarity measure for lag=5 pixels for D10, and (c) histogram of 7th Lacunarity measure for lag=5 pixels for D1, and (d) histogram of 1st Lacunarity measure for lag=15for D10.

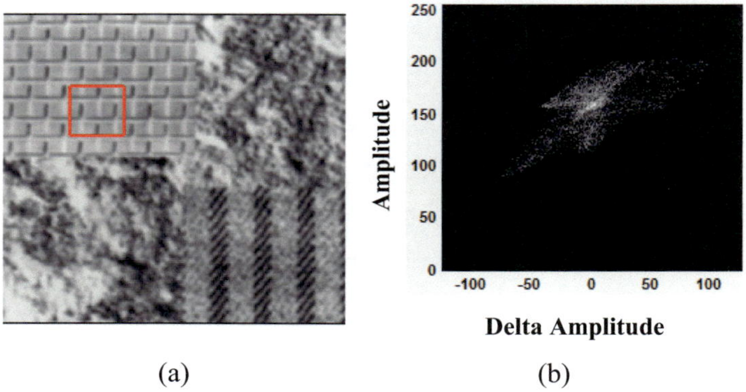

Figure 175: Convolutional window for texture processing and the resultant phase plot.

In the ***Segmentation Processing*** subsystem the ***Determine Measure Mixtures*** determines the parameters of the collection of unique textures within the image.

Fig. **178** (b) and (c) provide example accumulated histograms resulting from convolving the window across the entire image for a two of the possible texture measures, namely the Box Counting dimension and the Angular Second Moment. Clearly these histograms appear to be a mixture of histograms corresponding to the varying texture regions and the processing in this stage will estimate the parameters of these mixtures.

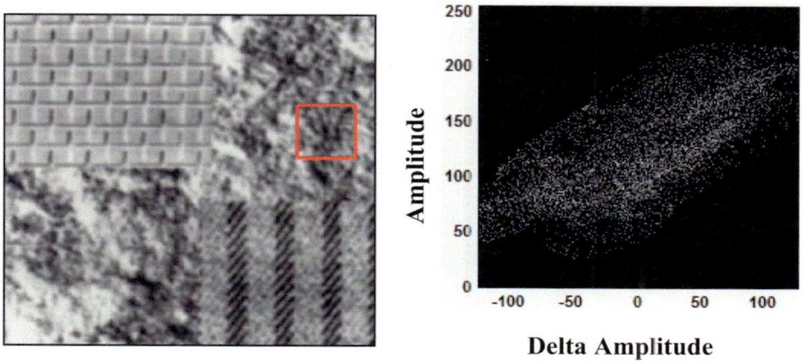

(a) (b)

Figure 176: Convolutional window for texture processing and the resultant phase plot.

For performing segmentation one must estimate the parameters of the mixtures within the feature histograms and the Gaussian Mixture Model algorithm is a very common methodology [125, 133]. One of the issues with GMM is that it does not provide a framework for estimating the actual model (*i.e.* number of mixtures) but only the parameters of the mixtures, but Zhang *et al.,* have developed a method in [133] for defining the model as well. Figueiredo and Jain previously addressed a general approach for defining the number of mixtures in a GMM in [134]. The GMM algorithm is based on the Expectation Maximization (EM) algorithm estimating the mixture of Gaussians that comprise an image, according to [118]:

$$p(x \mid \Theta) = \sum_{i=1}^{M} \alpha_i \cdot p_i(x \mid \vartheta_i) \tag{93}$$

where the α_i are the weighting factors, and ϑ_i are parameter estimates for each of the underlying Gaussians.

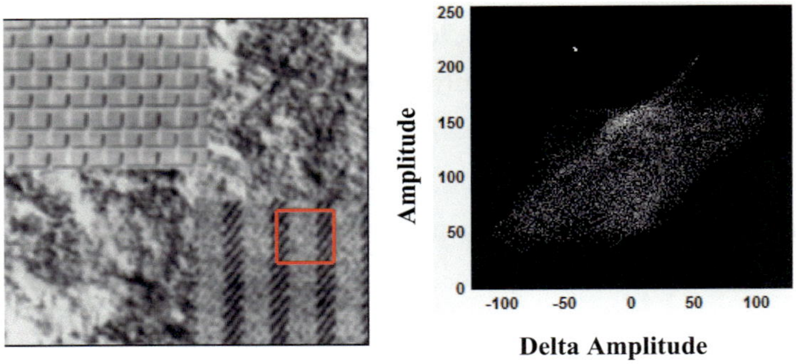

(a) (b)

Figure 177: Convolutional window for texture processing and the resultant phase plot.

(a)

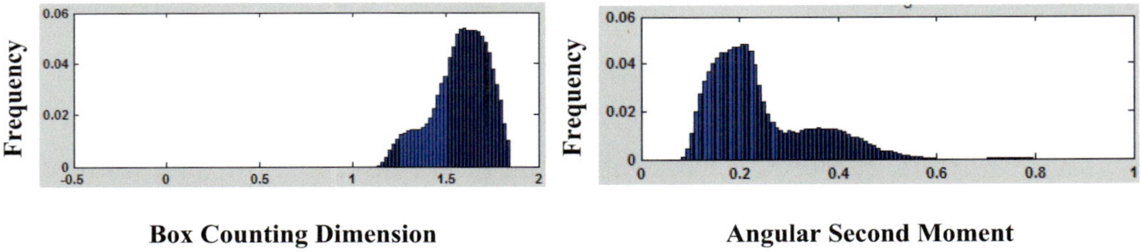

(b) (c)

Figure 178: Example test image for texture -based segmentation using a collage of the Brodatz images with example histograms of measures for the entire image, (a) the test image, (b) the histogram for the image using the Box Counting Dimension, and (c) the histogram for the image using the angular second moment.

One limitation is that for many textures and their measures, the resultant histograms are not normally distributed which can negatively impact the performance of the GMM algorithm. Referring back to Fig. **173** the reader can see the histograms for the Box Counting dimension and the homogeneity measures sometimes deviate from normal, particularly for the homogeneity measure in Fig. **173** (f). Other approaches to mixture analysis such the method proposed by Lee *et al.,* using Independent Components Analysis specifically for non-Gaussian signals is possible; however, it requires hundreds of iterations but does reduce to the GMM model when the underlying distributions are Gaussian [135]. Irrespective of the specific algorithm, the results from one of these labeling algorithms is a coarse region-labeled image where each pixel in the image is assigned a label based on its log-likelihood of being produced by one of the mixtures. Fig. **179** provides example segmentation processing where an image is composed of two distinct texture regions as shown in Fig. **179** (a). The resultant image of Box Counting values is provided in Fig. **179** (b), with the histogram of the Box Counting measures across the entire image provided in Fig. **179** (d), along with the detected Gaussian mixtures highlighted in green. The resultant labeled image is provided in Fig. **179** (c) with the boundaries of the two regions roughly following the actual boundaries in the original grayscale image.

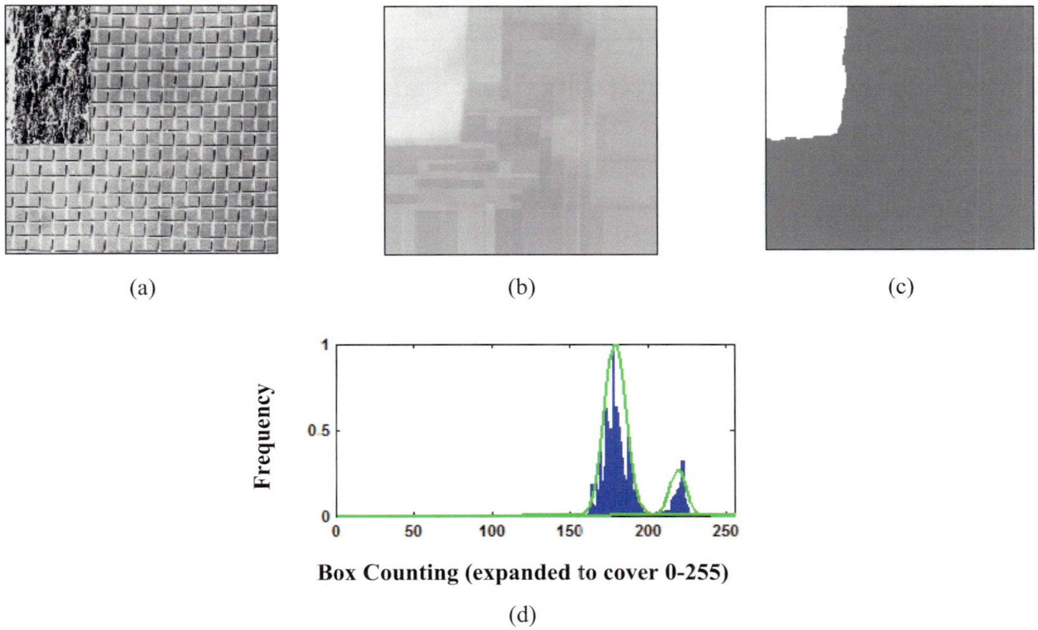

Figure 179: Segmentation using Box Counting measure: (a) Original image, (b) Box Counting measure image, (c) histogram of Box Counting measure, and (d) final segmentation into three mixtures.

A CHAOS-BASED APPROACH TO TEXTURE CLASSIFICATION

The unique aspect of the classification processing begins with the ***Compute Distances to Library Images*** function. The task is used to determine which texture from the library of training images is most similar to the current texture. The histograms created for the input image are compared to the histograms developed off-line for each image in the texture library. Since we are not comparing simple feature vectors such as means and variances, but rather complete histograms (approximated density functions) simple classifiers such as k-Nearest Neighbors or other feature-based classifiers are not suitable. Instead measures that compare the two histograms are required [136]. Since we know these histograms are often non-Gaussian, a non-parametric histogram comparison is required, and a popular measure is the Kolmogorov-Smirnov measure which compares the relative distance between two cumulative distribution functions (CDFs) of two random variables [137]. Fig. **180 (a)** and **(b)** provide histograms of the Box Counting measure for two different Brodatz images. Fig. **180**(c) provides the resultant approximations to the cumulative distribution functions and the green line highlights the largest difference between them which will be the Kolmogorov-Smirnov measure. Mathematically the Kolmogorov-Smirnov measure is defined as [137]:

$$D = \sup_{x}(|F_1(x) - F_2(x)|, \tag{94}$$

where the *supremum* function provides the maximum distance between the two distributions, $F_1(x)$ and $F_2(x)$. For a given confidence α the two distributions are considered to be different if [137]:

$$D_{1,2} > c(\alpha)\sqrt{\frac{n_1 + n_2}{n_1 n_2}}, \tag{95}$$

Where $c(\alpha)$ is the critical value defined for a particular confidence α and tables of these values are widely available [137]. For this particular application, n_1 and n_2 can be considered the same values since the number of samples (*i.e.* the number of windows convolved across the image for generating the histogram of measures) are so large.

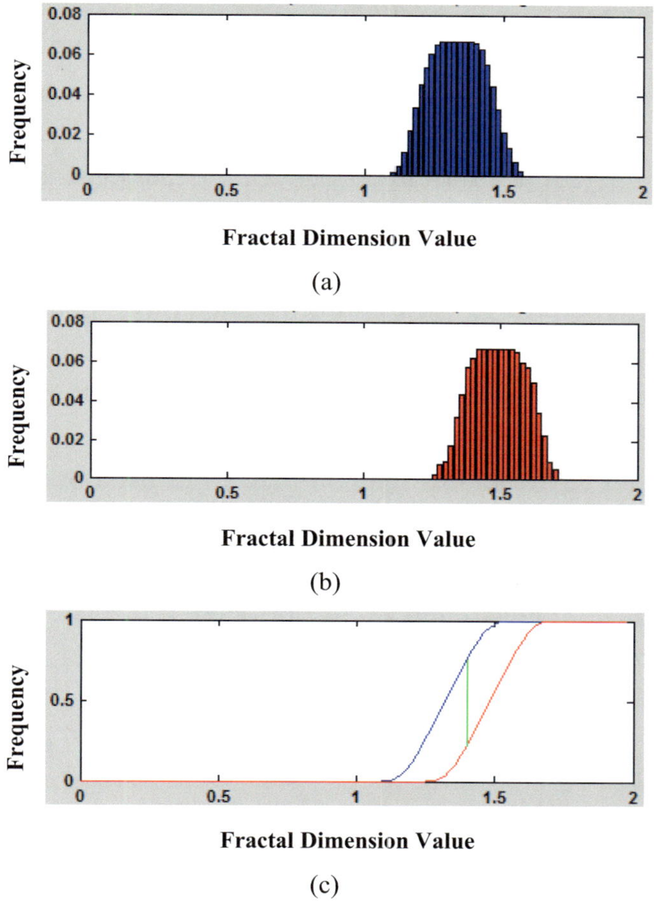

Figure 180: Example of K-S test for comparing two texture features, (a) Box Counting for Brodatz image D1, (b) Box Counting for Brodatz image D4, (c) CDFs with K-S distance highlighted in green.

There are two complicating issues with using the K-S statistic that must be addressed, (i) non-independence of the data samples, and (ii) multi-dimensional measures of fractality. The first issue with using the K-S statistic relates to the definition of n. It is assumed there are n independent identically distributed samples collected from each population. Since there is considerable overlap between the data windows used to generate the phase plots and compute the resultant measures, the samples are not independent. Thus the actual use of Equation (95) for determining whether the two distributions are identical within a particular confidence level is problematic; however, the use of Equation (94) and the general Kolmogorov-Smirnov measure to analyze the two distributions is still effective since the two distributions are generated using identical means. We will see in the following section that despite our inability to know the particular confidence level, the K-S test for the various texture measures is still an effective classifier.

The second issue is related to the multi-dimensionality of some of the texture measures. A definition of a multi-dimensional K-S statistic does not exist. The most common method for handling multi-dimensionality is to perform pair-wise analysis of all of the dimensions and then use the maximum value of the K-S measure. We do not advocate this method here since each of the dimensions is a distinctly different measure. Recall the Renyi spectrum where each positive value corresponds to a different fractal measure, and the negative values do not relate to any fractal values but rather provide a measure of a different characteristic completely. Instead we will create a vector of K-S measures on each of the specific measures and then compute the average K-S measure. We will show in the following section that this does indeed provide a quality classification metric.

TYPICAL SEGMENTATION RESULTS OF APPLYING CHAOS TO TEXTURE ANALYSIS

Test segmentation images were created using the Brodatz library image set. Regions were created corresponding to different textures and the segmentation test images are provided in Fig. **181** (a) and (b). The segmentation results are provided for both traditional texture measures, namely Angular Second Moment and Homogeneity, and for chaotic measures, namely the Box Counting method and Lacunarity. For the texture measures in each table we averaged the respective values over *5* step sizes (*5, 10, 15, 20*, and *25* pixels) and two angles (*0* and *90* degrees). For the Renyi spectrum the coefficients from *-5* to *5* were computed.

The values for the Lacunarity were calculated using a *50%* increase in box size from the initial size of two-by-two pixels, resulting in a ten element Lacunarity vector of [*2, 3, 5, 8, 12, 18, 27, 41, 62, 93, 140*] box sizes for which a single Lacunarity vector element is used for the segmentations.

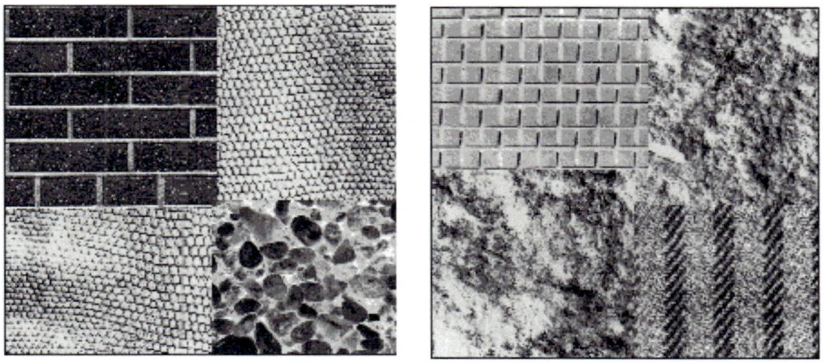

(a) (b)

Figure 181: The two test images for demonstrating the chaos-based segmentation.

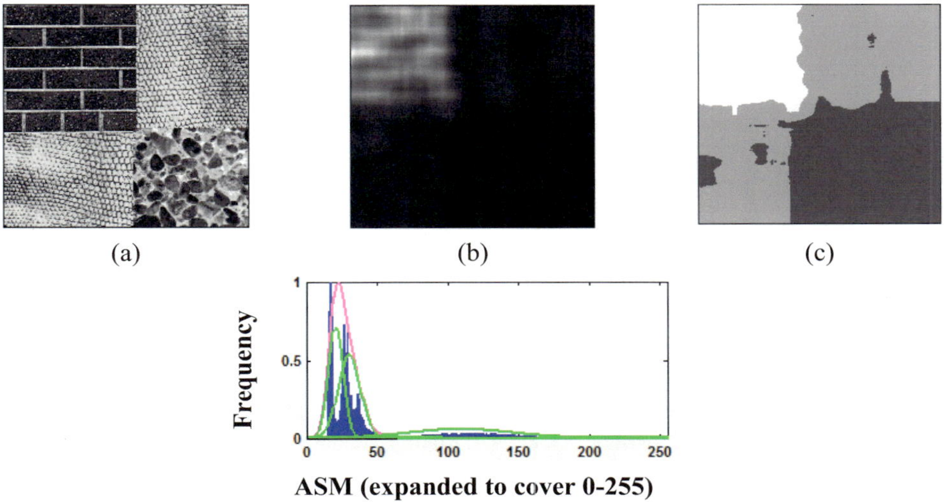

(d)

Figure 182: Segmentation using Angular Second Moment measure: (a) Original image, (b) ASM measure image, (c) histogram of ASM measure, and (d) final segmentation into three mixtures.

For simple comparison of the various measures when applied to segmentation, we will use the EM algorithm with Gaussian mixtures due to its ease of use. Fig. **182** through Fig. **185** provide example segmentations for the composite image in Fig. **181** (a) which to the human observer does appear to be relatively easy to segment.

Fig. **182** and Fig. **183** provide the results for two traditional texture measures applied to the phase space representation (Angular Second Moment and Homogeneity), and Fig. **184** Fig. **185** provide the results for two fractal measures applied to the phase space representations (Box Counting and the *9th* vector element of the Lacunarity). These segmentations are based on a single step size (*20* pixels) and a single angle (*0* degrees) which for this composite image produces reasonable segmentations. The resultant segmentations from each of the approaches are relatively equivalent. Interestingly, the Angular Second Moment provides one of the better segmentations.

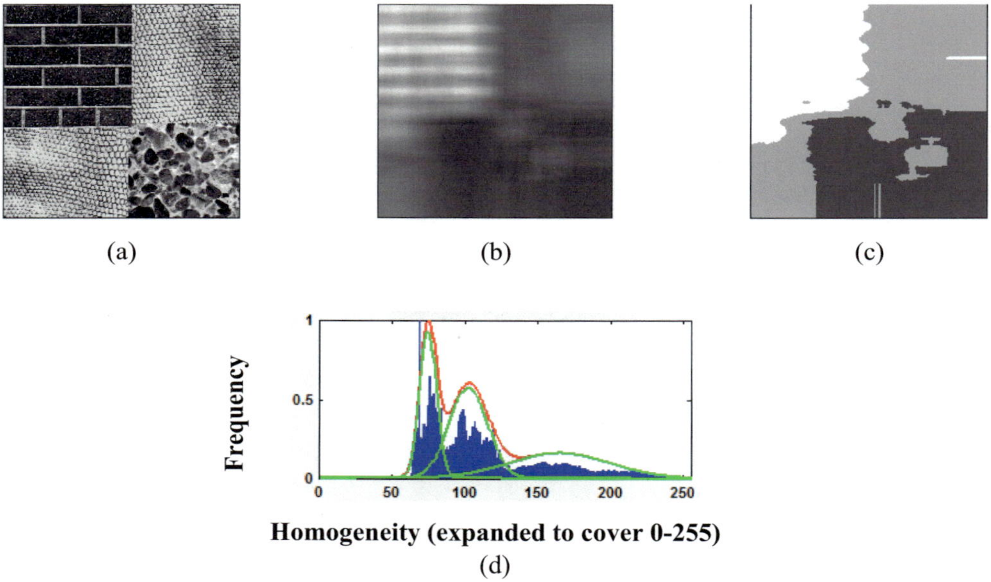

Figure 183: Segmentation using Homogeneity measure: (a) Original image, (b) Homogeneity measure image, (c) histogram of Homogeneity measure, and (d) final segmentation into three mixtures.

Fig. **186** through Fig. **189** provide example segmentations for the composite image in Fig. **181** (b) which is more difficult to segment due to the complexity of the textures in the upper right and lower left quadrants. Fig. **186** and Fig. **187** provide the segmentations for the traditional texture measures applied to the phase plot, namely Angular Second Moment and Homogeneity. Fig. **188** and Fig. **189** provide the segmentations for the fractal-based measures, namely Box Counting and Lacunarity.

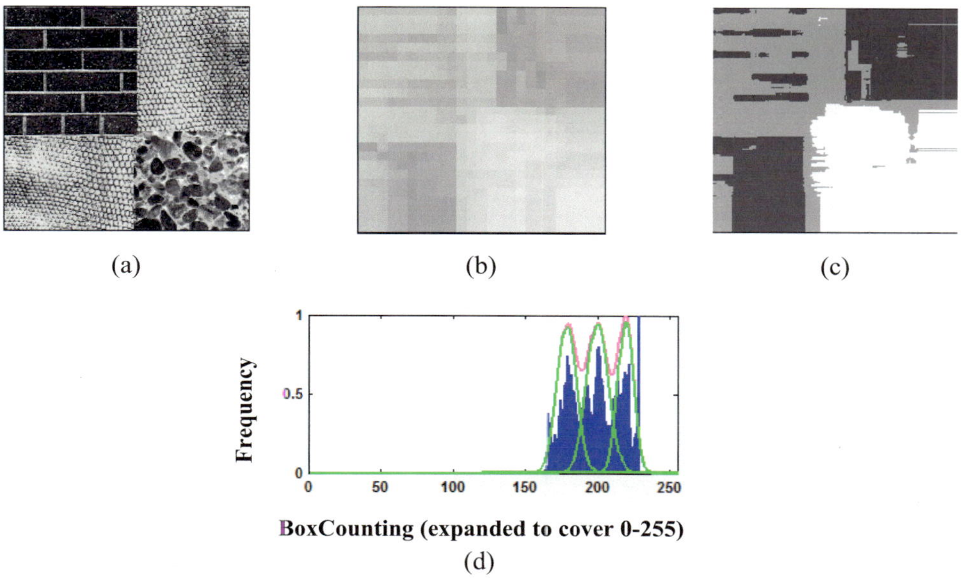

Figure 184: Segmentation using Box Counting measure: (a) Original image, (b) Box Counting measure image, (c) histogram of Box Counting measure, and (d) final segmentation into three mixtures.

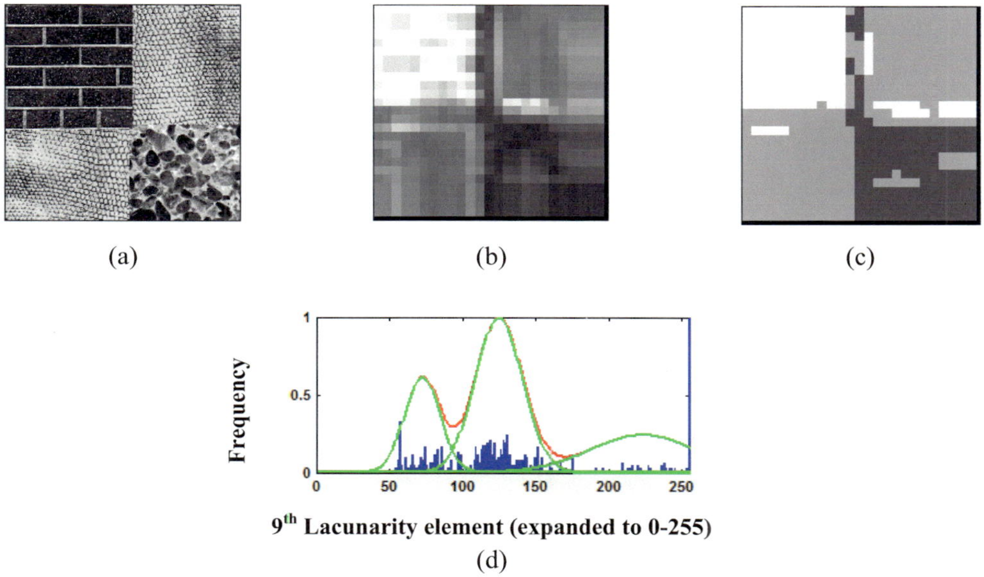

Figure 185: Segmentation using Lacunarity measure: (a) Original image, (b) Lacunarity measure image, (c) histogram of Lacunarity measure, and (d) final segmentation into three mixtures.

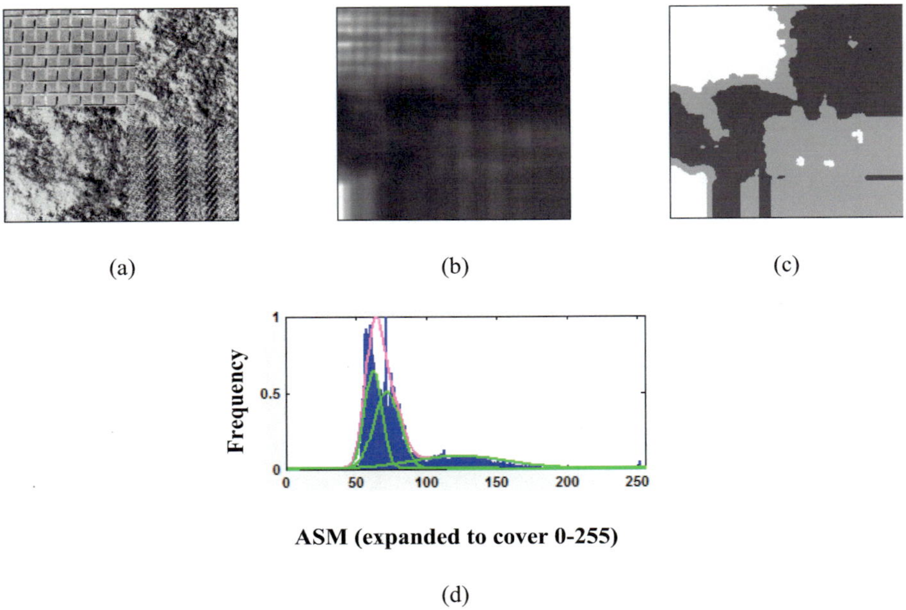

Figure 186: Segmentation using Angular Second Moment measure: (a) Original image, (b) ASM measure image, (c) histogram of ASM measure, and (d) final segmentation into three mixtures.

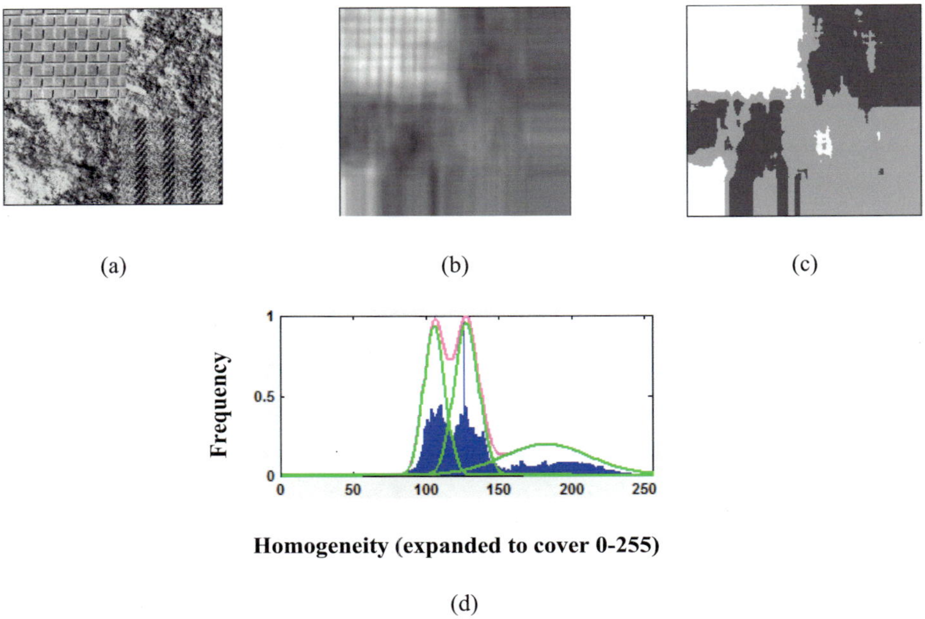

Figure 187: Segmentation using Homogeneity measure: (a) Original image, (b) Homogeneity measure image, (c) histogram of Homogeneity measure, and (d) final segmentation into three mixtures.

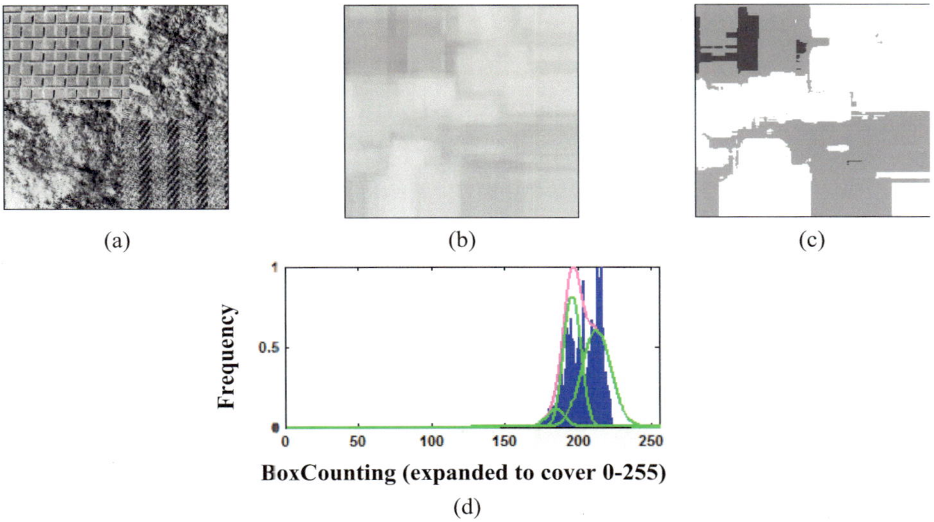

Figure 188: Segmentation using Box Counting measure: (a) Original image, (b) Box Counting measure image, (c) histogram of Box Counting measure, and (d) final segmentation into three mixtures.

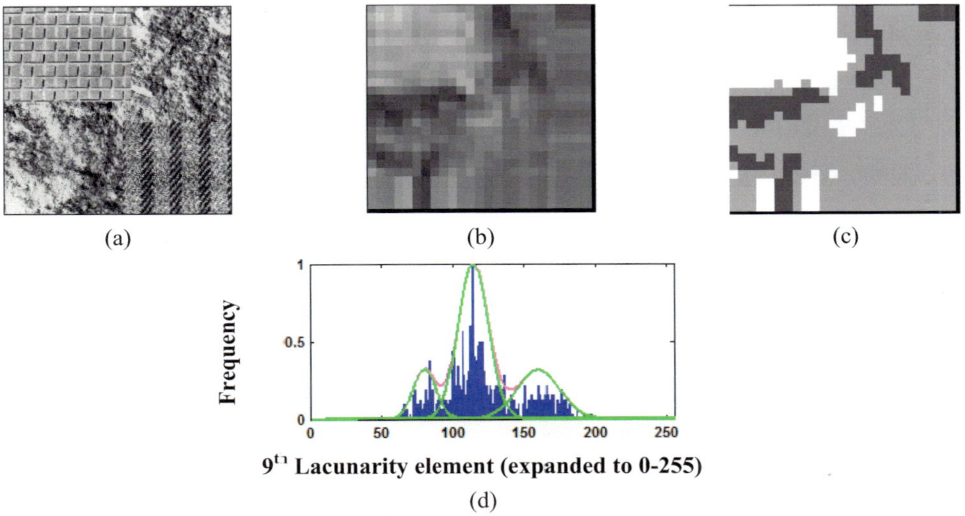

Figure 189: Segmentation using the 9th Lacunarity measure: (a) Original image, (b) Lacunarity measure image, (c) histogram of Lacunarity measure, and (d) final segmentation into three mixtures.

The resultant segmentations from each of the approaches are quite different for this more complex image with the fractal-based measures providing significantly poorer segmentations. Given the appearance of the measurement images in Fig.

188 (b) and Fig. **189** (b) it is difficult to even visually differentiate the regions in the composite image. Interestingly, the resultant measure histogram for the Lacunarity measure in Fig. **189** (c) does appear to fit a tri-modal Gaussian mixture however, the resultant segmentation is quite poor. Recall Fig. **174** showed the complex multimodal nature the Lacunarity measure can have, which certainly contributed to the poor segmentation; and this also probably contributed to the raw feature image in Fig. **189** (b) not being visually separable into the key regions. Once again, the Angular Second Moment provides one of the better segmentations.

TYPICAL CLASSIFICATION RESULTS OF APPLYING CHAOS TO TEXTURE ANALYSIS

Fig. **190** provides a sampling of the Brodatz texture library that we will use to provide results for employing the concepts of chaos theory to texture analysis. The approach we have taken is to divide each image into quarters and train the classifier on one of the quarters and then test the classifier on the remaining three quarters. This is intended to provide independence from the training data set and the test dataset. Table **7** through Table **12** provide the results for both traditional texture measures (Angular Second Moment and Homogeneity) and the measures related to analyzing phase plots for chaotic behavior, namely the Box Counting method, the Information Dimension, the Renyi spectrum, and Lacunarity. Along the columns of the table is each of the training images with the region used for training identified. The rows of the table provide the test results averaged over the three quadrants of the Brodatz images not used for training.

We computed the texture measures over *5* step sizes (*5, 10, 15, 20*, and *25* pixels) and two angles (*0* and *90* degrees).For the Renyi spectrum the coefficients from -*5* to *5* were computed. The values for the Lacunarity were calculated using a *50%* increase in box size from the initial size of two-by-two pixels, for a ten element Lacunarity vector of [*2, 3, 5, 8, 12, 18, 27, 41, 62, 93, 140*] box sizes. It is possible better performance can be achieved using additional angles and larger step sizes, but these sets of values provide a reasonable initial estimate of performance.

Table 7: Angular Second Moment K-S texture classification statistics

	D1 r1-c1	D2 r1-c2	D3 r1-c1	D4 r1-c1	D5 r1c1	D6 r1-c1	D7 r1-c1	D8 r1-c1	D9 r1c1	D10 r1-c2	D11 r1-c1	D12 r1-c1	D26 r1-c1	D30 r1-c2
D1 ~r1-c1	0.49	1.00	0.67	0.94	1.00	0.91	***0.21***	0.85	0.93	0.24	0.99	1.00	0.82	0.37
D2 ~r1-c2	0.93	***0.17***	0.92	0.78	0.44	0.95	0.29	0.57	0.83	0.38	0.49	0.41	0.93	0.58
D3 ~r1-c1	0.56	0.93	0.47	0.39	0.99	1.00	***0.26***	0.40	0.33	0.35	0.73	0.99	0.96	0.33
D4 ~r1-c1	0.52	0.95	0.42	0.70	1.00	1.00	***0.26***	0.46	0.49	0.34	0.80	0.99	0.95	0.34
D5 ~r1-c1	1.00	0.28	1.00	0.98	***0.12***	1.00	0.38	0.77	0.99	0.48	0.81	0.16	0.99	0.70
D6 ~r1-c1	1	1	1	1	1	***0.41***	0.67	1	1	0.70	1	1	0.53	0.97
D7 ~r1-c1	0.49	0.72	0.51	0.44	0.80	0.75	0.26	0.41	0.46	0.26	0.51	0.81	0.68	***0.25***
D8 ~r1-c1	0.69	0.77	0.61	0.34	0.91	0.99	0.26	***0.16***	0.36	0.36	0.48	0.90	0.96	0.36
D9 ~r1-c1	0.84	0.80	0.81	0.31	0.96	1.00	***0.30***	0.31	0.50	0.40	0.40	0.95	0.93	0.48
D10 ~r1-c2	0.36	0.94	0.31	0.56	0.99	0.86	***0.16***	0.51	0.52	0.21	0.80	0.98	0.77	0.24
D11 ~r1-c1	0.88	0.69	0.83	0.39	0.92	1.00	***0.30***	0.35	0.49	0.42	0.30	0.90	0.97	0.51
D12 ~r1-c1	0.91	0.26	0.92	0.88	0.17	0.99	0.34	0.66	0.90	0.44	0.72	***0.10***	0.97	0.62
D26 ~r1-c1	0.98	1.00	1.00	1.00	1.00	0.48	0.46	1.00	1.00	0.47	1.00	1.00	***0.18***	0.90
D30 ~r1-c2	0.41	0.80	0.41	0.34	0.88	0.88	0.14	0.40	0.36	0.19	0.54	0.90	0.82	***0.14***

In these tables the lowest K-S value corresponds to the best matching training image. These best match values are highlighted in bold and italics, and when these are incorrect they are further highlighted in red. In cases of ties in values, we default to the error case since the correct classification was not definitive. Notice that while the textures measures were defined for the GLCM, the Homogeneity measure, in particular, is equally effective for the phase space analysis. This underscores the equivalence between the two feature spaces that we had advocated earlier in Chapter 4. The Renyi spectrum results are also quite interesting when compared to the relatively poor results of the Box Counting Dimension and the Information Dimension provided in Tables **9** and **10** respectively. Recall that the zero and first order Renyi values are exactly the Box Counting and Information Dimension measures. This implies that the additional higher order and also negative order Renyi dimensions provide additional information for differentiating between two different chaotic trajectories, despite the fact that they are not considered accurate measures for differentiating between chaotic and non-chaotic trajectories.

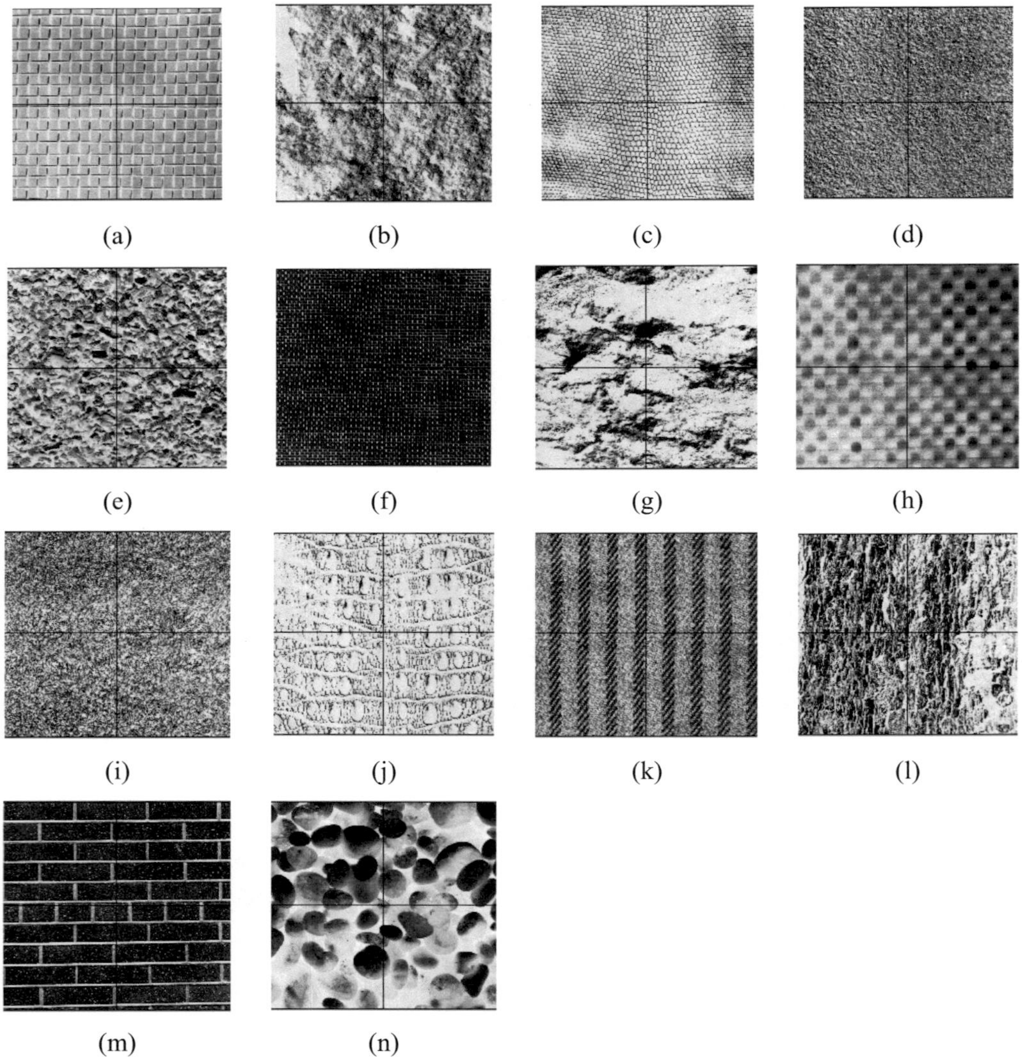

Figure 190: Textures from the standard Brodatz texture library showing the 2x2 grid with training performed using one grid and testing done on all four grids [90]: (a) D1, (b) D2, (c) D3 (d) D4, (e) D5, (f) D6, (g) D6, (h) D8, (i) D9, (j) D10, (k) D11, (l) D12, (m) D26, (n) D30.

It is also useful to analyze the errors for the various measures to better understand their performance. The Renyi spectrum and Lacunarity both have common errors in confusing images D4 and D9 and the confusion matrices in Tables **11** and **12**. If the reader will refer to Fig. **190** (d) and Fig. **190** (i) she will see these two images are quite common in texture. This is encouraging that these measures are confused on images that have very similar textures. This is in contrast to one of the errors for Homogeneity being confused between D2 and D4 which, referring to Fig. **190** (b) and Fig. **190** (d) we see are quite different.

Table 8: Homogeneity K-S texture classification statistics

	D1 r1-c1	**D2 r1-c2**	**D3 r1-c1**	**D4 r1-c1**	**D5 r1c1**	**D6 r1-c1**	**D7 r1-c1**	**D8 r1-c1**	**D9 r1c1**	**D10 r1-c2**	**D11 r1-c1**	**D12 r1-c1**	**D26 r1-c1**	**D30 r1-c2**
D1 ~r1-c1	0.31	0.55	0.58	0.90	1.00	0.69	0.46	0.68	0.85	*0.28*	0.81	0.98	0.68	0.52
D2 ~r1-c2	0.80	***0.26***	0.75	0.53	0.47	0.92	0.34	0.41	0.58	0.68	0.44	0.37	0.92	0.37
D3 ~r1-c1	0.50	0.34	***0.29***	0.46	0.84	0.93	0.31	0.54	0.41	0.44	0.57	0.83	0.88	0.46
D4 ~r1-c1	0.59	*0.28*	0.44	0.36	0.85	0.96	0.32	0.51	0.31	0.54	0.45	0.80	0.90	0.46
D5 ~r1-c1	0.97	0.39	0.87	0.80	***0.11***	1.00	0.54	0.67	0.90	0.87	0.71	0.56	1.00	0.57
D6 ~r1-c1	0.81	0.80	0.99	1.00	1.00	***0.22***	0.77	0.87	1.00	0.73	1.00	1.00	0.72	0.80
D7 ~r1-c1	0.52	0.32	0.52	0.51	0.77	0.73	***0.26***	0.37	0.46	0.41	0.58	0.67	0.75	0.29
D8 ~r1-c1	0.55	0.26	0.65	0.57	0.79	0.82	0.19	***0.14***	0.53	0.49	0.57	0.65	0.93	0.17
D9 ~r1-c1	0.72	0.25	0.59	*0.24*	0.81	0.98	0.31	0.43	0.33	0.63	0.43	0.67	0.94	0.41
D10 ~r1-c2	0.34	0.34	0.41	0.59	0.94	0.75	0.26	0.45	0.49	***0.25***	0.62	0.90	0.76	0.34
D11 ~r1-c1	0.68	0.28	0.65	0.46	0.71	0.95	0.42	0.49	0.49	0.59	***0.16***	0.72	0.84	0.49
D12 ~r1-c1	0.87	0.31	0.84	0.69	0.55	0.97	0.43	0.50	0.71	0.77	0.61	***0.21***	0.96	0.44
D26 ~r1-c1	0.77	0.75	0.90	0.97	1.00	0.69	0.78	0.94	0.97	0.65	0.89	1.00	***0.14***	0.84
D30 ~r1-c2	0.40	0.31	0.53	0.60	0.79	0.76	*0.19*	0.30	0.54	0.32	0.65	0.71	0.82	0.19

Table 9: Box Counting K-S texture classification statistics

	D1 r1-c1	D2 r1-c2	D3 r1-c1	D4 r1-c1	D5 r1c1	D6 r1-c1	D7 r1-c1	D8 r1-c1	D9 r1c1	D10 r1-c2	D11 r1-c1	D12 r1-c1	D26 r1-c1	D30 r1-c2
D1 ~r1-c1	0.15	0.87	*0.14*	0.41	0.90	0.88	0.87	0.39	0.33	0.62	0.57	0.96	0.38	0.95
D2 ~r1-c2	0.71	***0.12***	0.86	0.46	0.22	1.00	0.18	0.48	0.54	0.23	0.29	0.32	0.48	0.37
D3 ~r1-c1	*0.18*	0.80	0.29	0.30	0.85	0.91	0.81	0.32	0.22	0.52	0.47	0.92	0.28	0.91
D4 ~r1-c1	0.21	0.75	0.29	0.31	0.82	0.94	0.78	0.29	*0.19*	0.46	0.40	0.90	0.25	0.90
D5 ~r1-c1	0.88	0.16	0.97	0.70	***0.07***	1.00	0.08	0.69	0.76	0.48	0.54	0.10	0.70	0.13
D6 ~r1-c1	0.95	1.00	0.87	1.00	1.00	***0.19***	1.00	0.98	0.99	1.00	1.00	1.00	0.98	1.00
D7 ~r1-c1	0.74	0.16	0.85	0.56	0.12	0.98	***0.13***	0.56	0.62	0.36	0.42	0.22	0.57	0.26
D8 ~r1-c1	0.34	0.52	0.53	0.17	0.61	0.96	0.57	***0.12***	0.19	0.24	0.19	0.71	0.24	0.73
D9 ~r1-c1	0.35	0.50	0.57	*0.10*	0.62	0.99	0.58	0.17	0.18	0.18	0.15	0.72	0.15	0.75
D10 ~r1-c2	0.45	0.39	0.65	0.17	0.51	0.99	0.47	0.20	0.25	***0.10***	0.14	0.61	0.21	0.65
D11 ~r1-c1	0.36	0.51	0.56	*0.14*	0.63	0.99	0.59	0.17	0.17	0.22	0.17	0.73	0.26	0.76
D12 ~r1-c1	0.91	0.22	0.98	0.76	0.11	1.00	0.14	0.75	0.81	0.54	0.60	***0.07***	0.75	0.10
D26 ~r1-c1	0.29	0.55	0.50	0.15	0.66	0.97	0.62	0.23	0.14	0.25	0.25	0.75	***0.05***	0.77
D30 ~r1-c2	0.84	0.15	0.92	0.67	*0.11*	1.00	0.11	0.66	0.72	0.45	0.51	0.14	0.67	0.20

Table 10: Information Dimension K-S texture classification statistics

	D1 r1-c1	D2 r1-c2	D3 r1-c1	D4 r1-c1	D5 r1c1	D6 r1-c1	D7 r1-c1	D8 r1-c1	D9 r1c1	D10 r1-c2	D11 r1-c1	D12 r1-c1	D26 r1-c1	D30 r1-c2
D1 ~r1-c1	0.21	0.90	0.22	0.22	0.95	0.99	0.58	0.38	***0.19***	0.24	0.46	0.98	0.81	0.61
D2 ~r1-c2	0.71	***0.18***	0.66	0.65	0.29	0.99	0.24	0.51	0.68	0.60	0.44	0.37	0.96	0.26
D3 ~r1-c1	0.18	0.69	0.15	***0.13***	0.80	1.00	0.36	0.29	0.15	0.17	0.24	0.86	0.91	0.40
D4 ~r1-c1	***0.24***	0.90	0.27	0.33	0.95	1.00	0.60	0.45	0.25	0.27	0.50	0.97	0.78	0.63
D5 ~r1-c1	0.94	0.20	0.91	0.88	***0.08***	1.00	0.51	0.77	0.93	0.82	0.72	0.13	1.00	0.54
D6 ~r1-c1	1.00	1.00	1.00	1.00	1.00	***0.17***	0.97	0.99	1.00	0.99	1.00	1.00	0.68	1.00
D7 ~r1-c1	0.51	0.47	0.49	0.46	0.57	0.91	***0.24***	0.38	0.50	0.41	0.38	0.64	0.79	0.27
D8 ~r1-c1	0.32	0.57	0.38	0.34	0.69	1.00	0.25	***0.13***	0.32	0.28	0.23	0.77	0.92	0.22
D9 ~r1-c1	0.19	0.67	0.17	***0.16***	0.80	1.00	0.34	0.23	0.21	0.19	0.20	0.87	0.94	0.34
D10 ~r1-c2	0.26	0.60	0.25	0.23	0.71	0.99	0.28	***0.23***	0.25	0.24	0.23	0.79	0.88	0.30
D11 ~r1-c1	0.26	0.67	0.25	0.22	0.78	1.00	0.36	0.25	0.24	0.25	***0.19***	0.87	0.87	0.36
D12 ~r1-c1	0.91	0.19	0.88	0.86	0.14	1.00	0.49	0.75	0.90	0.80	0.72	***0.12***	1.00	0.52
D26 ~r1-c1	0.86	1.00	0.87	0.85	1.00	0.68	0.87	0.87	0.87	0.79	0.90	1.00	***0.13***	0.95
D30 ~r1-c2	0.37	0.49	0.39	0.35	0.60	0.99	***0.18***	0.18	0.36	0.28	0.26	0.67	0.91	0.20

Table 11: Averaged Renyi Spectrum K-S texture classification statistics

	D1 r1-c1	**D2 r1-c2**	**D3 r1-c1**	**D4 r1-c1**	**D5 r1c1**	**D6 r1-c1**	**D7 r1-c1**	**D8 r1-c1**	**D9 r1c1**	**D10 r1-c2**	**D11 r1-c1**	**D12 r1-c1**	**D26 r1-c1**	**D30 r1-c2**
D1 ~r1-c1	***0.31***	0.86	0.42	0.60	0.86	0.87	0.49	0.52	0.47	0.33	0.67	0.85	0.69	0.59
D2 ~r1-c2	0.69	***0.18***	0.77	0.41	0.29	0.71	0.39	0.39	0.50	0.61	0.36	0.28	0.61	0.48
D3 ~r1-c1	0.41	0.75	***0.24***	0.47	0.82	0.91	0.54	0.47	0.40	0.40	0.55	0.81	0.74	0.61
D4 ~r1-c1	0.35	0.64	0.52	0.39	0.70	0.78	0.43	0.35	*0.27*	0.42	0.42	0.68	0.61	0.51
D5 ~r1-c1	0.87	0.24	0.94	0.62	***0.13***	0.70	0.58	0.64	0.75	0.80	0.53	0.21	0.75	0.52
D6 ~r1-c1	0.87	0.72	0.95	0.72	0.70	***0.20***	0.70	0.74	0.78	0.83	0.68	0.74	0.49	0.69
D7 ~r1-c1	0.47	0.53	0.62	0.48	0.56	0.67	***0.23***	0.38	0.41	0.35	0.48	0.55	0.51	0.35
D8 ~r1-c1	0.40	0.50	0.56	0.31	0.59	0.77	0.33	***0.14***	0.25	0.42	0.31	0.57	0.57	0.44
D9 ~r1-c1	0.64	0.39	0.69	*0.29*	0.45	0.72	0.48	0.36	0.41	0.62	0.31	0.47	0.65	0.49
D10 ~r1-c2	0.36	0.72	0.37	0.49	0.77	0.86	0.39	0.41	0.41	***0.26***	0.51	0.77	0.66	0.49
D11 ~r1-c1	0.61	0.53	0.70	*0.35*	0.59	0.54	0.52	0.42	0.46	0.61	0.36	0.63	0.62	0.49
D12 ~r1-c1	0.76	0.22	0.86	0.55	0.20	0.73	0.45	0.52	0.60	0.69	0.51	***0.16***	0.67	0.49
D26 ~r1-c1	0.71	0.70	0.81	0.64	0.73	0.51	0.54	0.58	0.58	0.59	0.68	0.70	***0.13***	0.74
D30 ~r1-c2	0.51	0.48	0.67	0.41	0.49	0.66	*0.23*	0.38	0.45	0.40	0.40	0.51	0.63	0.24

Table 12: Averaged Lacunarity Vector K-S texture classification statistics

	D1 r1-c1	D2 r1-c2	D3 r1-c1	D4 r1-c1	D5 r1c1	D6 r1-c1	D7 r1-c1	D8 r1-c1	D9 r1c1	D10 r1-c2	D11 r1-c1	D12 r1-c1	D26 r1-c1	D30 r1-c2
D1 ~r1-c1	***0.24***	0.63	0.63	0.50	0.75	0.82	0.47	0.58	0.49	0.51	0.68	0.70	0.86	0.54
D2 ~r1-c2	0.61	***0.16***	0.32	0.44	0.34	0.49	0.48	0.26	0.53	0.75	0.25	0.27	0.97	0.61
D3 ~r1-c1	0.65	0.29	***0.13***	0.45	0.46	0.49	0.53	0.27	0.55	0.78	0.27	0.44	0.99	0.67
D4 ~r1-c1	0.54	0.57	0.55	0.17	0.78	0.82	0.39	0.50	***0.12***	0.61	0.62	0.66	0.97	0.54
D5 ~r1-c1	0.78	0.28	0.51	0.71	***0.12***	0.41	0.66	0.44	0.79	0.90	0.35	0.26	1.00	0.79
D6 ~r1-c1	0.84	0.46	0.54	0.77	0.43	***0.09***	0.71	0.53	0.82	0.93	0.46	0.43	1.00	0.84
D7 ~r1-c1	0.53	0.60	0.62	0.50	0.71	0.75	***0.30***	0.55	0.51	0.39	0.64	0.63	0.7[illegible]	0.34
D8 ~r1-c1	0.58	0.26	0.33	0.42	0.43	0.54	0.42	***0.19***	0.49	0.68	0.34	0.41	0.97	0.57
D9 ~r1-c1	0.52	0.54	0.48	***0.11***	0.76	0.78	0.42	0.46	0.15	0.64	0.58	0.64	0.93	0.58
D10 ~r1-c2	0.48	0.71	0.68	0.45	0.86	0.88	***0.31***	0.62	0.44	0.34	0.75	0.76	0.81	0.33
D11 ~r1-c1	0.73	0.22	0.27	0.58	0.31	0.43	0.60	0.32	0.68	0.87	***0.10***	0.30	1.00	0.73
D12 ~r1-c1	0.66	0.21	0.41	0.55	0.31	0.43	0.52	0.37	0.62	0.77	0.29	***0.19***	0.97	0.65
D26 ~r1-c1	0.88	1.00	1.00	0.97	1.00	1.00	0.85	0.99	0.97	0.71	1.00	0.99	***0.17***	0.76
D30 ~r1-c2	0.53	0.62	0.65	0.50	0.76	0.79	0.22	0.56	0.51	0.31	0.67	0.66	0.80	***0.18***

One of the strengths throughout the text of the chaos-based methods to traditional image processing techniques has been the robustness of the chaos-based approach to illumination. For motion segmentation the robustness is founded in the fact that illumination results in very non-chaotic phase space trajectories and hence is readily differentiated from motion. It is still important to ask what affect illumination will have on the accuracy of texture classification. Fig. **191** provides the classification accuracy of the Homogeneity and Lacunarity texture measures against the reduced Brodatz texture library shown in Fig. **190** for varying illumination amplitudes. Other traditional measures such as the Angular Second Moment were not included on the curve because their performance fell-off much more dramatically. The accuracies are plotted for image illumination reductions of *0.15* through *0.35* with the performance of the Lacunarity measure being more robust for through a *0.25* reduction in illumination while the Homogeneity measure experiences a steady reduction in performance. Clearly the Lacunarity measure provides a more graceful reduction in performance *versus* illumination. Direct illumination immunity is impossible of course because a *100%* amplitude reduction would clearly result in no visible texture; however, improved robustness to illumination variability is clearly possible with the chaos-based approach of analyzing the Lacunarity of the phase plot trajectory.

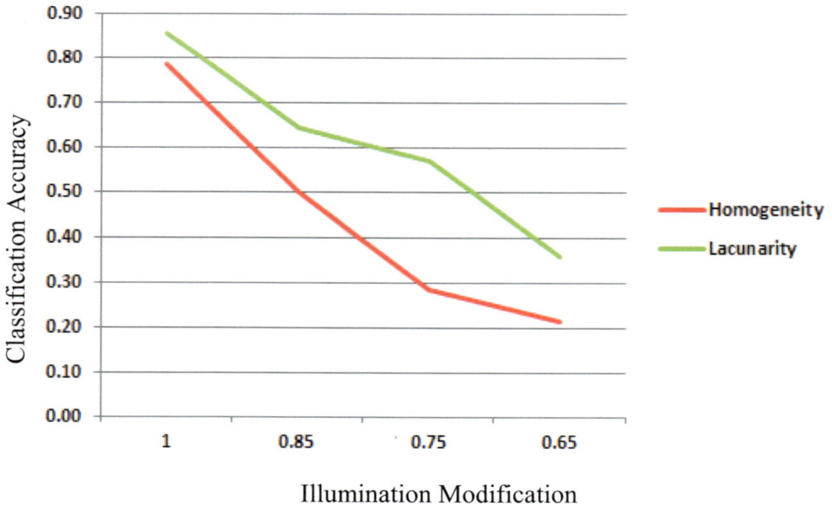

Figure 191: Classification accuracy of texture measures *versus* illumination factor.

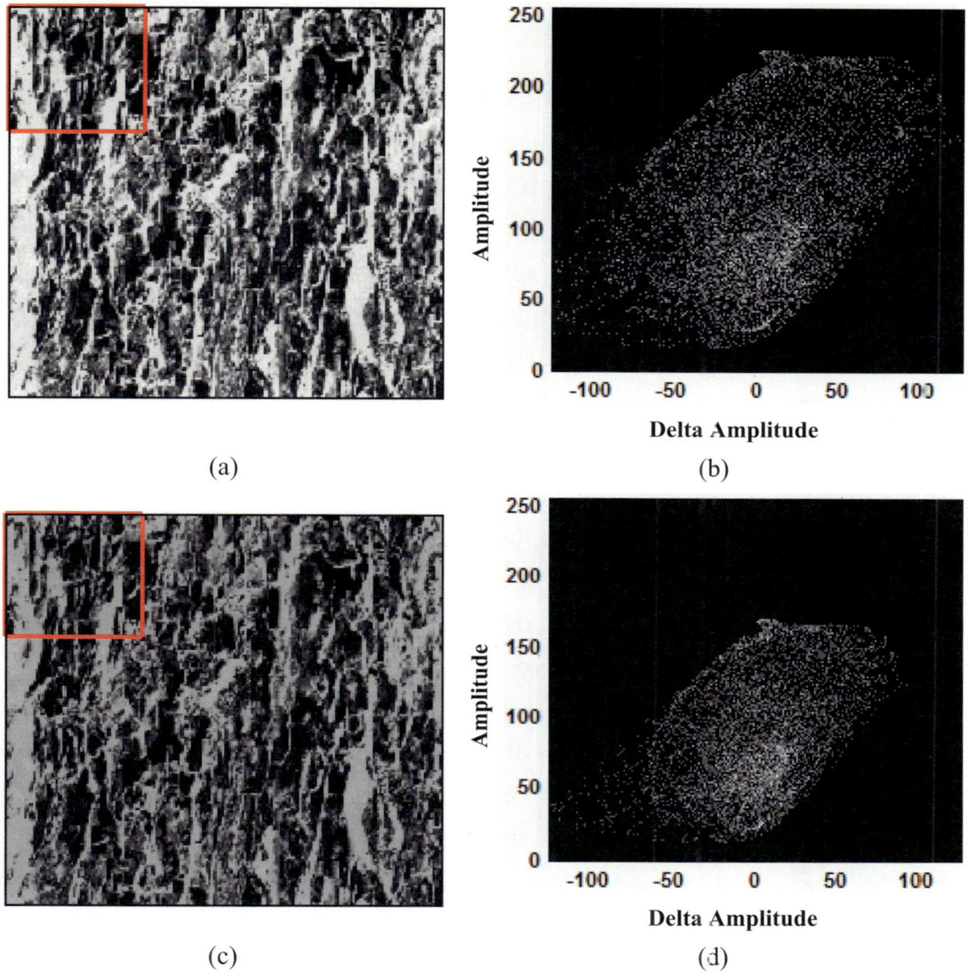

Figure 192: Effects of illumination on texture phase plots: (a) original texture image, (b) phase plot, (c) texture image with illumination reduced to 75% of original, and (d) phase plot of illumination reduced image.

Fig. **192** provides some insight into the robustness of the Lacunarity measure. Recall it is a measure captured at varying resolutions similar to the general fractal measures, but captures the internal structure of the phase plot trajectory. Illumination change results in a phase plot with similar structure with only a compression in the overall trajectory extent corresponding to the amount of illumination change. Thus the values for the Lacunarity are less affected by the overall illumination of the texture.

CONCLUDING REMARKS

This chapter introduced the concept of spatial chaos as a model for describing texture in images. The concept of the aperiodic forcing function being applied spatially rather than temporally was shown to be an interesting model for texture. We demonstrated the equivalence of the grey-level co-occurrence matrix (GLCM) and the phase plot representation and provided processing frameworks for applying the chaos-based concepts to both segmentation and classification of texture. Likewise applying the phase plot representation provided a natural understanding for the effectiveness of using multiple spatial lags to explore texture, as they relate to additional dimensions in phase space within which the various textures can be differentiated. The recognition of spatial chaos to describe texture in a manner analogous to temporal chaos describing motion now provides a unifying framework for computer vision. This is in contrast to the traditional haphazard collection of algorithms developed for each subfield of computer vision without relation to other subfields.

The results demonstrated that the traditional measures such as Angular Second Moment and Homogeneity are equally effective when applied to the phase plot as to the GLCM, particularly for texture segmentation. Additionally, we demonstrated that the new measures such as the Renyi Spectrum and Lacunarity of the phase plot are extremely effective measures for classification of a collection of the Brodatz texture images, with the Lacunarity measure being the most effective. Recall Lacunarity is a multi-resolution measure, and as texture can be readily characterized at multiple resolutions, these results are not surprising.

Lastly, we explored the common theme throughout the text of robustness of the proposed chaos-based methods to changes in illumination. The improved performance of the Lacunarity measure to other traditional texture measures such as Homogeneity demonstrated again that utilizing phase space representations and the related phase space descriptive algorithms can provide improved immunity to illumination. In the case of texture, full illumination immunity is not possible but improved robustness across a broad range of illumination values is possible.

Application of Chaos and Fractals to Computer Vision, 2014, 233-269

CHAPTER 9

Applications to Post-Attentive Vision – Employing Chaos for Image Registration and Object Tracking

Abstract: Image registration is a critical upper level vision task for many applications, as is the related task of object tracking. One of the simplest tracking algorithms is the correlation tracker which does not require prior object segmentation to successfully estimate motion parameters of possible objects of interest. For image registration there are two classes of algorithms, landmark or point-based and pixel-based. Pixel-based methods are popular in applications where reliable detection of landmark points is not feasible. As with the other computer vision tasks defined in the text, the performance of these pixel-based methods is sensitive to illumination change between the image pair being registered. Unfortunately illumination change is quite common in image registration problems, particularly in outdoor scene tracking. The popular measure of Mutual Information has been widely accepted as the standard measure for image registration; however, it is sensitive to illumination change. The chaos-based measures such as the Box Counting dimension and the Information Dimension will be applied to the image registration problem. The results obtained by these methods will be shown to be superior to the results provided by the traditional measures.

Keywords: Registration, mutual information, voxel-based registration.

REGISTRATION AND TRACKING

This chapter will address the application of chaos based techniques to object tracking. The specific approach to tracking investigated in this chapter will be that of correlation tracking, where image registration techniques are used to determine the motion vectors of the object of interest. Other approaches to tracking such as Kalman filter-based tracking of objects of interest *via* the centroid positions through the use of a state vector will not be addressed, nor will algorithms such as particle filter, mean-shift or active contours as there is no clear method for applying chaos theory to these methods. The purpose of this processing task in the vision hieracrchy is to identify the best transformations to convert one image in the sequence into the previous image in the sequence. This operation will result in motion vectors, zoom parameters, and rotation angles which can then be used by higher level vision processing to perform scene and motion understanding.

Michael E. Farmer

OVERVIEW OF ISSUES RELATED TO IMAGE REGISTRATION

The goals of image registration are to determine the optimal transformation required to map one image into another image. It is possible to characterize the image registration problem according to the characteristics of the image pair being registered, namely: (i) images of the same scene taken at different times, (ii) images of the same scene from different viewpoints, and (iii) images of the same scene from different sensors [138]. Category (i) image registration corresponds to applications such as surveillance for image change detection (abandoned bags, *etc.*) and image tracking for ego-motion detection or for object of interest tracking. The results of this chapter will concentrate on this category of image registration problems.

It is important to note that as Oldridge, *et al.,* state: "Systems for automatic image registration exist… however no single algorithm exists that will solve all types of registration [problems]" [142]. The performance of the various algorithmic approaches depend heavily on the types of variations that are present in the image pairs being registered, and Oldridge restates Brown's taxonomy of variations into three classes: "(i) variations due to differences in acquisition that cause the images to be misaligned, (ii) variations due to differences in acquisition that cannot be easily modeled such as lighting or camera extrinsics, and finally (iii) variations due to movement of objects within the scene" [142,143].

Mathematically, the image registration problem can be defined as [139]:

$$T_g^*(\cdot) = \arg\max_{T_g(\cdot)} \rho\left(I_R, T_g\left(I_t\right)\right) \tag{96}$$

where I_R is the reference image, I_t is the target image, $T_g()$ is a geometric transformation applied to the image, and ρ is the similarity measure between the reference image and the transformed image. There are many classes of registration algorithms to perform the transformations, calculate the resultant image similarity, and search through the similarity space, but a common taxonomy of algorithms common in computer vision is Point based and Voxel (or Pixel) based algorithms, which are defined by Maes, *et al.,* as [140]:

> "***Point based*** methods rely on manually indicated anatomical landmarks or automatically computed geometrically salient points".
>
> "***Voxel based*** registration methods optimize a functional measuring the similarity of all geometrically corresponding voxel pairs for some feature".

Alternatively these two approaches to image registration have been termed ***feature-based*** *versus* ***area-based*** by Zitova and Flusser in [138] or feature-based *versus* intensity-based by Dawn *et al.,* in [141]. Algorithms that rely on point or feature matching such as the Random Sample Consensus (RANSAC) or Scale-invariant Feature Transform (SIFT) algorithms will not be addressed here since they do not have a direct phase space correspondence. Area/intensity methods perform the registration of the image pairs without attempting to detect salient objects or features within the images such as edges, corners, *etc.* [138]. For medical image processing applications, area-based methods are the most popular due to there being no loss in data during feature selection, and also since they require little or no user interaction to select feature points [139]. Area methods often use windows of predefined size or entire images for the correspondence estimation. Throughout this text we have been using image decomposition into grid-cells to subdivide the images into smaller regions, and we will continue to do so for image registration. For ego motion detection different regions of the image are often experiencing different transformations, and for object tracking, the objects of interest are often much smaller than the entire image field of view.

Two limitations of the area-based methods identified by Zitova and Flusser in [138] are: (i) the inability of simple shaped areas (such as the rectangles used in our grid-cells) to capture complex transformations, and (ii) the 'remarkableness' of the window content. They further comment in [138]: "there is high probability that a window containing a smooth area without any prominent details [will be present]". The second issue regarding remarkableness is even more important for feature-based methods. In these methods a lack of 'remarkable' features will make even the identification of a useful feature impossible. Region or area methods, on the other hand, can utilize slowly changing patterns to still accomplish a reasonable registration. The first issue regarding an inability to handle complex transformations can also be minimized by using smaller regions where combinations of simpler transformations can be employed. We will show for ego-motion detection this is a very feasible approach even in the presence of image-wide perspective effects.

Zitova and Flusser identify a third weakness of area methods namely, "classical area-based methods such as cross-correlation exploit image intensities directly for matching without any structural analysis. Consequently, they are sensitive to the intensity changes, introduced for instance by noise, varying illumination, and/or by using different sensor types" [138]. Likewise recall from Brown's taxonomy of registration problems the second set of problems directly identified changes due to illumination as being particularly problematic. This is clearly a critically important issue that can be addressed through the application of the chaos-theoretic methods since one of the strengths of the chaos-based approach shown in this text has been its inherent immunity to varying illumination. Thus their observation of sensitivity to illumination and different sensor types is not caused by the area-based methods themselves but rather by the similarity measure they employ, such as simple correlation measures or Mutual Information.

For the voxel, area, or intensity-based methods a key element of the algorithm is the selection of a similarity measure as it plays a critical role in Equation (96). Numerous metrics have been proposed for area-based registration including: sum of absolute differences, sum of squared differences, ratio-image uniformity, cross-correlation, Fourier transform-based phase correlation, Mutual Information, and Normalized Mutual Information [139]. Mutual Information is probably the most popular measure for this class of image registration algorithms [38,140,144, 145]. Throughout the text we have demonstrated the efficacy of a chaos-theoretic approach over traditional approaches, including Mutual Information based approaches, and in this chapter we will once again explore the benefits of our chaos-theoretic approach. Recall its strength lies in its analysis in terms of the fact that chaotic behavior in phase space can be directly attributed to information creation. Pluim, *et al.,* explored additional information-theoretic measures applied to image registration in [146]. Rather than focusing on information creation as the source of differences between image pairs, they address the divergence in the histograms of the two images and use the *f*-Information measures to quantify the divergence. In the next section we will discuss the properties of Mutual Information and the equivalent properties of the two common chaos-theoretic measures using the global fractal measures of the phase plot between the reference image and the target image, namely the Box Counting dimension and the Information Dimension.

CHARACTERISTICS OF MEASURES FOR REGISTRATION SIMILARITY TESTING

While there are many interesting properties of mutual information, the following three are particularly useful for image registration of two images A and B: [38, 75]:

$$I(A,B) = I(B,A) \tag{97}$$

$$I(A,A) = H(A) \tag{98}$$

$$I(A,B) \leq H(A) \tag{99}$$

Equation (97) establishes symmetry of the Mutual Information operator between two images, and this property also applies to the proposed chaos-based approaches. The property of Equation (98) establishes the condition for meeting the upper bounds of the Mutual Information operator by the comparison of an image with itself. Equation (99) establishes the fact that by comparing any image with a different image the Mutual Information will be at most that of the image compared with itself and otherwise will be less than that value. This is a key parameter for using Mutual Information to search for optimal registration parameters as it establishes the rule that the result will always be less than that of a perfect match. Thus when using Mutual Information for registration searching we will seek to maximize the value.

Fortunately, these three key properties also have analogies in chaos-based analysis and the properties defined in Equations (98) and (99) are even simpler in definition. The chaos-based properties are defined in terms of the fractal dimension, F_D of the phase plots of the two images, A and B, as follows [147]:

$$F_D\left(A_{\text{phase plot}}, B_{\text{phase plot}}\right) = F_D\left(B_{\text{phase plot}}, A_{\text{phase plot}}\right) \tag{100}$$

$$F_D\left(A_{\text{phase plot}}, A_{\text{phase plot}}\right) = 1 \tag{101}$$

$$F_D\left(A_{\text{phase plot}}, B_{\text{phase plot}}\right) \leq 2 \tag{102}$$

Thus the lower bounds on the registration value between two images is actually ***independent*** of the image being analyzed when applying the chaos-based approach. Likewise, the greatest difference between two images is also independent of the two images and only relies on the fact that the most complicated phase space trajectory will completely fill the entire phase space, resulting in a fractal dimension of two. Based on Equation (102) when using the chaos-based image registration we will be trying to minimize the fractal dimension, which is opposite to the approach for Mutual Information.

As we demonstrated throughout the text, there are numerous methods for computing the fractal dimension of a phase plot. The first question is whether a local or a global measure is required for the registration task. Since correlation trackers and registration algorithms in general are interested in the relative transformation of one complete image relative to another complete image a global fractal measure will be required. There were a host of global measures of the fractal dimension which are possible candidates for a chaos-based registration approach. As voxel-based registration is basically a search performed to determine the transformation required to convert one image into a second image, a scalar-valued measure of fractal dimension of the phase plot is required. This makes sense since Mutual Information which is quite popular is a scalar value also. The requirement of a scalar value limits the choices available for suitable fractal dimensional measures to be those such as Box Counting, Information Dimension, and Correlation Dimension. Other issues such as the robustness to illumination, quality of the resultant search space, and application domain (object tracking *versus* ego-motion estimation) will all be deciding factors as to which of these fractal measures is most appropriate, and these issues will be addressed in the following sub-chapters.

CHARACTERISTICS OF SEARCH SPACES FOR REGISTRATION

A critical issue when performing automated searching for registration parameters is the quality of the search space available for determining the best registration between the two images. Poorly behaved search spaces have many local minima within which a search engine can become trapped, leading to erroneous registration parameter estimation. We will see that there is a significant difference in the quality of the search space for ego-motion estimation between the Box Counting method and the other global fractal dimensional measures; however we will also later see that the Box Counting method has its own advantages in terms of robustness to illumination changes.

Recall the Box Counting method examines the extent of the phase space trajectory in terms of its completeness of coverage of the entire phase space. It treats any region of the phase space trajectory equally in terms of its occupation of the varying sized boxes used to cover the space. Thus a single excursion of the trajectory through a region of phase space provides as much impact on the calculation as a dense region of many closely spaced trajectory elements. We will see that this causes the search spaces for the Box Counting method to be quite complex and not well-behaved for ego-motion estimation; however, for object tracking the difference is only of slightly lower quality. Other measures such as the Information Dimension, in particular, provide a weighting to the fractal dimension calculation based on the density of the trajectory within the regions of interest. Thus a single excursion of the phase space trajectory has a minimal impact on the fractal dimension calculation when using Information Dimension compared to what a densely spaced trajectory region would have.

The search space quality of Box Counting *versus* Information Dimension can be seen by considering the example of the moving vehicle in Fig. **193**. For this image pair, a 3-dimensional search space is constructed consisting of shifts in the row and column directions and zoom inward and outward. The reduced search space corresponding to the row and column shift for Mutual Information, Box Counting, and Information Dimension are provided in Fig. **194**. As can be seen by comparing the search surfaces of each method in Fig. **194**, the Box Counting fractal dimension tends to create a more textured and unsmooth surface which can negatively impact simple search algorithms such as hill-climbing algorithms. Fig. **195** provides the complete collection of slices across the row-column dimensions for each zoom increment for the Box Counting method and the surface is highly textured with numerous small local minima.

(a) (b) (c) (d)

Figure 193: Recall common scene of moving object: (a) first image with motion [67], (b) next image with motion, (c), cleaned segmented image used for the registration, and (d) the original phase plot.

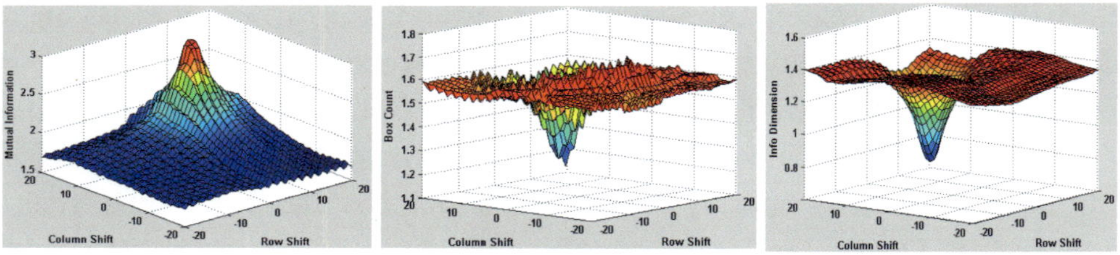

(a) (b) (c)

Figure 194: Example correlation-tracker registration search surfaces for row and column shifting: (a) Mutual Information, (b) Box Counting, and (c) Information Dimension.

The complexity of the search spaces associated with the various fractal dimensional measures can also be seen when considering ego-motion estimation for a moving camera. A typical pair of images from an ego-motion application can be found in Fig. **196** (a) and (b). Fig. **197** shows the resulting search spaces for the row shift-column shift transformation space within which the optimal transformation must be detected for the upper right-most grid cell shown in Fig. **196** (c) and (d). In these search spaces the Box Counting method results in a considerably more complex highly textured search space. Again this is due to the binary nature of the Box Counting method in considering a region of phase space when any amount of trajectory enters the region. Note, however, the oscillations in the Mutual Information search space would also make a simple gradient ascent algorithm struggle.

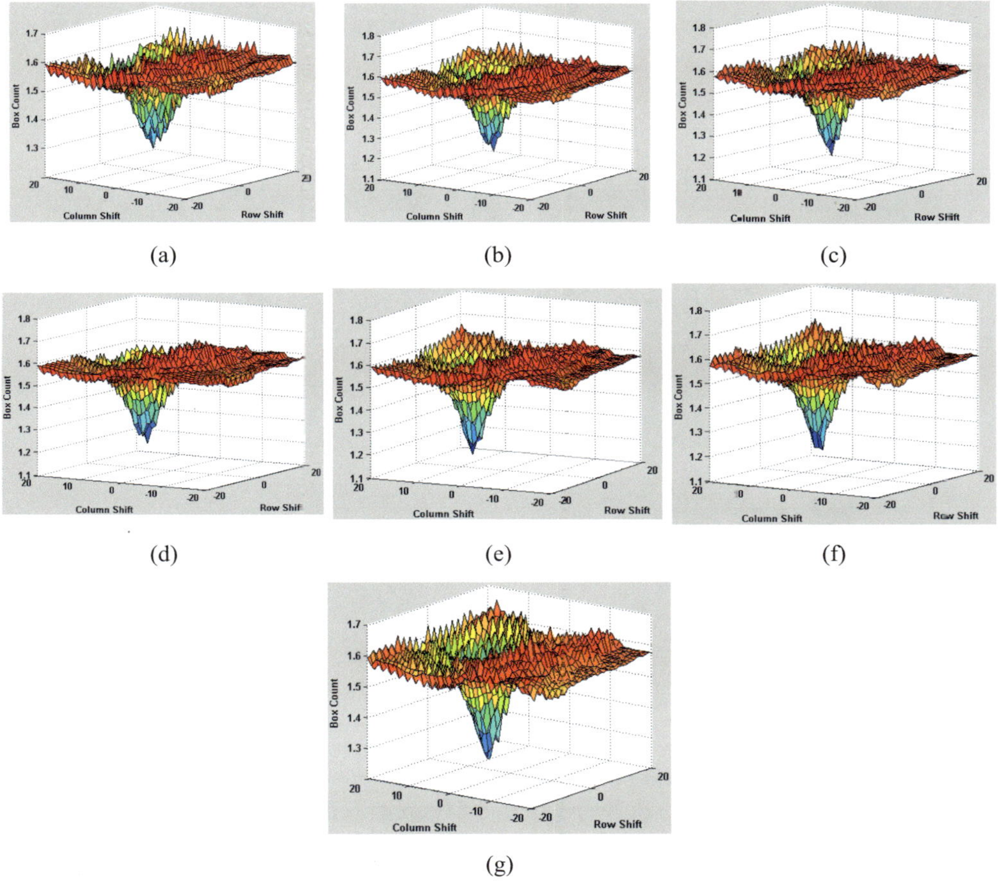

Figure 195: The complete search space for the Box Counting method consisting of the row-column axes slices for each zoom factor for the moving object in Fig. **193**: (a) zoom=-3%, (b) zoom=-2%, (c) zoom=-1%, (d) zoom=0%, (e) zoom=+1%, (f) zoom=+2%, and (g) zoom=+3%.

The Information Dimension search space in Fig. **197** (c) is clearly the most well-behaved search space. Fig. **198** (b) through (d) show the resultant motion vectors for the three methods, with the results being relatively comparable between the three methods. Box Counting, however, is the only method to capture the slight zoom in the image pair as the camera moved through the scene. Fig. **199** (a) shows the original phase plot and (b) and (c) show the final phase plots after the best motion estimates were applied to the second image in the pair using Mutual Information in (b) and Box Counting in (c). The consolidation of the phase plot to the central axis demonstrating the similarity between the final transformed image and the original image as this phase space structure is indicative of an image being compared to itself.

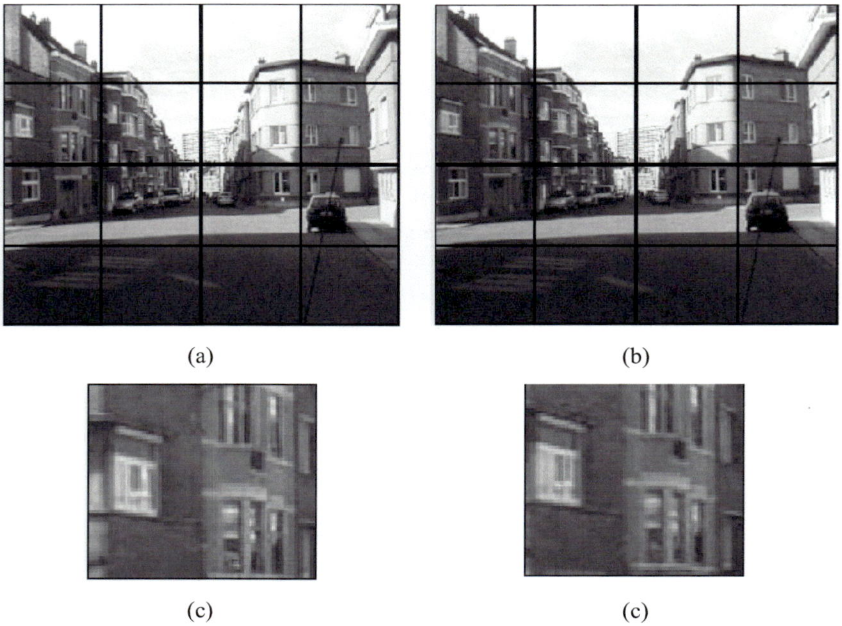

Figure 196: Image sequence for ego motion estimation [148], (a) first image, (b) second image, (c) upper left (row=2, col=2) grid cell from (a), and (d) upper left (row=2, col=2) grid cell from (b).

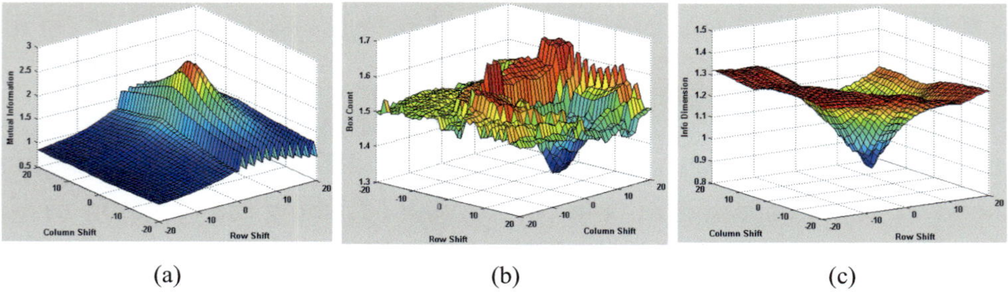

Figure 197: Example ego-motion detection from moving camera sequence registration search surfaces from Fig. **196**: (a) Mutual Information, (b) Box Counting, and (c) Information Dimension.

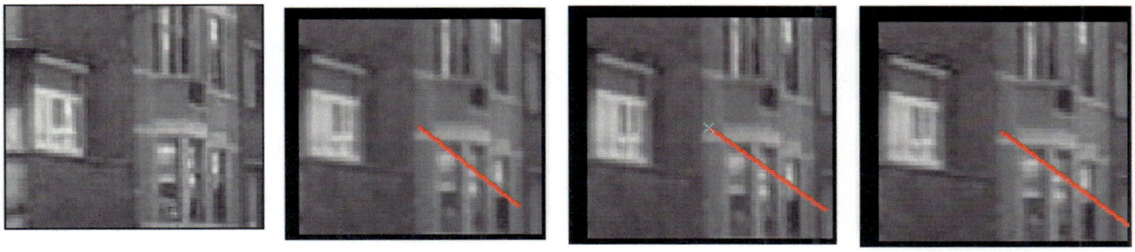

(a) (b) (c) (d)

Figure 198: Example ego motion tracker registration results for the image pair in Fig. **196** [148]: (a) first image, (b) second image with directional vectors showing best shift and zoom of image to match first image using Mutual Information ($\Delta R = 5, \Delta C = 7, \Delta Z = 0\%$), (c) second image with directional vectors showing best shift and zoom of image to match first image using Box Counting ($\Delta R = 5, \Delta C = 8, \Delta Z = -1\%$), and (d) second image with directional vectors showing best shift and zoom of image to match first image using Information Dimension ($\Delta R = 6, \Delta C = 9, \Delta Z = 0\%$).

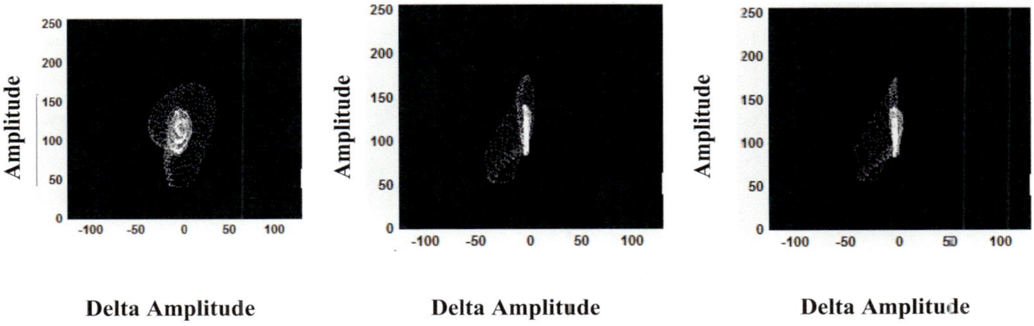

(a) (b) (c)

Figure 199: Example phase plots and resultant difference image from motion detection with global illumination change: (a) phase plot from original image pair, (b) phase plot from best resultant match of two images using Mutual Information, and (c) phase plot from best resultant match of two images using Box Counting.

The complete search spaces for all three methods are provided in Fig. **200**, Fig. **201**, and Fig. **202**. When reviewing the search spaces recall that for the fractal dimension methods the optimal registration parameters can be found at the minimum of the search space, while for Mutual Information the optimal parameters are located at the maximum of the search space. Overall the behavior of the Information Dimension's search space makes it an attractive choice for image registration. In the following sub-chapter we will see that under spatially varying illumination change and motion, issues arise with both the Mutual Information and Information Dimension measures that do not arise with the Box Counting method.

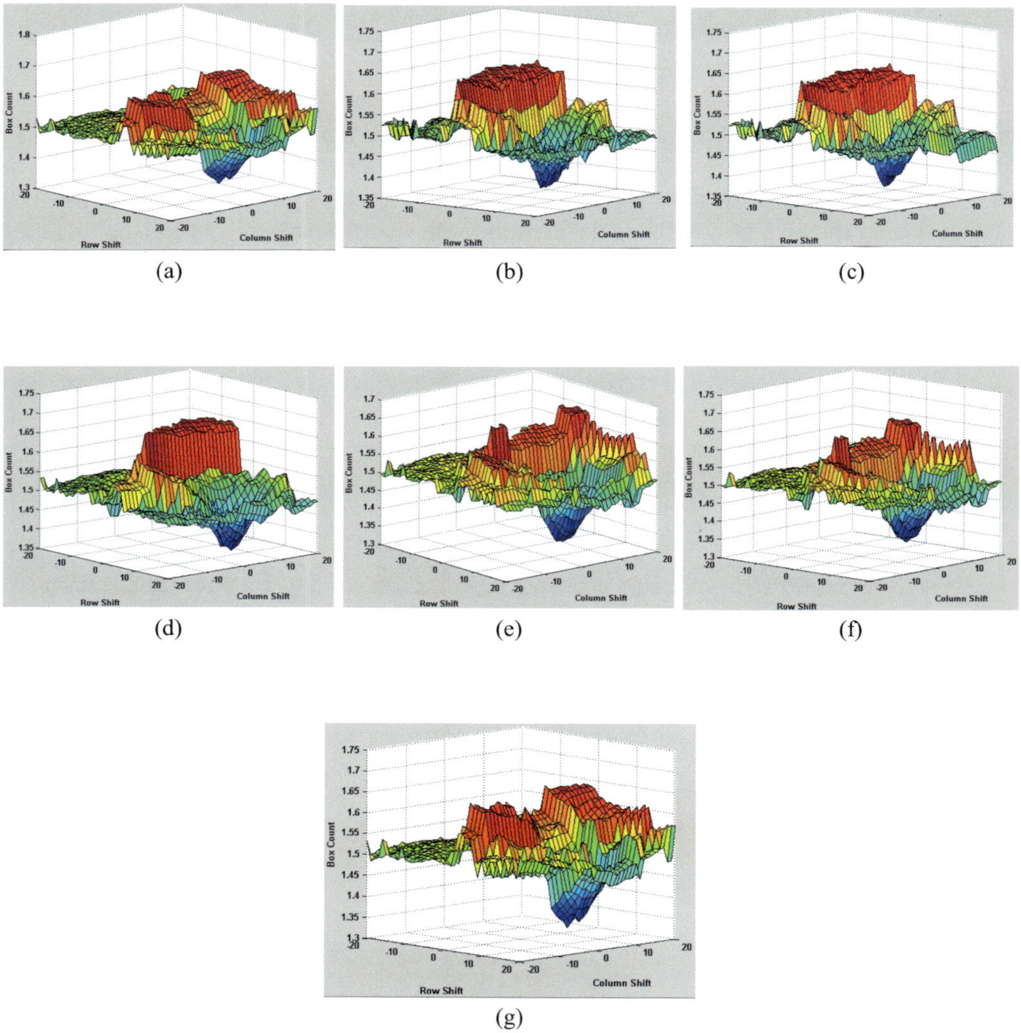

Figure 200: The complete search space for the Box Counting method consisting of the row-column axes slices for each zoom factor for the ego motion analysis in Fig. **196**: (a) zoom=-3%, (b) zoom=-2%, (c) zoom=-1%, (d) zoom=0%, (e) zoom=+1%, (f) zoom=+2%, and (g) zoom=+3%.

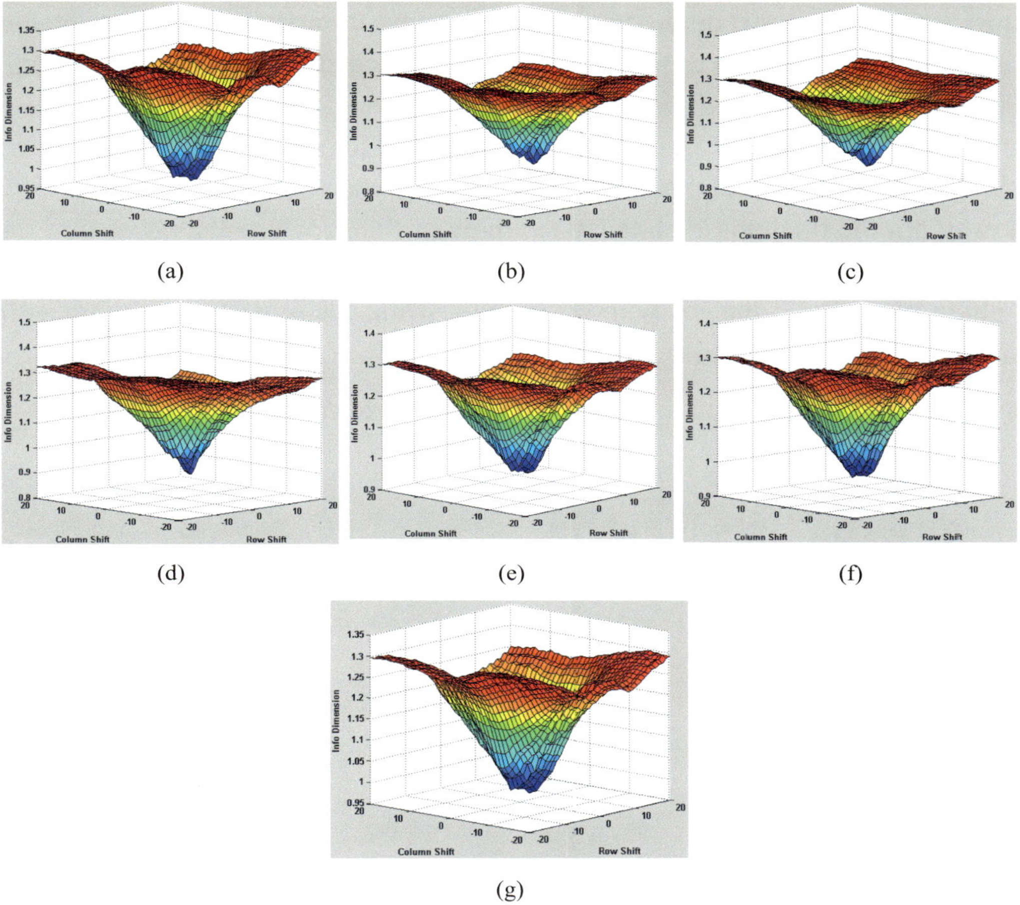

Figure 201: The complete search space for the Information Dimension method consisting of the row-column axes slices for each zoom factor for the ego motion analysis in Fig. **196**: (a) zoom=-3%, (b) zoom=-2%, (c) zoom=-1%, (d) zoom=0%, (e) zoom=+1%, (f) zoom=+2%, and (g) zoom=+3%.

One other key issue to address is the behavior of the registration algorithms in situations where there are considerable amounts of relatively uniform background and only a small region where there is actual change in the images. Notice in Fig. **196** (a) and (b) the second grid cell along the top row of the image contains very little building and large amounts of sky. The image pair for this grid cell and the resultant phase plot between the original image pair is provided in Fig. **203**. The registration results for the three methods, Mutual Information, Box Counting, and Information Dimension are provided in Fig. **204** where the final translation vectors are superimposed on the transformed images. Clearly there is considerable variability in the outcomes of the three methods, which can be seen by the varying offsets of the building roofline in the three resultant transformed images. These results are further verified in Fig. **205** where the difference images for the three methods with their resultant sum of absolute difference value are provided. Fig. **206** provides the final phase plots for the three methods, where the phase plot for the Box Counting method demonstrates a very clear vertical line corresponding to the phase plot of two images with no change, while the other two methods still exhibit dispersion in the phase plot.

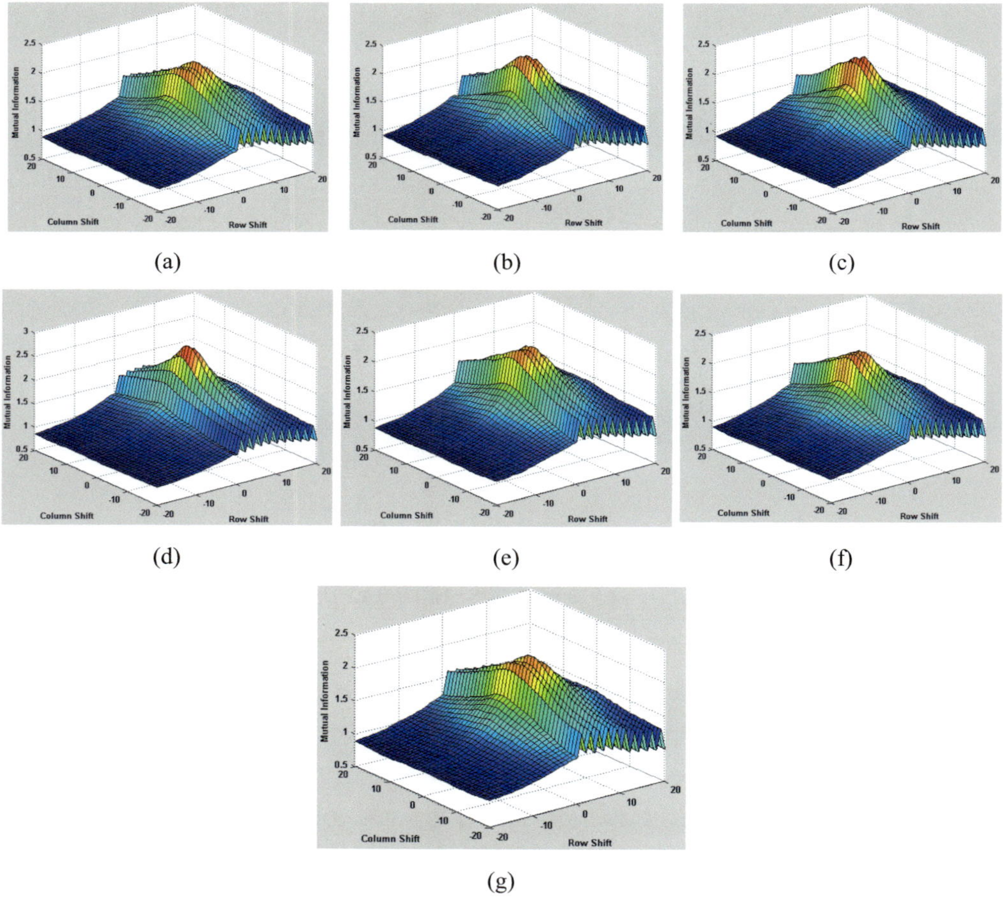

Figure 202: The complete search space for Mutual Information consisting of the row-column axes slices for each zoom factor for the ego motion analysis in Fig. **196**: (a) zoom=-3%, (b) zoom=-2%, (c) zoom=-1%, (d) zoom=0%, (e) zoom=+1%, (f) zoom=+2%, and (g) zoom=+3%.

(a) (b) (c) (d)

Figure 203: Recall grid cell of building edge from Fig. **196**: (a) first image in registration sequence, (b) next image, (c), difference image, and (d) the original phase plot.

(a) (b) (c) (d)

Figure 204: Example ego motion tracker registration results for the image pair in Fig. **196**: (a) first image, (b) second image with directional vectors showing best shift to match first image using Mutual Information ($\Delta Row = 3, \Delta Col = 1$), (c) second image with directional vectors showing best shift to match first image using Box Counting ($\Delta Row = 6, \Delta Col = 4$), and (d) second image with directional vectors showing best shift to match first image using Information Dimension ($\Delta Row = 9, \Delta Col = 5$).

Insight into the performance of the three algorithms can be gained when analyzing the original phase plot in Fig. **203** (c). Notice in the upper portion of the phase plot there is a region that is quite dense and centered on the zero-change axis of the phase plot. This region of the phase plot corresponds to the relatively bright background portion of the original grayscale images in Fig. **203** (a) and (b). Recall from Chapter 5 that phase plots that exhibit this behavior are multi-fractal in nature and multi-fractal phase plots cause the estimates of density-based measures such as the Information Dimension to be inaccurate. This region of the phase plot is generated by the relatively large regions of the image where there was no change. These regions dominate the calculation of Mutual Information as well. This dramatic superiority in the results from the Box Couunting method is due to the fact that the chaos-based methods focus on the ***creation of new information*** and hence are able to detect small changes in the scene from the resultant excursion of the trajectory in phase space. On the other hand, Mutual Information is overwhelmed by the mutually common background data between the two images.

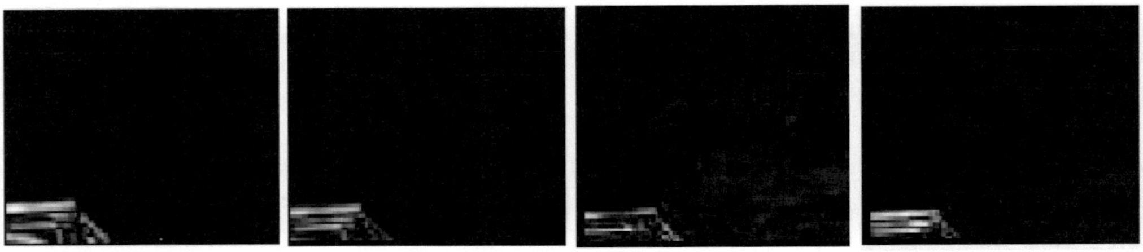

(a) (b) (c) (d)

Figure 205: Example ego motion tracker registration results for the image pair in Fig. **196**: (a) original difference image (original SAD =48486), (b) difference image for Mutual Information (residual SAD=33816), (c) difference image for Box Counting (residual SAD=22548), and (d) difference image for Information Dimension (residual SAD=26331).

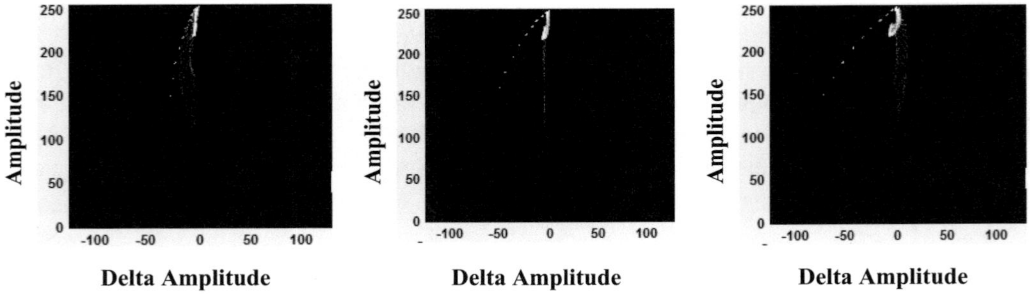

(a) (b) (c)

Figure 206: Example phase plots and resultant difference image from motion detection with global illumination change: (a) phase plot from best resultant match of two images using Mutual Information, and (b) phase plot from best resultant match of two images using Box Counting, and (c) phase plot from best resultant match of two images using Information Dimension.

To better understand the results produced by each of the methods it is interesting to examine the decision surfaces produced by Mutual Information and the two proposed chaos-based methods in Fig. **207**. In Fig. **207** (a) the surface for Mutual Information has an interesting structure, where there is a sharp peak corresponding to the background and then a minor hump in the search surface to the left of this peak that actually corresponds to the motion of the buildings. The height of the peak corresponding to no motion relative to the correct peak is due to the significantly larger amount of background in the image relative to salient regions with motion. In the two search surfaces for Box Counting and Information Dimension shown in Fig. **207** (b) and (c), there is a distinct minima at the proper location to capture the motion vector. In neither of the chaos-based methods is the search space corrupted by the extensive unchanged background regions of the images.

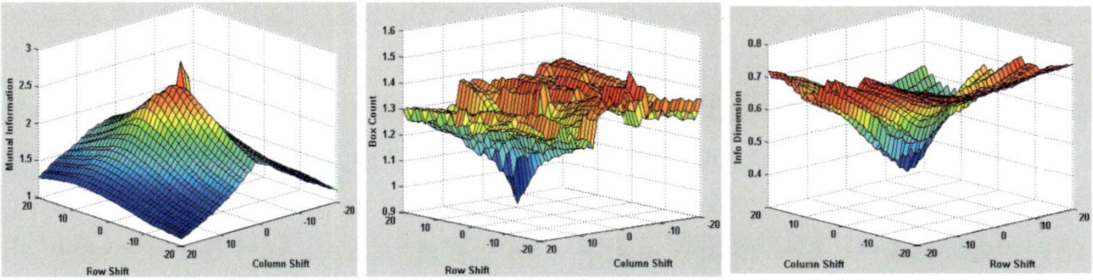

(a) (b) (b)

Figure 207: Decision surface from ego-motion detection from moving camera sequence for the (1, 2) grid cell: (a) surface for Mutual Information, (b) surface for Box Counting, and (c) Information Dimension [147].

So far we have developed a basic understanding of the behaviors of the search spaces for moving objects in scenes and for ego-motion of entire scenes. Since throughout this text we have demonstrated the issues that arise from interesting illumination change in image sequences, and how the proposed chaos-based analysis of these sequences can help to resolve these issues, we will now investigate the effects of illumination change on the task of image registration.

BEHAVIOR OF SEARCH SPACES UNDER ILLUMINATION CHANGE

One common issue in image registration is that the images of interest are not taken at the same time, and possibly from a different viewing angle which can result in global illumination changes. We expect traditional methods such as the Mutual Information approach to have difficulties in images with illumination change as Zitova and Flusser noted, "classical area-based methods…exploit…image intensities, without any structural analysis.

Consequently, they are sensitive to … *varying illumination*" [138]. Likewise the findings in the research efforts of a variety of other researchers including Brown [143] and Oldridge [142] also confirm it is difficult to separate the effects of image transformations from illumination.

Fig. **208** (a) and (b) show a laboratory generated example of an image pair with global illumination changes and a moving object simultaneously occurring in the field of view [147]. Fig. **209** (a) and (b) provide the histograms of each of these images showing the clear compression along the x-axis in the histogram due to the global illumination decrease. Fig. **209** (c) provides the phase plot for the image pair. Note the distinct diagonal line in the phase plot corresponding to the multiplicative global illumination change experienced in the second image in Fig. **208** (b) relative to the first image in Fig. **208** (a). As we learned in Chapter 4, the illumination effects are superimposed on the motion effects in phase space resulting in distinct regions of fractal and non-fractal behavior. Recall from Chapter 5 when we discussed the effects of simultaneous presence of illumination and motion on the calculation of the fractal dimension, we found that the non-fractal components of the phase plot reduced the fractal dimension when compared to images with only motion present. We also know from Zitova and Flusser, Brown, and Oldridge that Mutual Information-based registration techniques are highly sensitive to illumination change [138, 142, 143].

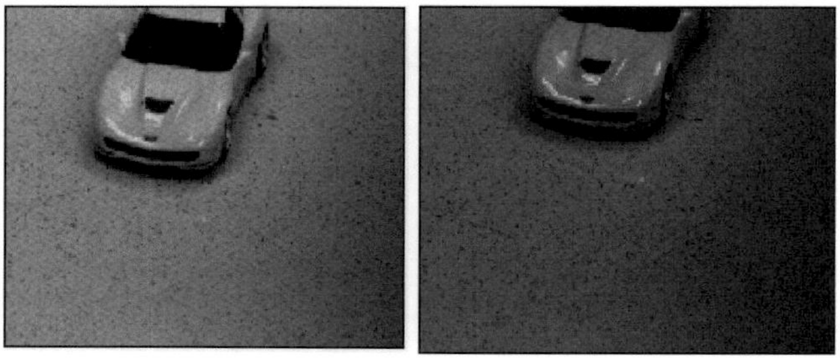

(a) (b)

Figure 208: Example of registration-based tracking of moving object with *global* temporal illumination effects present [24]: (a) first image of moving object, and (b) second image of moving object image (vehicle is moving in reverse).

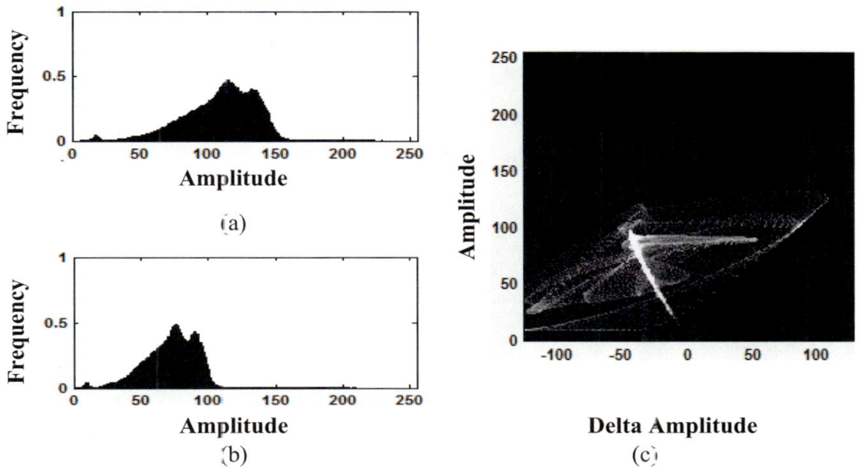

Figure 209: Grayscale characteristics of moving object with *global* temporal illumination effects present: (a) histogram of first image, (b) histogram of second image, and (c) phase plot (note strong diagonal line from the multiplicative global illumination change).

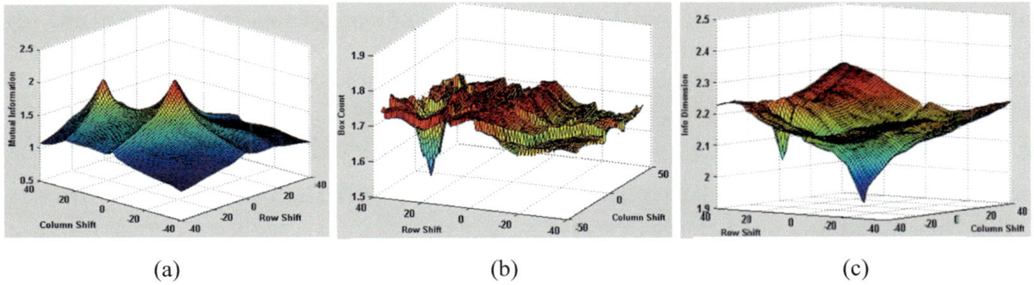

Figure 210: Example correlation-tracker registration search surfaces for row and column shifting: (a) Mutual Information, (b) Box Counting, and (c) Information Dimension [147].

Fig. **210** provides the search spaces for the registration problem in Fig. **208** for the Mutual Information, Box Counting and Information Dimension measures. In Fig. **210** (a) and Fig. **210** (b) we see that the search surface for both the Mutual Information and Information Dimensions have two distinct peaks, one corresponding to the illumination change and one due to the actual motion present in the image. Fig. **210** (b) provides the search space for the Box Counting measure and we see it has a single peak corresponding to the motion, and it effectively ignores the illumination effects. The quality of the estimated registration can be verified in Fig. **211** (c) and (d) where we show the initial and final difference images between the two images in Fig. **208** (a) and (b). Notice that the final difference image is quite uniform in amplitude, with only the illumination change present. The final phase plot corresponding to the estimated registration is provided in Fig. **211** (b) and the non-fractal diagonal region corresponding to the global illumination is clearly visible.

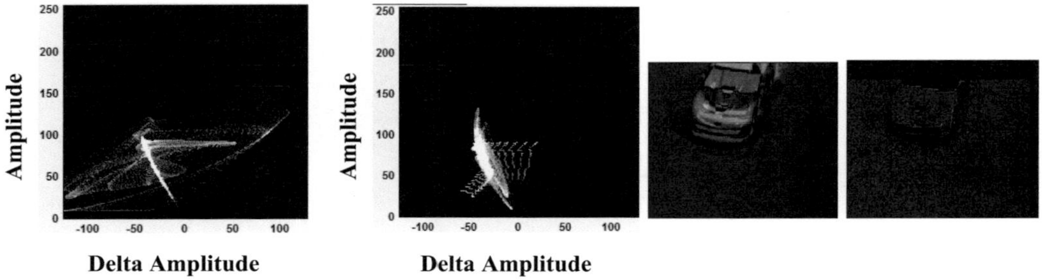

(a) (b) (c) (d)

Figure 211: Example phase plots and resultant difference image from motion detection with global illumination change: (a) phase plot from original image pair, (b) phase plot from best resultant match of two images, (c) initial difference image of two original input images, and (d) final difference image after correction from motion determined using Box Counting (Note constant amplitude difference across image due to global illumination change).

Fig. **211** (a) shows that the presence of globally varying illumination changes produce non-fractal regions in phase space. These non-fractal regions then bias the calculation of the global fractal dimension by lowering its value. The biasing of the global fractal measures then corrupt the search space to varying degrees based on the actual measure used. Since the Box Counting method only relies on the spatial extent of the phase plot it is more robust to the presence of these dense non-fractal regions. This is in stark contrast to using the Information Dimension or Correlation Dimension measures which are both negatively impacted by these dense non-fractal regions.

Therefore for registration-based tracking applications where spatio-temporally varying illumination may be present some form of phase plot preprocessing to remove these regions is recommended. Fig. **212** (a) shows the resultant best matching phase plot where the non-fractal regions have been removed during the registration search process, and Fig. **212** (b) provides the *improved* complete search space for the Information Dimension. Likewise, Fig. **213** summarizes all the detected motion vectors for the Mutual Information, Box Counting, and the illumination pre-processed Information Dimension. The results for the Box Counting method and the Information Dimension method are now identical. Unfortunately, Mutual Information has no underlying mechanism for correcting for spatio-temporally varying illumination.

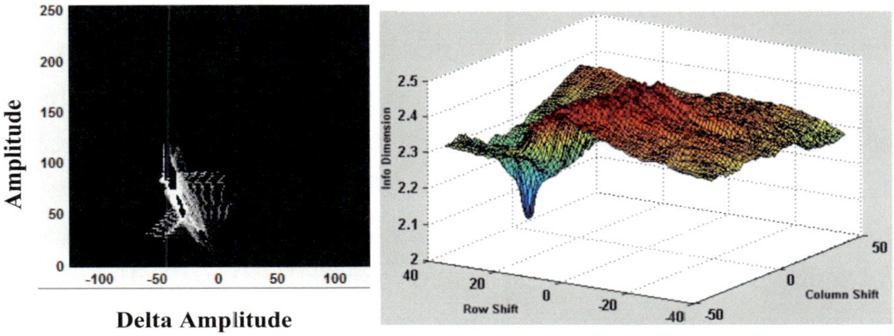

(a) (b)

Figure 212: Results for illumination-corrected Information Dimension measure: (a) final phase plot for illumination-corrected Information Dimension with low fractal regions removed and(b) resultant decision surface showing motion as only remaining minimum in the search space.

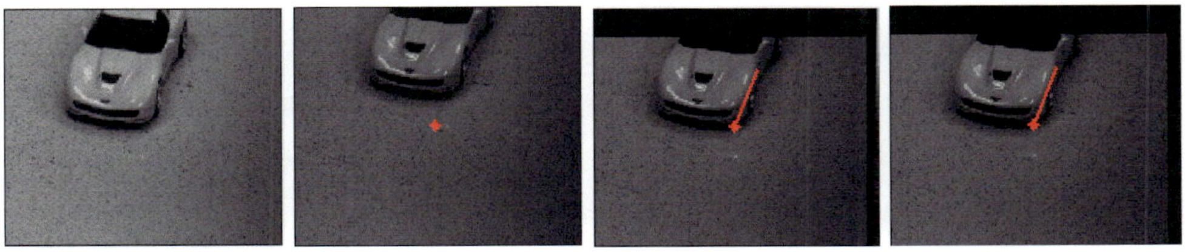

(a) (b) (c) (d)

Figure 213: Example correlation-tracker cleaned segmented images from the spatio-temporal illumination and motion laboratory scene from Fig. **214**: (a) first image, (b) second image with directional vectors showing best shift of image to match first image using Mutual Information ($\Delta R = 0, \Delta C = 0$), (c) second image with directional vectors showing best shift of image to match first image using Box Counting ($\Delta R = 29, \Delta C = -13$), and (d) second image with directional vectors showing best shift of image to match first image using illumination-corrected Information Dimension ($\Delta R = 29, \Delta C = -13$).

For the chaos-based methods, there are three clear options for image pair registration that may be experiencing global illumination changes:

(i) Rely on the Box Counting method,

(ii) Use a local fractal measure to pre-process the phase plot to remove these regions, and

(iii) Use an illumination model-based region blocking approach to remove the regions.

As we saw earlier, spatio-temporally varying illumination can cause even greater complexities in various computer vision tasks than global illumination, and image registration is no different. Moving illumination bands caused by a variety of application dependent effects can all contribute spatio-temporally varying illumination patterns in images. A partial list of such illumination effects include reflections off of windshields of passing vehicles, headlights panning across an image at dusk, subway car headlights illuminating the station, and shadows cast from direct sunlight obscuration. These spatio-temporal patterns will then complicate registration and tracking tasks when using traditional computer vision techniques. Fig. **214** (a) and (b) provide two images in a sequence where there is a vehicle moving to the top of the image and a spatio-temporally varying illumination band moving on the opposite direction and passing over the vehicle of interest. This laboratory image set allows us to carefully test the effects of motion and illumination change in a controlled setting. Fig. **215** (a) and (b) provide the grid cells of the image about the object of interest and Fig. **215** (c) provides the phase plot. Notice the existence of both the complex phase space trajectory of the moving object and the compacted region due to the moving illumination.

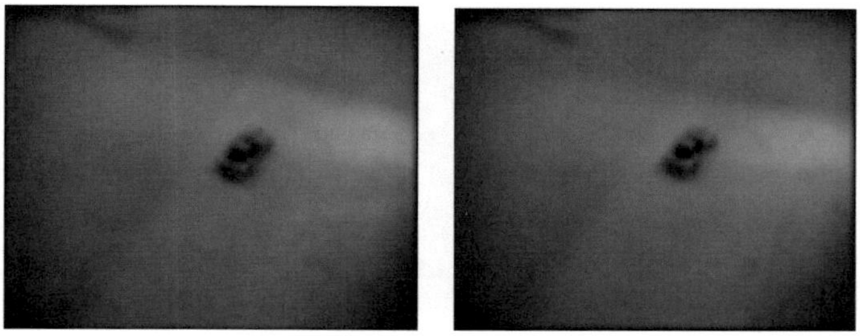

(a) (b)

Figure 214: Example of registration-based tracking of moving object with spatio-temporal illumination effects present [24]: (a) first complete image and (b) second complete image (Note motion of illumination band between image (a) and image (b).

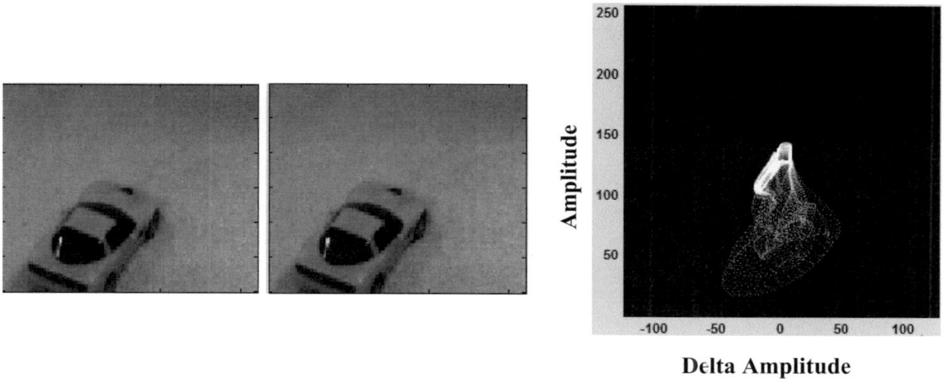

(a) (b) (c)

Figure 215: Example of registration-based tracking of moving object with spatio-temporal illumination effects present [24]: (a) first grid cell about moving object, (b) second grid cell about moving object image, and (c) phase plot.

Fig. **216** provides the search spaces of the row and column translational transformations to perform the registration-based tracking function. Fig. **216** (a) shows the search space for the Mutual Information measure. Unlike the smooth, well-behaved search spaces that were shown in Fig. **202** the search space in Fig. **216** (a) is not only highly complex, but also has its best registration at the point of no change between the images. Notice, however a slight rise in the search space in the lower left-hand side that actually corresponds to the motion of the vehicle. Unfortunately, the effects of the illumination band overwhelm the effects of the moving vehicle and the resulting transformation values for the Mutual Information measure are incorrect as can be seen in Fig. **217** (b) which shows no motion was detected.

Fig. **216** (b) provides the search space for this motion scene for the Box Counting method, and Fig. **217** (c) shows the resultant motion vector for the vehicle. Note the Box Counting method correctly calculated the best match, and the decision surface in Fig. **216** (b) appears roughly equivalent in behavior to the decision surfaces for the moving vehicle scene provided Fig. **193** which were provided in Fig. **195**. Fig. **216** (c) provides the decision surface for the Information Dimension. This surface is particularly interesting because the correct decision point can be seen in the image; however, the minimum for this surface is actually along the far right boundary of the image in Fig. **216** (c). This minimum in the decision surface resulted in the erroneous motion estimation vector provided in Fig. **217** (d).

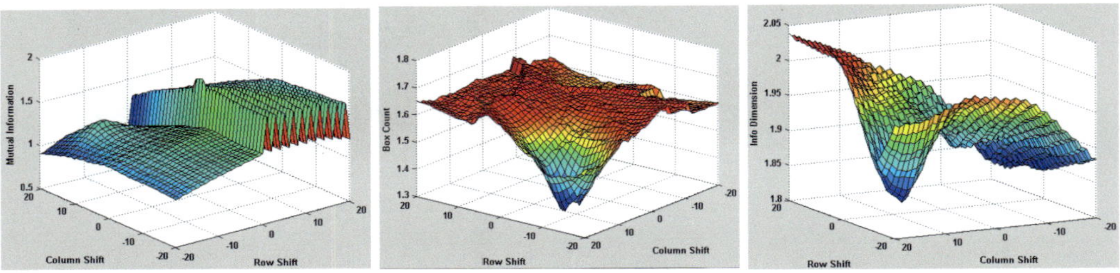

(a) (b) (c)

Figure 216: Example correlation-tracker registration search surfaces for row and column shifting: (a) Mutual Information, (b) Box Counting, and (c) Information Dimension.

As with performing image registration under the global illumination, one must first remove the non-fractal regions of the phase plot when using Information Dimension. Fig. **218** (a) shows the resultant search space for Information Dimension after illumination removal using a local fractal measure was applied, and this is clearly different from the corrupted search space shown in Fig. **216** (c). The resultant detected motion vector is superimposed over the corrected image in Fig. **218** (b) and we see the detected vector is identical to the vector detected by the Box Counting method.

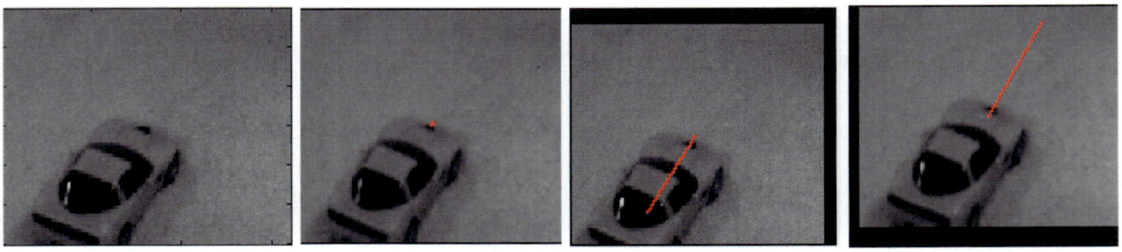

(a) (b) (c) (d)

Figure 217: Example correlation-tracker cleaned segmented images from the *spatio-temporal* illumination and motion laboratory scene from Fig. **214**: (a) first image, (b) second image with directional vectors showing best shift of image to match first image using Mutual Information ($\Delta R = 0, \Delta C = 0$), (c) second image with directional vectors showing best shift of image to match first image using Box Counting ($\Delta R = 16, \Delta C = -12$), and (d) second image with directional vectors showing best shift of image to match first image using Information Dimension ($\Delta R = -19, \Delta C = 13$).

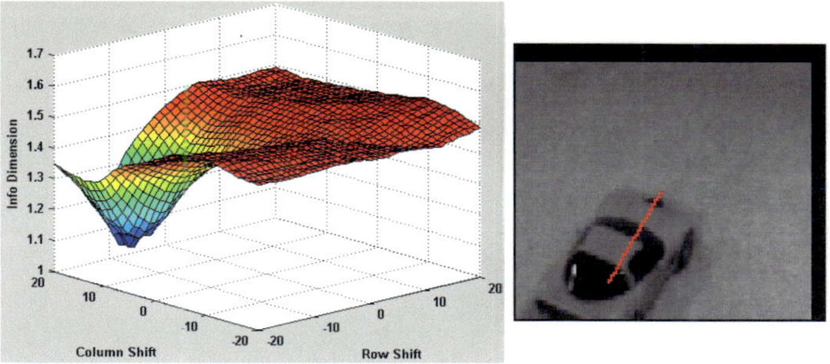

(a) (b)

Figure 218: Results of registration from *improved* surface after background removal for Information Dimension : (a) decision surface for Information Dimension after non-fractal components of phase plot are removed and (b) resultant best motion estimation vector ($\Delta R = 16, \Delta C = -11$).

In the following section we will define an algorithm for performing chaos-based image registration and then we will provide example results of applying the chaos-based methods to the problems of registration-based tracking and ego-motion estimation. We will show how the chaos-based approach is uniquely able to remove background artifacts such as the above demonstrated illumination effects.

A CHAOS-BASED ALGORITHM FOR REGISTRATION AND TRACKING

A proposed processing flow for registration and correlation tracking is provided in Fig. **219**. This is a general framework that provides the mechanisms for iterating the transformation parameters, for computing the new phase plot, and for calculating the resultant fractal dimension. The inputs to this algorithm are either an entire image or individual grid cells depending on the application. Individual grid cells are useful for applications such as ego-motion estimation where the different regions of the image experience different effects. Fig. **196** provides an ego-motion example where specific grid cell motions are provided in Fig. **229** and Fig. **232.** The combined motion vector from all the grid cells can provide a composite motion vector to define the ego-motion. For other image registration applications, the use of the complete image may be more appropriate. In either of these cases, the image is initially low-pass filtered to reduce the effects of noise on the phase plot. For correlation tracking applications, the inputs to the algorithm defined in Fig. **219** may be the segmented outputs from the motion segmentation processing defined in Chapter 8.

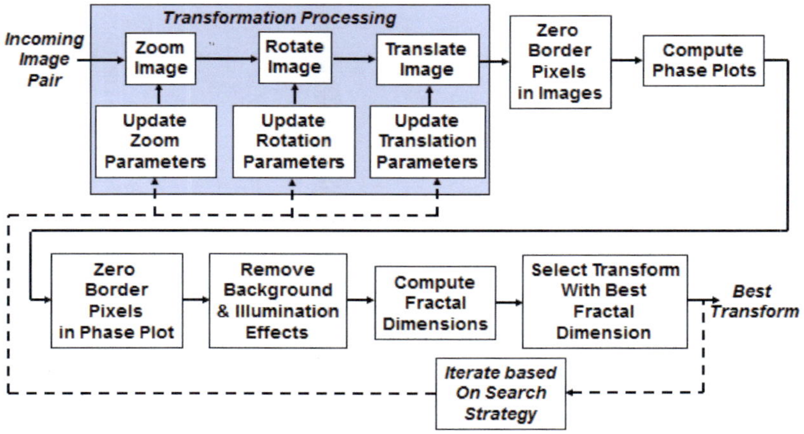

Figure 219: Processing for complete search for chaos-based image registration and correlation tracking [147].

The processing in Fig. **219** begins with the traditional image processing steps defined in ***Image Transformation Processing***. This processing is responsible for two tasks: (i) updating the parameters of the various transformation candidates and (ii) executing those transformations on the image. The available transformation operations are zoom, rotation, and translation, and they are performed in this order. The zoom operation accounts for motion perpendicular to the imaging plane of the sensor which results in objects in the image increasing or decreasing in size. The zoom transformation provides not only a bi-directional inward and outward zooming function, but also a unidirectional inward and outward zoom that can provide a stretching function in either the row or column directions if desired. This stretching function has proven useful for objects that may be rotating about their own perpendicular axis resulting in slight changes in the width of the object of interest. The rotation processing is then performed to account for rotations of the object in the image frame. Once these operations are performed, the shift transformations applied. The reader is referred to any standard image processing or computer graphics textbook for the details of each these transformations.

Prior to the generation of the phase plots in ***Compute Phase Plots*** the borders of the images are masked in the ***Zero Border Pixels in Images*** processing block to ensure that the two images in the image pair correspond to the same regions and that no pixels map to empty space. This step is only applied for ego-motion applications where the entire grid-cell is used for the registration processing. In this processing block a mask is generated that corresponds to the transformed image region of the gird-cell and this mask is then applied to the original image in a simple pixel-level masking operation.

For pre-segmented scenes such as for object tracking, the differences in regions can be removed more simply with the ***Zero Border Pixels in Phase Plot*** processing block. This processing block is performed for the pre-segmented object tracking applications. Examples of these border edge effects are provided in Fig. **220** and the effects in phase space are provided in Fig. **221** (a) with the cleaned phase space provided in Fig. **221** (b).

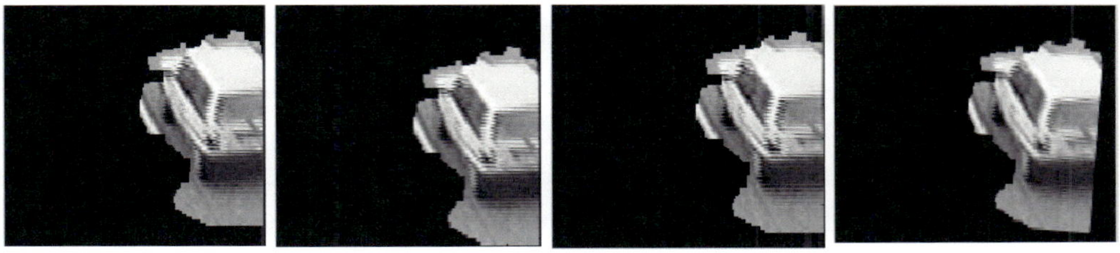

(a) (b) (c) (d)

Figure 220: Resulting border effects from image transformations, (a) original image, (b) translation downward, (c) zoom and (d) rotation.

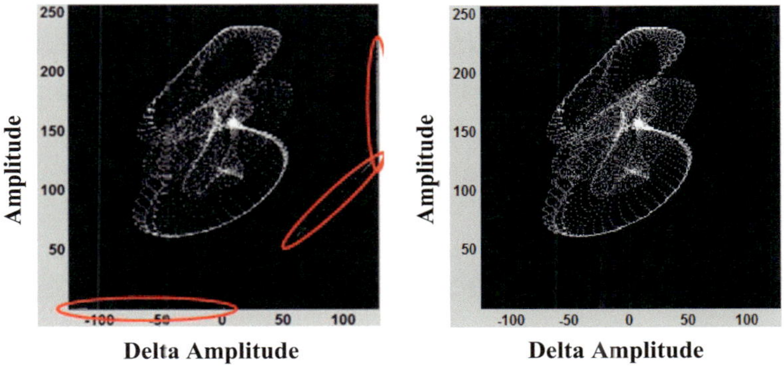

(a) (b)

Figure 221: Effects in phase space of edge effects due to mismatch between base image and transformed image, (a) corrupted phase space with regions of border effects highlighted and (b) cleaned phase space with all edge effects removed.

The algorithm for removal of these artifacts is quite simple as they occupy two primary regions in the periphery of the phase space as highlighted in Fig. **221** (a). The pixels along the bottom of the phase plot have amplitude of zero and a negatively valued change since they were non-zero in the first image. There is also a peak in the phase plot at (0, 0) that corresponds to background pixels in the first image that remain background in the subsequent image. The other artifact is the straight line that has slope equal to one, which terminates and runs along the far right vertical axis. This line corresponds to pixels that had zero amplitude in the original image and non-zero amplitude in the subsequent image therefore representing a change exactly equal to their amplitude (hence the unit-slope of the line).

The ***Compute Fractal Dimensions*** in Fig. **219** has been discussed in detail throughout the text and will not be addressed further here. The ***Remove Background and Illumination Effects*** detects the non-fractal regions in the phase plot that would correspond to global or spatially varying illumination conditions. For this processing we use a *local* fractal measure to segment non-fractal regions from the phase plot prior to calculation of the main global fractal dimension used for the registration metric. This is required only when using density measures such as the Information Dimension rather than the Box Counting method. While this step adds significant processing complexity to the registration, it ensures very accurate registration for the density-based measures.

The final processing block is the ***Iterate Based on Search Strategy*** block. The search strategy employed in pixel-level registration and tracking frameworks is quite flexible. At every iteration of the transformation parameters the second image in the image pair in the ***Image Transformation Processing*** region of the processing.

TYPICAL RESULTS OF APPLYING CHAOS TO REGISTRATION AND TRACKING

To demonstrate the effectiveness of the chaos-based registration we will test the algorithm on both object tracking and scene tracking for ego-motion estimation.

For object tracking we will test the algorithm on two classes of objects, rigid, and non-rigid. The rigid objects will be the vehicle scenes used throughout the text and the non-rigid object will be a human walking and turning.

CORRELATION-BASED OBJECT TRACKING USING CHAOS

The vehicle tracking will use the image set from Fig. **193**. The result of the transformations to align the two segmented vehicle images in Fig. **193** (a) and (b) compresses the phase plot significantly in this case as can be seen in Fig. **222** (b) which clearly shows a significant reduction in the space-filling nature of the phase space trajectory. The actual transformation vectors which verify the motion of the vehicle through the image scene can be seen in Fig. **223** (b) through (c) for Mutual Information, Box Counting, and Information Dimension measures. Likewise Fig. **224** (b) through (d) provides the difference images resulting from the transformations detected by each of the methods. For this relatively simple straightforward registration and tracking application all three methods produce similar results.

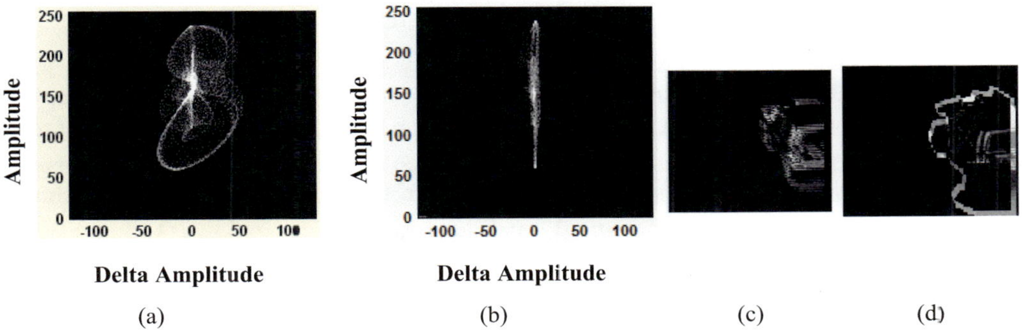

Figure 222: Example phase plots and resultant difference image from correlation-tracker registration: (a) phase plot from original image pair, (b) phase plot from best resultant match of two images, (c) initial difference image of two original input images, and (d) resultant difference image of two original input images.

The image sequence for the non-rigid object, namely the human subject is provided in Fig. **225**, (a) and (b) with the segmented image provided in (c) and the initial phase plot in (d). Notice the arms of the subject are moving and the handbag she is carrying is also moving relative to her center of mass. Also she is slightly rotating to her right which causes a slight compression in the x-direction (column wise) of the image. Fig. **226** (a) shows the initial phase plot and Fig. **226** (b) shows the final phase plot after the optimal transformations have been applied. Notice as before the compression of the phase plot towards the vertical axis as the two images more closely resemble each other after the image transformations have been applied. Likewise, Fig. **226** (c) shows the initial difference image and Fig. **226** (d) shows the final difference image. Fig. **227** provides the comparison of resultant corrected images with the shift vectors overlaid on the images. Note the similarity of parameter estimations again amongst the three measures. Fig. **228** provides the difference images for the original image pair (Fig. **228** (a)) and the resultant difference images from each of the three registration metrics. All three approaches compare favorably in terms of these difference images, as well.

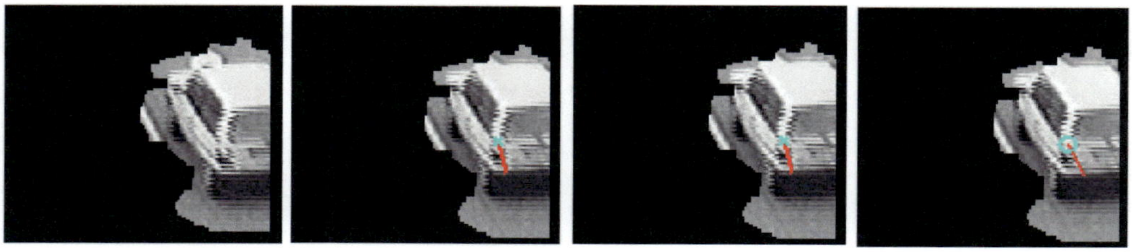

(a) (b) (c) (d)

Figure 223: Example correlation-tracker cleaned segmented images from the Reinhofen traffic scene from Fig. **193** [67]: (a) first image, (b) second image with directional vectors showing best shift of image to match first image using Mutual Information ($\Delta R = 4, \Delta C = 1, Zoom = -1$), (c) second image with directional vectors showing best shift to match original image using Box Counting ($\Delta R = 4, \Delta C = 1, Zoom = -1$), and (d) second image with directional vectors showing best shift of image to match first image using Information Dimension ($\Delta R = 4, \Delta C = 2, Zoom = +1$).

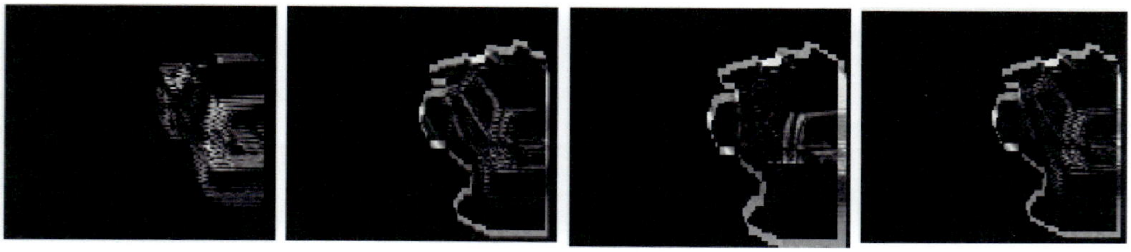

(a) (b) (c) (d)

Figure 224: Difference images for the moving vehicle detection application: (a) original difference image, (b) difference image from correction by Mutual Information processing, (c) difference image from correction by Box Counting method and (d) difference image from correction by Information Dimension.

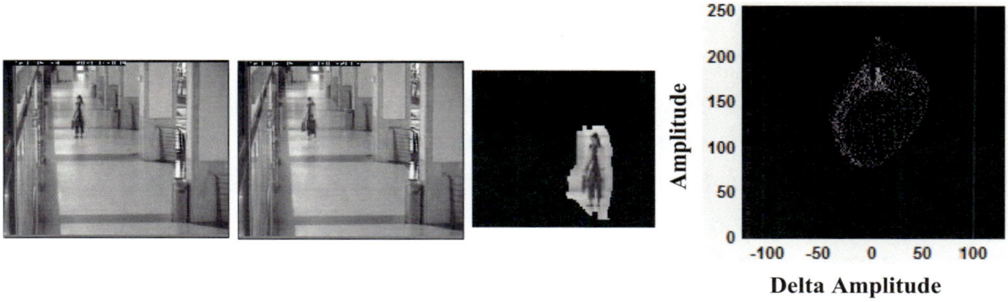

(a) (b) (c) (d)

Figure 225: Non-rigid object scene: (a) first image with motion [80], (b) next image with motion, (c), cleaned segmented image used for registration-based tracking, and (d) the original phase plot.

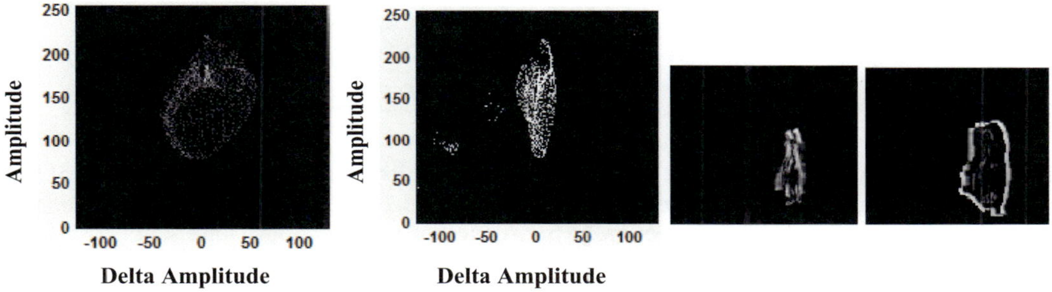

(a) (b) (c) (d)

Figure 226: Example phase plots and resultant difference image from correlation-tracker registration on non-rigid (human) objects: (a) phase plot from original image pair, (b) phase plot from best transformation between the two images, (c) initial difference image of two original input images, and (d) resultant difference image of two input images after application of the best transformation parameters.

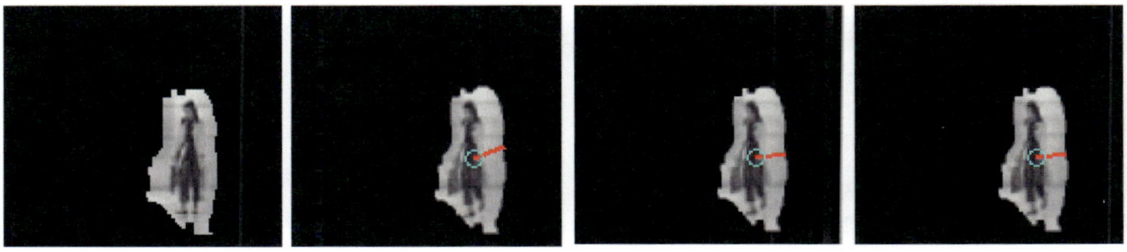

(a) (b) (c) (d)

Figure 227: Example correlation-tracker cleaned segmented images from the human subjects from Fig. **225**: (a) first image, (b) second image with directional vectors showing best shift of image to match first image using Mutual Information ($\Delta R = -1.5, \Delta C = 4.5, Zoom(column) = -3$), (c) second image with directional vectors showing best shift of image to match first image using Box Counting ($\Delta R = -.5, \Delta C = 4.5, Zoom(column) = -3$), and (d) second image with directional vectors showing best shift of image to match first image using Information Dimension ($\Delta R = -.5, \Delta C = 4.5, Zoom(column) = -3$).

Note in general for non-rigid objects (human subjects) the quality of the final mutual information or fractal dimensional values will be less-optimal when compared to the measures for rigid bodies, however, the important characteristic is the relative change in structure of the phase plot as the motion estimation process is executed. For large non-rigid, possibly articulated, objects within a scene it would be possible to divide the motion segmented region into grid cells. These cells can then be separately iterated through the transform processing to detect the optimal transformation.

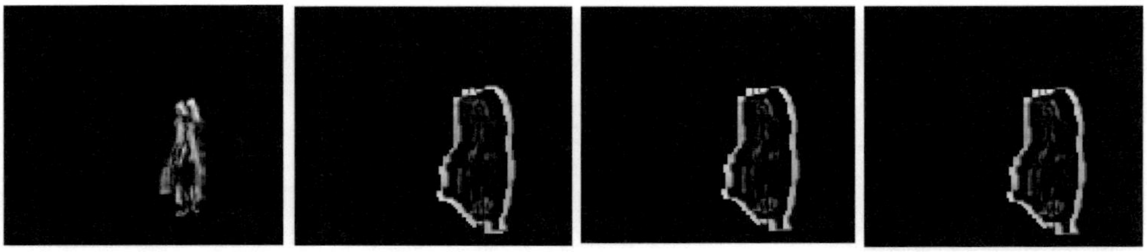

(a) (b) (c) (d)

Figure 228: Difference images for the human subjects application: (a) original difference image, (b) difference image from correction by Mutual Information processing, (c) difference image from correction by Box Counting method and (d) difference image from correction by Information Dimension.

IMAGE REGISTRATION FOR EGO-MOTION DETECTION USING CHAOS

The last application to demonstrate the chaos-based registration is the ego-motion estimation problem shown in Fig. **196**. For the initial tests, two grid cells in the upper right and upper left of the image are utilized to demonstrate the expanding nature of the image motion as a camera moves through a scene. For the image in the upper right hand corner, the resulting transformations to map the two images from the sequence are provided in Fig. **229** (b) through (d) for each of the registration metrics employed. Again note the similarity in performance of the three methods. The transformations used for this registration are shifting in the row and column dimensions independently and zooming of the image. The resulting transformed images still have some differences from the original image since the underlying barrel distortion of the images was not corrected for. A more complex set of allowable transformations could better convert the second image into the first image; however, the main goal is to understand the macro-level motion experienced between the frames rather than perfectly matching the two images. The transformation vectors in all three resulting images are commensurate with the forward direction ego-motion of the camera and the outer corners of the image scene move outward in a radial direction with a slight overall zooming of the image as well.

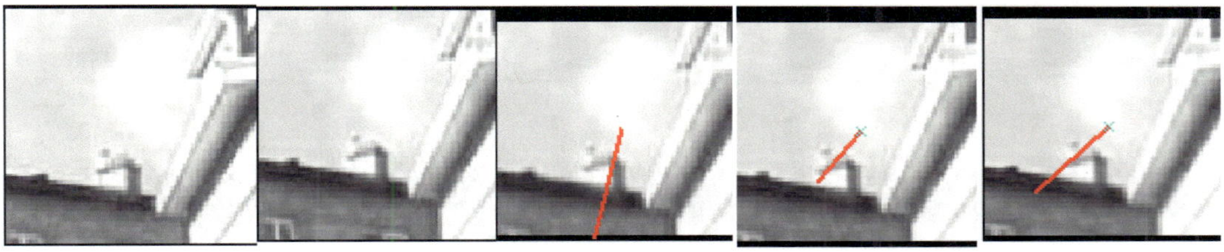

(a) (b) (c) (d) (e)

Figure 229: Example ego-motion detection from moving camera sequence [148]: (a) original image grid cell, (b) second image grid cell, and (c) second image with directional vectors showing best shift of image to match first image using Mutual Information ($\Delta R = 10, \Delta C = -1, Zoom = 1.0$), (d) second image with directional vectors showing best shift of image to match first image using Box Counting ($\Delta R = 6, \Delta C = -6, Zoom = 1.05$), and (e) second image with directional vectors showing best shift of image to match first image using Information Dimension ($\Delta R = 4.0, \Delta C = -5.0, Zoom = 1.04$).

The effectiveness of the chaos-based registration is further verified in Fig. **230** (a) and (b). Note the phase plots demonstrate the expected compression of the phase space trajectory to a vertical line as the transformation of the second image matches the first image. The resulting difference images from using the Box Counting measure are provided in Fig. **230** (c) and (d). For comparison, Fig. **231** (b) through (d) provides all of the resulting difference images from the optimal transformations detected using each of the three methods, Mutual Information, Box Counting and Information Dimension.

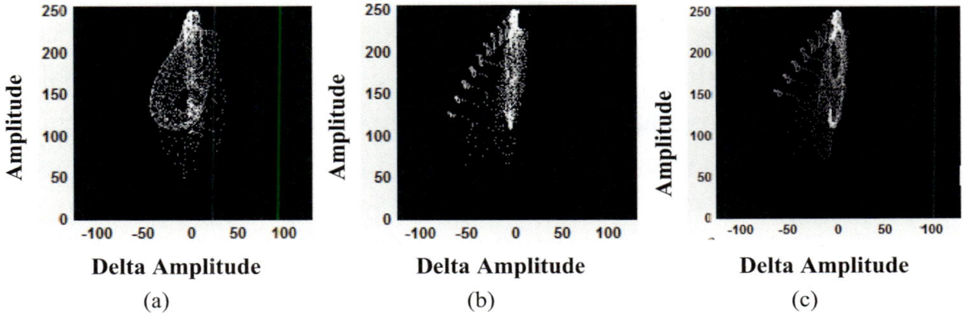

Figure 230: Example of phase plots from ego-motion detection : (a) original phase plot, (b) phase plot from Mutual Information best match, and (c) phase plot from Information Dimension best match.

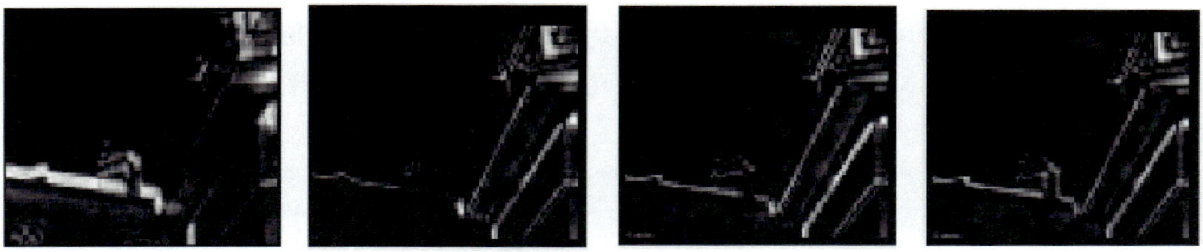

(a) (b) (c) (d)

Figure 231: Difference images for ego-motion detection application: (a) original difference image, (b) difference image from correction using Mutual Information processing, (c) difference image from correction using the Box Counting method and (d) difference image from correction using the Information Dimension.

(a) (b) (c) (d) (e)

Figure 232: Upper right grid cell image to test ego-motion detection from moving camera sequence [148]: (a) original image grid cell, (b) second image grid cell, and (c) second image with directional vectors showing best shift of image to match first image using Mutual Information ($\Delta R = 4, \Delta C = 3.5, Zoom = 1.01$), (d) second image with directional vectors showing best shift of image to match first image using Box Counting ($\Delta R = 4, \Delta C = 4, Zoom = 1.01$), and (e) second image with directional vectors showing best shift of image to match first image using Information Dimension ($\Delta R = 4.5, \Delta C = 3.5, Zoom = 1.01$).

The validity of the motion vectors is further confirmed by Fig. **232** (b) through (d) which shows the resulting relative motion detection for the upper left grid cell. In this grid cell, the resultant motion vectors are moving outward radially as expected for the corner regions of an image where the sequence is experiencing a forward direction ego-motion of the camera. Fig. **233** (a) provides the original phase plot and Fig. **233** (b) shows the corrected phase plot when using the Box Counting method. Fig. **233** (c) shows the original difference image and the resultant difference image after the application of the image transformation determined by the Box Counting method.

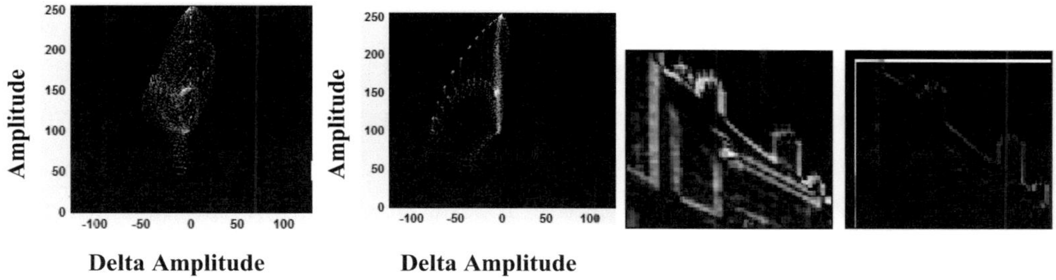

(a) (b) (c) (d)

Figure 233: Example phase plots and resultant difference image from ego-motion detection from moving camera sequence: (a) phase plot from original image pair, (b) phase plot from best resultant match of two images, (c) initial difference image of two original input images, and (d) final difference image after correction from motion determined using Box Counting.

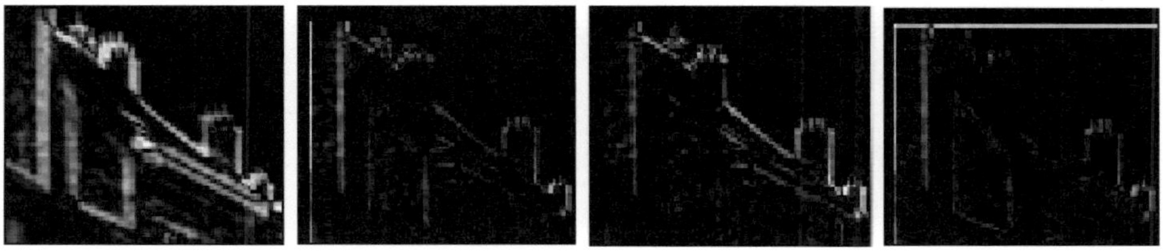

(a) (b) (c) (d)

Figure 234: Difference images for ego-motion detection application: (a) original difference image, (b) difference image from correction by Mutual Information processing, (c) difference image from correction by Box Counting method and (d) difference image from correction by Information Dimension.

For comparison, Fig. **234** (a) through (d) provide the similar results on this image pair when the motion parameters are estimated using the traditional Mutual Information. As can be surmised from the nearly identical motion vectors shown in Fig. **232** (b) through (d), the resultant difference images between these two methods are nearly identical. These example images, however, are relatively straightforward where there is significant structural content in the images and there are no non-motion effects such as illumination to confound the traditional methods.

Fig. **235** provides the complete motion vector estimation for the ego-motion application. The motion vectors for each grid cell are provided for each method. Notice in general the results are consistent between the traditional Mutual Information method and the chaos-based methods in terms of the direction of the vectors and their amplitudes. The obvious exception is the middle two grid cells in the upper row where there was no motion detected by Mutual Information. The reason for this was the confounding influence of large non-changing background regions in the images that overwhelm the Mutual Information calculation. In general the complete set of motion vectors for the Box Counting method provides a better representation of the actual ego-motion since it is immune to the influences of large regions of monotone unchanging background.

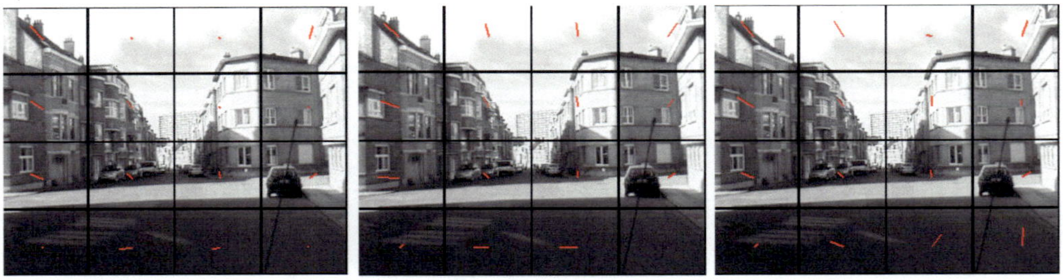

(a) (b) (c)

Figure 235: Complete motion vector estimations for the ego-motion detection application [148]: (a) results using Mutual Information, (b) results using Box Counting method, and (c) results using Information Dimension.

CONCLUDING REMARKS

The problem of image registration has common applications in both the implementation of the correlation-tracker for object tracking and in scene registration for ego-motion estimation. In both cases the approach is to utilize pixel-based methods to determine the optimal set of image transformations to transform the second image in a sequence into the initial image. The gold standard for such approaches to date has been the use of Mutual Information to compare the two images. We showed two situations where the traditional Mutual Information method was at a significant disadvantage to the chaos-theoretic approach defined in this text, (i) scenes with small regions of change in large uniform backgrounds, and (ii) scenes when either global or spatio-temporal illumination changes were present in addition to the motion of the object of interest. Both of these situations can frequently occur in real-world tracking and ego-motion applications.

For the correlation tracking application, we provided results for two target types, namely rigid body objects (vehicles) and non-rigid bodies (humans). The results for the fractal methods compared favorably with the Mutual Information methods for both the Box Counting method and the Information dimension. All three methods provided similar vectors defining the transformations which the image sequence has undergone. For the ego-motion estimation application, a sequence of image scenes with a camera moving with both translations through the image scene and rotations as the camera changed directions was used. Again the chaos-based algorithms were compared with the Mutual Information measure, and the results compared favorably.

In both of these cases the chaos-based Box Counting method significantly outperformed Mutual Information. The Information Dimension approach initially performed poorly as well, however, when a proposed background and illumination removal method is applied, the Information Dimension method also significantly outperformed Mutual Information. The advantage of the chaos-based methods lies in the fact that in phase space the effects of illumination and motion are dramatically different and hence can be easily removed. Traditional grayscale methods throughout the text have been shown to be inferior since they cannot readily distinguish the effects of illumination from the effects of motion.

 Application of Chaos and Fractals to Computer Vision, 2014, 270-303

CHAPTER 10

More Applications to Post-Attentive Vision – Chaos Theory and Object Recognition

Abstract: The application of concepts from chaos theory to a broad range of lower level computer vision has proven useful throughout the text so far. These tasks have included motion detection and segmentation, texture analysis and image registration and tracking. The application of chaos theory to the higher level computer vision task of pattern recognition has also been an area of active research. This is particularly true in the area of chaotic neural networks based on the known chaotic behavior of biological neural systems. Pattern recognition can be considered an optimization problem where the best matching pattern maximizes the probability of correct classification. The application of optimization algorithms such as genetic algorithms to pattern recognition has also proven fruitful, and the dependence of these algorithms on random number generation for processes such as mutation makes them logical candidates for improvements using chaos theory to develop more robust random behavior. In this chapter the application of chaos theory to neural networks and genetic algorithms for the high level computer vision function of object recognition will be explored.

Keywords: Classification, pattern recognition, optimization, neural networks, genetic algorithms, chaotic mutation, chaotic neural networks, chaotic genetic algorithms.

RECOGNITION AS AN OPTIMZATION PROBLEM

Concepts from the field of chaos theory and the related field of multi-fractal analysis have proven useful throughout the text for a broad variety of computer vision applications. The flow of the text began with low-level image processing functions, such as motion detection and texture analysis, and advanced through the vision hierarchy into higher level vision functions such as registration and object tracking. This final chapter is devoted to exploring the application of chaos theory to the high level vision task of object recognition. In Chapter 8 we exploited the ideas of spatial chaos and the analysis of chaos in phase space to create features useful for texture recognition. The results of applying chaos-related features to recognize textures were shown to be quite positive. Chaos-related features have also been successfully applied to other recognition tasks, such as EEG, ECG, and seismic signal recognition [149]. Li *et al.,* in [150] have

Michael E. Farmer

also applied chaos theory to the task of feature selection to improve the results of a face recognition task. Wang and Wang applied chaos to determining the optimal number of input features required for pump diagnostics based on the embedding dimension of the chaotic input signals [151]. They then used the embedding dimension to determine the optimal number of Support Vector Machine classifiers needed to process these signals in a parallel classifier architecture. This chapter is devoted to applying chaos theory to the recognition algorithms rather than applying chaos theory to developing or selecting features that may be used in traditional pattern recognition frameworks.

A related class of algorithms which have shown improvement through the application of chaos theory has been optimization algorithms. This area of research is of interest to our exploration of chaotic pattern recognition since Hornegger and Niemann note [152] that, "Optimization algorithms are very much a part of pattern recognition and computer vision". Recall the basic classification algorithm can be framed as the following optimization problem [152]:

$$\kappa = \arg\max_{\lambda} \left(p\left(\Omega_{\lambda} \mid O, B_{\lambda}, R, T\right)\right), \tag{103}$$

where κ is the output classification, Ω_{λ} is the set of possible object classes, B_{λ} is the collection of measures, and R and T are optional rotation and translation operators. Optimization algorithms also clearly find a place in computer vision applications such as image segmentation, image registration, feature selection, and classifier training. Optimization algorithms have also been applied to Machine Learning in general as noted by Bennett and Parrado-Hernandez in [122]. Genetic algorithms have been used in [159] for the training of Support Vector Machines (SVMs) and for training neural networks in [160]. Wang and Meng in [156] applied Particle Swarm Optimization to training SVMs.

Caponetto *et al.,* have noted that: "The convergence properties [of optimization algorithms]...are strongly connected to the random sequence applied... during a run" [157]. He noted that the strength of the randomness of these sequences can be improved through the introduction of chaos. Fig. **236** shows the effect on the performance of a neural network-based optimization algorithm when employing chaotic noise *versus* traditional Gaussian random noise. The algorithm was applied to two traditional problems, the traveling salesman problem and the quadratic assignment problem. In both cases we see that the chaotic noise was more powerful than traditional pseudo-random noise and led to greater solvability. Azamimi *et al.,* in [158] show that adding chaotic noise to the popular Back Propagation (BP) training algorithm for the multi-layer perceptron (MLP) improves the rate of convergence of the training over the conventional BP approach. The convergence rates of chaotic *versus* traditional BP algorithms are shown in Fig. **237**. Chen and Zhou and Chen in [153, 154] developed general search algorithms using simulated annealing algorithms based on chaotic neural networks. A very thorough application of chaos theory to optimization algorithms based on neural networks can be found in the survey paper by Ikeguchi *et al.,* [155]. Another popular optimization algorithm is the Particle Swarm Optimization algorithm whose performance has also been improved through the addition of chaos [156]. Interestingly, Ikeguchi *et al.,* note: "the temporal structure of the chaotic noise is important in the chaotic search" [155]. Interestingly they also noted that randomizing the order of chaotically generated noise actually reduced performance [155]. We will see later in this chapter that the chaotic sequences created by chaotic maps such as the logistics map are integral to creating chaotic classifier systems.

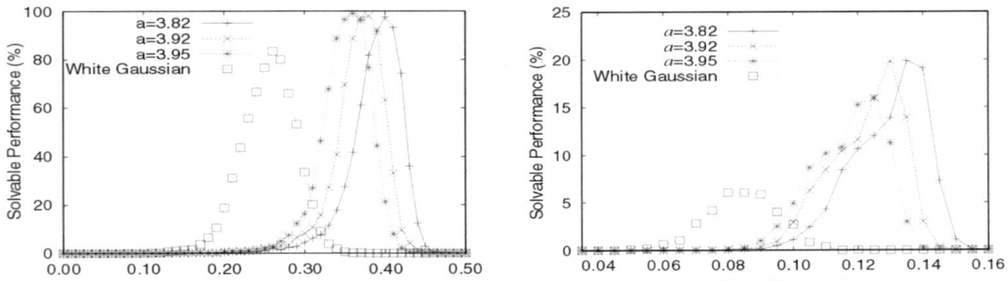

(a) (b)

Figure 236: Effects of chaotic noise rather than random noise on performance of neural network-based optimization algorithm for (a) traveling salesman problem and (b) a quadratic assignment problem [155].

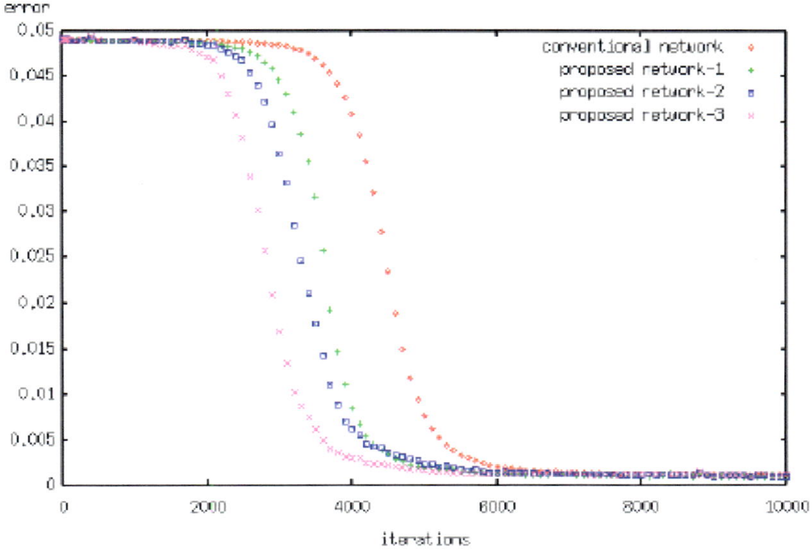

Figure 237: Effects of chaotic noise on the convergence of the Back Propagation algorithm for three different chaotic noise inputs *versus* traditional random noise, network 1 inserts noise after input layer, network 2 inserts noise before output layer, and network 3 inserts noise at both input and output layers [158].

We have seen numerous authors benefitting from applying chaos theory to a variety of optimization algorithms. The focus of this chapter, however, will be focused on employing concepts from chaos theory to pattern classification algorithms rather than general optimization algorithms. Two classifier approaches where chaos theory has found utility are neural networks and genetic algorithms [161-165, 170]. It is quite natural to explore the benefits of chaos in neural networks since these algorithms are inspired by biological neural systems which have been shown to employ chaotic signals. Genetic algorithms employ the randomness in tasks such as mutation. We noted earlier that random effects can be strengthened with the application of chaos [164, 165]. Other approaches to applying optimization algorithms to classification involve the use of swarm intelligence, either directly in particle swarm optimization-based classification in [166] or in ant colony optimization in [167]; however, these applications are not common. We will focus this chapter on exploring the use of chaos for improving neural networks and genetic algorithms as they are considerably more common approaches. Note that chaotic neural networks have become an incredibly active area of research deserving of a dedicated book unto itself so the coverage of the topic in this chapter will be constitute an overview of the subject.

CHAOS-BASED NEURAL NETWORKS FOR CLASSIFICATION AND OBJECT RECOGNITION

Recall in Chapter 2 we saw there was considerable evidence from neural research that the signals in biological neural pathways exhibited chaotic behavior [3, 4, 42-44, 48, 52]. While conventional neural networks have found immense popularity in the optimization and pattern recognition communities, there are still well-known problems with neural networks in some applications. Popular neural network models include the multi-layer perceptron (MLP) and the Hopfield network. The MLP is a feed-forward network and hence cannot in its basic form create chaotic dynamics. Architectures based on modifying the feed-forward multi-layer perceptron architecture to provide feedback are shown in Fig. **238**. A global mechanism is provided as in Fig. **238** (b) to provide this feedback. The architecture in Fig. **238** (a) takes a different approach. Here the inputs are sequenced with varying time delays similar to the varying time delays used to create the phase plots throughout the text. Note however these approaches are less common in chaotic neural network research and will not be discussed further.

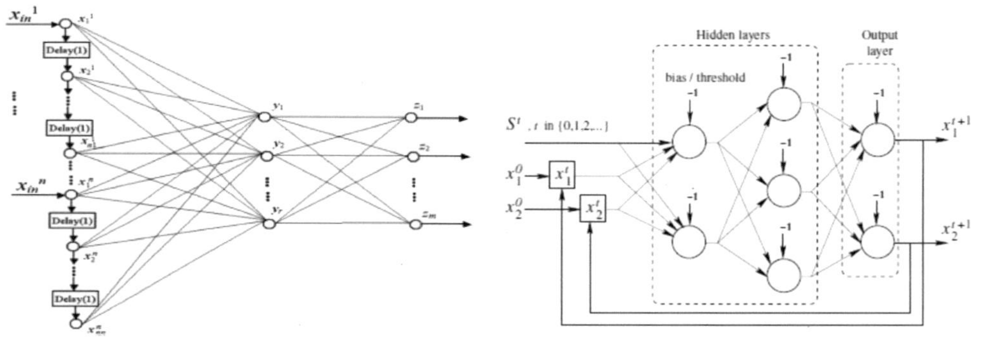

(a) (b)

Figure 238: Alternate chaotic neural network architectures based on MLP, (a) a sequentially time delayed MLP network topology [172] and (b) an MLP with a global feedback term [173].

The Hopfield architecture is the most popular approach for chaotic networks because as Zhao states in [168], "the basic idea for retrieving patterns is similar to a physical system whose phase space dynamics is dominated by locally stable states as a general content addressable memory". Mirzaei and Safabakhsh note in [169] that Hopfield networks applied to optimization problems often fail to converge or converge to solutions that are far from optimal. They also note that chaotic versions of these networks "can store more memory patterns than the conventional Hopfield networks since there is an infinite number of unstable periodic orbits which represent specific internal states of a system" [169]. Likewise, Taherkhani *et al.,* note that "A bounded nonlinear dynamic feedback system can become chaotic and, thus, dynamic feedback neural networks can show chaotic behavior" [170]. Zhao also notes that when Hopfield networks behave chaotically there are "itinerant orbits that visit nearly all the memory patterns, the so-called chaotic wandering" [168].

The recurrent Hopfield network is provided in Fig. **239** (a). The structure of the neurons within these architectures can be found in Fig. **239** (b). The standard Hopfield network differs slightly from this figure in that the standard Hopfield neuron does not have ego-feedback into each neuron but only feedback from all other neurons. Chaotic neural networks will add ego-feedback to each neuron as well. In general any attractor neural network, namely a network that employs feedback can be extended to employ chaos. In these attractor networks, pattern recognition is accomplished by presenting an incoming pattern to the network, and then the network progresses to "an invariable state, namely an attractor" [171]. The attractors correspond to specific learned patterns. This approach was employed by Chartier and Proulx in their non-linear dynamic recurrent associative memory (NDRAM) which is an attractor-based associative memory [171]. We will show in the subsequent sections of this chapter that the results of this attractor architecture are superior to traditional non-self-feedback network architectures. These networks have the potential for more robust convergence to correct solutions and higher performance when they are extended to employ chaotic attractors.

There are two common classes of chaotic neural networks, defined by *where* chaos is employed and *how* chaos is employed. The first class of algorithms is that in which chaotic dynamics is generated within the network. The second class of algorithms is that in which *external* chaotic noise is fed into the network [169]. In this text we will focus on the networks that employ chaotic dynamics within the network since these chaotic dynamics networks have shown considerable promise in computer vision-related applications.

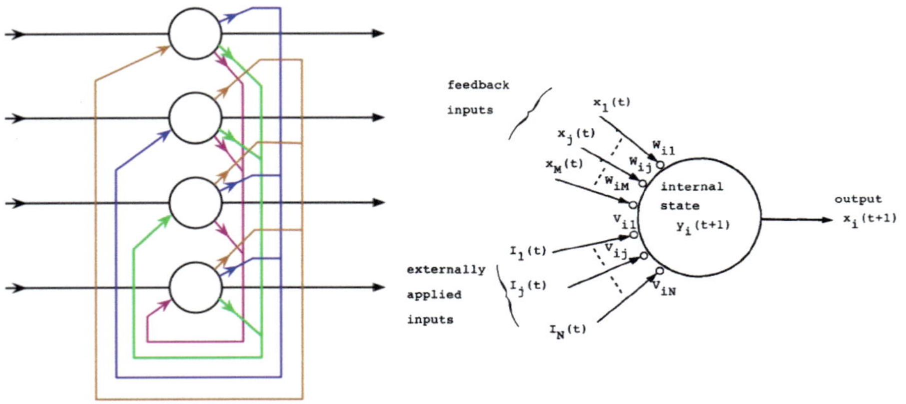

(a) (b)

Figure 239: Architecture for recurrent neural networks, (a) the Hopfield network topology and (b) the general artificial neuron with feedback [161].

Of the class of networks where chaotic dynamics is generated within the network, there are again generally two classes of chaotic neural networks defined by their network topology, (i) those based on the Hopfield network with the addition of the self-feedback term and (ii) those based on more general collections of neurons with chaotic dynamics. If chaotic dynamics is used within a network then the activation of the chaotic dynamics must be controlled to facilitate this transitioning between chaotic and non-chaotic behavior. The various chaotic neural networks proposed by researchers primarily differ by their methods and mechanisms employed to perform this control function.

Zhao notes that chaotic neural networks operate in two modes, (i) a chaotic phase, and (ii) a non-chaotic phase. This is analogous to the biological systems described by Freeman in [43, 168]. In the non-chaotic phase the networks behave as a conventional associative memory, while in the chaotic phase the networks employ the chaotic wandering. This wandering allows the networks to visit greater reaches of the search space more efficiently, resulting in faster convergence and improved performance [168].

The simplest architectures for chaotic neural networks consist of collections of bifurcating neurons proposed by researchers such as Zhao in [168], Taherkhani *et al.,* in [170], and Del-Moral-Hernandez in [174]. While any chaotic dynamics map would work, many of the efforts are based on the simple logistics map which is defined as [174]:

$$x(t+1) = \mu \cdot x(t)(1 - x(t)), \tag{104}$$

where μ is the chaotic attractor parameter and $x(t)$ is the iterated value producing the chaotic effect. The logistics map is one of the period-doubling bifurcating chaotic maps. Its phase space plot is provided in Fig. **240** (a) where the effects for varying μ are clearly visible. Del-Moral-Hernandez uses the two periodic points highlighted in Fig. **240** (a) to represent the binary values of *0* and *1* for encoding binary strings. Zhao employs four periodic points highlighted in Fig. **240** (b) to represent four grayscale levels for the highly quantized images provided in Fig. **241** [168].

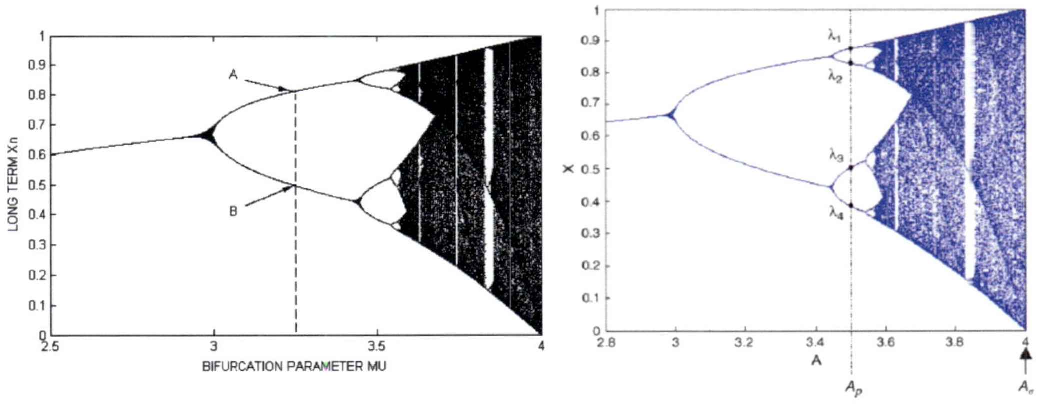

(a) (b)

Figure 240: Bifurcation structure of the logistics map, (a) two periodic points used by Del-Moral-Hernandez [174] and (b) four periodic points used by Zhao [168].

In the Zhao architecture there is a neuron assigned to each pixel in the image, and each pixel can attain one of four grayscale values that correspond to the abovementioned bifurcation points. Zhao employs the logistics map with an additional control parameter $z_i(\tau)$ in the form [168]:

$$x_i(t+1) = z_i(\tau)\cdot x_i(t)\left(1 - x_i(t)\right), \tag{105}$$

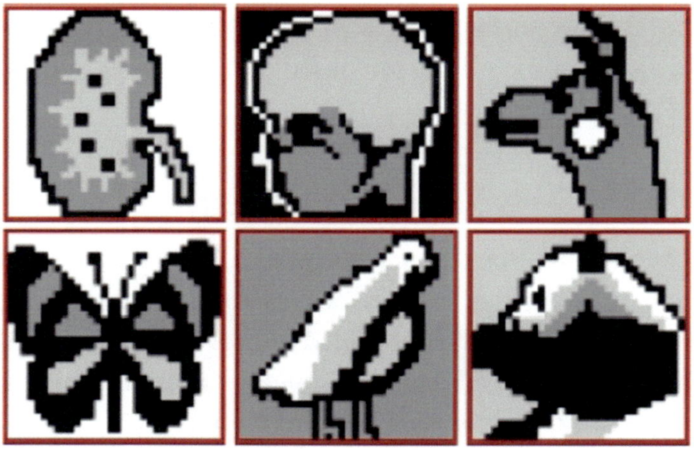

Figure 241: Four grayscale quantized images used by Zhao [168].

The term $z_i(\tau)$ can take on two values based on the desired chaotic *versus* non-chaotic behavior shown in Fig. **240** (b); either A_p for the periodic values corresponding the the final convergence to a grayscale value, or A_c for the chaotic value to facilitate chaotic wandering. The transition between these two values is determined by the following rule [168]:

$$z_i(\tau) = \begin{cases} A_p & \left| s\left(x_i(t)\right) - \sum_{j=1}^{N} w_{ij} s\left(x_j(t)\right) \right| < \delta \\ A_c & otherwise \end{cases} \tag{106}$$

The function $s(x_i(t))$ is an enumerated function with four values corresponding to the four actual grayscale values of the input images. The selection of the specific value is based on the closest bifurcation point $x_i(t)$ at that time interval.

The network stores a set of M patterns in a matrix of patterns, P. The weights w_{ij} used in Equation (106) are then computed using Hebbian learning according to [168, 174]:

$$w_{ij} = \sum_{k=1,M} (P_{i,k} P_{j,k}), \quad i \neq j, \tag{107}$$

where $P_{i,k}$ is the ith element of the kth training pattern. When the difference between the input image values and any of the pattern values (captured in the weights) is large, $z_i(\tau) = A_c$ and the neuron wanders chaotically. As the difference converges (*i.e.* the neuron value approaches that of a stored pattern) $z_i(\tau) = A_p$ and the neuron enters the periodic dynamics indicative of a pattern being recognized. Recall this is identical to the behavior of biological systems proposed by Freeman in [43].

Del-Moral-Hernandez [174] and the Taherkhani *et al.,* [170] employ similar collections of simple bifurcating neurons in differing architectures provided in Fig. **242**. As with Zhao these networks are collections of simple Logistic Map nodes but the chaotic behavior is controlled by an external controller. In the Taherkhani architecture, as with Zhao, there is a logistic map-based neuron assigned to each pixel in an image. Each neuron is responsible for reconstructing a particular pixel in the input image to match a stored image *via* [170]:

$$x_{n[0]} = x_t + D, \tag{108}$$

where $x_{n[0]}$ is the amplitude value of a pixel in the input image, x_t is the amplitude of the same pixel in the target image, and D is the difference between the stored and modified pixel. The pixel amplitudes are adapted based on a modification of the logistics function provided in Equation (105) to allow increasing or decreasing of pixel amplitudes according to [170]:

$$x_{i[t+1]} = \alpha_i \left\{ A_i \left[\left(\Delta x_{i[t]} / \alpha_i + 0.5 \right) \left(0.5 - \Delta x_{i[t]} / \alpha_i \right) \right] - 0.5 \right\}, \tag{109}$$

where A_i is the attractor parameter, set in their case to 4 for maximal chaotic behavior, and α_i is a control parameter. The neurons remain in a chaotic mode to enhance search. In this model the *extent* of the allowed changes in the pixel amplitudes is adjusted *via* the parameter α_i. This provides a cooling function where pixel amplitudes can change by large amounts when they are far from the target, and then they are changed by smaller amounts as the input pattern converges to a stored pattern. These α_i are determined for each pixel by the supervisor based on the displacement values *D*. If the ith element of *D* corresponding to a particular pixel falls below a threshold, then Equation (109) is deactivated and the value $x_{i[t+1]} = x_{i[t]}$.

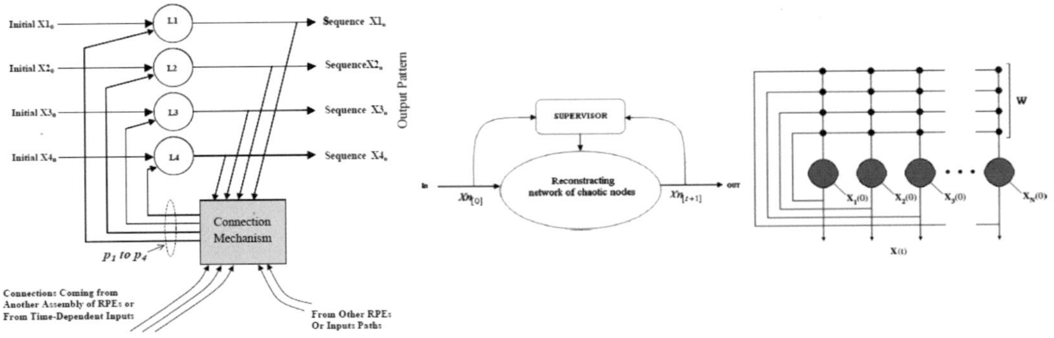

(a) (b)

Figure 242: Architectures for utilization of collection of logistics map-based chaotic nodes, (a) [174], (b) the collection of Logistic map based neurons controlled by a supervisor and (c) the recurrent architecture for the supervisor in (b) [170].

The approach by Del-Moral-Hernandez [174] is interesting in that it more closely mimics the biological model of Freeman in [43]. It employs chaotic Recursive Processing Elements (RPE) based on the logistics map. Taherkhani varies the range of values over which the pixel amplitude values could vary, while Del-Moral-Hernandez varies the chaotic behavior of each neuron by varying the logistics map parameter μ in Equation (104). When performing a pattern recognition task, the RPEs in the system begin in a chaotic state, and then transition over time to the non-chaotic period-doubling region of the Logistic Map shown as points *A* and *B* in Fig. **240**. This allows the system to quite naturally encode binary strings where *A* corresponds to a *0* and *B* corresponds to a *1*. The system uses the chaotic region of the map to explore transitioning bit values between the two allowed values. The input pattern sets the initial values of the *x(t)* in Equation (105). Over time the μ in each node settles to a minimum value where the chaotic behavior converges to the stable period-doubling points identified in Fig. **240**.

In this architecture the relative disagreement between a given node i and the remaining nodes in the architecture is used to drive each individual node's chaotic parameter. The difference in each node is computed according to [174]:

$$d_i = -\left(x_i - k_1\right)\left(\sum_j w_{ij}\left(x_j - k_1\right)\right) + k_2, \tag{110}$$

and d_i is used to calculate the chaotic parameter μ according to [174]:

$$\Delta\mu_i = d_i c - e. \tag{111}$$

In Equation (110) k_1 is the average of the x variables and k_2 is an offset to make the minimum d_i zero. The term $-e$ in Equation (111) drives the parameter μ low into non-chaotic behavior in situations of low disagreement with a stored pattern. Once again this behavior is similar to the behavior of biological systems identified by Freeman where neural systems begin in a chaotic state and converge to periodic orbits upon the recognition of a known pattern [43, 168].

One critical issue that the authors note is that the performance of the network degrades as more patterns are trained. The w_{ij} in Equation (110) are elements of the weight matrix W that encodes the specific patterns to be recognized by the system and defined by Equation (107). Notice Equation (107) has a summation over the number of stored patterns. As the number of patterns increase the values of the weight correspondingly increase which affects the chaotic behavior through Equation (110) and Equation (111). To offset this growing amplitude with more patterns they simply scale the Hebbian weights in Equation (107) by $1/\sqrt{M}$.

The above approaches have employed the basic architecture of traditional artificial neural network architectures. These architectures loosely model the macroscopic structure of biological neural systems. It is also possible to integrate chaotic behavior into models that more closely mimic biological systems. Detailed models of biological neuronal behavior were modeled by the Hodgkin-Huxley and the FitzHugh-Naguma equations, however, these models are far too complex for artificial neural networks [161]. Caianiello developed an extended McCulloch-Pitts neuron which attempted to develop a simplified model of these biological models [161]. This model was further modified by Naguma and Sato, and this biologically inspired model of neuronal signal behavior serves as the basis for the work of Aihara for the basic feedback neuron provided in Fig. **239** (b) [161]. The model was further refined in his work with Adachi in [175]. The Aihara/Adachi model has served as the basis for many researchers in chaotic neural networks. A simplified version of the original Aihara equation for the internal state of a chaotic neuron is defined by [161, 176]:

$$y_i(t+1) = ky_i(t) + \alpha\left(\sum_{j=1}^{M} w_{ij}x_j(t) + I_i\right) - z_i x_i(t) \tag{112}$$

where the $y_i(t)$ are the internal state values, $x_i(t)$ are the outputs of the neurons, I_i is bias for each neuron, k is a damping factor for the neuron, α is a scaling factor for the inputs, and the w_{ij} are the connection weights. The term z_i is the self-feedback connection weight. This term provides the control required to drive the dynamics of the network between the chaotic and non-chaotic behavior. The output of each neuron is defined to be [161]:

$$x_i(t+1) = 1\Big/\left(1 + \mathrm{e}^{-y_i(t+1)/\varepsilon}\right), \tag{113}$$

where ε controls the steepness of the output function.

The last term in Equation (112) has been modified by Chen and Aihara to provide more complex chaotic behavior. Their modified model generates transient chaotic behavior by replacing $z_i x_i(t)$ with the time-dependent term $z_i(t)x_i(t)$ where [176]:

$$z_i(t+1) = (1-\beta)z_i(t) \tag{114}$$

with β being a damping factor. The term $z_i(t)$ is equivalent to the temperature of an annealing process. It drives the network from a chaotic network to a traditional

Hopfield network as its amplitude is reduced. Mirzaei and Safabakhsh in [169] have successfully used this model for the development of a chaotic string edit algorithm.

Other authors such as Qin and Oommen have argued that this basic Aihara/Adachi approach is actually not purely chaotic but only quasi-chaotic. They extended the basic Aihara/Adachi approach further to provide true chaotic behavior in [61]. First they rewrite the internal state for the neurons as being the sum of two distinct states where the single parameter k in Equation (112) is replaced by two terms k_r and k_f, with the result being [61]:

$$\begin{aligned} x_i(t+1) &= f\left(\eta_i(t+1)+\xi_i(t+1)\right) \\ \eta_i(t+1) &= k_f\eta_i(t)+\left(\sum_{j=1}^{M} w_{ij}x_j(t)\right) \\ \xi_i(t+1) &= k_r\xi_i(t)-\alpha x_i(t)+a_i \end{aligned} \tag{115}$$

Then they modify these internal states by having them updated based on the results of a single neuron, the Nth neuron rather than being updated by each individual neuron. They do this by modifying the first term in each equation by [61]:

$$\begin{aligned} \eta_i(t+1) &= k\eta_N(t)+\ldots \\ \xi_i(t+1) &= k\xi_N(t)+\ldots \end{aligned} \tag{116}$$

They then analyzed the chaotic behavior of this system and verified it has two positive Lyapunov exponents, which is indicative of truly chaotic behavior. They further enhance the chaotic behavior by replacing Equation (114) with the logistics map [61]:

$$z_i(t+1)=\beta\cdot 4\cdot z_i(t)\left(1-z_i(t)\right), \tag{117}$$

where the factor 4 provides maximal chaotic behavior and, β is a damping factor to transition the behavior to periodic states. They also modify the traditional Hebbian learning. First they normalize the patterns between *-1* and *1* rather than between *0* and *1* for Adachi. Then they normalize the weights in a manner similar to Del-Moral-Hernandez in [174]. The result is newly defined network weights [177]:

$$w_{ij} = \frac{1}{M} \sum_{k=1,M} (2P_{i,k} - 1)(2P_{j,k} - 1), \quad i \neq j, \tag{118}$$

They demonstrate that the Lyapunov exponents of this network architecture are truly chaotic and the system does not become periodic for any conditions other than the trained pattern being found [61, 177]. In other words all of the quasi-chaotic behavior has successfully been removed.

Crook *et al.,* used an interesting feedback method of control based on its biological plausibility [178]. They defined a nonlinear dynamic state (NDS) neuron model based on the Rossler attractor. The system is driven by the Rossler attractor's chaotic dynamics into a potentially large number of unstable periodic orbits (UPOs). Each of these UPOs produces a temporal periodic output pattern of spikes corresponding to a stored pattern, reminiscent of Freeman's observations of biological neural systems [43]. They note "The set of UPOs in a stabilized network is designated a pattern, in much the same way as the set of stabilized activations of neurons within a Hopfield network is regarded as a pattern" [178]. Specific input patterns are recognized by the system based on the times that these spikes are generated throughout the network. Fig. **243** (a) provides the phase plot of the internal dynamics of a typical neuron. Fig. **243** (b) provides a typical spike train produced by the system. Note the upper portion of the graph shows the spikes that pass the output threshold of the neuron and are transmitted to the neurons connected to it in the network. The lower portion of the time series in Fig. **243** (b) represents the chaotic wandering produced by the attractor.

The basic Rossler equations for three variables $x(t)$, $y(t)$ and $z(t)$are defined as [1]:

$$\frac{dx}{dt} = -y(t) - z(t)$$
$$\frac{dy}{dt} = x(t) + ay(t) \qquad (119)$$
$$\frac{dz}{dt} = b + z(t)(x(t) - c)$$

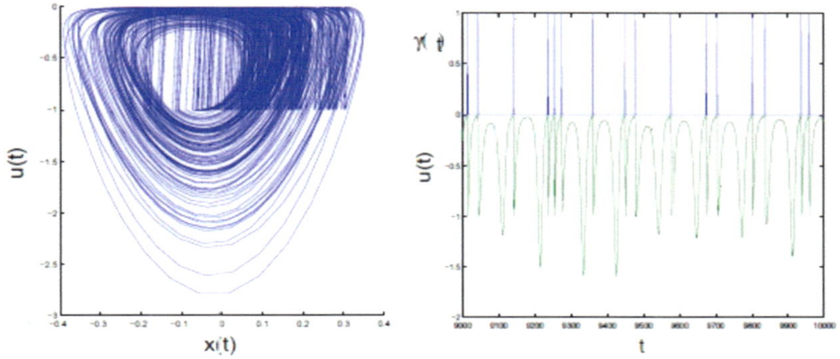

(a) (b)

Figure 243: Example of generation of spike trains, (a) phase plot of neuron and (b) resultant spike train when internal neuron voltage exceeds threshold [178].

The internal state of the neuron is defined by three parameters *u(t)*, *x(t)* and *y(t)* based on the Rossler variables. The term *u(t)* parallels the term *z(t)* in the Rossler equations. It is the internal voltage which drives the external spike trains according to [178]:

$$u_i(t+1) = \begin{cases} \eta_0 & : u_i(t) > \theta \\ u_i(t) + d\left(v + u_i(t)(-x_i(t)) + ku_i(t)\right) & : u_i(t) \le \theta \\ +w_i\Omega_i(t) + I_i(t) & \end{cases} \qquad (120)$$

The terms *x(t)* and *y(t)* govern the chaotic dynamics of the neuron based on [178]:

$$x_i(t+1) = x_i(t) + b(-y_i(t) - u_i(t)) \qquad (121)$$

and

$$y_i(t+1) = y_i(t) + c(x_i(t) + ay_i(t)) \qquad (122)$$

The last term in Equation (120), $I_i(t)$, is the total input for each neuron at a particular time. It is defined to be the weighted sum of all spike train inputs and any external inputs. The external inputs are provided by patterns of interest being applied to the network. It is defined mathematically to be [178]:

$$I_i(t) = \sum_{j=1}^{n} w_{ij}\gamma_j(t-\tau_j) + E_i(t) \tag{123}$$

The spike train outputs, $\gamma_j(t)$, from each neuron are generated based on a simple threshold test of $u(t)$ against a firing threshold θ according to [178]:

$$\gamma_j(t) = \begin{cases} 1 & : u_i(t) > \theta \\ 0 & : u_i(t) \le \theta \end{cases} \tag{124}$$

w_{ij} is the inter-neuron weighting and w_{ii} is the feedback weighting into the neuron. There are additional weighting terms in Equation (120), w_i. These terms are internal neuronal weights. These weights push the internal dynamics of the neuron so it produces spikes consistent with the global network pattern.

The term $\Omega_i(t)$ in Equation (120) controls activation of the feedback term based on the following rule [178]:

$$\Omega_i(t) = \begin{cases} 1 & : N_i(t) = \chi_j \ \ \& \, t \in S_i(\chi_j) \\ 0 & : otherwise \end{cases} \tag{125}$$

$N_i(t)$ is the pattern identification that the neuron i believes it is converging towards at time t. The term $S_i(\chi_j)$ is the collection of firing times for neuron i for pattern χ_j [178]. During training against a particular pattern χ_j, each neuron develops a table of all of the firing times of spikes it receives from all of the neurons in the network, including its self-feedback. When in test mode, if a trained pattern is applied to the network, it causes its respective spike trains to be generated and $\Omega_i(t) = 1$.

We have seen a variety of methods for employing chaos theory into neural networks. These various algorithms all employ some form of feedback in the network to drive the chaotic behavior. The specific architectures used to embed this feedback vary amongst researchers. They vary from simple linear weightings of outputs of the neuron to more complicated functions of the outputs based on chaotic maps such as the logistics map and the Rossler equations. Later in the chapter we will provide examples of applications of these neural networks to various pattern recognition problems related to computer vision. First we will investigate the use of chaos theory to extend another class of algorithms useful for pattern recognition, the genetic algorithm.

CHAOS-BASED GENETIC ALGORITHMS FOR CLASSIFICATION AND OBJECT RECOGNITION

Genetic algorithms are a type of probabilistic search algorithm that is based on the biological processes of evolution and natural selection [179]. Conventional genetic algorithms have been used for computer vision tasks such as image segmentation by various authors, including Angelina *et al.,* in [180]. They have also been used for image classification applications such as by Khoo and Suganthan in [181] and Auwatanamongkol in [182]. Lastly they have also been used for an integrated segmentation-classification system by Farmer and Shugars in [183].

A key challenge to applying genetic algorithms to any classification problem is to map the classification problem into one of matching chromosomes consisting of binary strings. The more common approaches to encoding computer vision classification problems are to encode the boundary of the given objects of interest in the image into sequences of line segments. This approach can either be performed after an initial segmentation or directly on edge-enhanced images. These line segments can be encoded either as sequences of (x, y) vertex locations as developed in [181] and shown in Fig. **244**, or as sequences angles between sequential line segments as in [182]. Another encoding approach used in [183] and provided in Fig. **245** initially performs a low level image labeling into blobs of common grayscale value. They then use a binary string to identify whether a particular region is retained as belonging to the classified object. This approach integrates the tasks of image segmentation and object classification.

In another approach Garai and Chauhduri encoded the set of translational and rotational transformations that best transform the incoming edge detected image into a training image as shown in Fig. **246** [186]. They encoded the transformation information as a series of bits for each aspect of the transformation as follows:

$$C_i = \{x_{i1},\dots,x_{im},y_{i1},\dots,y_{im},\theta_{i1},\dots,\theta_{im}\} \tag{126}$$

The fitness function calculates the cumulative distance between all the points within the edge map of the transformed input image and the edge maps of the training images.

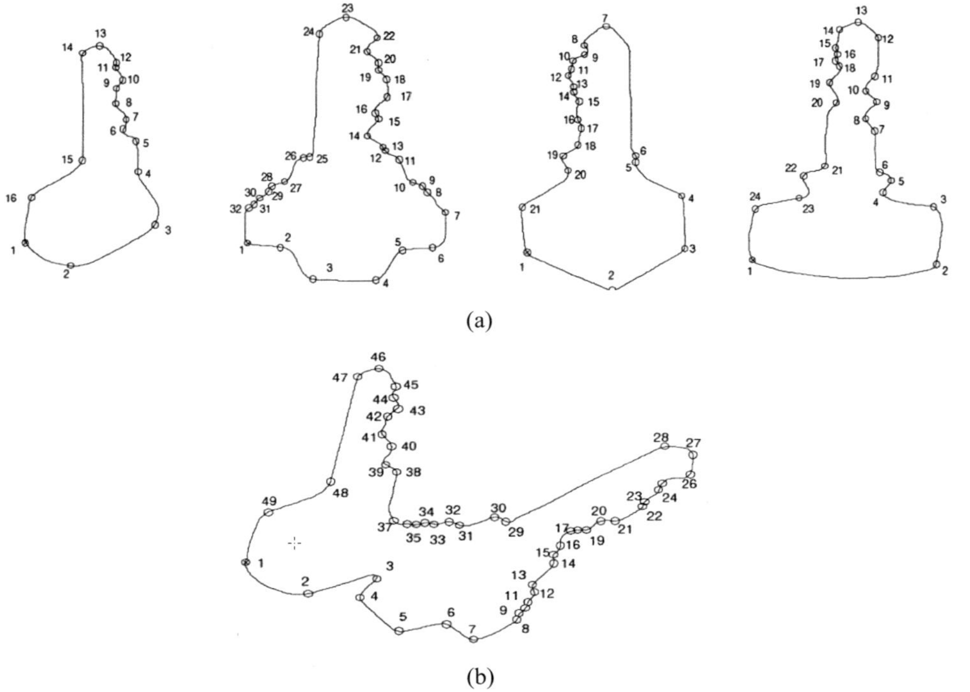

Figure 244: Example boundary encoding genetic algorithm pattern recognition problem, (a) training edge encoded images of keys and (b) test image with multiple keys present [181].

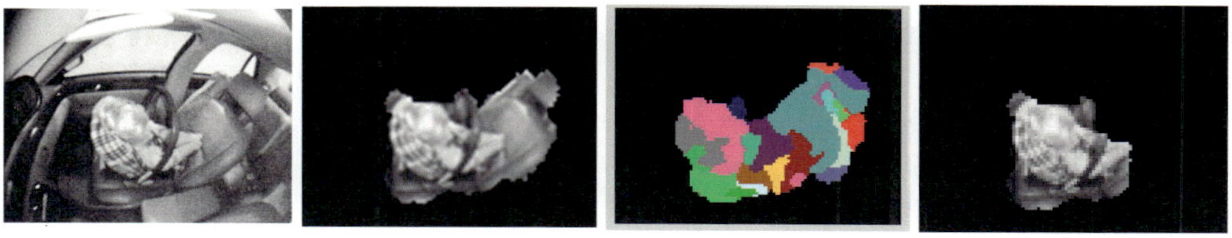

(a) (b) (c) (d)

Figure 245: Example region-based encoding genetic algorithm pattern recognition problem, (a) input image, (b) background-reduced image, (c) region encoded image, and (d) final best segmentation for best class (infant seat) [183].

(a) (b) (c)

Figure 246: Example transformation-based encoding genetic algorithm pattern recognition problem, (a) original image, (b) edge detected image, and (c) based transformed input-training image match [186].

Genetic algorithms rely on randomization as a key aspect of their design since they are a class of stochastic or probabilistic search algorithms. Zhang *et al.,* in [165] note that "taking advantage of chaotic randomicity, periodicity, and regularity…is… beneficial…to GA". Likewise, Jin-Yu *et al.,* reinforce this idea when they state: "Chaos has randomicity, ergodicity, and regularity. Based on these characteristics of chaos, using chaotic variables to optimize search is no doubt better than random search". [120]

As Caponetto *et al.,* discuss in [157], genetic algorithms can rely on randomization in the following portions of the algorithm:

(i) initial population generation,

(ii) mating pair selection when using roulette wheel method,

(iii) selection of cross-over points, and

(iv) mutation of the chromosomes.

As we mentioned at the beginning of this chapter, chaotic noise can be more powerful and random than traditional pseudo-random noise. Consequently, genetic algorithms can be improved through employing chaos in each of the above operations. The processing flow for a typical chaotic genetic algorithm (CGA) is provided in Fig. **247**. Note the same basic structure of traditional genetic algorithms is followed. In the figure we highlight the portions of the processing that have been identified as relying on randomization and thus being candidates for improving through chaos. Additionally we included two additional steps that various authors have employed to enhance the population diversity, namely chaotic population disturbance and chaotic population control. Note there is no standard definition of what steps comprise a CGA. Various authors have attempted to introduce the benefits of chaos into the GA through various combinations of the above mechanisms.

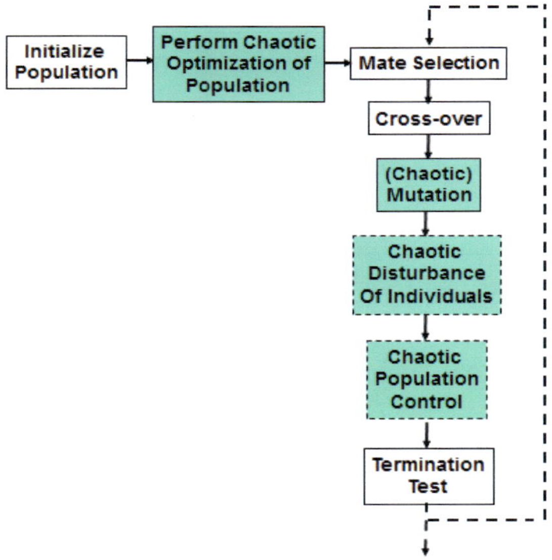

Figure 247: Typical processing flow for chaotic genetic algorithm [188].

The use of chaotic operators to improve the randomness and uniformity of coverage of the initial population has been exploited by many authors [120, 164, 165, 188, 189]. Ma notes that: "Natural populations are so dynamic that one of the first experimental evidences of chaos in nature was discovered by a theoretical ecologist" [184]. Fig. **248** shows two instances of chaos improving the distribution of the population. Fig. **248** (b) very clearly shows that the uniformity of coverage of the initial population using chaos is better than the coverage of a traditional pseudo-randomly generated population. Wang and Wu note: "the ergodic property of chaos phenomenon is used to optimize the quality of the initial population" [188].

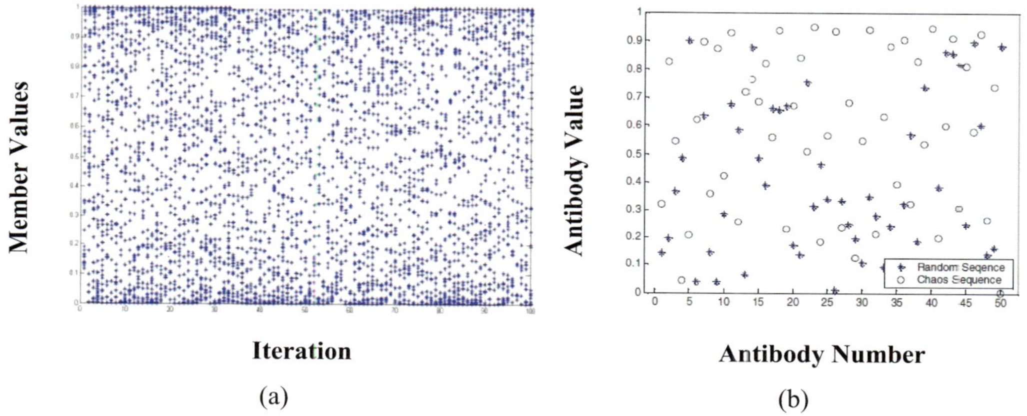

Figure 248: Examples of uniformity of initial population based on chaotic population generation: (a) ergodicity of sequence used to map initial population [120] and (b) comparison of uniformity of coverage of random *versus* chaotically generated initial population [164].

One key issue with applying chaos to the genetic algorithm population creation is that the structure of the chromosome for a particular application is determined by that application's specific data needs and may not be directly suited to manipulation by a chaotic function. Therefore the first step in many chaotic genetic algorithms is to perform a mapping of the problem-driven chromosome into a domain better suited for iterating with a chaotic function. The initial population can be considered a collection of vectors, Y whose range is *[a, b]* [189]:

$$Y = \left\{ y_1^0, y_2^0, \ldots y_i^0, \ldots y_N^0 \right\} \in [a, b] \tag{127}$$

The first step is to convert this arbitrary range of values into the range [0, 1] to create a new population according to [189]:

$$\beta_i^0 = \frac{y_i^0 - a}{b - a} \tag{128}$$

Once the variables are converted to the normalized range of *[0, 1]* they can be infused with a chaotic disturbance. The most common method for infusing a chaotic disturbance into the population is to propagate each of the initial population's members along the trajectory of a chaotic map. The most common map to use is the Logistic Map [165,189]:

$$\beta_i^{u+1} = \mu \cdot \beta_i^u \left(1 - \beta_i^u\right), \tag{129}$$

where μ is the chaotic parameter. Equation (129) becomes chaotic when $\mu > 3.57$ [165], and the majority of authors select $\mu = 4$ which is where the logistic mapping achieves the point of greatest ergodicity [120]. Equation (129) is iterated a number of times for each population sample β_i^u to drive each of the chromosome along the chaotic trajectory to differing points in the sample space. This exploits the characteristic of a chaotic system that small changes in initial conditions can lead to large divergences over time [1]. Note the various genetic operators, and most importantly, the fitness function calculation must be performed on the actual chromosomes and not these chaotic versions created by Equation (128). Therefore after the population has been 'ergodicized' using Equation (129) it is returned to the original problem space according to [165, 189]:

$$Y_i^0 = \beta_i^0 \cdot (b - a) + a \tag{130}$$

Once this population is returned to the original problem space the traditional GA operators of selection, crossover and mutation can be applied.

The next mechanism shown in Fig. **247** to employ chaos theory in genetic algorithms is to apply chaotic mutation to the individual genes in the chromosomes. Some of the earliest work in chaotic genetic algorithms was by Determan and Foster where they explored the use chaos in mutation. They employed an embedded additional gene field within all population members' chromosomes. This subfield encoded a bifurcation parameter of the logistics function to control each individual's mutation rate [185]. They developed populations of mixtures of chaotically and non-chaotically mutated members and demonstrated that a mix of the two provides an effective balance between exploration and exploitation of the search space. Garai and Chaudhuri note in [186] that "as the system goes towards convergence it is better to increase the rate of the mutation probability". They found that improving the randomness of the mutation operation through the application of chaos theory improved the population's diversity.

Chaotic mutation was also exploited by Wang *et al.,* in [190] and Yang *et al.* in [191]. Their chaotic mutation begins with the standard Logistic mapping [190]:

$$l_n' = \mu \cdot l_n \left(1 - l_n\right), \tag{131}$$

where μ is the chaotic attractor value, and l_n is an iterated value from some initial l_0. The mutation operator is defined for the jth gene of the ith chromosome, $x_i(j)$ according to [190]:

$$x_i'(j) = x_i(j) + \sigma_i(j) \cdot K_{ij}, \tag{132}$$

where $\sigma_i(j)$ is the scale of the mutation and K_{ij} is adjusted to vary across the range *[-1, 1]* by [190]:

$$K_{ij} = 2 \cdot l_n - 1 \tag{133}$$

To ensure smaller amounts of mutation are used later in the evolutionary process, the mutation scale factor $\sigma_i(j)$ is adjusted according to [190]:

$$\sigma_{i,t}(j) = \sigma_{i,0}(j) \cdot A \cdot \left(e^{-Bt} + C\right), \tag{134}$$

where t is the number of the current generation, and A, B, and C are parameters for tailoring the behavior. The term e^{-Bt} provides a cooling function to reduce the amount of change as time progresses.

The next mechanism for employing chaos in genetic algorithms highlighted in Fig. **247** is to apply an additional chaotic disturbance to the chromosome after the final mutation. Note this approach only tends to be used if traditional mutation is applied rather than chaotic mutation. Gao and Zheng in [187], Wang and Wu in [188], and Gao *et al.,* in [189] all employ some type of chaotic population disturbance. One approach to population disturbance is to apply a mixing of the most recent optimal solution with other solutions in the population. Gao and Zheng employ a decaying weighting factor that eventually ignores the optimal solution and only considers each population member on its own merit according to [187]:

$$\beta_k' = \alpha \cdot \beta_k + (1-\alpha) \cdot \beta^*, \tag{135}$$

where β_k is a given solution at the kth iteration of the algorithm and β^* is the current best member of the population. Note both β_k and β^* are the remapped versions of the chromosome using Equation (128). Alternatively, a chaotic offset can be directly applied to some subset of the top individuals of the search space population using [188]:

$$x_k' = x_k^* + \alpha \cdot u_{k,i}, \tag{136}$$

where x_k^* is a given member of a subset of the most fit members of the population at the kth iteration of the algorithm and $u_{k,i}$ is a Logistic Map-based chaotic disturbance. In both Equation (135) and Equation (136) α is a decaying mixing factor that monotonically reduces as the population iteration increases. This is employed because early in the genetic process the solutions will most likely be further from the optimal solution and need larger changes [187, 188]:

$$\alpha = 1 - \left[\frac{k-1}{k} \right]^m \tag{137}$$

Other approaches to chaotic population disturbance do not mix the optimal members with the remaining members of the population but rather directly modify members based on their relative fitness. Gao and Zheng, apply a chaotic disturbance to the chromosomes of each of the lower 90% fittest members of the population at the end of each epoch [187]. Alternatively Wang and Wu in [188] apply a chaotic disturbance to the members with the *best* fitness rather than the lowest fitness. In all cases the chaotic disturbance is applied through the following steps: (i) convert the chromosome to be disturbed into one suitable for chaotic processing using Equation (128), (ii) advance each converted chromosome along a chaotic map using Equation (129), and then return the chromosome to its native form using Equation (130).

One additional mechanism highlighted in Fig. **247** to employ chaos in genetic algorithms is to control the size of the population rather than the makeup of the population. Ma proposed using the logistics map to control the size of the population much the way natural populations grow and shrink based on the efficacy of their mating and the cooperation of the environment [184]. In many genetic algorithm implementations the population is of a fixed size. The population members initially mate and grow the population. Then the population is reduced back to the original population size through a broad range of strategies that vary from only allowing children to advance to allowing older population members to advance if they pass the fitness threshold. Rather than maintaining a fixed population, Ma found that: "dynamic populations controlled (modeled) by the Logistic Chaos Map model significantly outperform the fixed-size populations" [184]. They employ the logistics map because they note: "the Logistic map is the foundation for most analytic and deterministic [biological] population dynamics models" [184]. Ma dynamically modifies the size of the population by first mapping it to a variable x_i which ranges from *0* to *1* as was accomplished with Equation (128) earlier. Then at each epoch of the genetic algorithm they update the population based on [184]:

$$x_{i+1} = \mu \cdot x_i \left(1 - x_i\right) \tag{138}$$

Unlike the use of the logistics map in other portions of the GA processing, the value $\mu = 4$ is not allowed for population management. They found the optimal performance when the control parameter was set to just match the onset of chaos, namely $\mu = 3.57$ [184]. They also found, however, that there was not a significant variation in performance across the broad range of values of $2 \leq \mu < 3.83$.

TYPICAL RESULTS OF APPLYING CHAOS TO OBJECT RECOGNITION

In this section we will first demonstrate the performance of chaotic neural networks to a set of computer vision applications. Then we will demonstrate the performance of chaotic genetic algorithms. Recall that non-chaotic attractor networks were proposed by Chartier and Proulx where the attractors correspond to specific learned patterns [171]. They tested their architecture on a character recognition task and compared the results to traditional non-attractor, *i.e.* non-self-feedback networks. The results are provided in Fig. **249** (b) which shows the recall performance on an associative memory problem. In this figure noise of increasing amplitude is being used to corrupt the test image, and the recall rate is determined. As we can see from the figure the NDRAM architecture was significantly more robust to increasing noise levels compared to traditional architectures [171].

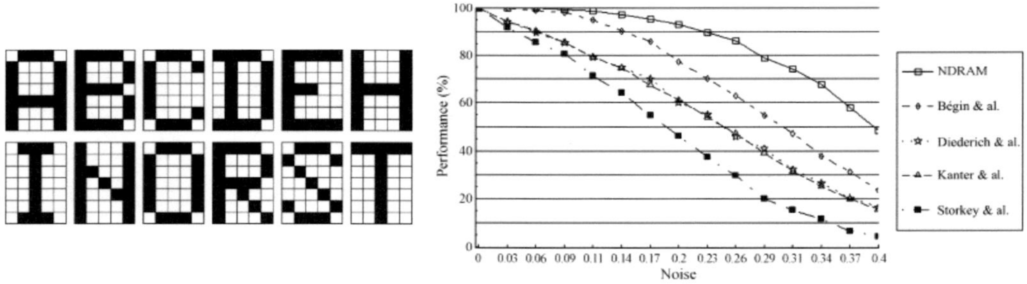

(a) (b)

Figure 249: Example results of attractor-based Associative memory by Chartier, (a) training data set and (b) results with varying amounts of noise when compared to non-attractor methods [171].

Recall however, that the basic NDRAM attractor architecture relied on non-chaotic attractors. By enhancing the architecture and employing chaotic behavior, the overall performance can be improved even further. The simplest chaotic model discussed was that of Zhao in [168]. Their logistics map-based neurons significantly improved the performance over traditional linear associative memories as can be seen in both Fig. **250** and Fig. **251**. In Fig. **250** (d) the recognition performance of the Zhao chaotic network is compared to a traditional linear associative memory. It is clear that for increasing noise levels (D-axis) the chaotic network significantly outperforms the traditional network. Likewise in Fig. **251** the Zhao network is shown to considerably outperform a traditional Hopfield network in a character recognition task.

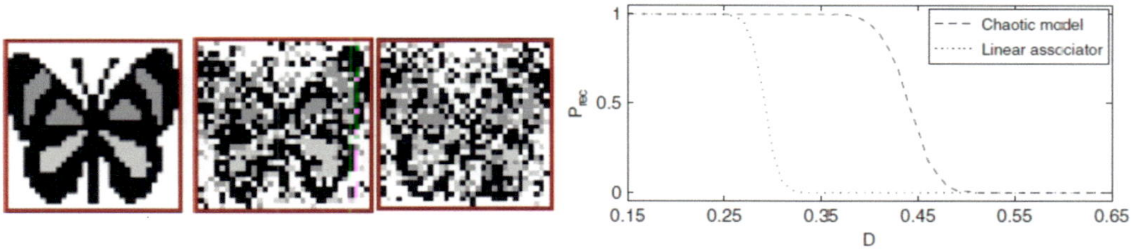

(a) (b) (c) (d)

Figure 250: Example results of chaotic associative memory by Zhao *versus* a traditional linear associative memory, (a) training data set and (b) D=0.3 noise corruption, (c) D=0.4 noise corruption, and (d) results compared to non-chaotic methods [168].

Taherkhani combined a collection of simple chaotic neurons with a controller based on the above NDRAM attractor network [170]. By combining both the chaotic neurons and an external controller they further improved the results over either of the Zhao or NRDAM architectures as is shown in Fig. **251**. They also dramatically outperform the traditional Hopfield network.

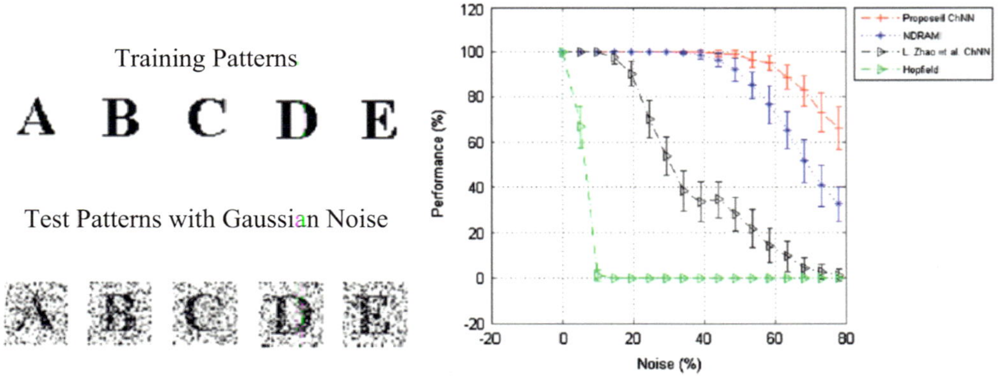

(a) (b)

Figure 251: Example results of chaotic associative memory by Taherkhani *versus* non-chaotic attractor and traditional Hopfield network, (a) training and test data sets and (b) results with varying amounts of noise when compared to non-chaotic methods [170].

Fig. **252** (a) provides the results of the architecture proposed by Del-Moral-Hernandez in recovering noisy patterns compared to the traditional Hopfield network. They show that as bit-flipping noise in a grayscale image increases, the chaotic neural networks significantly outperform the traditional neural network architectures.

Fig. **253** summarizes the performance of the Aihara-based model of chaotic neural network developed by Qin and Oommen in [177]. Fig. **253** (a) provides the training and test patterns provided to the network where the first test pattern is the number *4* with 30% noise added to it. The second test pattern, the number *5*, is not in the training set. Fig. **253** (b) shows the output of the four possible outputs of the system when the number *4* is input to the network. Recall this network converges to a solution when it enters a periodic output signal state [177]. As can be seen in the figure the network developed a periodic output for the 4th training sample which was the correct classification. Fig. **253** (c) shows results when a noisy version of number *4* is input to the system. Note once again the network generates the same periodic output for the 4th training sample. The output in Fig. **253** (d) shows that when a test image that was not included in the network training is provided to the network (the number '*5*'). None of the possible training pattern outputs enter a periodic output state.

The results provided are for a variety of neural network architectures employing chaotic dynamics. They show that for many applications the integration of chaos into the neural network architecture can lead to significant performance improvements over traditional network architectures.

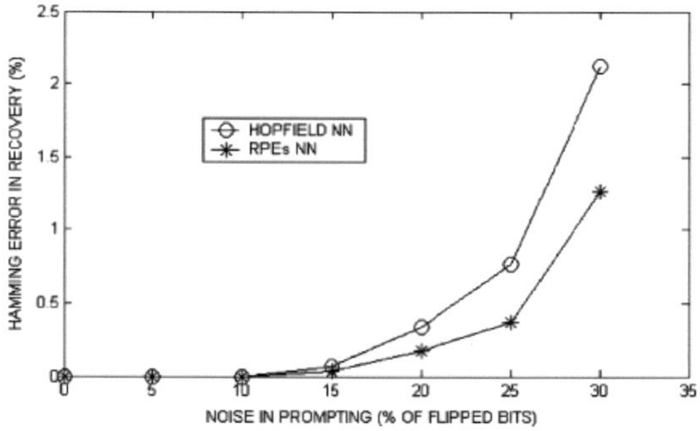

Figure 252: Performance of Del-Moral-Hernandez network *versus* traditional Hopfield network [174].

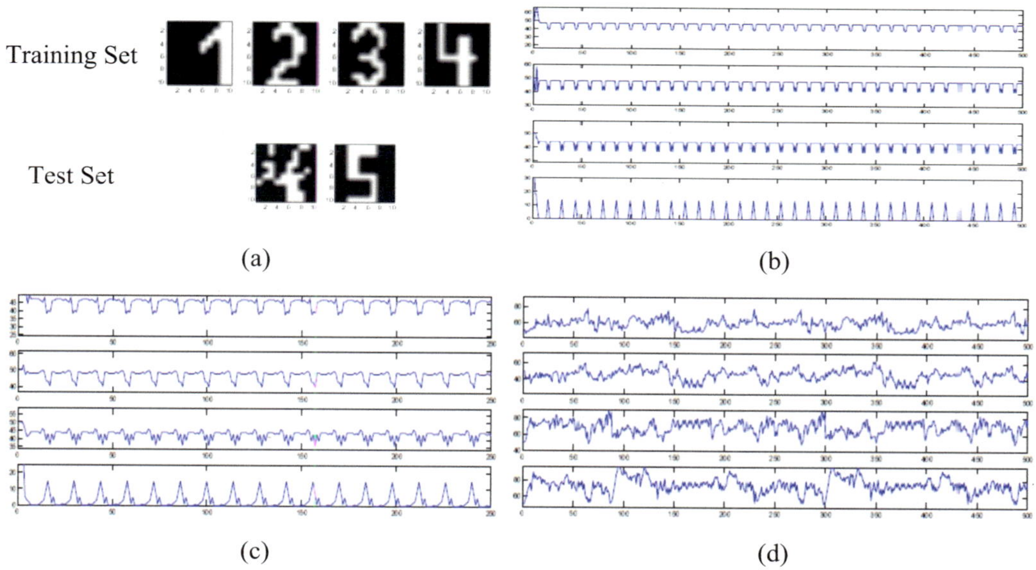

Figure 253: Demonstration of the Aihara-based network developed by Qin and Oommen, (a) training and test images, (b) output for training sample 4 provided to the network, (c) output for test sample 1 (a noisy number '*4*') provided to the network, and (d) output for the second test sample which was not included in the training set [177].

The results of integrating chaos theory into genetic algorithms are also quite positive. Two common complaints of traditional genetic algorithms are: (i) slow convergence and (ii) convergence to non-global minima. Fig. **254** provides examples of the improved convergence behavior of the chaotic genetic algorithm when compared to traditional optimization algorithms. Fig. **254** (a) compares the clustering performance of a chaotic genetic algorithm to a collection of feedforward neural networks. In all cases the CGA has improved variance in the cluster memberships which resulted in a significant reduction in the number of iterations required for convergence to a solution. In Fig. **254** (b) the performance of a set of genetic algorithms using a variety of both traditional pseudo-random number and chaotic random number generators are evaluated. All of the chaotic generators outperformed the traditional generator in terms of the best population member *versus* GA epoch when tested on a function minimization application. These improvements are quite dramatic, and the number of required iterations for convergence is dramatically reduced compared to traditional methods in these figures.

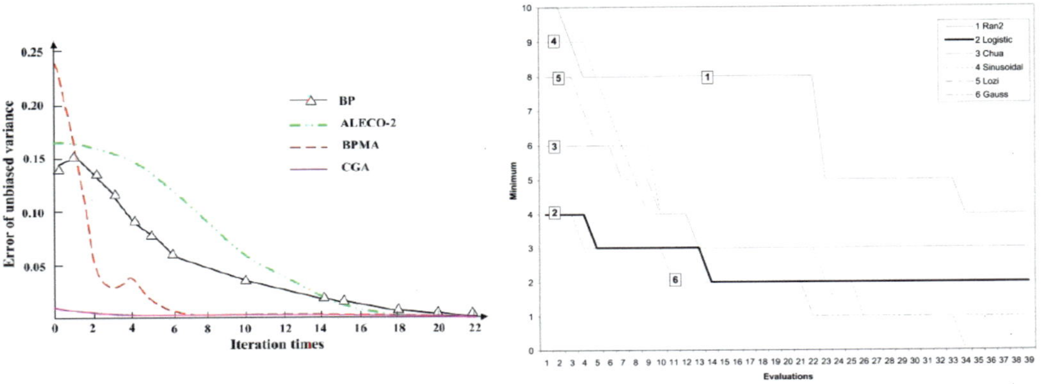

(a) (b)

Figure 254: Improvement in convergence behavior for chaotic genetic algorithm, (a) error in clustering algorithm comparing [188] and (b) optimization of the De Jong function in a minima search when comparing the logistics map to a traditional pseudo-random number generator and other chaotic random number generators [157].

While not a recognition problem, path planning is a basic optimization problem that has been widely researched. Fig. **255** shows the performance of a chaotic GA *versus* a traditional GA for a path planning problem. The improvement of the path for the chaotic algorithm shown in Fig. **255** (b) is clear when compared to the traditional algorithm in Fig. **255** (a).

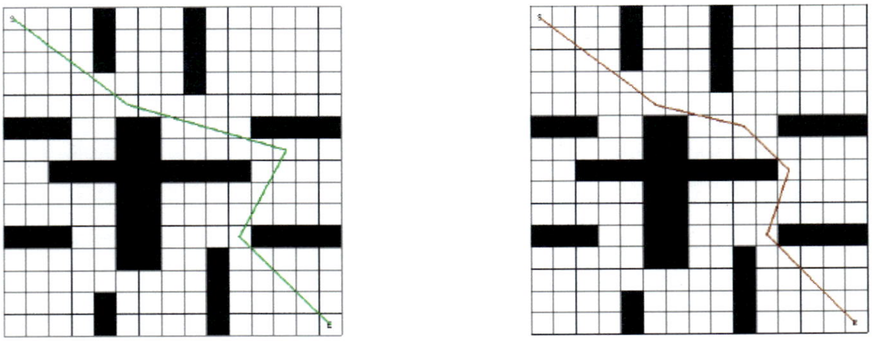

(a) (b)

Figure 255: Path planning results improved with the introduction of chaos into the Genetic Algorithm, (a) traditional GA and (b) reduced path length with chaotic GA [192].

Fig. **256** (a) shows a collection of training images used in a face recognition application that has been solved using a chaotic GA. These face images are all different views of a single person. The GA was used for performing the feature selection for the classification problem. The performance of the chaotic GA (labelled PCA-ICGA in the figure) is tested for a varying number of features being retained for classification. In each instance, the set of features selected by the chaotic GA outperforms the features found using other traditional methods.

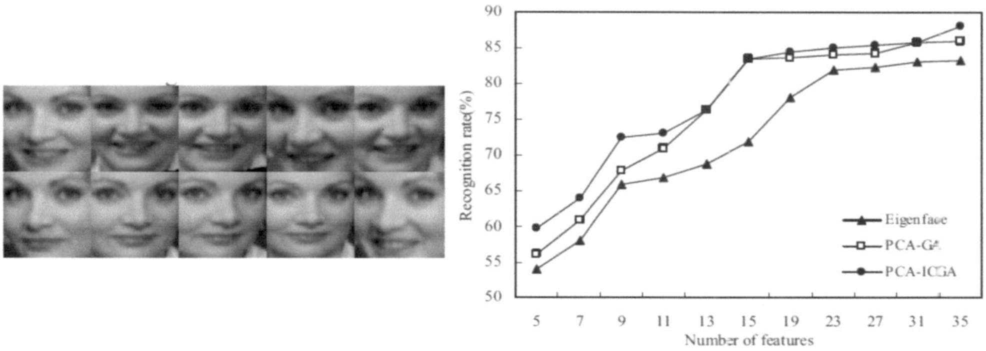

(a) (b)

Figure 256: Results for feature selection and classification using chaotic GA, (a) example faces from single person and (b) resulting recognition rate showing improved performance for chaotic GA [150].

In this section we saw that adding chaos to traditional algorithms to solve optimization problems and related pattern recognition problems can improve performance over the baseline algorithms. The improvement in neural networks by integrating chaotic behavior is not surprising given the evidence of chaotic signals in biological pathways. Likewise employing chaos theory in genetic algorithms lead to performance improvements due to greater 'randomness' of the underlying random numbers used for the various tasks in the GA algorithms.

CONCLUDING REMARKS

In this chapter we explored the application of chaos theory to the computer vision task of pattern recognition. The two main approaches to pattern recognition discussed in this chapter are neural networks and genetic algorithms. Given the research into the chaotic behavior of electrical signals within biological neural pathways it is not surprising that artificial neural network researchers began employing chaotic dynamics to improve the functioning of their systems. Also given the ability of chaotic systems to uniformly explore large expanses of phase space it was expected that chaos can improve the power of pseudo-random number generation. As genetic algorithms rely so heavily on random inputs for controlling mutation and initial population generation, it is not surprising that they have benefited from employing chaotic dynamics as well.

While chaos theory has been used to improve the back-propagation algorithm for training multi-layer perceptrons, the bulk of the research in chaotic neural networks has been in improving recurrent neural networks. These networks often employ variations of the Hopfield network architecture since chaotic systems rely on feedback to create the non-linear behaviors. Approaches vary broadly in the particular implementation of chaos in neural networks but they do employ common chaotic functions such as the logistics map and the Rossler function to facilitate the chaotic dynamics within the neurons. The systems in general exploit the transitioning from chaotic to non-chaotic behavior as they perform the recognition task in a manner analogous to biological systems. Recall biological systems begin in an ambient chaotic state and then converge to periodic states upon recognition of a particular pattern. By beginning in states of chaos, these systems are able to rapidly explore large regions of their classification space quickly and reduce the effects of local minima that commonly negatively impact the performance of traditional neural networks.

Researchers in chaotic genetic algorithms exploit the improved randomness of chaotic functions to improve many aspects of these algorithms. The performance of the systems is positively impacted by using chaos in the initial population generation to improve the population's diversity through a more complete coverage of the search space. Chaotic maps have also been used to improve the randomness of the cross-over selection points and the mutation operators by many researchers. Additionally some researchers further randomize the search population at the end of the mutation stage with an additional chaotic disturbance of the population by propagating population members along chaotic map trajectories. As the population matures over time, the chaotic behavior of these systems is cooled in much the same way cooling is used in simulated annealing to ensure the system is not too random and not converging to solutions.

The results for both chaotic neural networks and chaotic genetic algorithms have been positive for improving the recognition accuracy of object classification systems. Note the mechanism with which chaos theory has been employed by classification systems is more direct than its application to the other aspects of computer vision. In pattern recognition the chaotic dynamics are directly inserted into the recognition processing. In other portions of the text the differences between chaotic and non-chaotic behavior have been exploited to improve the specific tasks at hand by for example differentiating the effects of illumination and motion. In these chaotic recognition systems, the transition to non-chaotic behavior is exploited to drive the system to converge to final solutions. In all applications throughout the text, however, the exploitation of concepts from chaos theory has helped to improve the robustness of specific computer vision tasks.

REFERENCES

[1] H.O. Peitgen, H. Jurgens, and D. Saupe, *Chaos and Fractals*, Springer, 1992.
[2] O. LeMeur, P. LeCallet, D. Barba, and D, Thoreau, "A coherent computational approach to model bottom-up visual attention", *IEEE Trans. on Pattern Analysis and Machine Intelligence*, vol. 28, no. 5, pp. 802-817, 2006.
[3] H. Korn and P. Faure, "Is there chaos in the brain? II. Experimental evidence and related models", *C.S. Biologies*, No. 326, pp. 787-840, 2003.
[4] N. Nagao, H. Nishimura, and N. Matsui, "A neural chaos model of multistable perception", *Neural Processing Letters*, vol. 12, no. 3, pp. 267-276, 2000.
[5] J.L.P. Velazquez, "Brain, behaviour, and mathematics: are we using the right approaches?", *Physica D*, No. 212, pp. 161-182, 2005.
[6] A.L. Perrone, "Applications of chaos theory to lossy image compression", *Nuclear Instruments and Methods in Physics Research A*, vol. 389, pp. 221-225, 1997.
[7] M. Bouab, M. Khamadja, and S. Amira-Biad, "A robust chaotic image watermarking technique based on HVS and differential affine motion estimation", *Procs. IEEE Intl. Conf. on Signal Processing and Communications*, pp. 1387-1390, 2007.
[8] A. H. Abdullah, R. Enayatifar, and M. Lee, "A hybrid genetic algorithm and chaotic function model for image encryption", *Intl. Journal of Electronics and Communications*, vol. 66, pp. 806-816, 2012.
[9] C. H. Yuen, O. Y. Lui, and K. W. Wong, "Hybrid fractal image coding with quadtree-based progressive structure", *Journal of Visual Communications and Image Recognition*, vol. 24, pp. 1328-1341, 2013.
[10] A. Pentland, Fractal-based description of natural scenes", *IEEE Trans. On Pattern Analysis and Machine Intelligence*, vol. 6, no. 6, pp. 661-674, 1984.
[11] R. Lopes and N. Betrouni, "Fractal and multifractal analysis: A review", *Medical Image Analysis*, Vol. 13, pp. 634-649, 2009.
[12] P. Campisi, E. Maiorana, and A. Neri, "Video textures fractal modeling", *IEEE Signal Processing Letters*, vol. 14, no. 6, pp. 405-408, 2007.
[13] M. Varma and R. Garg, "Locally invariant fractal features for statistical texture classification", *Proc. IEEE Intl. Conference on Computer Vision*, pp. 1-8, 2007.
[14] W. Wang, M. Suzuki, and F. Ren, "Texture image retrieval based on gray-primitive co-occurrence matrix", *IEEE Intl. Conference on Natural Language Processing and Knowledge Engineering*, pp. 1-4, 2010.
[15] Z. Hai-ying, X. Zheng-guang, and Penghong, "A texture feature extraction based on two fractal dimensions for content-based image retrieval", *Proc. IEEE World Congress on Computer Science and Information Engineering*, pp. 117-121, 2008.
[16] I.R. Reljin, B. Reljin, I. Pavlovic, and I. Rakocevic, "Multifractal analysis of gray-scale images", *Proc. of the IEEE 10th Mediterranean Electrotechnical Conference*, vol. 2, pp. 490-493, 2000.
[17] C. Canus and J. L. Véhel, "Change Detection in Sequences of Images by Multi-fractal Analysis", *Proc. IEEE Intl. Conf. On Acoustics, Speech and Signal Processing*, pp. 2172-2175, 1996.
[18] S. Siddiqui and W. Kinsner, "Modeling of multifractal object boundaries", *Proc. of the IEEE Canadian Conference on Electrical and Computer Engineering*, vol. 2, pp. 1403-1408, 2003.

Michael E. Farmer

[19] S. He, S. Yang, A. Shi, and T. Li, "A Novel Image Moving Sea Targets Detection Method Based on Natural Measure Feature", *Procs. IEEE Intl. Symposium on Information Science and Engineering*, pp. 397-400, 2008.

[20] D. P. Subha, P. K. Joseph, R. A. U, and C. M. Lim, "EEG Signal Analysis: A survey", *Journal of Medical Systems*, vol. 34, pp. 195-2112, 2010.

[21] H.D.I Abarbanel, *Analysis of Observed Chaotic Data*, Springer, 1996.

[22] T. Tel and M. Gruiz, *Chaotic Dynamics*, Cambridge, 2006.

[23] P. Coullet, C. Elphick, and D. Repaux, "Nature of spatial chaos ", Phys. Rev. Letters, vol. 58, no. 5, pp.431-434, 1987.

[24] M. Farmer, "Multi-fractal and chaotic phenomena of motion in image sequences: Foundations", *Proc. of the IEEE International Conference on Acoustic, Speech, and Signal Processing,* 2007.

[25] S. Beauchemin and J. Barron, "The computation of optical flow," ACM Computing Surveys, vol. 27, no. 3, pp. 433-467, 1996.

[26] Y. Xu, A.K. Roy-Chowdhury, "The joint illumination and motion space of video sequences", *Proc. of the IEEE Intl. Conf. on Image Processing*, 2005.

[27] M. J. Black, D.J. Fleet, and Y. Yacoob, "Robustly estimating changes in image appearance", *Computer Vision and Image Understanding*, vol. 78, pp. 8-31, 2000.

[28] R. Mester, T. Aach, and L. Dumbgen, "Illumination-invariant change detection using a statistical colinearity criterion", *Proc. 23rd Symposium DAGM on Pattern Recognition*, pp. 170-177, 2001.

[29] Z. Zivkovic and F. van der Heijden, "Efficient adaptive density estimation per image pixel for the task of background subtraction", *Pattern Recognition Letters*, Vol. 27, No. 7, pp. 773-780, 2006.

[30] J. Pilet, C. Strecha, and P. Fua, "Making background subtraction robust to sudden illumination changes", *Proc. Of European Conference on Computer Vision*, pp. 567-580, 2008.

[31] C-C Chen and J.K. Aggarwal, "As adaptive background initialization algorithm with objects moving at different depths", *Proc. Intl. Conference on Image Processing*, pp. 2664-2667, 2008.

[32] I. Sato, Y. Sato, and K. Ikeuchi, "Illumination from Shadows", *IEEE Trans. on Pattern Analysis and Machine Intelligence*, Vol. 25, No. 3, pp. 290-300, 2003.

[33] Y. Tian, R.S. Feris, H. Liu, A. Hamparar, and M-T. Sun, "Robust detection of abandoned and removed objects in complex surveillance videos", *IEEE Trans. On Systems, Man, and Cybernetics-Part C: Applications and Reviews*, future issue, 2010.

[34] K. Sung, Y. Hwang, and I-S Kweon, "Robust background maintenance for dynamic scenes with global intensity level changes", *Proc. 5th Intl. Conf on Ubiquitous Robots and Ambient Intelligence*, pp. 759-762, 2008.

[35] J. Shi and J. Malik, "Normalized cuts and image segmentation", *IEEE Trans. on Pattern Analysis and Machine Intelligence*, vol. 22, No. 8, pp. 888-905, 2000.

[36] A.C. Lindgren, M. T. Johnson, and R. J. Povinelli, "Speech recognition using reconstructed phase space features", *Proc. IEEE Intl. Conf. on Acoustic, Speech, and Signal Processing*, pp. I-60-I-63, 2003.

[37] F. Fotopoulou, I. Theodorakopoulos, and G. Econonou, "Fusion in phase space for shape retrieval", *Proc. 19th European Signal Processing Conference*, pp. 936-940, 2011.

[38] J.P.W. Pluim, J.B.A. Maintz, M.A. Viergever, "Mutual Information Based Registration of Medical Images: A Survey", *IEEE Trans. on Medical Imaging*, vol. 22, no. 8, pp. 986-1004, 2003.

[39] J.P. Eckmann and D. Ruelle, "Ergodic theory of chaos and strange attractors ", *Reviews of Modern Physics*, vol. 57, no. 3, pp. 617-656, 1985.

[40] J.M. Wolfe and T.S. Horowitz, "What attributes guide the deployment of visual attention and how do they do it?", *Neuroscience*, vol. 5, pp. 1-7, 2004.

[41] J.M. Wolfe, "Visual Attention", in *Seeing*, 2nd Edition, Editor K.K. DeValois, Academic Press, pp. 335-386, 2000.

[42] W. J. Freeman, "The physiology of perception", *Scientific American*, vol. 264, no. 2, pp. 78-85, 1991.

[43] W. J. Freeman, "Tutorial on neurobiology: from single neurons to brain chaos", *Intl. Journal of Bifurcation and Chaos in Applied Sciences and Engineering*, vol. 2, pp. 451-482, 1992.

[44] L. Cauller, "Layer I of primary sensory neocortex: where top-down converges upon bottom-up". *Behav Brain Research,* vol. 71, no. (1-2), pp. 163–70, 1995.

[45] B. Brogaard, "Are there unconscious perceptual processes?", *Consciousness and Cognition*, vol. 20, pp. 449–463, 2011.

[46] A. Clark, "Perception, action, and experience: Unraveling the golden braid", *Neuropsychologia,* vol. 47, pp. 1460–1468, 2009.

[47] R. A. Brooks, "A robust layered control system for a mobile robot". *IEEE Journal of Robotics and Automation*, RA-2, pp. 14-23, 1986.

[48] X. Zhang, L. Zhaoping, T. Zhou, and F. Fang, "Neural activities in V1 create a bottom-up saliency map", *Neuron*, Vol. 73, pp. 183-192, 2012.

[49] M.C. Park, K.J. Cheoi, and T. Hamamoto, "A smart image sensor with attention module", *Proc. of the 7th IEEE Workshop on Computer Architecture for Machine Perception*, pp. 46 - 51, 2005.

[50] Y. Zheng, J. Gao, J.C. Sanchez, J.C. Principe, and M.S. Okun, "Multiplicative multifractal modeling and discrimination of human neural activity", *Physics Letters A*, vol. 344, pp. 253-264, 2005.

[51] M. Farmer, "Chaotic phenomena from motion in image sequences, *Procs. of the IEEE Intl. Joint Conf. on Neural Networks*, pp. 835-840, 2007.

[52] S. Ishizuka and H. Hayashi, "Chaotic and phase locked responses of the somatosensory cortex to a periodic medial lemniscus stimulation in the anesthetized rat", Brain Research, vol. 723, pp. 46-60, 1996.

[53] S. Ishizuka and H. Hayashi, "Chaotic mossy fiber stimulation efficiently increases the frequency of epileptiform bursts in rat CA3 hippocampal slices", *International Congress Series*, vol. 1291, pp. 93–96, 2006.

[54] J-H Cho and S-D Kim, "Object detection using multi-resolution mosaic in image sequences", *Signal Processing: Image Communication*, vol. 20, pp. 233-253, 2005.

[55] L. Zhang, T. Sakurai, H. Miike, "Detection of motion fields under spatio-temporal non-uniform illumination", *Image and Vision Computing*, Vol. 17, pp. 309-320 1999.

[56] R. Basri and D.W. Jacobs, "Lambertian reflectance and linear subspaces", *IEEE Trans. on Pattern Analysis and Machine Intelligence*, Vol. 25, No. 2, pp. 218-233, 2003.

[57] W. Klonowski,"Chaotic dynamics applied to signal complexity in phase space and in time domain", *Chaos, Solitons, and Fractals*, vol. 14, pp. 1379-1387, 2002.

[58] W. Klonowski, "Signal and image analysis using chaos theory and fractal geometry," *Mach. Graphics Vis.*, vol. 9,no. 1–2, pp. 403–431,2000.

[59] C-K. Peng, S.V. Buldyrev, A.L. Goldberger, S. Havline, R.N. Mantegna, M. Simons, and H.E. Stanley, "Statistical properties of DNA sequences", Physica A, vol. 221, pp. 180-192, 1995.

[60] T. Mattfeldt, "Spatial pattern analysis using chaos theory: A nonlinear deterministic approach to the histological texture of tumours", *Fractals in Biology and Medicine Mathematics and Biosciences in Interaction*, pp. 50-72, 1998.

[61] K. Qin and B. J. Oommen, "Chaotic and pattern recognition properties of a network of logistic neurons", Procs. of the 2nd IEEE Intl. Conf. on Computer Engineering and Technology, vol. 3, pp. 82-87, 2010.

[62] B. Chirikov, "Pseudochaos in statistical physics", *Intl. Conf. on Nonlinear Dynamics, Chaotic and Complex Systems*, 1995.

[63] P.V. McDonough, J.P. Noonan, and G.R. Hall, "A new chaos detector", *Computers in Electrical Engineering*, vol. 21, no. 6, pp. 417-431, 1995.

[64] M. Farmer, "Quantization effects in applying chaos theory to the detection of motion in image sequences", *Proc. IEEE Intl. Conference on Digital Signal Processing*, pp. 1-6, 2009.

[65] P.A. Bromiley, N.A. Thacker and E. Bouhova-Thacker, "Shannon Entropy, Renyi Entropy, and Information", *Tina Memo No. 2004-004*, 2004.

[66] C. Tricot, *Curves and Fractal Dimension*, Springer-Verlag, 1995.

[67] H.-H. Nagel, Universitat Karlsruhe, "http://i21www.ira.uka.de/image_sequences/".

[68] J. Theiler, "Estimating fractal dimension", Journal of the Optical Society of America, Vol. 7, No. 6, pp. 1055-1073, 1990.

[69] K. Falconer, *Fractal Geometry: Mathematical Foundations and Applications*, John Wiley & Sons Ltd., West Sussex, 2nd Edition, 2003.

[70] A. Materka, M. Strzelecki, Texture Analysis Methods – A Review, Technical University of Lodz, Institute of Electronics, *COST B11 Report*, Brussels, 1998.

[71] N. Sanchez, A.J Alfaro, and E. Perez, "The fractal dimension of projected clouds", *The Astrophysical Journal*, vol. 625, pp. 849-856, 2005.

[72] D. Amarasinghe and U. Sonnadara, "Predicting three-dimensional fractal dimensions of electrical discharges using two-dimensional projections", Journal of Science, Eastern University of Sri Lanka, vol. 6, pp.57-67, 2009.

[73] B. Mandlebrot, *The Fractal Geometry of Nature*, New York, Freeman and Co. 1983.

[74] M. Farmer, "A chaos theoretic analysis of motion and illumination in video sequences", *Journal of Multimedia*, vol. 2, no. 2, pp.53-64, 2007.

[75] D. Russakoff, C. Tomasi, T. Rohlfing, and C.R. Maurer, "Image similarity using mutual information of regions", *Proc. of the 8th European Conf. on Computer Vision,* pp. 596-607, 2004.

[76] L. Florack, "Modeling Foveal Vision", F. Sgallari, A. Murli, and N. Paragios (Eds.): *Proc. of the International Conference on Scale Space and Variational Methods in Computer Vision*, LNCS 4485, pp. 919–928, Springer-Verlag, 2007.

[77] S. Gould, J. Arfvidsson, A. Kaehler, B. Sapp, M. Messner, G. Bradski, P. Baumstarck, S. Chung and A.Y. Ng, "Peripheral-Foveal Vision for Real-time Object Recognition and Tracking in Video", *Proc. of the* International Joint Conference on Artificial Intelligence, pp. 2115-2121, 2007.

[78] M.T. Rosenstein and J. J. Collins, "Visualizing the effects of filtering chaotic signals", In *Computers & Graphics*, vol. 18, no. 4, pp. 587-592, 1994.

[79] T. Randen and J. H. Husøy, "Filtering for Texture Classification: A Comparative Study", IEEE Trans. On Pattern Analysis and Machine Intelligence, vol. 21, no. 4, pp. 291-310, 1999.

[80] CAVIAR project/IST 2001 37540, http://homepages.inf.ed.ac.uk/rbf/CAVIAR/.

[81] W.A.P. Smith and E.R. Hancock, "A unified model of specular and diffuse reflectance for rough, glossy surfaces", *Proc. IEEE Conference on Computer Vision and Pattern Recognition*, pp. 643-650, 2009.

[82] M. Oren and S.K. Nayar, "Diffuse reflectance from rough surfaces", *Proc. IEEE Conference on Computer Vision and Pattern Recognition*, pp. 763-764, 1993.

[83] M.R. Bales, D. Forsthoefel, D.S. Wills, and L.M. Wills, "The Georgia Tech IlluminationTransition (GTILT) Dataset," Mobile Vision Embedded Systems Lab (MoVES), Georgia Institute of Technology, http://www.ece.gatech.edu/research/labs/pica/GTILT.html, November 2012.

[84] M. R. Bales, D. Forsthoefel, D. S. Wills, and L. M. Wills, "Illumination change compensation techniques to improve kinematic tracking", *IEEE Workshop on Applications of Computer Vision*, pp. 434-439, 2011.

[85] I-Lids dataset for AVSS 2007.

[86] M. Farmer, "A Comparison of a Chaos-theoretic Method for Pre-attentive Vision with Traditional Grayscale-based Methods", *Proc. IEEE Intl. Conference on Advanced Video and Signal-based Surveillance*, pp. 337-342, 2011.

[87] WILD:Weather and Illumunation Database, Columbia University, http://www.cs.columbia.edu/CAVE/software/wild.

[88] C.A. Bouman and M. Shapiro, "A multi-scale random field model for bayesian image segmentation, " *IEEE Trans. on Image Processing*, vol. 3, no. 2, pp. 162-177, Mar. 1994.

[89] Y. Hu, C Zhao, and H. Wang, "Directional analysis of texture images using gray level co-occurrence matrix", *Proc. IEEE Pacific-Asia Workshop on Computational Intelligence and Industrial Applications*, pp. 277-281, 2008.

[90] Brodatz texture images, http://www.ux.uis.no/~tranden/brodatz.html

[91] W. Qiao, H. Wang, X. Wu, and H. Wang, "Crowd target extraction and density analysis based on FTLE and GLCM", *Proc. IEEE Intl. Conf. on Signal and Image Analysis*, pp. 1-4, 2009.

[92] D. Terzopoulos, "Co-occurrence analysis of speech waveforms", *IEEE Trans. On Acoustics, Speech, and Signal Processing*, vol. ASSP-33, no. 1, pp. 5-30, 1985.

[93] R. Haralick, K. Shanugam, and I. Dinstein, "Textural features for image classification", *IEEE Trans. On Systems, Man and Cybernetics*, vol. SMC-3, no. 6, pp. 610-621, 1973.

[94] A. Bourissou, K. Pham, W. C. Au, J. A. Kong, and T. L. Toan, "Classification of a polarimetric SAR image using fractal concepts", *Procs. of the IEEE Intl. Geoscience and Remote Sensing Symposium*, pp. 1599-1601, 1993.

[95] S. Novianto, Y. Suzuki, and J. Maeda, "Near optimum estimation of local fractal dimension for image segmentation", *Pattern Recognition Letters*, vol. 24, pp. 365-374, 2003.

[96] K. Kim, S. Jeong, B. T. Chun, J. Y. Lee, and Y. Bae, "Efficient video image retrieval by using local co-occurrence matrix texture features and normalized correlation", *Proc. IEEE TENCON*, pp. 934-937, 1999.

[97] J.H. Kim, S.C. Kim, and T.J. Kang, "Fractal dimension co-occurrence matrix method for texture classification", *Proc. IEEE TENCON Conference, Region 10*, pp. 1-4, 2006.

[98] C. Poynton, "The rehabilitation of gamma", *Proceedings of SPIE/IS&T Conference on Human Vision and Electronic Imaging III*, vol. 3299, 1998.

[99] M. Ogier, "Gamma Correction: what to know, and why it's as important as ever", http://www.planetanalog.com/document.asp?doc_id=528110&site=planetanalog.

[100] "Korea University Elevator Scenes", Courtesy of Hanseok Ko, Korea University, video taken in 2011".

[101] L. Barreira, Y. Pesin, and J. Schmeling, "On a general concept of multifractality: multifractal spectra for dimensions, entropies, and Lyapunov exponents", *Chaos*, vol. 7, pp. 27-38, 1997.

[102] W. Kinsner, "A unified approach to fractal dimensions", *Proc. IEEE Conf. on Cognitive Informatics*, pp. 58-72, 2005.

[103] B.R. Hunt and V.Y. Kaloshin, "How projections affect the dimension spectrum of fractal measures", *Nonlinearity*, vol. 10, pp. 1031-1046, 1997.

[104] A.J. Roberts, "Use the information dimension, not the Hausdorff", *Nonlinear Sciences*, 2005.

[105] S.A. Borovkova, "Review of correlation dimension estimators", http://dissertations.ub.rug.nl/FILES/faculties/science/1998/s.a.borovkova/c2.pdf

[106] M.Cross, http://crossgroup.caltech.edu/Chaos_Course/Lesson9/Dimension.pdf.

[107] M-P. Dubuisson and R.C. Dubes, "Efficacy of fractal features in segmenting images of natural textures", *Pattern Recognition Letters*, vol. 15, pp. 419-431, 1994.

[108] S. W. Myint and N. Lam, "A study of lacunarity-based texture analysis approaches to improve urban image classification", *Computers, Environment and Urban Systems*, vol. 29, pp. 501-523, 2005.

[109] K. I. Kilic and R.H. Abiyev, "Exploiting the synergy between fractal dimension and lacunarity for improved texture recognition", *Signal Processing*, vol. 91, pp. 2332-2334, 2011.

[110] R. A. Feagin, "Relationship of second-order lacunarity, Hurst exponent, Brownian motion, and pattern organization", *Physica A*, vol. 328, pp. 315-321, 2003.

[111] B. Mandlebrot, "Measures of fractal lacunarity: Minkowski content and alternatives", *Progress in Probability*, vol. 37, pp. 15-42, 1995.

[112] http://www.fp.ucalgary.ca/mhallbey/tutorial.htm.

[113] A. Wolf, J.B. Swift, H.L Swinney, and J.A. Vastano, "Determining Lyapunov exponents from a time series", Physica 16D, pp. 285-317, 1985.

[114] M. T. Rosenstein, J. J. Collins, and C. J. De Luca, "A practical method for calculating largest Lyapunov exponents from small data sets", *Physica D 65,* pp. 117-134, 1993.

[115] E. Trucco and A. Verri, *Introductory Techniques for 3-D Computer Vision*, Prentice Hall, 1998.

[116] R.J. Radke, S. Andra, O.Al-Kofahi, and B. Roysam, "Image change detection algorithms: A systematic survey", *IEEE Trans. on Image Processing*, vol. 14, no. 3, pp. 294-307, 2005.

[117] M. Farmer, Robust Pre-attentive Attention Direction Using Chaos Theory for Video Surveillance, *Applied Mathematics*, Scientific Research Press, September, 2013.

[118] J.A. Blimes, "A gentle tutorial of the EM algorithm and its application to parameter estimation for Gaussian mixture and hidden Markov models", *Tech Report TR-97-021*, Dept. of Electrical Engineering and Computer Science, Univ. of Washington, April 1998.

[119] K. Melkemi, M. Batouche and S. Foufou, "Chaotic multi-agent system approach for MRF-based image segmentation", Procs. of the 4th IEEE Intl. Conf. on Image and Signal Processing and Analysis, pp. 268-273, 2005.

[120] Z. Jin-Yu, C. Yan and H. Xian-Xiang, "IR thermal image segmentation based on enhanced genetic algorithms and two-dimensional classes square error", Procs. IEEE Intl. Conf. on Information and Computing Science, pp. 309-312, 2009.

[121] C. Ma, C. Liu, S. Ma and C. Jiang, "The application of a new entropy function and mutative scale chaos optimization strategy in the two-dimensional entropic image segmentation", Procs. of the IEEE Intl. Conf. on Computational Intelligence and Security, pp. 1647-1652, 2006.

[122] K. P. Bennett and E. Parrado-Hernandez, "The interplay of optimization and machine learning research", Journal of Machine Learning Research, vol. 7, pp. 1265-1281, 2006.

[123] M. Farmer, X. Lu, H. Chen, and A. Jain" Robust motion-based image segmentation using fusion", *Proc. of the IEEE International Conference on Image Processing*, pp. 3375 - 3378, 2004.

[124] M. Farmer and C. Yuan, "An algorithm for motion and change detection in image sequences based on chaos and information theory", *Proc. of SPIE Conference on Imaging Science and Technology*, vol. 6812, Image Processing: Algorithms and Systems VI, pp. 68120K-1- 68120K-12, 2008.

[125] Y. Jian, "Texture image segmentation based on Gaussian mixture models and gray level co-occurrence matrix", *Procs. of the Third International Symposium on Information Science and Engineering*, pp. 149-152, 2010.

[126] K. Wang and H. Xie, "Texture Image Segmentation Using Fully Global Minimization Active Contour Model", *Procs. of the Intl. Conf. on Multimedia Technology (ICMT)*, pp. 2649-2653, 2011.

[127] H. Zhu and O. Basir, "Proximity measure image based region merging for texture segmentation through Gabor filtering and watershed transform", *Procs. of the IEEE Conf. on Robotics,Intelligent, Systems, and Signal Processing*, pp. 742-747, 2003.

[128] Y. Yang and Shawn Newsam, "Comparing SIFT Descriptors and Gabor texture features for classification of remote sensed imagery", *Procs. of the IEEE Intl. Conf. on Image Processing*, pp. 1852-1855, 2008.

[129] J. Filip and M. Haindl, "Bidirectional texture function modeling: A state of the art survey", *IEEE Trans. On Pattern Recognition and Machine Intelligence*, vol. 31, no. 11, 1921-1940, 2009.

[130] A. Dixit and N. P. Hedge, "Image Texture Analysis-Survey", Procs. of the *Third Intl. Conf. on Advanced Computing and Communication Technologies (ACCT)*, pp. 69-76, 2013.

[131] M. H. Yap, H. Ugail, R. Zwiggelaar, and B. Rajoub, "A Short Review of Methods for Face Detection and Multifractal Analysis", *Procs. of the IEEE Intl. Conference on CyberWorlds*, pp. 231-236, 2009.

[132] J. Melendez, D. Puig, M. A. Garcia, Gabor-based texture classification through efficient prototype selection *via* normalized cut", *Procs. of the IEEE Intl. Conf. on Image Processing*, pp. 1385-1388, 2009.

[133] X. Zhang, X. Yang, P. Chen, and L. Jiao, "A complete unsupervised learning of mixture models for texture image segmentation", *Procs. of the IEEE Congress on Image and Signal Processing*, pp. 605-609, 2008.

[134] M.A.T. Figueiredo and A.K. Jain, "Unsupervised learning of finite mixture models", *IEEE Trans. on Pattern Analysis and Machine Intelligence*, vol 24, no. 3, pp. 381-396, Mar. 2002.

[135] T.W. Lee, M.S. Lewicki, and T.J. Sejnowski, "ICA mixture models for unsupervised classification of non-Gaussian classes and automatic context switching in blind signal separation", *IEEE Trans. on Pattern Analysis and Machine Intelligence*, vol. 22, no. 10, pp.1078–1089, 2000.

[136] R. O. Duda, P. E. Hart, D. G. Stork, *Pattern Classification*, 2nd Edition, Wiley, 2001.

[137] R. J. Larsen and M. L. Marx, *Introduction to Mathematical Statistics and Its Applications*, 5th Edition, Prentice Hall, 2011.

[138] B. Zitova′ and.J Flusser, "Image registration methods: a survey", *Image and Vision Computing*, vol. 21, pp. 977–1000, 2003.

[139] F. Khalifa, G.M. Beache, G. Gimelfarb, J.S. Suri, and A.S. El-Baz, "State of the art medical image registration methodologies: a survey", *Multi Modality State-of-the-art Medical Image Segmentation and Registration Methodologies: Vol. 1*, Springer Science and Business, 2011.

[140] F. Maes, D. Vandermeulen, and P. Suetens, "Medical image registration using mutual information", Proceedings of the IEEE, Vol. 91, No. 10, pp. 1699-1722, 2003.

[141] S. Dawn, V. Saxena, and B. Sharma, "Remote sensing image registration techniques: a survey", LNCS 6134, pp. 103–112, 2010.

[142] S. Oldridge, G. Miller, and S. Fels, "Automatic Classification of Image Registration Problems", *Proceedings of International Conference on Computer Vision Systems*, LNCS 5815, pp. 215–224, 2009.

[143] L.G. Brown, "A survey of image registration techniques", *ACM Computing Surveys*, vol. 24, pp. 325–376, 1992.

[144] P. Viola, "Alignment by maximization of mutual information", *A.I. Tech Report No. 1548, Artificial Intelligence Laboratory*, MIT, June 1995.

[145] Z. Gao, B. Gu, and J. Lin, " Mono-modal image registration using mutual information based methods", *Image and Vision Computing*, vol. 26, pp. 164–173, 2008.

[146] J.P.W. Pluim, J.B.A. Maintz, and M. A. Viergever, "f-Information measures in medical image registration", *IEEE Trans. On Medical Imaging*, vol. 23, no. 12, pp. 1508-1516, 2004.

[147] M. Farmer, "Illumination Invariant Intensity-based Image Registration Using Chaos Theory", *Proceedings of the IEEE Intl. Conf. on Acoustics, Speech, and Signal Processing*, 2013.

[148] http://www.vision.ee.ethz.ch/datasets/index.en.html.

[149] Z. Jinkui, C. Yi, W. Ying, "Chaotic analysis of seismic time series and short-term prediction with RBF neural networks", *Procs. of the Third Intl. Conf. on Genetic and Evolutionary Computing*, pp. 506-509, 2009.

[150] M. Li, W. Du and L. Yuan, "Feature selection of face recognition based on improved chaos genetic algorithms", *Procs. of the 3rd IEEE Intl. Symposium on Electronic Commerce and Security*, pp. 74-78, 2010.

[151] Z. Wang and Z. Wang, "Chaotic parallel support vector machine and its application for fault diagnosis of hydraulic pump", *Procs. of the IEEE Conf. on Prognostics and Health Management*, pp. 1-6, 2013

[152] J. Hornegger and H. Niemann, "Optimzation problems in statistical object recognition", *Energy Minimization Methods in Computer Vision and Pattern Recognition, Lecture Notes in Computer Science* Volume 1223, pp 311-326, 1997.

[153] S. S. Chen, "Chaotic Simulated Annealing by a Neural Network with a Variable Delay: Design and Application", *IEEE Trans. On Neural Networks*, vol. 22, no. 10, pp. 1557-1565, 2011.

[154] C. Zhou and T. Chen, "Chaotic neural networks and chaotic annealing", *Neurocomputing*, vol. 30, pp. 293-300, 2000.

[155] T. Ikeguchi, M. Hasegaw, T. Kimura, T. Matsuura, and K. Aihara, "Theory and applications of chaotic optimization methods", in *Innovative Computing Methods and Applications*, Springer-Verlag, pp. 131-161, 2011.

[156] S. Wang and B. Meng, "Chaotic particle swarm optimization algorithm for support vector machine", IEEE, pp. 1654-1657, 2006.

[157] R. Caponetto, L. Fortuna, S. Fazzino, nad M. Xibilia, "Chaotic sequences to improve the performance of evolutionary algorithms", *IEEE Trans. on Evolutionary Computation*, vol. 7, no. 3, pp. 289-304, 2003.

[158] A. Azamimi, Y. Uwate and Y. Nishio, "Effect of chaos noise on the learning ability of back propagation algorithm in feed forward neural network", *Procs. of the IEEE Intl. Colloquium on Signal Processing and its Applications*, pp. 78-81, 2010.

[159] A. Ebrahimzadeh and V. Ranaee, "Recognition of control chart patterns using genetic algorithm and support vector machine", *Procs. of the IEEE Intl. Conf. on Networked Digital Technologies*, pp. 489-492, 2009.

[160] Y. Tai-shan, "An improved genetic algorithm and its blending application with neural network", *Procs. of the IEEE Intl. Workshop on Intelligent Systems and Applications*, pp. 1-4, 2010.

[161] K. Aihara, T. Takabe, and M. Toyoda, "Chaotic neural networks", Physics Letters A, vol. 144, no. 6, pp. 333-340, 1990.

[162] A. Azamimi, Y. Uwate, and Y. Nishio, "Effect of chaos noise on the learning ability of back propagation algorithm in feed forward neural network", Procs. of the IEEE Intl. Colloquium on Signal Processing and its Applications, pp. 78-81, 2010.

[163] Y. He and L. Wang, "Chaotic neural networks and their applications", Procs. of the IEEE World Congress on Intelligent Control and Automation, pp. 826-830, 2000.

[164] J. Zhang, T. Li, N. Zhang, D. Wang, and S. Liu, "An immune evolutionary algorithm based on chaos mutation", Procs. of the IEEE Conf. on Intelligent Systems Design and Applications, pp.925-929, 2006.

[165] J. Zhang, X. Liu, T. Li, N. Zhang, N. Liu, and C. Xu, "A genetic algorithm based on immune and chaos", Procs. of the IEEE Intl. Conf. on Natural Computation, pp. 239-243, 2007.

[166] I. De Falco, A. Della Cioppa, E. Tarantino, "Evaluation of Particle Swarm Optimization Effectiveness in Classification", in *Fuzzy Logic and Applications, Lecture Notes in Computer Science*, Vol. 3849, pp 164-171, 2006.

[167] A. Tayade and L. Ragha, "Ant colony optimization as an adaptive classifier, *Procs. of the IEEE Intl. Conf. on Communication, Information, and Computing Technology*, pp. 1-6, 2012.

[168] L. Zhao, J.C.G. Caceres, A.P.G. Damiance Jr., and H. Szu, "Chaotic dynamics for multi-value content addressable memory", *Neurocomputing*, vol. 69, pp. 1628-1636, 2006.

[169] A. Mirzaei and R. Safabakhsh, "Optimal matching by transiently chaotic neural network", *Applied Soft Computing*, vol. 9, pp. 863-873, 2009.

[170] A. Taherkhani, S.A. Seyyedsalehi, and A.H. Jafari, "Design of a chaotic neural network for training and retrieval of grayscale and binary patterns", Neurocomputing, vol. 74, pp. 2824-2833, 2011.

[171] S. Chartier and R. Proulx, "NDRAM: Nonlinear dynamic recurrent associative memory for learning bipolar and non-bipolar correlated patterns", *IEEE Trans. on Neural Networks*, vol. 16, no. 6, pp. 1393-1400, 2005.

[172] G. Xu, "G-S chaotic neural networks and its applications", *Procs. of the IEEE Intl. Conf. on Computer and Communication Technologies in Agriculture Engineering*, pp. 120-122, 2010.

[173] J. M. Bahi, C. Guyeux, and M. Salomon, "Neural Networks and Chaos: Construction, Evaluation of Chaotic Networks, and Prediction of Chaos with MultiLayer Feedforward Network", *Chaos*, vol. 22, no. 1, pp. 1-9, 2012.

[174] E. Del-Moral-Hernandez, "Non-homogeneous neural networks with chaotic recursive nodes: Connectivity and multi-assemblies structures in recursive processing elements architectures", *Neural Networks*, vol. 18, pp. 532-540, 2005.

[175] M. Adachi and K. Aihara, "Associative dynamics in a chaotic neural network", *Neural Networks*, Vol. 10, No. 1, pp. 83-98, 1997.

[176] L. Chen and K. Aihara, "Chaos simulated annealing by a neural network model with transient chaos", *Neural Networks*, vol. 8, no. 6, pp. 915-930, 1995.

[177] K. Qin and B. J. Oommen, "Ideal Chaotic Pattern Recognition Using the Modified Adachi Neural Network", *Chaotic Modeling and Simulation (CMSIM)*, vol. 4, pp. 701-710, 2012.

[178] N. Crook, W.J. Goh, and M. Hawarat, "Pattern recall in networks of chaotic neurons", *Biosystems*, vol. 87, pp. 267-74, 2005.

[179] David E. Goldberg, *Genetic Algorithms in Search, Optimization and Machine Learning*, Addison-Wesley Longman, Inc., 1989.

[180] S. Angelina, L.P. Suresh, and S.H.K. Veni, "Image segmentation based on genetic algorithm for region growth and region merging", *Procs. of the IEEE Intl. Conf. on Computing, Electronics, and Electrical Technologies*, pp. 970-974, 2012.

[181] K. G. Khoo and P. N. Suganthan, "Structural pattern recognition using genetic algorithms with specialized operators", *IEEE Trans. On Systems Man and Cybernetics – Part B: Cybernetics*, vol. 33, no. 1, pp. 156-165, 2003.

[182] S. Auwatanamongkol, "Pattern recognition using genetic algorithms", *Proc. of IEEE World Congress on Evolutionary Computation*, pp. 822-828, 2000.

[183] M. Farmer and D. Shugars, "Application of genetic algorithms for wrapper-based image segmentation and classification", *Proc. of IEEE World Congress on Evolutionary Computation,* 2006.

[184] Z. Ma, "Chaotic populations in genetic algorithms", *Applied Soft Computing*, vol 12, pp. 2409–2424, 2012.

[185] J. Determan and J. A. Foster, "Using chaos in genetic algorithms", *Procs. of the IEEE Congress on Evolutionary Computation*, pp. 2094-2101, 1999.

[186] G. Garai and B. B. Chaudhuri, "A cascaded genetic algorithm for efficient optimization and pattern matching", *Image and Vision Computing*, vol. 20, pp. 265-277, 2002.

[187] Y. Gao and T. Zheng, "Improved genetic algorithms based on chaotic mutation operation and its application", *Procs. of the IEEE Intl. Conf. on Multimedia*, pp. 1-3, 2010.

[188] S. Wang and Y.Wu, "Clustering analysis based on chaos genetic algorithm", *Procs. of the IEEE Chinese Control and Decision Conference*, pp. 16-19, 2010.

[189] M. Gao, J. Xu, J. Tian, and H. Wu, "Path planning for mobile robot based on chaos genetic algorithm", *Procs. of the 4th IEEE Intl. Conf. on Neural Computation*, pp. 409-413, 2008.

[190] X. Wang, P. Liu, and M. Huang, "A QoS multicast routing algorithm based on shrinking-chaotic-mutation evolutionary algorithm in IP/DWDM optical internet", *Procs. of the Sixth IEEE Intl. Conf. on Parallel and Distributed Computing*, pp. 698-702, 2005.

[191] M. Yang, H. Huang, and G. Xiao, "A novel dynamic particle swarm optimization algorithm based on chaotic mutation", *Procs. of the IEEE Second Intl. Workshop on Knowledge Discovery and Data Mining*, pp. 656-659, 2009.

[192] G. Ye and G. Tao, "Improved genetic algorithms based on chaotic mutation operation and its application", *Procs. of the IEEE Intl. Conf. on Multimedia Technology*, pp. 1-3, 2010.

Author Index

Subject Index

A

B

C

Michael E. Farmer

D

E

F

G

H

I

J

L

M

N

O

P

Q

R

Made in the USA
Las Vegas, NV
03 November 2026

57424626R00200